Sacraments and Worship

Sacraments and Worship

The Sources of Christian Theology

Edited by Maxwell E. Johnson

WESTMINSTER
JOHN KNOX PRESS
LOUISVILLE · KENTUCKY

1st edition
Published by Westminster John Knox Press
Louisville, Kentucky

12 13 14 15 16 17 18 19 20 21—10 9 8 7 6 5 4 3 2 1

Book design by Drew Stevens
Cover design by Eric Walljasper, Minneapolis, MN
Cover illustration: © Manuela Krause / istockphoto.com

Library of Congress Cataloging-in-Publication Data

Sacraments and worship / edited by Maxwell E. Johnson. — 1st ed.
    p. cm. — (The sources of Christian theology)
    Includes bibliographical references (p.   ) and index.
    ISBN 978-0-664-23157-6 (alk. paper)
    1. Sacraments (Liturgy)—History—Sources. I. Johnson, Maxwell E., 1952-
    BV800.S23 2011
    234'.1609—dc23

                                                                        2011039962

♾ The paper used in this publication meets the minimum requirements of the American National Standard for Information Sciences—Permanence of Paper for Printed Library Materials, ANSI Z39.48-1992.

Contents

Series Introduction

The Sources of Christian Theology is a series of books to provide resources for the study of major Christian doctrines. The books are edited by expert scholars who provide an extended introductory discussion of the important dimensions of the doctrine. The main focus of each volume is on selections of source materials. These are drawn from major Christian theologians and documents that convey essential elements of theological formulations about each doctrine. The editor provides context and backgrounds in short introductory materials prior to the selections. A bibliography for further study is included.

There is no substitute in theological study for a return to the "sources." This series provides a wide array of source materials from the early church period to the present time. The selections represent the best Christian theological thinking and display the range of ways in which Christian persons have thought about the issues posed by the major aspects of Christian faith.

We hope that those interested in the study of Christian theology will find these volumes rich and valuable resources. They embody the efforts of Christian thinkers to move from "faith" to "understanding."

Donald K. McKim
Westminster John Knox Press

Introduction

This volume is somewhat different than other volumes in this series, which take one particular doctrine or theological topic (e.g., creation, Christology, or eschatology) and treat it from a variety of different authors and perspectives over the wide sweep of the Christian tradition. In this volume there is no single "doctrine" or issue that provides its overall content or focus. Rather, as a collection of texts concerned specifically with sacraments and Christian worship, it is more of an introductory companion for the study of the history and theology of Christian worship from the New Testament until today. That is, the primary focus of this volume is the history and theology of the individual sacraments and their liturgical context in the church's worship.

The discipline of liturgical study can be undertaken from different methodological perspectives, namely, liturgical history, liturgical theology, and ritual studies. By training and conviction I approach liturgical study from a strongly historical and theological perspective, an approach—thanks to my formation by such great liturgiologists as Paul Bradshaw, Robert Taft, and Gabriele Winkler—that is called *Liturgiewissenschaft* or "comparative liturgy," the term used by the founder of this school or method, Anton Baumstark (+1948).[1]

What this means concretely is that one must attend to the great variety that actually exists—liturgically and theologically—in the sources of the various Christian traditions, as that variety is revealed to us by study of those documents themselves. That is, one cannot study simply *the* history or *the* theology of baptism, confirmation, Eucharist, or anything else in liturgy, for that matter, as though there was and is a single line of development. One can study only the *histories* and *theologies* of those sacramental ceremonies and activities of the church as they actually appear in history, and one must do this not only chronologically but also geographically within the various rites of the churches, those distinct ecclesial ways of being Christian,[2] in both East and West.

Paul Bradshaw has cautioned against scholarship assuming a monolinear developmental model in the evolution of liturgy, criticizing the all-too-common assumption by some that there has always been such a thing as *the* liturgy of *the* church, a divinely instituted "*sacred* liturgy," an

---

1. See Anton Baumstark, *Comparative Liturgy*, rev. Bernard Botte; English edition by F. L. Cross (London: A. R. Mowbray, 1958).
2. See Aidan Kavanagh, *On Liturgical Theology* (New York: Pueblo, 1984), 100.

assumption that treats the role of historical research into the actual state of liturgical development as largely irrelevant to the faith-based conviction that there is a fundamental continuity of the church's liturgy through the ages. Such an uncritical, almost liturgical fundamentalist, approach, often based on a rather romantic vision of what has been assumed to be *the* liturgical practice of *the* early church, has fostered a mentality in approaches to liturgical study that either tends to ignore practices that obscure this romantic vision or seeks to "restore" the "true pattern" by writing off "Reformation developments as being the death of the authentic Christian liturgy . . . seen essentially as the work of fallible humans in contrast to the divine character attributed to the shaping of . . . worship."[3] Bradshaw writes:

> [N]ot only is the fundamental continuity of liturgical practice assumed without historical research, but historical research itself does not give us grounds for concluding that there is any fundamental continuity, except in the very broadest of terms. The "deep structures" running through liturgy are very few indeed if we apply the test of universal observance to them. There are very few things that Christians have consistently done in worship at all times and in all places. Of course, the task is made somewhat easier if one restricts one's vision to just a single ecclesiastical tradition and ignores all the rest, but even there the genuine historical continuities are generally fewer than the often sweeping generalizations of liturgical theologians seem to suggest.[4]

Elsewhere he argues that

> the past does not hold all the solutions to today's questions, and all too often it seems that the makers of modern rites have sought to restore the ancient pattern for its own sake, without adequate consideration as to whether it accords with the current theological climate, our own cultural situation, or present needs.[5]

Robert Taft makes a similar point, saying:

> As a historian of Christian liturgical traditions, it is my unshakeable conviction that a tradition can be understood only genetically, with reference to its origins and evolution. Those ignorant of history are prisoners of the latest cliché, for they have nothing against which to test it. That is what a knowledge of the past can give us. . . . [T]he past is always instructive, but not necessarily normative. What we do today is not ruled by the past but by the adaptation of the tradition to the needs of the present. History can only help us decide what the essentials of that tradition are, and the parameters of its adaptation.[6]

---

3. Paul Bradshaw, "Difficulties in Doing Liturgical Theology," *Pacifica* 11 (June 1998): 185.

4. Ibid., 184–85.

5. Paul Bradshaw, "Liturgical Use and Abuse of Patristics," in Kenneth Stevenson, ed., *Liturgy Reshaped* (London: SPCK, 1982), 144.

6. Robert Taft, *The Liturgy of the Hours in East and West: The Origins of the Divine Office and Its Meaning for Today* (Collegeville, MN: Liturgical Press, 1986), xiv–xv.

If such methodological caution is necessary, however, and if "history can only help us decide what the essentials of that tradition are, and the parameters of its adaptation," this only serves to make the contemporary historical study of the sacraments and Christian worship all the more necessary precisely for the very recovery of those essentials, broadly and ecumenically understood, today. The great liturgical theologian Geoffrey Wainwright has written: "Without the heartbeat of the sacraments at its center, a church will lack confidence about the gospel message and about its own ability to proclaim that message in evangelism, to live it out in its own internal fellowship, and to embody it in service to the needy."[7] And, further: "A deeper re-plunging into its own tradition will, in my judgment, be necessary if the church is to survive in recognizable form, particularly in our western culture."[8]

The "tradition" into which, according to Wainwright, the church is to replunge itself so that the sacraments become again its heartbeat, is the church's classic liturgical tradition as that tradition is revealed in all its rich diversity and variability in the sources. Robert Taft has defended strongly the need for this historical approach in service to the church:

> [A]midst all the contemporary talk of "relevance" in matters liturgical it remains my firm conviction that nothing is so relevant as knowledge, nothing so irrelevant as ignorance. So I think that in matters of pastoral relevance there is still something we can learn from comparative liturgical scholarship across a broad range of traditions. . . . [P]ractice is determined not by the past but by tradition, which encompasses not only past and present, but theological reflection on both. That is why the Catholic Church has never been guided by a retrospective ideology. Tradition is not the past; it is the Church's self-consciousness *now* of that which has been handed on to her not as an inert treasure but as a dynamic inner life. . . . Theology must be reflection on the whole of that reality, the whole of tradition, not on just its present manifestation. One of the great contemporary illusions is that one can construct a liturgical theology without a profound knowledge of the liturgical tradition. So in spite of the (to me) rather perplexing discomfort that many Americans seem to have with history, there can be no theology without it. . . . Christian liturgy is a given, an object, an already existing reality like English literature. One discovers what English literature is only by reading Chaucer and Shakespeare and Eliot and Shaw and the contemporaries. So too with liturgy. If we want to know what Christmas and Chrismation, Eucharist and Easter mean, we shall not get far by studying anthropology or game-theory, or by asking ourselves what we *think* they mean. We must plunge into the enormous stream of liturgical and patristic evidence and wade through it piece by piece, age by age,

---

7. Geoffrey Wainwright, "The Sacraments in Wesleyan Perspective," in Geoffrey Wainwright, *Worship with One Accord: Where Liturgy and Ecumenism Embrace* (New York: Oxford University Press, 1997), 106.

8. Geoffrey Wainwright, "Renewing Worship: The Recovery of Classical Patterns," in *Worship with One Accord*, 138.

ever alert to pick up shifts in the current as each generation reaches for its own understanding of what it is we are about.[9]

Within that "tradition," especially the liturgical tradition—even if we do not know from the earliest period what exactly constituted Christian initiation (whether water bath or not, anointings or not), what the precise relationship between Sabbath and Sunday was among early Christians, what the earliest culinary contents of the Eucharist were, how "the" great prayer of thanksgiving was offered at the meal, or how the earliest communities were "ordered" in terms of ministry—the fact remains that all our evidence, from at least Justin Martyr on through the Reformation, indicates the existence of some kind of "baptismal" rite of incorporation, the existence of the Christian churches assembling together on Sundays and other feasts to hear the Word and share in some form of eucharistic Meal, the existence of patterns for daily prayer (whether private or communal), some form of "order," and some form of ministry to the poor. All this points, indeed, to some kind of universal pattern of worship that the diverse churches of Christian antiquity saw as constituting a type of universal norm, which determined authentic Christian worship and transcended local diversity and variety, that which Gordon Lathrop has referred to today as an ecumenical "ordo" of and for Christian worship.[10]

If our evidence for specific ritual detail is not what we wish it would be, baptismal rites of incorporation, a relationship established between the church and time (Sundays, feasts, seasons, the structure of the week, and daily prayer), and the centrality of Word and Meal in Sunday worship, even if active participation in the Meal itself was to dwindle from the late fourth century on, do witness to the existence of some kind of *ordo*. The diversity we encounter in the churches of the first few centuries then is, precisely, a diversity in *how* baptism and its various encompassing rites are celebrated, *how* Sunday and festival observance is structured (e.g., whether Pascha on a calendrical date [14 Nisan] or a Sunday), *how* the Meal is celebrated and its gifts gathered and distributed, *how* the Meal prayers are to be prayed and what their various structural components were, and *how* the various ministries of *episkopé* (oversight) and *diakonia* (service) might be ordered.

But no one, to my knowledge, actually questioned the very existence, structure, and contents of Christian worship as having to do with baptism, Word, Eucharist, days and seasons, daily prayer, or the need for ordering the tasks of *episkopé* and *diakonia* or ministry to the sick, reconciliation,

---

9. Robert Taft, *Beyond East and West: Problems in Liturgical Understanding*, 2nd rev. and enlarged ed. (Rome: Edizioni Orientalia Christiana, 1997), 13–14.

10. Gordon Lathrop, *Holy Things: A Liturgical Theology* (Minneapolis: Fortress Press, 1993). For a summary of Lathrop's approach see later in this book, chapter 2, pp. 74–76. And for a critique from a Free Church perspective, see chapter 2, pp. 90–93.

marriage, and burial of the dead. These, it seems, were givens and are constitutive parts of the inherited tradition, which may indeed serve to shape and govern present experience. To that end, Lathrop's model of the *ordo* remains not only one of "the finest available description[s] of classical Christian worship,"[11] but commends itself as a most fruitful model in the contemporary search for some kind of ecumenical-liturgical "norm."

Recent developments in Christian worship around the world—for example, the increasing phenomenon of megachurches, the church growth movement, the development of "seeker services," and the increasing notion across ecclesial lines that the church's liturgy is but "one" of several options for "worship"—challenge the historic priority of sacramental worship. What appears to be at stake in this, I would submit, is a particular theological understanding of how God is believed to act in the world and church.

That is, the classic sacramental-liturgical tradition claims that God acts primarily vis-à-vis creation and humanity through means, instruments, and mediation, in ways that are described as both incarnational and sacramental. So the theologian, grounded in and formed by what today might be called the ecumenical-liturgical-sacramental tradition, can no more view that foundational understanding of how God is believed to act as one "option" among several than she or he can fly in the face of canon, creed, and confession without thereby denying his or her own identity and separating himself or herself from the historic orthodox Christian faith. As Ruth Meyers has written of this sacramental view:

> The ordinary elements of water, bread, and wine allow us to encounter Christ in ways readily accessible to our senses. *We meet Christ not in some abstract spiritual way, but in these very tangible substances that by their use in worship permeate the very core of our being.* An expansive use of these symbols helps us glimpse the infinite, incomprehensible, overflowing love of God in Christ Jesus.[12]

I would suggest that it is here especially where a volume on sacraments and Christian worship belongs rightly in a series devoted to the "sources" of Christian theology. For what we are dealing with in the history of sacraments and Christian worship is precisely "theology," that is, what the liturgy says and expresses theologically about God and God's relationship with the world through Christ and the Holy Spirit. As a *locus theologicus* (theological source), the church's worship has always carried the church's

---

11. James White, "How Do We Know It Is Us?" in E. Byron Anderson and Bruce T. Morrill, eds., *Liturgy and the Moral Self: Humanity at Full Stretch before God* (Collegeville, MN: Liturgical Press, 1998), 55–66.

12. Ruth Meyers, "Responses," in Gordon Lathrop, ed., *Open Questions in Worship*, vol. 1: *What Are the Essentials of Christian Worship?* (Minneapolis: Augsburg/Fortress, 1994), 27 (emphasis added).

doctrinal expressions and at the same time helped in developing those doctrinal expressions.

Especially with regard to the challenges of doctrinal heresy, Christian worship was not only formed by, but also helped in forming, orthodox Christian teaching. Orthodox Trinitarian and christological doctrine developed, in part at least, from the church at prayer, as the baptismal-creedal profession of faith gave rise to the "official" creeds themselves, as prayer *to* Christ contributed to understanding his *homoousios* with the Father, as the Holy Spirit's "divine" role in baptism shaped the theology of the Spirit's divinity, and as early devotion to Mary as *Theotokos* gave rise to the decree of Ephesus in 431.

While in Byzantine Greek "orthodoxy" really means "right thinking," this "right thinking" often developed from the doxology of the church, including the sense expressed still by Russian Orthodoxy of giving "right glory" or right *doxa* to God *and* orthodox belief (*Pravoslavie*), where several of the central Christian doctrines were prayed liturgically long before they were formalized dogmatically. So it has been through the ages. The practice of Christian worship forms the belief of the church (*ut legem credendi lex statuat supplicandi*, in the words of Prosper of Aquitaine[13]). In turn, worship itself is formed further by that belief and, further still, continues to form people into believers and disciples of the crucified and risen Lord.

If, thanks to historical scholarship, the "deeper re-plunging into its own tradition" envisioned by Wainwright is a much more complex endeavor today than it has ever been before, thanks to that same scholarship on the diversity of liturgical sources, the treasures to be uncovered there for Christianity and its worship life are richer than we may have so far imagined. The goal in all this, of course, is faithfulness, fidelity to the God who acts and works for human salvation through sacraments, people, and communities and to the sacramental worldview that continues to define and characterize classic Christianity in spite of its manifold diversity. This goal is well summarized in the words of Frank Senn, who writes that

> the church must provide what people lack in order to offer meaning for their lives: a narratable world—a worldview that provides coherent meaning and a way of enacting it. If the world has come apart in postmodern nihilism, the church must redo the world. It must provide an aimless present with a usable past and a hope-filled future. . . . And if we face in our society's religiosity a gnostic tendency to seek to escape from the threats of natural decay, temporal limitations, and political responsibility, *this can be at least countered with attention to the sacramental life, the historic liturgy, and traditional ecclesiastical polity.*[14]

---

13. See later in this book, chapter 2, p. 51.

14. F. Senn, *Christian Liturgy: Catholic and Evangelical* (Minneapolis: Fortress Press, 1997), 698 (emphasis added).

May this collection be a helpful resource in bringing about that worthy goal.

The particular shape and contents of this collection owe their immediate origins to the work of another of my former teachers, Professor James F. White (+2004), who taught at the University of Notre Dame from 1983 until his retirement in 1999. In many ways, this volume is but a significantly expanded and revised version of his 1992 *Documents of Christian Worship: Descriptive and Interpretive Sources*.[15] But if White's book clearly serves here as a core document, this volume is significantly different as well. That is, while White limited himself to what he called "descriptive and interpretive sources," this work also includes many liturgical texts themselves, in an effort to provide an accessible guide to various liturgical prayers and collections of prayers and rites from within the distinct Christian liturgical traditions of both East and West, Orthodox, Catholic, and Protestant.

Further, although *Documents of Christian Worship* did contain a chapter on "Sacraments in General,"[16] this volume not only offers additional historical texts but provides selections from contemporary influential sacramental theologians as well. At the same time, this volume includes a chapter altogether reflecting the discipline of liturgical theology (chapter 2), offering, as it were, a historical overview of the discipline from Athanasius of Alexandria to a postmodern approach to the subject from the recent writings of my Notre Dame colleague Nathan Mitchell. Similarly, each chapter is provided with its own brief introduction, locating the particular documents of the chapter in their historical, liturgical, and theological contexts; each document or group of documents within the chapter is provided with short introductory and contextual comments, dealing with issues regarding the date of the document, its contents, or its influence in the wider tradition. Each chapter, or major section of a chapter, is provided with a select bibliography on the topic(s), which can be found on pages 409–14. In this way, it is intended that this volume might be of greater benefit to the reader and to those who might use it in a course.

The task of producing a volume such as this is not possible without the great assistance of others. Here I want to acknowledge and express my deep gratitude to those who have been extraordinarily helpful to me: first, to my *Doktoralvater* and now Notre Dame colleague Paul F. Bradshaw, who has read every word of this work and has made invaluable suggestions about the inclusion and exclusion of various documents (throughout the work but especially with regard to chapters 5 and 6) as well as concerning the overall context and presentation; second, to my former research

---

15. James F. White, *Documents of Christian Worship: Descriptive and Interpretive Sources* (Louisville, KY: Westminster/John Knox Press, 1992).

16. Ibid., 119–34.

assistant, Annie Vorhes McGowan, a recent graduate of the liturgical studies doctoral program at Notre Dame, who was invaluable in tracking down and scanning texts, in proofreading, and, certainly not least, in contacting publishers for copyright permissions to reproduce their materials here (without Annie, this work would not have been completed); third, to my research assistant, Nathanael Marx, who continued Annie's work superbly, not least, providing his own translations of Latin texts for inclusion in this volume (see pp. 361–63); to my current research assistant, Cody Unterseher, whose invaluable assistance has included both the preparation of the index and proofreading; and, fourth, to Westminster John Knox Press for providing me with an electronic copy of James F. White, *Documents of Christian Worship: Descriptive and Interpretive Sources* (without having this text to use as a core document with several important texts already included, I doubt that I would have agreed so willingly to take on this project); and, finally, to Don McKim of Westminster John Knox Press for inviting me to do this collection and to Dilu Nicholas for organizing the copyright permissions and taking care of the necessary financial arrangements with other publishers. To all these people I am very grateful.

Abbreviations

The following abbreviations are used for texts frequently cited.

ACC   Alcuin Club Collections

ACW   Ancient Christian Writers series. Westminster, MD: Newman Press, 1946–.

AGLS   Alcuin/GROW Liturgical Study. Cambridge: Grove Books, Ltd.

ANF   *The Ante-Nicene Fathers: Translations of the Writings of the Fathers Down to A.D. 325.* 10 vols. Edited by Alexander Roberts, James Donaldson, et al. Edinburgh: T. & T. Clark, 1885–1897. Reprinted Grand Rapids: Eerdmans, 1985–1987.

DBL   *Documents of the Baptismal Liturgy.* ACC 79. 3rd edition revised and expanded. Edited by E. C. Whitaker and Maxwell E. Johnson. London: SPCK, 2003.

FC   *Fathers of the Church: A New Translation.* Washington, DC: Catholic University of America, 1947–.

GLS   Grove Liturgical Study. Cambridge: Grove Books, Ltd.

LCC   *The Library of Christian Classics.* 26 vols. Ed. John Baillie, John T. McNeill, and Henry P. Van Dusen. Philadelphia: The Westminster Press; London: SCM Press, 1953–1966.

LW   *Luther's Works.* American ed. 55 vols. Edited by Jaroslav Pelikan. Philadelphia and St. Louis: Fortress Press and Concordia Publishing House, 1955–1986.

LWSS   *Living Water: Sealing Spirit: Readings on Christian Initiation.* Edited by Maxwell E. Johnson. Collegeville, MN: The Liturgical Press / Pueblo, 1995.

NPNF[1] *A Select Library of the Nicene and Post-Nicene Fathers of the Christian Church.* First Series. 14 vols. Edited by Philip Schaff. Edinburgh: T. & T. Clark, 1886–1889.

NPNF[2] *A Select Library of the Nicene and Post-Nicene Fathers of the Christian Church.* Second Series. 14 vols. Ed. Philip Schaff and Henry Wace. Edinburgh: T. & T. Clark. 1890-1900. Reprinted Grand Rapids: Eerdmans, 1985–1987.

OCA   Orientalia Christiana Analecta. Rome: Pontificium Institutum Orientalium Studiorum.

PEER   *Prayers of the Eucharist: Early and Reformed.* 3rd edition. Edited by R. C. D. Jasper and G. J. Cuming. Collegeville, MN: The Liturgical Press, Pueblo, 1990.

PG   *Patrologia cursus completus. Series Graeca.* 161 vols. Edited by J.-P. Migne. Paris: Migne, 1857–1866.

PL   *Patrologia cursus completes. Series Latina.* 221 vols. Edited by J.-P. Migne. Paris: Migne, 1844–1855.

SC   *Sources chrétiennes.* Paris: Les Éditions du Cerf, 1943–.

CHAPTER 1

Sacraments in General and Sacramental Theology

Scholastic theological approaches to the study of the sacraments and to sacramental theology began with a treatise or section entitled *Sacramenta in generis*, that is, "Sacraments in general," before going on to treat the individual sacraments themselves in subsequent sections. This volume is no exception. Beginning with Augustine's famous and ecumenically influential definition that "the word is joined to the element and the result is a sacrament, itself becoming, in a sense, a visible word," this chapter proceeds historically through the patristic and medieval periods, the latter of which witnesses the development of "seven sacraments," thanks to the *Sentences of Peter the Lombard* and Thomas Aquinas's *Summa*.

In the next section the challenge to the medieval sacramental system represented by Luther's 1520 *Babylonian Captivity* and the works of other Protestant reformers and the renewed defense of the seven sacraments at the Council of Trent leads through the subsequent centuries to what has been called the Copernican revolution in modern sacramental theology, especially in light of the Second Vatican Council in the Roman Catholic Church in the early 1960s.

The final section of this chapter, then, provides selections from contemporary influential sacramental theologians such as Karl Rahner on the relationship of the church and sacrament, James F. White on the numbering of sacraments from an ecumenical Protestant perspective, Louis-Marie Chauvet on the relationship between Word and sacrament, and others, including a contemporary feminist approach offered by Susan Ross and an Eastern theological perspective from M. Daniel Findikyan. Thus this chapter provides a concise overview of the historical development and particular issues that constitute that area of study called sacramental theology.

|

Definitions of a Sacrament,
Key Concepts, and the Number of Sacraments
in Early and Medieval Theologians

|

EARLY THEOLOGIANS

Augustine of Hippo

Augustine treats the notion of what constitutes a "sacrament" in several of his writings, rather than in a special treatise on the sacraments.

Augustine of Hippo, *Treatise on the Gospel of John*, LXXX, 3 (ca. 416), trans. Paul F. Palmer, in *Sacraments and Worship* (London: Darton, Longman & Todd, 1957), 127–28.

Why does He not say: you are clean because of the baptism with which you were washed, but says: "because of the word that I have spoken to you" [John 15:3], unless the reason is that even in water it is the word that cleanses? Take away the word and what is water but water? The word is joined to the element and the result is a sacrament, itself becoming, in a sense, a visible word as well. . . . Whence this power of water so exalted as to bathe the body and cleanse the soul, if it is not through the action of the word; not because it is spoken, but because it is believed? . . . This word of faith is of such efficacy in the Church of God that it washes clean not only the one who believes in the word, the one who presents [the child for baptism], the one who sprinkles [the child], but the child itself, be it ever so tiny, even though it is as yet incapable of believing unto justice with the heart or of making profession unto salvation with the lips. All this takes place through the word, concerning which the Lord says: "You are already clean because of the word that I have spoken to you."

Augustine of Hippo, *Against Faustus the Manichaean*, XIX, 11 (ca. 398), trans. Bernard Leeming, in *Principles of Sacramental Theology* (London: Longmans, 1960), 562–63.

In no religion, whether true or whether false, can men be held in association, unless they are gathered together with a common share in some visible signs or sacraments; and the power of these sacraments is inexpressibly effective, and hence if contemned is accounted to be a sacrilege.

Augustine of Hippo, *Questions on the Heptateuch*, III, 84 (ca. 410),
trans. Bernard Leeming, in *Principles of Sacramental Theology*, 563.

How, then, do both Moses and the Lord sanctify? . . . Moses, by
the visible sacraments through his ministry; God by invisible grace
through the Holy Spirit, wherein is the whole fruit of the visible sacraments; for without that sanctification of invisible grace, what use
are visible sacraments?

Augustine of Hippo, *Commentary on the Psalms*, LXXIII, 2 (ca. 416),
trans. Paul F. Palmer, in *Sacraments and Worship*, 128–29.

If we weigh well the two testaments, the old and the new, the sacraments are not the same, nor are the promises made the same. . . .
The sacraments are not the same, since there is a difference between
sacraments that give salvation and those that promise a Saviour. The
sacraments of the New Law give salvation, the sacraments of the Old
Law promised a Saviour.

Augustine of Hippo, *On Baptism against the Donatists*, IV, II, 18 (ca. 400),
trans. Paul F. Palmer, in *Sacraments and Worship*, 123.

When baptism is given in the words of the gospel, no matter how
great the perverseness of either minister or recipient, the sacrament
is inherently holy on His account whose sacrament it is. And if any
one receives baptism from a misguided man, he does not on that
account receive the perversity of the minister, but only the holiness of the mystery, and if he is intimately united to the Church in
good faith and hope and charity, he receives the remission of his
sins. . . . But if the recipient himself is perverse, that which is given is
of no profit while he remains in his perversity; and yet that which is
received does remain holy within him, nor is the sacrament repeated
when he has been corrected.

Augustine applies the terminology of "sacrament" to the annual celebration of the Pascha.

Augustine of Hippo, *Letter 55 to Januarius* 1, 2; in *Easter in the Early Church:
An Anthology of Jewish and Early Christian Texts*, selected, annotated, and introduced
by Raniero Cantalmessa (Collegeville, MN: Liturgical Press, 1993), 108–9.

Here you must know, first of all, that the Lord's birthday is not celebrated in a sacrament but his birth is simply remembered, and for
this it was only necessary to mark with festive devotion each year the
day on which the event took place. But there is a sacrament in any

celebration when the commemoration of the event is done in such a way as to make us understand that it signifies something that is to be taken in a holy manner. This is in fact how we keep the Pascha. Not only do we call to mind again what happened, that is, that Christ died and rose again, but we also do not leave out the other things about him which confirm the signification of the sacraments. For, since he "died for our sins and rose for our justification," as the apostle says, a certain passage from death to life has been consecrated in the passion and resurrection of the Lord.

Leo I

Leo's statement "What was visible in our Redeemer when on earth has become operative in sacramental signs" has become a standard and key text in sacramental and liturgical theology.

Leo I, *De Ascensione Domini* II, in *Benedictine Daily Prayer: A Short Breviary*, ed. Maxwell E. Johnson (Collegeville, MN: Liturgical Press, 2006), 300-301.

The Lord's resurrection brought us joy; so should his ascension, as we recall the event that exalted our lowly nature beyond the angels and highest created powers to the Father's side. These divine actions provide a sure foundation; through them God's grace works marvelously to keep our faith firm, our hope confident, and our love ardent, even though the visible events as such are now a part of history.

It takes great strength of mind and a faithful and enlightened heart to believe without hesitation in what escapes the bodily eye and to desire unswervingly what cannot be seen. Yet how could our hearts be inflamed and how could one be justified by faith if our salvation arose only from what is visible? Therefore, what was visible in our Redeemer when on earth has become operative in sacramental signs [*Quod itaque Redemptoris nostri conspicuum fuit, in sacramenta transivit*]. And, in order that faith might become stronger and more perfect, teaching replaces sight, and the hearts of the faithful are illumined by God to accept its authority.

Even the blessed Apostles, despite the signs they saw and the sermons they heard, were fearful when the Lord suffered, and did not accept his resurrection unhesitatingly. So much did his ascension influence them, however, that all fear was turned to joy. Their minds contemplated the divine Christ at the Father's side; no earthly trial could distract them from the fact that Christ had not left the Father when he descended nor left the disciples when he returned.

Therefore, beloved, the Son of Man who is Son of God has in an ineffable way become more present to us in his Godhead now that he has departed from us in his humanity. Faith now reaches to the Son, who is equal to the Father, and no longer needs the bodily presence of Jesus, in which he is less than the Father. For though his incarnate nature continues to exist, faith is summoned to touch the only-begotten Son, not with bodily sense but with spiritual understanding.

MEDIEVAL THEOLOGIANS

The definition of what constitutes a sacrament becomes more precise.

Hugh of St. Victor

Hugh of St. Victor, *On the Sacraments of the Christian Faith*, I, 9 (1140), trans. Roy J. Deferrari, in *Hugh of Saint Victor on the Sacraments of the Christian Faith* (Cambridge: Medieval Academy of America, 1951), 155.

Now if any one wishes to define more fully and more perfectly what a sacrament is, he can say: "A sacrament is a corporeal or material element set before the senses without, representing by similitude and signifying by institution and containing by sanctification some invisible and spiritual grace." This definition is recognized as so fitting and perfect that it is found to befit every sacrament and a sacrament alone. For every thing that has these three is a sacrament, and every thing that lacks these three can not be properly called a sacrament.

For every sacrament ought to have a kind of similitude to the thing itself of which it is the sacrament, according to which it is capable of representing the same thing; every sacrament ought to have also institution through which it is ordered to signify this thing and finally sanctification through which it contains that thing and is efficacious for conferring the same on those to be sanctified.

Peter Lombard

Peter Lombard, "Distinction I," 2–7, trans. Owen R. Ott, in *The Four Books of Sentences*, IV (ca. 1152), in LCC 10:338–41.

"A sacrament is a sign of a sacred thing" [Augustine]. However a sacrament is also called a sacred secret just as it is called a sacrament of the deity, so that a sacrament both signifies something sacred and is something sacred signified; but now it is a question of a sacrament as a sign.

Again, "A sacrament is the visible form of an invisible grace" [Augustine].

"A sign is something beyond the appearance, which it presses on the senses, for it makes something else enter thought" [Augustine].

"Some signs are natural, such as smoke signifying fire; others are given" [Augustine] and of those which are given, certain ones are sacraments, certain ones are not, for every sacrament is a sign, but not conversely.

A sacrament bears a likeness of that thing, whose sign it is. "For if sacraments did not have a likeness of the things whose sacraments they are, they would properly not be called sacraments" [Augustine]. For that is properly called a sacrament which is a sign of the grace of God and a form of invisible grace, so that it bears its image and exists as its cause. Sacraments were instituted, therefore, for the sake, not only of signifying, but also of sanctifying. . . .

"The sacraments were instituted for a threefold cause: as a means of increasing humility, as a means of instruction, and as a spur to activity" [Hugh of St. Victor]. . . .

"Moreover, there are two constituents of a sacrament, namely, words and things: words such as the invocation of the Trinity; things such as water, oil, and the like."

Now there remains to be seen the difference between the old sacraments and the new, so that we may call sacraments what in former times used to signify sacred things, such as sacrifices and oblations and the like.

Augustine, indeed, briefly indicated the difference between these, when he said, "While the former only promised and signified, the latter gave salvation."

Nevertheless there was among them a certain sacrament, namely circumcision, conferring the same remedy against sin which baptism now does. . . .

Through circumcision, from the time of its institution, the remission of original and actual sin for young and old was offered by God, just as now it is given in baptism.

Peter the Lombard is the first to articulate a list of seven sacraments for the Western church.

Peter Lombard, "Distinction II," 1, trans. Owen R. Ott, in LCC 10:344–45.

Now let us approach the sacraments of the new law, which are: baptism, confirmation, the bread of blessing, that is the eucharist, penance, extreme unction, orders, marriage. Of these, some provide a remedy against sin and confer assisting grace, such as baptism;

others are only a remedy, such as marriage; others strengthen us with grace and power, such as the eucharist and orders.

If it is asked why the sacraments were not instituted soon after the fall of man, since righteousness and salvation are in them, we say that the sacraments of grace were not to be given before the coming of Christ, who brought grace, for they receive power from his death and Passion. Christ did not wish to come before man was convinced that neither the natural nor the written law could support him.

"Marriage, however, was certainly not instituted before sin [the fall] as a remedy, but as a sacrament and a duty" [Hugh of St. Victor]; after sin, indeed, it was a remedy against the corrupting effect of carnal concupiscence, with which we shall deal in its place.

Peter Lombard, "Distinction IV," 1, trans. Elizabeth Frances Rogers, in *Peter Lombard and the Sacramental System* (Merrick, NY: Richwood Publishing Co., 1976), 95.

[Baptism]: Here we must say that some receive the sacrament and the thing [*res*], some the sacrament and not the thing, some the thing and not the sacrament.

Peter Lombard, "Distinction VIII," 6–7, trans. Elizabeth Frances Rogers, in *Peter Lombard and the Sacramental System*, 122.

[Eucharist]: Now let us see what is the sacrament and what the thing [*res*]: "The sacrament is the visible form of invisible grace" [Augustine]; the form therefore of the bread and wine which appears here is the sacrament, that is "the sign of a sacred thing, because it calls something to mind beyond the appearance which it presents to the senses." Therefore the appearances "keep the names of the things which they were before, namely, bread and wine."

"Moreover the thing [*res*] of this sacrament is two-fold: one, what is contained and signified, the other what is signified but not contained. The thing contained and signified is the flesh of Christ which he received from the Virgin and the blood which he shed for us. The thing signified and not contained is the unity of the Church in those who are predestined, called, justified, and glorified."

Peter Lombard, "Distinction XXIII," 3, trans. Elizabeth Frances Rogers, in *Peter Lombard and the Sacramental System*, 221.

[Extreme unction] This sacrament of the unction of the sick is said to have been instituted by the apostles. For James says: "Is any sick among you?" [James 5:14].

Peter Lombard, "Distinction XXIV," 1–3, trans. Owen R. Ott, in LCC 10:349.

[Ordination] Let us now enter upon the consideration of sacred orders.

There are seven degrees or orders of spiritual function, as is plainly handed down by the writings of the holy Fathers and is shown by the example of our head, namely, Jesus Christ. He exhibited the functions of all in himself and left to his body, which is the Church, the same orders to be observed.

Moreover there are seven on account of the sevenfold grace of the Holy Spirit, and those who are not partakers of the Spirit approach ecclesiastical orders unworthily. . . .

In the sacrament of the sevenfold Spirit there are seven ecclesiastical degrees, namely, doorkeeper, lector, exorcist, acolyte, subdeacon, deacon, priest; all, however, are called clerics, that is, those chosen by lot [Acts 1:26].

Peter Lombard, "Distinction XXIV," 11, trans. Elizabeth Frances Rogers,
in *Peter Lombard and the Sacramental System*, 231.

Wherefore also among men of old times bishops and presbyters were the same, because it is the name of a dignity, not of an age.

Peter Lombard, "Distinction XXIV," 12–16, trans. Owen R. Ott, in LCC 10:350–51.

Although all spiritual states are sacred, the canons well conclude that only two are so called, namely, the diaconate and the presbyterate; for "it is written that the primitive Church had these alone" [Gratian]. . . . The Church appointed subdeacons and acolytes for itself as time went on" [Gratian].

If it is asked what that which is called an order is, it can definitely be said that it is a certain sign, that is, a sacred something, by which spiritual power and office are handed to the ordinand. Therefore a spiritual character in which there is an increase of power is called an order or grade.

And these orders are called sacraments because in receiving them a sacred thing, grace, which the things that are there done figure, is conferred.

There are certain other names, not of orders, but of dignities and offices. "Bishop" is both the name of a dignity and of an office. . . .

"The bishop is the chief of priests, as it were the path of those who follow. He is also called the highest priest; for he makes priests and deacons, and distributes all ecclesiastical orders" [Isidore of Seville].

Thomas Aquinas

Thomas Aquinas, *Summa Theologica*, Part III, 61–65
(ca. 1271), trans. Fathers of the English Dominican Province
(New York: Benziger Bros., 1947), 2:2352–79.

Question 61: First Article: "Whether Sacraments Are Necessary for Man's Salvation?" . . .

I answer that, Sacraments are necessary unto man's salvation for three reasons. The first is taken from the condition of human nature which is such that it has to be led by things corporeal and sensible to things spiritual and intelligible. . . . The second reason is taken from the state of man who in sinning subjected himself by his affections to corporeal things. . . . The third reason is taken from the fact that man is prone to direct his activity chiefly toward material things. . . .

Question 62: First Article: "Whether the Sacraments Are the Cause of Grace?" . . .

I answer that, We must needs say that in some way the sacraments of the New Law cause grace. For it is evident that through the sacraments of the New Law man is incorporated with Christ. . . .

Fourth Article: "Whether There Be in the Sacraments a Power of Causing Grace?" . . .

I answer that, . . . If we hold that a sacrament is an instrumental cause of grace, we must needs allow that there is in the sacraments a certain instrumental power of bringing about the sacramental effects. . . .

Sixth Article: "Whether the Sacraments of the Old Law Caused Grace?" . . .

I answer that, It cannot be said that the sacraments of the Old Law conferred sanctifying grace of themselves, i.e., by their own power: since thus Christ's Passion would not have been necessary. . . .

Question 63: First Article: "'Whether a Sacrament Imprints a Character on the Soul?" . . .

I answer that, . . . Since, therefore by the sacraments, men are deputed to a spiritual service pertaining to the worship of God, it follows that by their names the faithful receive a certain spiritual character. . . .

Fifth Article: "Whether a Character Can Be Blotted Out from the Soul?" . . .

I answer that, . It is clear that the intellect being perpetual and incorruptible, a character cannot be blotted out from the soul. . . .

Sixth Article: "Whether a Character Is Imprinted by Each Sacrament of the New Law?" . . .
I answer that, . . . These three sacraments imprint a character, namely, Baptism, Confirmation, and Order. . . .

Question 64: Second Article: "Whether the Sacraments Are Instituted by God Alone?" . . .
I answer that, . . . Since, therefore, the power of the sacrament is from God alone, it follows that God alone can institute the sacraments. . . .

Fifth Article: "Whether the Sacraments Can be Conferred by Evil Ministers?" . . .
I answer that, . . . The ministers of the Church can confer the sacraments, though they be wicked. . . .

Seventh Article: "Whether Angels Can Administer Sacraments?" . . .
I answer that, . . . It belongs to men, but not to angels, to dispense the sacraments and to take part in their administration. . . .

Ninth Article: "'Whether Faith Is Required of Necessity in the Minister of a Sacrament?" . . .
I answer that, . . . Wherefore, just as the validity of a sacrament does not require that the minister should have charity, and even sinners can confer sacraments, . . . so neither is it necessary that he should have faith, and even an unbeliever can confer a true sacrament, provided that the other essentials are there. . . .

Question 65: First Article: "Whether There Should Be Seven Sacraments?" . . .
I answer that, As stated above, the sacraments of the Church were instituted for a twofold purpose: namely, in order to perfect man in things pertaining to the worship of God according to the religion of Christian life, and to be a remedy against the defects caused by sin. And in either way it is becoming that there should be seven sacraments. . . .

Third Article: "Whether the Eucharist Is the Greatest of the Sacraments?" . . .
I answer that, Absolutely speaking, the sacrament of the Eucharist is the greatest of all the sacraments: and this may be shown in three ways. First of all because it contains Christ Himself substantially. . . . Secondly, this is made clear by considering the relation of the sacraments to one another. For all the other sacraments seem to be

ordained to this one as to their end. . . . Thirdly, this is made clear by considering the rites of the sacraments. For nearly all the sacraments terminate in the Eucharist. . . .

Fourth Article: "Whether All the Sacraments Are Necessary to Salvation?" . . .

I answer that, . . . In the first way, three sacraments are necessary for salvation. Two of them are necessary for the individual; Baptism, simply and absolutely; Penance, in the case of mortal sin committed after Baptism; while the sacrament of Order is necessary to the Church, since *where there is no governor the people shall fall* (Prov. 11:14).

But in the second way the other sacraments are necessary. For in a sense Confirmation perfects Baptism; Extreme Unction perfects Penance; while Matrimony, by multiplying them, preserves the numbers in the Church.

Council of Florence

This fifteenth-century decree becomes the classic statement of the definition and number of the sacraments in the West.

Council of Florence, "Decree for the Armenians" (1439), trans. from *Enchiridion: Symbolorum Definitionum et Declarationum*, ed. Henry Denzinger and Adolf Schönmetzer, 33rd ed. (Freiburg: Herder, 1965), 332–33.

Fifthly, we have set down in briefest form the truth about the sacraments of the Church for the easier instruction of the Armenians at present or in the future. There are seven sacraments of the new law: namely, baptism, confirmation, eucharist, penance, extreme unction, ordination and marriage. These differ much from the sacraments of the old law. The latter did not cause grace but only served as a figure of the passion of Christ. Ours truly contain grace and confer it on those who worthily receive it.

Of these, five pertain to the spiritual perfecting of individuals; the other two are ordained to the governing and increase of the Church. Through baptism we are spiritually reborn; through confirmation we are made to grow in grace and are strengthened in faith. When we have been reborn and strengthened, we are sustained by the divine nourishment of the eucharist. But if through sin we incur sickness of the soul, through penance we are made healthy; we are healed, spiritually and physically according as the soul needs, through extreme unction. Through ordination the Church is governed and increased spiritually, through marriage it grows physically.

All these sacraments are made complete by three things, namely things or matter, words or form, and the person of the minister performing the sacrament with the intention of doing what the Church does. If any of these is absent, the sacrament is not complete.

Among these sacraments there are three—baptism, confirmation, and ordination—which impose on the soul indelibly a character, a certain spiritual sign distinguished from all others. These are not repeated for the same person. The other four do not impose a character and allow repetition.

|

The Protestant and Catholic Reformations

|

THE PROTESTANT REFORMATION

Martin Luther and the Lutheran Reforms

Luther attacks the sacramental system of the medieval Western church and yet articulates a sacramental principle of a biblical "single sacrament" (i.e., Christ himself), which will become common in modern sacramental theology.

Martin Luther, *Babylonian Captivity of the Church* (1520), trans. A. T. W. Steinhäuser, Frederick C. Ahrens, and Abdel Ross Wentz, in LW 36:18, 91–92,106–7,117–18,123–25.

To begin with, I must deny that there are seven sacraments, and for the present maintain that there are but three: baptism, penance, and the bread. All three have been subjected to a miserable captivity by the Roman curia, and the church has been robbed of all her liberty. Yet, if I were to speak according to the usage of the Scriptures, I should have only one single sacrament [Christ, I Tim. 3:16], but with three sacramental signs, of which I shall treat more fully at the proper time. . . .

Confirmation
It is amazing that it should have entered the minds of these men to make a sacrament of confirmation out of the laying on of hands. . . .

I do not say this because I condemn the seven sacraments, but because I deny that they can be proved from the Scriptures. Would that there were in the church such a laying on of hands as there was in apostolic times, whether we chose to call it confirmation or healing! But there is nothing left of it now but what we ourselves have invented to adorn the office of bishops, that they may not be entirely without work in the church. . . .

For to constitute a sacrament there must be above all things else a word of divine promise, by which faith may be exercised. . . .

These things cannot be called sacraments of faith, because they have no divine promise connected with them, neither do they save, but the sacraments do save those who believe the divine promise.

Marriage

Not only is marriage regarded as a sacrament without the least warrant of Scripture, but the very ordinances which extol it as a sacrament have turned it into a farce. Let us look into this a little.

We have said that in every sacrament there is a word of divine promise, to be believed by whoever receives the sign, and that the sign alone cannot be a sacrament. . . .

Ordination

Of this sacrament the church of Christ knows nothing; it is an invention of the church of the pope. Not only is there nowhere any promise of grace attached to it, but there is not a single word said about it in the whole New Testament. Now it is ridiculous to put forth as a sacrament of God something that cannot be proved to have been instituted by God. . . . We ought to see that every article of faith of which we boast is certain, pure, and based on clear passages of Scripture. But we are utterly unable to do that in the case of the sacrament under consideration. . . .

The Sacrament of Extreme Unction

To this rite of anointing the sick the theologians of our day have made two additions which are worthy of them: first, they call it a sacrament, and second, they make it the last sacrament. . . .

I still would say, that no apostle [James] has the right on his own authority to institute a sacrament, that is, to give a divine promise with a sign attached. For this belongs to Christ alone. . . .

There are still a few other things which it might seem possible to regard as sacraments; namely, all those things to which a divine promise has been given, such as prayer, the Word, and the cross. . . .

Nevertheless, it has seemed proper to restrict the name of sacrament to those promises which have signs attached to them. The remainder, not being bound to signs, are bare promises. *Hence there are, strictly speaking, but two sacraments in the church of God—baptism and the bread.* For only in these two do we find both the divinely instituted sign and the promise of forgiveness of sins. The sacrament of penance, which I added to these two, lacks the divinely instituted visible sign, and is, as I have said, nothing but a way and a return to baptism. Nor can the scholastics say that their definition fits penance, for they too ascribe to the true sacraments a visible sign, which is to impress upon the senses the form of that which it effects invisibly. But penance or absolution has no such sign. Therefore they are compelled by their own definition either to admit that penance is not a sacrament and thus to reduce their number, or else to bring forth another definition of a sacrament.

Baptism, however, which we have applied to the whole of life, will truly be a sufficient substitute for all the sacraments which we might need as long as we live. And the bread is truly the sacrament of the dying and departing; for in it we commemorate the passing of Christ out of this world, that we may imitate him. . . . Thus he clearly seems to have instituted the sacrament of the bread with a view to our entrance into the life to come. For then, when the purpose of both sacraments is fulfilled, baptism and bread will cease.

Martin Luther, *The Large Catechism* (1529), trans. Theodore G. Tappert, in *The Book of Concord* (Philadelphia: Fortress Press, 1959), 436.

It remains for us to speak of our two sacraments, instituted by Christ. Every Christian ought to have at least some brief, elementary instruction in them because without these no one can be a Christian, although unfortunately in the past nothing was taught about them.

Augsburg Confession

Augsburg Confession (1530), Articles VII, VIII, IX, X, XI, and XXVIII, in trans. Theodore G. Tappert, *The Book of Concord*, 32–34, 81.

Article VII. It is also taught among us that one holy Christian church will be and remain forever. This is the assembly of all believers [or "saints"] among whom the Gospel is preached in its purity and the holy sacraments are administered according to the Gospel. For it is sufficient [*satis est*] for the true unity of the Christian church that the Gospel be preached in conformity with a pure understanding of it and that the sacraments be administered in accordance with the divine Word [or, "are administered rightly"].

Art. VIII. . . . [B]ecause in this life many false Christians, hypocrites, and even open sinners remain among the godly, the sacraments are efficacious even if the priests who administer them are wicked men. . . .

Art. IX. It is taught among us that Baptism is necessary and that grace is offered through it. Children too should be baptized, for in baptism they are committed to God and become acceptable to him. On this account the Anabaptists who teach that infant Baptism is not right are rejected.

Art. X. It is taught among us that the true body and blood of Christ are really present in the Supper of our Lord under the form of bread and wine and are there distributed and received. The contrary doctrine is therefore rejected.

Art. XI. It is taught among us that private absolution should be retained and not allowed to fall into disuse. However, in confession it is not necessary to enumerate all trespasses and sins, for this is impossible. Ps. 19:12, "Who can discern his errors?"

Art. XXVIII. Our teachers assert that according to the Gospel the power of keys or the power of bishops is a power and command of God to preach the Gospel, to forgive and retain sins, and to administer and distribute the sacraments. . . .This power of keys or of bishops is used and exercised only by teaching and preaching the Word of God and by administering the sacraments . . . In this way are imparted not bodily but eternal things and gifts, namely, eternal righteousness, the Holy Spirit, and eternal life. These gifts cannot be obtained except through the office of preaching and of administering the sacraments.

Apology to the Augsburg Confession

The Lutheran confessional tradition leaves the door open as to the number of sacraments in the church.

> *Apology to the Augsburg Confession* (1531), Art. VII, VIII, and XIII,
> in trans. Theodore G. Tappert, *The Book of Concord*, 173, 211–13.

Art. VII and VIII. . . . They [i.e., the ordained] do not represent their own persons but the person of Christ, because of the church's call, as Christ testifies (Luke 10:16), "He who hears you hears me." When they offer the Word of Christ or the sacraments, they do so in Christ's place and stead.

Art. XIII. The genuine sacraments, therefore, are Baptism, the Lord's Supper, and absolution (which is the sacrament of penitence), for these rites have the commandment of God and the promise of grace, which is the heart of the New Testament. When we are baptized, when we eat the Lord's body, when we are absolved, our hearts should firmly believe that God really forgives us for Christ's sake. . . .

. . . If ordination is interpreted in relation to the ministry of the Word, we have no objection to calling ordination a sacrament. The ministry of the Word has God's command and glorious promise: "The Gospel is the power of God for salvation to every one who has faith" (Rom. 1:16), again, "My word that goes forth from my mouth shall not return to me empty, but it shall accomplish that which I purpose, and prosper in the thing for which I sent it" (Isa. 55:11). If ordination is interpreted this way, we shall not object either to calling the laying on of hands a sacrament. The church has the command to appoint ministers; to this we must subscribe wholeheartedly, for we know that God approves this ministry and is present in it. . . .

. . . Ultimately, if we should list as sacraments all things that have God's command and a promise attached to them, then why not prayer, which can most truly be called a sacrament? It has both the command of God and many promises. . . . No intelligent person will quibble about the number of sacraments or the terminology, so long as those things are kept which have God's command and promise.

Ulrich Zwingli

Zwingli's approach to the sacraments focuses on their being "memorials."

Ulrich Zwingli, *Commentary on True and False Religion* (1525), trans. Samuel Macauley Jackson and Clarence Nevin Heller (Durham, NC: Labyrinth Press, 1981), 184.

The sacraments are, then, signs or ceremonials—let me say it with the good permission of all both of the new school and the old—by which a man proves to the Church that he either aims to be, or is, a soldier of Christ, and which inform the whole Church rather than yourself of your faith. For if your faith is not so perfect as not to need a ceremonial sign to confirm it, it is not faith. For faith is that by which we rely on the mercy of God unwaveringly, firmly, and singleheartedly, as Paul shows us in many passages.

So much for the meaning of the name. Christ left us two sacraments and no more, Baptism and The Lord's Supper. By these we are initiated, giving the name with the one, and showing by the other that we are mindful of Christ's victory and are members of His Church. In Baptism we receive a token that we are to fashion our lives according to the rule of Christ; by the Lord's Supper we give proof that we trust in the death of Christ, glad and thankful to be in that company which gives thanks to the Lord for the blessing of redemption which He freely gave us by dying for us. The other sacraments are rather ceremonials, for they have no initiatory function in the Church of God. Hence it is not improper to exclude them; for they were not instituted by God to help us initiate anything in the Church.

John Calvin

John Calvin has a much higher appreciation for sacramental signs than does Ulrich Zwingli.

John Calvin, *Institutes of the Christian Religion*, IV, 14, 1–26 (1559), trans. Ford Lewis Battles, in LCC 21:1277–1303.

Chapter XIV. The Sacraments.
1. First, we must consider what a sacrament is. It seems to me that a simple and proper definition would be to say that it is an outward sign by which the Lord seals on our consciences the promises of his good will toward us in order to sustain the weakness of our faith; and we in turn attest our piety toward him in the presence of the Lord and of his angels and before men. Here is another briefer definition: one may call it a testimony of divine grace toward us, confirmed by an outward sign, with mutual attestation of our piety toward him. Whichever of these definitions you may choose, it does not differ in meaning from that of Augustine, who teaches that a sacrament is a "visible sign of a sacred thing," or "a visible form of an invisible grace," but it better and more clearly explains the thing itself. . . .

3. But as our faith is slight and feeble unless it be propped on all sides and sustained by every means, it trembles, wavers, totters, and at last gives way. Here our merciful Lord, according to his infinite kindness, so tempers himself to our capacity that, since we are creatures who always creep on the ground, cleave to the flesh, and, do not think about or even conceive of anything spiritual, he condescends to lead us to himself even by these earthly elements, and to set before us in the flesh a mirror of spiritual blessings. For if we were incorporated (as Chrysostom says), he would give us these very things naked and incorporeal. Now, because we have souls engrafted in bodies, he imparts spiritual things under visible ones. . . .

7. It is therefore certain that the Lord offers us mercy and the pledge of his grace both in his Sacred Word and in his sacraments. But it is understood only by those who take Word and sacraments

with sure faith, just as Christ is offered and held forth by the Father to all unto salvation, yet not all acknowledge and receive him. In one place Augustine, meaning to convey this, said that the efficacy of the Word is brought to light in the sacrament, not because it is spoken, but because it is believed. . . .

9. But the sacraments properly fulfill their office only when the Spirit, that inward teacher, comes to them, by whose power alone hearts are penetrated and affections moved and our souls opened for the sacraments to enter in. If the Spirit be lacking, the sacraments can accomplish nothing more in our minds than the splendor of the sun shining upon blind eyes, or a voice sounding in deaf ears. Therefore, I make such a division between Spirit and the sacraments that the power to act rests with the former, and the ministry alone is left to the latter—a ministry empty and trifling, apart from the action of the Spirit, but charged with great effect when the Spirit works within and manifests his power. . . .

17. Therefore, let it be regarded as a settled principle that the sacraments have the same office as the Word of God: to offer and set forth Christ to us, and in him the treasures of heavenly grace. . . .

They do not bestow any grace of themselves, but announce and tell us, and (as they are guarantees and tokens) ratify among us, those things given us by divine bounty. . . .

God therefore truly executes whatever he promises and represents in signs; nor do the signs lack their own effect in proving their Author truthful and faithful. . . .

20. These [circumcision, purifications, sacrifices, and other rites] were the sacraments of the Jews until the coming of Christ. When at his coming these were abrogated, two sacraments were instituted which the Christian church now uses, Baptism and the Lord's Supper [Matt. 28:19; 26:26–28]. I am speaking of those which were established for the use of the whole church. I would not go against calling the laying on of hands, by which ministers of the church are initiated into their office, a sacrament, but I do not include it among the ordinary sacraments. In what place the rest of what are commonly considered sacraments should be held, we shall soon see.

Yet those ancient sacraments looked to the same purpose to which ours now tend: to direct and almost lead men by the hand to Christ, or rather, as images, to represent him and show him forth to be known. . . . There is only one difference: the former foreshadowed Christ promised while he was as yet awaited: the latter attest him as already given and revealed.

21. When these things are individually explained, they will become much clearer.

For the Jews, circumcision was the symbol by which they were admonished that whatever comes forth from man's seed, that is, the whole nature of mankind, is corrupt and needs pruning. Moreover, circumcision was a token and reminder to confirm them in the promise given to Abraham of the blessed seed in which all nations of the earth were to be blessed [Gen. 22:18], from whom they were also to await their own blessing. Now that saving seed (as we are taught by Paul) was Christ [Gal. 3:16]. . . .

26. It is good that our readers be briefly apprised of this thing also: whatever the Sophists have dreamed up concerning the *opus operatum* is not only false but contradicts the nature of the sacraments, which God so instituted that believers, poor and deprived of all goods, should bring nothing to it but begging. From this it follows that in receiving the sacraments believers do nothing to deserve praise, and that even in this act (which on their part is merely passive) no work can be ascribed to them.

Church of Scotland

The Church of Scotland stands with Calvin's theological focus.

Church of Scotland, *The Scotch Confession of Faith* (1560), in trans. Philip Schaff, *The Creeds of Christendom* (Grand Rapids: Baker Book House, 1969), 3:467–68 (spelling, capitalization, and punctuation modernized).

Article XXI. Of the Sacraments
As the fathers under the law, besides the verity of the sacrifices, had two chief sacraments, to wit, circumcision and the Passover, the despisers and contemners whereof were not reputed for God's people; so do we acknowledge and confess that we now in the time of the Evangel have two chief sacraments, only instituted by the Lord *Jesus* and commanded to be used of all they that will be reputed members of his body, to wit Baptism and the Supper or Table of the Lord *Jesus*, called the Communion of his Body and his Blood. And these sacraments, as well of Old as of New Testament, now instituted of God, not only to make any visible difference betwixt his people and they that were without his league: But also to exercise the faith of his children, and, by participation of the same sacraments, to seal in their hearts the assurance of his promise, and of that most blessed conjunction, union, and society, which the elect have with their head *Christ Jesus*. And thus we utterly damn the vanity of they that affirm sacraments to be nothing else but naked and bare signs.

Church of England

While only baptism and Lord's Supper are retained as official sacraments of the "Gospel," the Church of England underscores that the sacraments are effectual signs of grace by which God works.

Articles of Religion (1563), in *The Book of Common Prayer* (Oxford, 1784); bracketed items omitted or modernized by John Wesley (1784), in *John Wesley's Sunday Service* (Nashville: United Methodist Publishing House, 1984), 311–12.

Article XXV [XVI]. Of the Sacraments.

Sacraments ordained of Christ, [be] not only badges or tokens of Christian men's profession; but rather they [be] certain [sure witnesses, and effectual] signs of grace, and God's good will towards us, by the which he doth work invisibly in us, and doth not only quicken, but also strengthen and confirm our Faith in him.

There are two Sacraments ordained of Christ our Lord in the Gospel; that is to say, Baptism, and the Supper of the Lord.

Those five commonly called Sacraments, that is to say, Confirmation, Penance, Orders, Matrimony, and Extreme Unction, are not to be counted for Sacraments of the Gospel, being such as have grown partly of the corrupt following of the Apostles, partly are states of life allowed in the Scriptures: but yet have not like nature of [Sacraments with] Baptism, and the Lord's Supper, [for that] they have not any visible sign or ceremony ordained by God.

The Sacraments were not ordained [of] Christ to be gazed upon, or to be carried about; but that we should duly use them. And in such only as worthily receive the same, they have a wholesome effect or operation: but they that receive them unworthily, purchase to themselves [damnation], as Saint *Paul* saith.

THE CATHOLIC REFORMATION

Council of Trent

The Council of Trent reaffirms the traditional seven sacraments, including their institution by Christ.

The Canons and Decrees of the Council of Trent (1547), in *The Creeds of Christendom*, 2:119–22.

Seventh Session, held March 3, 1547

Canon I.—If any one saith, that the sacraments of the New Law were not all instituted by Jesus Christ, our Lord; or, that they are more, or less, than seven, to wit, Baptism, Confirmation, the Eucharist, Penance, Extreme Unction, Order, and Matrimony; or even that any one of these seven is not truly and properly a sacrament: let him be anathema.

Canon II.—If any one saith, that these said sacraments of the New Law do not differ from the sacraments of the Old Law, save that the ceremonies are different, and different the outward rites: let him be anathema.

Canon III.—If any one saith, that these seven sacraments are in such wise equal to each other, as that one is not in any way more worthy than another: let him be anathema.

Canon IV.—If any one saith, that the sacraments of the New Law are not necessary unto salvation, but superfluous; and that without them, or without the desire thereof, men obtain of God, through faith alone, the grace of justification;—though all [the sacraments] are not indeed necessary for every individual: let him be anathema.

Canon V.—If any one saith, that these sacraments were instituted for the sake of nourishing faith alone: let him be anathema.

Canon VI.—If any one saith, that the sacraments of the New Law do not contain the grace which they signify; or, that they do not confer that grace on those who do not place an obstacle thereunto; as though they were merely outward signs of grace or justice received through faith, and certain marks of the Christian profession, whereby believers are distinguished amongst men from unbelievers: let him be anathema.

Canon VII.—If any one saith, that grace, as far as God's part is concerned, is not given through the said sacraments, always, and to all men, even though they receive them rightly but [only] sometimes, and to some persons: let him be anathema.

Canon VIII.—If any one saith, that by the said sacraments of the New Law grace is not conferred through the act performed, but that faith alone in the divine promise suffices for the obtaining of grace: let him be anathema.

Canon IX.—If any one saith, that, in the three sacraments, to wit, Baptism, Confirmation, and Order, there is not imprinted in the soul a character, that is, a certain spiritual and indelible sign, on account of which they can not be repeated: let him be anathema.

Canon X.—If any one saith, that all Christians have power to administer the word, and all the sacraments: let him be anathema.

Canon XI.—If any one saith, that, in ministers, when they effect, and confer the sacraments, there is not required the intention at least of doing what the Church does: let him be anathema.

Canon XII.—If any one saith, that a minister, being in moral sin,—if so be that he observe all the essentials which belong to the effecting, or conferring of, the sacrament,—neither effects, nor confers the sacrament: let him be anathema.

Canon XIII.—If any one saith, that the received and approved rites of the Catholic Church, wont to be used in the solemn administration of the sacraments, may be contemned, or without sin be omitted at pleasure by the ministers, or be changed, by every pastor of the churches, into other new ones: let him be anathema.

|

The Seventeenth and Eighteenth Centuries

|

The Puritans

The Calvinist tradition remains among the Puritans.

The Puritans, *Westminster Confession of Faith* (1647),
in *The Creeds of Christendom*, 3:660–61.

Chapter XXVII. Of the Sacraments.
1. Sacraments are holy signs and seals of the covenant of grace, immediately instituted by God, to represent Christ and his benefits, and to confirm our interest in him: as also to put a visible difference between those that belong unto the Church and the rest of the world; and solemnly to engage them to the service of God in Christ, according to his Word.

II. There is in every sacrament a spiritual relation or sacramental union, between the sign and the thing signified; whence it comes to pass that the names and the effects of the one are attributed to the other.

III. The grace which is exhibited in or by the sacraments, rightly used, is not conferred by any power in them; neither doth the efficacy of a sacrament depend upon the piety or intention of him that doth administer it, but upon the work of the Spirit, and the word of institution, which contains, together with a precept authorizing the use thereof, a promise of benefit to worthy receivers.

IV. There be only two sacraments ordained by Christ our Lord in the gospel, that is to say, Baptism and the Supper of the Lord: neither of which may be dispensed by any but by a minister of the Word lawfully ordained.

V. The sacraments of the Old Testament, in regard to the spiritual things thereby signified and exhibited, were, for substance, the same with those of the New.

Robert Barclay, Society of Friends

External sacraments have ceased in favor of the inward workings of God's Spirit.

Robert Barclay, *An Apology for the True Christian Divinity* (English trans. from Latin, 1678; Manchester: William Irwin, 1869), 215, 222, 240, 257, 280.

Proposition Eleventh. Concerning Worship.
All true and acceptable worship to God is offered in the inward and immediate moving and drawing of his own Spirit, which is neither limited to places, times, nor persons. . . .

And there being many joined together in the same work, there is an inward travail and wrestling; and also, as the measure of grace is abode in, an overcoming of the power and spirit of darkness; and thus we are often greatly strengthened and renewed in the spirits of our minds without a word, and we enjoy and possess the *holy fellowship*, and *communion of the body and blood of Christ,* by which our inward man is nourished and fed; which makes us not to dote upon outward *water,* and *bread* and *wine,* in our spiritual things. . . .

He [God] causeth the inward life (which is also many times not conveyed by the outward senses) the more to abound, when his children assemble themselves diligently together to wait upon him; so that *as iron sharpeneth iron* [Prov. 27:17], the seeing of the faces one of another, when both are inwardly gathered unto the life, giveth occasion for the life secretly to arise, and pass from vessel to vessel. And as many candles lighted, and put in one place, do greatly augment the light, and make it more to shine forth, so when many are gathered together into the same life, there is more of the glory of God, and his power appears to the refreshment of each individual; for that he partakes not only of the light and life raised in himself but in all the rest. And therefore Christ hath particularly promised a blessing to such as assemble together in his *name,* seeing he will be *in the midst of them,* Matt. 18:20. . . .

Proposition Twelfth. Concerning Baptism.
And this baptism is a pure and spiritual thing, to wit, the baptism of the Spirit and fire, by which we are buried with him, that being washed and purged from our sins, we may *walk in newness of life;* of

which the baptism of John was a figure, which was commanded for a time, and not to continue for ever. As to the baptism of *infants*, it is a mere human tradition, for which neither *precept* nor *practice* is to be found in all the scripture. . . .

Proposition Thirteenth. Concerning the Communion, or Participation of the Body and Blood of Christ.
The *communion* of the body and blood of Christ is *inward* and *spiritual*, which is the participation of his flesh and blood, by which the *inward man* is daily nourished in the hearts of those in whom Christ dwells; of which things the *breaking of bread* by Christ with his disciples was a *figure*, which even they who had received the substance used in the church for a time, for the sake of the weak; even as *abstaining from things strangled, and from blood; the washing one another's feet, and the anointing of the sick with oil*; all which are commanded with no less authority and solemnity than the former; yet seeing they are but *shadows* of better things, they cease in such as have obtained the *substance*.

Immanuel Kant

The Enlightenment values the sacraments chiefly as moral exhortations.

Immanuel Kant, *Religion within the Limits of Reason Alone* (1793), trans. Theodore M. Greene and Hoyt H. Hudson (New York: Harper & Row, 1960), 182–89.

There can, indeed, be three kinds of *illusory faith* that involve the possibility of our overstepping the bounds of our reason in the direction of the supernatural (which is not, according to the laws of reason, an object either of theoretical or practical use). *First*, . . . (the faith in *miracles*). *Second*, . . . (the faith in *mysteries*). *Third*, the illusion of being able to bring about, through the use of merely natural means, an effect which is, for us, a mystery, namely the influence of God upon our morality (the faith in *means of grace*). . . . It still remains, therefore, for us to treat of the means of grace, (which are further distinguished from *works of grace*, i.e., supernatural moral influences in relation to which we are merely passive; but the imagined experience of these is a fanatical illusion pertaining entirely to the emotions).

1. *Praying*, thought of as an *inner formal* service of God and hence as a means of grace, is a superstitious illusion. . . .

2. *Church-going*, thought of as the ceremonial *public service of God* in a church, *in general*, [only as] a *means of grace*, is an illusion.

3. The ceremonial initiation, taking place but once, into the church . . . community, that is, one's first acceptance as a member of a church (in the Christian Church through *baptism*) is a highly significant ceremony which lays a grave obligation either upon the initiate, if he is in a position himself to confess his faith, or upon the witnesses who pledge themselves to take care of his education in this faith. This aims at something holy (the development of a man into a citizen in a divine state) but this act performed by others is not in itself holy or productive of holiness and receptivity for the divine grace in this individual; hence it is no *means of grace*, however exaggerated the esteem in which it was held in the early Greek church, where it was believed capable, in an instant, of washing away all sins—and here this illusion publicly revealed its affinity to an almost more than heathenism superstition.

4. The oft-repeated ceremony (*communion*) of a *renewal, continuation, and propagation of this churchly community* under laws of *equality*, a ceremony which indeed can be performed, after the example of the Founder of such a church (and, at the same time, in memory of him), through the formality of a common partaking at the same table, contains within itself something great, expanding the narrow selfish, and unsociable cast of mind among men, especially in matters of religion, towards the idea of a cosmopolitan *moral community*; and it is a good means of enlivening a community to the moral disposition of brotherly love which it represents. But to assert that God has attached special favors to the celebration of this solemnity, and to incorporate among the articles of faith the proposition that this ceremony, which is after all but a churchly act, is, in addition, a *means of grace*—this is a religious illusion which can do naught but work counter to the spirit of religion. *Clericalism* in general would therefore be the dominion of the clergy over men's hearts, usurped by the dint of arrogating to themselves the prestige attached to exclusive possession of means of grace.

All such artificial self-deceptions in religious matters have a common basis. Among the three divine attributes, holiness, mercy, and justice, man habitually turns directly to the second in order thus to avoid the forbidding condition of conforming to the requirements of the first. . . .

To this end man busies himself with every conceivable formality, designed to indicate how greatly he *respects* the divine commands, in order that it may not be necessary for him to *obey* them; and, that his idle wishes may serve also good to make good the disobedience of these commands, he cries: "Lord, Lord," so as not to have to "do the will of his heavenly Father" (Mt. 7:21). . . . He busies himself

with piety (a passive respect for the law of God) rather than with
virtue. . . .

When the illusion of this supposed favorite of heaven mounts to
the point where he fanatically imagines that he feels special works
of grace within himself (or even where he actually presumes to be
confident of a fancied occult *intercourse* with God), virtue comes at
last actually to arouse his loathing and becomes for him an object of
contempt.

|

The Modern Period: A New Era
in Sacramental Theology

|

Edward Schillebeeckx

Dominican theologian Edward Schillebeeckx sets the agenda for contemporary Roman Catholic and ecumenical sacramental thinking by focusing
on the language of personal encounter in the sacraments.

Edward Schillebeeckx, OP, *Christ the Sacrament of the Encounter with God* (1960),
trans. Paul Barrett et al. (New York: Sheed & Ward, 1963), 15–17, 44–45.

The man Jesus, as the personal visible realization of the divine grace
of redemption, is *the* sacrament, the primordial sacrament, because
this man, the Son of God himself, is intended by the Father to be
in his humanity the only way to the actuality of redemption. "For
there is one God, and one mediator of God and men, the man Christ
Jesus" [I Tim. 2:5]. Personally to be approached by the man Jesus
was, for his contemporaries, an invitation to a personal encounter
with the life-giving God, because personally that man was the Son
of God. Human encounter with Jesus is therefore the sacrament of
the encounter with God, or of the religious life as a theologal [*sic*]
attitude of existence towards God. Jesus' human redeeming acts are
therefore a "sign and cause of grace." "Sign" and "cause" of salvation are not brought together here as two elements fortuitously conjoined. Human bodiliness is human interiority itself in visible form.

Now because the inward power of Jesus' will to redeem and of
his human love is God's own saving power realized in human form,
the human saving acts of Jesus are the divine bestowal of grace itself

realized in visible form; that is to say they cause what they signify; they are sacraments. . . .

From this account of the sacraments as the earthly prolongation of Christ's glorified bodiliness, it follows immediately that the Church's sacraments are not things but encounters of men on earth with the glorified man Jesus by way of a visible form. On the plane of history they are the visible and tangible embodiment of the heavenly saving action of Christ. They are this saving action itself in its availability to us; a personal act of the Lord in earthly visibility and open availability.

Here the first and most fundamental definition of sacramentality is made evident. In an earthly embodiment which we can see and touch, the heavenly Christ sacramentalizes both his continual intercession for us and his active gift of grace. Therefore the sacraments are the visible realization on earth of Christ's mystery of saving worship. "What was visible in Christ has now passed over into the sacraments of the Church" [Ascension Day sermon of Leo I].

The fact which we must now begin to analyze in detail is therefore this: Through the sacraments we are placed in living contact with the mystery of Christ the High Priest's saving worship. In them we encounter Christ in his mystery of Passover and Pentecost. The sacraments *are* this saving mystery in earthly guise. This visible manifestation is the visible Church.

Karl Rahner

The highly influential Jesuit theologian Karl Rahner grounds the sacraments in the sacramental nature of the church expressing itself sacramentally rather than in explicit dominical institution.

Karl Rahner, SJ, *The Church and the Sacraments*, Quaestiones Disputatae 9 (London: Search Press, Ltd., 1963), 38–41.

[W]e must distinguish between two aspects: the dependence of the actual manifestation on what is manifesting itself, and the difference between the two. To cite a comparable relationship, a spiritual being is an intellectual substance, yet only constitutes itself as such, as mind, by there emanating from it what is not identical with itself, its really distinct power of knowing. A proportionately similar relation holds between phenomenon and underlying reality. Hence it is possible to perceive why the symbol can be really distinct from what is symbolized and yet an intrinsic factor of what is symbolized. . . .

What is manifesting itself posits its own identity and existence by manifesting itself in this manifestation which is distinct from itself. An example of this relationship is available for the scholastic philosopher in the relation between soul and body. The body is the manifestation of the soul, through which and in which the soul realizes its own essence. The sign is therefore a cause of what it signifies by being the way in which what is signified effects itself. The kind of causality expressed in such a conception of symbolism occurs on various levels of human reality. In substantial being (body as the sign or symbol of the soul); in the sphere of activity (bodily gesture through which the inner attitude itself which is expressed by it first attains its own full depth). . . .

. . . This concept of the intrinsic symbol . . . must now be employed if we are to grasp what characterizes sacramental causation, and if we are to do this on the basis of the ecclesiological origin of the sacraments. The Church in her visible historical form is herself an intrinsic symbol of the eschatologically triumphant grace of God; in that spatio-temporal visible form, this grace is made present. And because the sacraments are the actual fulfillment, the actualization of the Church's very nature, in regard to individual men, precisely in as much as the Church's whole reality is to be the real presence of God's grace, as the new covenant, these sacramental signs are efficacious. Their efficacy is that of the intrinsic symbol. Christ acts through the Church in regard to an individual human being, by giving his action spatio-temporal embodiment by having the gift of his grace manifested in the sacrament. This visible form is itself an effect of the coming of grace; it is there because God is gracious to men; and in this self-embodiment of grace, grace itself occurs. The sacramental sign is cause of grace in as much as grace is conferred by being signified. And this presence (by signifying) of grace in the sacraments is simply the actuality of the Church herself as the visible manifestation of grace. Consequently the converse holds. The relation between the Church as the historical visible manifestation of grace and grace itself, one of reciprocal conditioning, extends into the relation between sacramental sign and grace conferred. The sign effects grace, by grace producing the sacrament as sign of the sanctification effected. This, of course, can only be said if the Church as an entity is truly and inseparably connected with grace. Only then is her act, when it is an unconditional realization of her essence (that is of the Church as the presence of grace), essentially and irrevocably a manifestation of grace, so that the manifestation necessarily renders present what is manifested. . . .

. . . From the principle that the Church is the primal sacrament it would be possible to see that the existence of true sacraments in the strictest traditional sense is not necessarily and always based on a definite statement, which has been preserved or is presumed to have existed, in which the historical Jesus Christ explicitly spoke about a certain definite sacrament. This would have its importance for apologetics of a less anxious and worried kind in the history of dogma, in the matter of the institution of all the sacraments by Christ. A fundamental act of the Church in an individual's regard, in situations that are decisive for him, an act which truly involves the nature of the Church as the historical, eschatological presence of redemptive grace, is *ipso facto* a sacrament, even if it were only later that reflection was directed to its sacramental character that follows from its connection with the nature of the Church. The institution of a sacrament can . . . follow simply from the fact that Christ founded the Church with its sacramental nature. It is clear too that, properly understood, the treatise *De sacramentis in genere* is not an abstract formulation of the nature of the individual sacraments, but is part of the treatise *De ecclesia*. It rightly precedes doctrine about the individual sacraments; it does not follow as a subsequent secondary generalization; for only on the basis of the doctrine about the Church, the fundamental sacrament, can the sacramentality of several sacraments be recognized at all.

Mark Searle

Searle provides a succinct summary of contemporary sacramental theology.

Mark Searle, "Infant Baptism Reconsidered," in *LWSS*, 365.

During the past twenty or thirty years sacramental theology has undergone an enormous transformation. Undoubtedly the leading indicator if not the cause of this transformation is the abandonment of the questions and vocabulary of Scholasticism in favor of more existentialist and personalist approaches to understanding what sacraments are and how they function in the Christian life. What began as a recovery of the ecclesial dimension of the sacraments quickly led to further shifts: from speaking of sacraments as "means of grace" to speaking of them as encounters with Christ himself; from thinking of them primarily as acts of God to thinking of them mainly as celebrations of the faith community; from seeing sacraments as momentary incursions from another world to seeing them as manifestations of the graced character of all human life; from interpreting them as remedies for sin and weakness to seeing them as promoting growth in Christ.

J. D. Crichton

The influence of both Schillebeeckx and Rahner is obvious in Crichton's helpful summary of contemporary Roman Catholic approaches to sacramental theology today.

J. D. Crichton, "A Theology of Worship," in C. Jones, G. Wainwright,
E. Yarnold, and P. Bradshaw, eds., *The Study of Liturgy*, rev. ed.
(New York: Oxford University Press, 1992), 23.

The ultimate subject of the liturgical celebration . . . is . . . Christ who acts in and through his Church. Obviously his action is invisible, but the people of God, his body, is a visible and structured community and over the whole range of its liturgical action, which . . . consists of both word and sacrament, manifests Christ's presence, shows forth the nature of his activity, which is redemptive, and by his power makes his redeeming work effectual and available to men and women today. It is for these reasons that the Church is called the "sacrament of Christ." Like him it is both visible and invisible, and its sole raison d'être is to mediate his saving love to humankind. . . . From Christ, the sacrament of the Father and of his saving purpose, to the Church, which is the sacrament of Christ, and then to the liturgy, which exists to manifest and convey the redeeming love of God, the line is clear. The liturgy then is essentially and by its nature sacramental. . . . It addresses a word to us but it embodies this word in actions, gestures and symbols; . . . [and] the gesture or thing (water, bread, wine) forces us to attend to the word, enables us to grasp its import and to appropriate its content.

James F. White

James White (+2004) offers a modern Protestant way to rethink the number and definition of the sacraments.

James F. White, *Sacraments as God's Self-Giving*
(Nashville: Abingdon Press, 1983), 70–75.

Throughout most of the history of Christianity, the number of sacraments was not defined. Over the centuries, Christians recognized a variety of ways God's self-giving was experienced in worship. Dozens of these forms have been called sacraments at one time or another. Augustine applied the term to an assortment of objects and sign-acts: the giving of salt in baptism, the use of ashes for penitents, recital of creeds and the Lord's Prayer, the baptismal font, and Easter Day. Each of these sacred signs represents something inward and spiritual. For the seven following centuries there was still considerable latitude; as late as 1140, Hugh of St. Victor could consider genuflection, the blessing of palms, the receiving of ashes, and reciting creeds as sacraments. Almost to the end of the twelfth century (1179), the third Lateran Council could still speak of instituting priests in office or burial of the dead as sacraments.

Such latitude seems strange today, so familiar are we with sharply restricted lists. . . . Yet almost a dozen centuries passed before the Church felt any need to systematize what is experienced in the sacraments. The experience of God's self giving in the sacraments is primary; theological systematization was a rather late secondary concern.

The key figure who pulled together the wide assortment of theological reflections about what the Church experienced in the sacraments . . . was a twelfth-century theologian, Peter Lombard, a professor in Paris and (briefly) bishop. . . . In order to systematize what the Church had been experiencing in sacraments, Peter found it necessary to list them. "Now let us approach the sacraments of the new law, which are: baptism, confirmation, the bread of blessing, that is the eucharist, penance, extreme unction, orders, marriage." By the following century the list had become standard, so that the Council of Trent in the sixteenth century could anathematize anyone claiming "that they are more, or less, than seven."

But one step Peter Lombard did not take—he did not find it necessary to affirm that all seven sacraments were instituted by Jesus Christ himself. Indeed, he tells us that the unction of the sick was said to be "instituted by the apostles," though Lombard is clear that Christ instituted baptism and the eucharist. . . .

The problem would be much simpler if we were to admit several levels of authority for sacraments. We suggest that they be looked at as dominical, apostolic, and natural. In relation to Christ's institution of baptism and the eucharist, we seem to have ample evidence, and thus we shall call them *dominical sacraments*. . . .

. . . But scripture gives us not only Christ's words but records his actions and intentions. We have, for example, abundant examples of Christ's forgiving sin. Certainly there is ample evidence of Jesus' ministry of forgiveness (e.g., Matt. 9:2), or of Jesus' will that his disciples should do likewise (John 20:23). Nor is there any doubt of the apostles fulfilling the Lord's intention (Acts 13:38; 26:18). . . . The apostles and their followers carried on Jesus' work of forgiveness as has the Church ever since. . . . Thus the apostolic practice is evidence of obedience to what the early Church considered to be the will of Christ. And on this basis the practice was retained by the Church.

Closely related is Christ's work of healing; examples abound of his healing work and his sending the disciples to do likewise: "the sick on whom they lay their hands will recover" (Mark 16:18). The apostolic Church obeyed these intentions to heal faithfully. . . . James 5:13–16 speaks of what had later apparently become routine healing by elders in local congregations.

The evidence of ordination is equally indirect and equally strong. Jesus obviously chose people to be his disciples (Mark 1:16–20) and sent them on mission (6:7–13), having first empowered them. . . . John makes it more formal: Jesus greets the disciples and commissions them, "As the Father sent me, so I send you," and transmits the Holy Spirit (John 20:21–22). Apostolic practice did likewise. Suitable people were chosen, there was prayer and the laying on of hands (Acts 6:3–6). . . . As the Lord had done, so did the apostolic Church in choosing representative persons to carry out its mission.

In these three examples—reconciliation, healing, and ordination—we have cases of apostolic practice continuing the intentions and actions of Jesus. Thus, though we cannot call them sacraments of dominical institution . . . , we can call them *apostolic sacraments* since their institution can be based on evidence of apostolic practice. . . .

. . . [T]here is one more type of sacrament. We prefer to speak of the Christian marriage ceremony and Christian burial as *natural sacraments*. Both have been listed as Christian sacraments, Christian burial as late as the Third Lateran Council in 1179, and matrimony made the Tridentine list. . . .

. . . In these cases, we are dealing with life events common to all humanity. In virtually every society there are rites of marriage and observance at the time of death. It is no surprise that Christians have adapted the wedding customs and burial practices of Jewish and Roman cultures (and almost every culture in the world) to their own purposes.

The humanity of the sacraments is reflected in the Church's celebration of normal and necessary human passages that are common to all people as witnesses to God's self-giving. Not every human rite of passage has been so treated by Christians. . . . But marriage and death have been treated as moments we can call natural sacraments. In them, the Church sees God's work through the community of faith in supporting people as they enter new relationships to each other and the community. . . .

. . . There is no reason to be too precise about God's actions now than there was in the first twelve Christian centuries. We would rather leave the number of sacraments once again indeterminate.

Susan A. Ross

Susan A. Ross, "God's Embodiment and Women," in *Freeing Theology:*
The Essentials of Theology in Feminist Perspective, ed. Catherine Mowry LaCugna
(San Francisco: HarperSanFrancisco, 1993), 198–99, 206–7; endnotes from 208–9.

The challenge of feminism to Christian theology is the expression of the full humanity of women and men, not only "in Christ" but in society and in the church. What has hampered this realization in Catholic theology in particular is a historical reliance on a theology of natural law that regards biological sex differences as essential factors in the significance of human nature, resulting in differential treatment of women and men. Women's "nature" is understood (as in the writings of John Paul II) to be primarily oriented toward childbearing and rearing, thus relegating women to the sphere of the home.[1] The vocations of religious women are sometimes seen as extensions of this maternal role, as pope John Paul II points out. In addition, the almost primeval character of religious symbolism has been infected by the pervasive influence of sexism. The resistance not only by many men but by many women to use feminine imagery for God suggests that our language and vision need reeducation.[2]

Where a sacramental feminist theology begins, then, is in the basic conviction of the full humanity of women and the recognition that the meaning associated with sex differences over the centuries is highly suspect. This meaning, usually seen as complementarity, is rooted in history and culture and therefore its claim to understand women's supposedly essential and timeless nature is without an adequate basis. In addition to this challenge comes the conviction of the interconnectedness of human life and of human and nonhuman life. Much of feminist thought over the last twenty years has pointed out the distinctive nature of women's experiences and has thus opened itself to criticism that these distinctive elements look suspiciously like stereotypically feminine qualities attributed to women by men. But what distinguishes these efforts are, first, the concern to know and value women's experiences and not to model expectations for women on male experience alone; and, second, a recognition of the ambiguity of women's experience. That is, because women have been both included in and excluded from the category men and have been included in the structures of society as domestic shapers of culture

---

1. John Paul II, "*Mulieris Dignitatem:* On the Dignity and Vocation of Women," *Origins* 18, no. 17 (Oct. 6, 1988).

2. Margaret Miles, *Image as Insight: Visual Understanding in Western Christianity and Secular Culture* (Boston: Beacon Press, 1985).

yet excluded from public positions of power, women have developed a dual consciousness, an awareness of "twoness"—in short, a sense of radical ambiguity that does not lend itself easily to strategies of separation and isolation.[3]

What some psychologists label as the greater permeability of women's ego boundaries, and what some ethicists have labeled as the inability of women to make clear moral distinctions, have been understood to handicap women. But women's sense of ambiguity, reluctance to make separations, and tendency to identify with the other are closer to the heart of Christian sacramentality than the strict separations that have become pervasive in much sacramental theology and practice. Such a sense of interconnection and an appreciation of the often conflicting realities that coexist in such interconnection is characteristic of much of contemporary feminist theory in psychology, literary theory, history, and ethics. These ideas have important implications for sacramental theology as well.[4]

———

Certain issues remain critical in any continuing reflection on women and the sacramental life of the church.

1. The meaning of the Incarnation and its connection with theological anthropology are at the core of sacramental theology. The recognition that God took on human (not specifically male) flesh is central, as is the recognition that the historical and social constructions of gender have played crucial roles in maintaining assumptions about women's so-called proper role in the church. The threats to women's full humanity have been recognized especially in the last one hundred and fifty years. While differences between men and women remain a controversial subject, traditional notions of complementarity are no longer adequate. Differences have most often been seen from a male perspective, so that women's awareness of their own experience has only recently begun to emerge. The postmodern focus on the multiplicity and diversity of human experience offers one way of accounting for difference without the stereotyped categories of complementarity. This focus also opens up the consideration of human experience from the perspectives of race and class as well as gender.

2. The influential role of symbolic expression and the recognition of the ways in which gender is an unacknowledged dimension of that expression require careful interdisciplinary analysis. Literary, psychoanalytic, and social critiques have revealed hidden biases in

3. See Elizabeth Fox-Genovese, *Feminism without Illusions: A Critique of Individualism* (Chapel Hill: University of North Carolina Press, 1991).

4. See Susan A. Ross, "Sacraments and Women's Experience," *Listening* 28 (1993): 52–64.

so-called universal expressions of human experience in novels, in psychological analyses of human development, and in the dynamics of social groups. Theologians need to be especially attentive to the contributions of their colleagues in these fields, since they can shed needed light on central theological questions. Sacramental theology, because of its reliance on studies of symbol and metaphor and its rootedness in human developmental processes, can especially benefit from such collaborative work.

3. The connection between sacramental praxis and social justice has received renewed emphasis since the rise of the liberation movements of the 1960s. Tissa Balisuriya writes that "the Eucharist has to be related positively to human life if it is to be faithful to its origins and its performance."[5] In more traditional language, sacraments must effect what they signify. The disjunction between social praxis and ecclesiology maintained in *Inter Insigniores* will no longer suffice as an adequate explanation for "sacramental sex discrimination." As long as sacramental theology continues to privilege the experience of men over women, there will not be a just sacramental praxis.

To a great extent, reflection on women and sacraments is at a very early stage. The depth of symbolic meaning precludes rapid change or change by fiat, but the realization that the structures of the imagination are deeply rooted should not be allowed to inhibit all changes. Openness to new developments, continuing reflection on women's experience, and careful scrutiny of our theological and symbolic heritage will work to transform the ways in which we live out the Christian belief that Christ lives among us, in the flesh and blood of the church.

M. Daniel Findikyan

Armenian Apostolic priest M. Daniel Findikyan directs attention to the presence of the phrase "unfailing Word" in Eastern Christian sacramental texts as a way of understanding anew the relationship between word and sacrament.

M. Daniel Findikyan, "The Unfailing Word in Eastern Sacramental Prayers," in Maxwell E. Johnson and L. Edward Phillips, eds., *Studia Liturgica Diversa: Essays in Honor of Paul F. Bradshaw* (Portland: Pastoral Press, 2004), 179–80, 188–89.

One of the enduring issues in the field of liturgical theology is the relationship between Word and Sacrament. Having roots reaching back to medieval Catholic and Reformation polemics, the problem

---

5. Tissa Balisuriya, *The Eucharist and Human Liberation* (Maryknoll, NY: Orbis Books, 1979), 86.

continues to attract the attention of Protestant and Catholic theologians, not to mention a few Orthodox scholars, who are beginning to add their voices to the fray.

Recent scholarship in liturgical theology is clearly attempting to reconcile what has been, at times in the history of Christian dogma, a stated or perceived divorce of Word and Sacrament in the life of the Church of Jesus Christ. In a fine summary of the vast scholarship on the issue, Andrew Ciferni has recently written: "There is hardly a single Christian church which would today admit to an opposition between word and sacrament. These are no longer considered independent and different manners of divine self-communication but complementary realities incapable of accomplishing their task without reciprocal penetration."[6]

The very rubric "Word and Sacrament," however, is in need of clarification and delimitation, since it has come to characterize an array of diverse theological issues. These include, but are by no means limited to the proper balance in the liturgical service between the ritual act on the one hand, and the proclamation of the word, often understood either as the homily or as the reading of sacred scripture, on the other hand. In theological discussions of this sort "word" and "sacrament" are inevitably, at least on some level, viewed in opposition, as discrete entities in need of reconciliation. Reformation-era polemics, which tended to absolutize one or the other of the two entities as normative or primary, have given way, in modern sacramental theology, to a variety of solutions that attempt to articulate the modality of "reciprocal penetration" of Word and Sacrament, which the modern scholarly consensus increasingly holds as the key to an authentic and accurate understanding of how, in the words of Peter Fink, "the whole church, assembled of its faith and its mission, embod[ies] and make[s] accessible the saving work of Christ."[7]

I do not presume here to make any landmark contribution to this great theological discussion, but rather to invite attention to an interesting little textual formula observable in a number of Armenian and other eastern sacramental prayers, which may shed light on the relationship of word and sacrament. It is the explicit reference to the "unfailing" or "infallible" Word of the Lord, which numerous prayers invoke as the ultimate authority and power justifying the sacramental action or claim. As a characteristic of the liturgical text itself, the observation I shall make regarding the Word-Sacrament relationship stems directly from the *lex orandi*, a foundation which

---

6. Andrew D. Ciferni, O. Praem., "Word and Sacrament" in *The New Dictionary of Sacramental Worship* (henceforth *NDSW*), ed. Peter E. Fink, SJ (Collegeville, MN: Liturgical Press, 1990), 1320.
7. Peter E. Fink, SJ, "Sacramental Theology after Vatican II," in *NDSW*, 1109–10.

much contemporary sacramental theology seeks and espouses, but which has, in fact, been only marginally achieved. After presenting some examples of this liturgical formula in various liturgical texts, I shall conclude by suggesting, in the most tentative way, what its implications may be for our understanding of the ongoing theological discourse regarding "word" and "sacrament." . . .

. . . What, then, is to be made of all this? At the very least we have drawn attention to a phrase from sacred scripture that seems to reflect a traditional attitude of liturgical prayer in the Deuteronomic school; which finds its way into some of the earliest extant sacramental texts, and from there into a remarkable number of sacramental prayers of various rites, the Armenian Rite in particular. Such an ancient common liturgical thread is of interest if for no other reason than that.

The "unfailing word" may indeed, however, have greater significance for our understanding of the sacraments within the life of the church; and, perhaps, for a renewed appreciation of an eventual patristic, or first-millennium theology of the sacraments that is firmly rooted in the *lex orandi*. In light of the tentative nature of my observations, instead of conclusions I should like to offer a few propositions that seem to emerge from the invocation of the "unfailing word" in the prayers we have analyzed.

1. The "unfailing word" clarifies the proverbial problem in sacramental theology of the relationship between divine initiative and the ecclesial response of faith in the sacraments, the *ex opere operato/ operantis* dispute. The only guarantee of the sacrament's efficacy is the church's faith in the Lord's promises. Implied in these prayers' appeal to the "unfailing word" is a total rejection of any sense of "automatic efficacy" for the sacraments. The only criterion for sacramental efficaciousness, in other words, is the "unfailing word," the church's faith that God will do what God promised to do. The role of the faithful in the sacramental encounter is not merely gratefully to accept or internalize some abstract notion of grace, either intellectually or emotionally, but in faith to proclaim and profess the word of the Lord. Here, embedded in the *lex orandi*, is tangible evidence for the assertion in *Sacrosanctum concilium* 59 that: "[The sacraments] not only presuppose the faith, but through words and things also nourish it, strengthen it and express it. That is why they are called sacraments of faith."[8]

2. The invocation of the "unfailing word" *de facto* repudiates the notion that the sacrament is magic, or that the minister is a magician.

---

8. *Vatican Council II: The Conciliar and Post-Conciliar Documents*, new rev. ed., Austin Flannery, OP, ed. (Collegeville, MN: Liturgical Press, 1992), 20.

The church and her ministers' only claim is for what the Lord himself has already promised by his word, and what, therefore, none other than the Lord can accomplish.

3. . . . [T]he logical arguments that culminate in the invocation of an "unfailing word" of the Lord virtually compel the Lord to act, in a way that is very reminiscent of Deuteronomic prayer, but startlingly bold and perhaps refreshing when compared with the sappy tone of much contemporary liturgical prayer.

4. The invocation of the word of the Lord in the anamnetic context of the sacramental prayer text serves to contextualize the sacrament in the divine economy of salvation history. The sacrament is far more than a visible vehicle for invisible grace, but an extension and perpetuation, in the church's time and space, of Christ's redemptive, loving activity based upon a specific promise by the word of the Lord. The word of the Lord, in other words, is fully harmonized within, and justifies the sacrament in its narrative prayer.

5. Finally, the "unfailing word" reconciles the word-sacrament dichotomy. The sacrament is a proclamation of the word of God, the celebration of the sacrament a profession of fidelity to that divine Word. Catholic, Orthodox and Protestant theologians have long asserted that "the liturgy of the Word is as sacramental as the Sacrament is 'evangelical'," as one theologian has put it.[9] But they have done so largely by intuition, without grounding their arguments in the liturgical texts themselves.[10]

Yet behind the early and widespread invocation of the "unfailing word" in liturgical texts lie an ancient, biblical theology of the sacraments and perhaps the seeds of a truly "ecumenical" sacramental theology that responds to the concerns of classical Protestantism without sacrificing or mitigating the centrality of sacramental life for the church.

---

9. Alexander Schmemann, *For the Life of the World* (Crestwood, NY: St. Vladimir's Seminary Press, 2000), 32–33.

10. Suffice it to mention four theologians who, in different ways, seek to reconcile Word and Sacrament, but without reference to the texts of the sacramental prayers. In this way their work is emblematic of much recent scholarship in this field. Catholic perspectives include Karl Rahner, "The Word and the Eucharist," in *Theological Investigations IV* (Baltimore: Helicon Press, 1960), 253–86, and Edward Kilmartin, SJ, "A Modern Approach to the Word of God," in *The Sacraments: God's Love and Mercy Actualized*, Francis A. Eigo, OSA, ed. (Philadelphia: Villanova University Press, 1979), 59–109. An Orthodox perspective is offered by John Breck, "The Sacramental Power of the Word," in *The Power of the Word* (Crestwood, NY: St. Vladimir's Seminary Press, 1995), 11–22. For an enlightening view from a Protestant author, see Daniel Shin, "Some Light from Origen: Scripture as Sacrament," *Worship* 75 (1999): 399–425.

Louis-Marie Chauvet

Louis-Marie Chauvet, noted French Roman Catholic sacramental theologian, returns to Augustine to elucidate the meaning of sacrament in relationship to the Word.

Louis-Marie Chauvet, *The Sacraments: The Word of God at the Mercy of the Body* (Collegeville, MN: Liturgical Press, Pueblo, 2001), 47–48.

The Sacrament, "Precipitate" of the Scriptures
The word of God does not reach us except through the sacramental mediation of the Scriptures read in church; conversely, the sacraments are like the precipitate (in the chemical sense) of the Scriptures as word. Of course, sacraments are rites, and we cannot understand them theologically without most carefully taking into account their ritual modality. However, although every sacrament is a rite, the rite becomes a sacrament only if it is converted by the word and the Spirit.

Word and Sacrament
That every sacrament is a sacrament of the word, is attested by the *lex orandi* ("the rule of prayer") of the church. The story of Emmaus already reflects a practice where the "breaking of the bread" followed the readings of Moses and the Prophets interpreted in the homily. The sequence Liturgy of the Word/Liturgy of the Sacrament, which is observed not only at Mass but also in every sacramental celebration, is not arbitrary. Is the sacrament anything else, according to Augustine's formula, than a *visibile verbum*, a "visible word," or rather the very word made visible? "In the name of the Father, and of the Son, and of the Holy Spirit," which is the sacramental word of baptism and reconciliation, is a synthesis of the Christian reading of all the Scriptures to such a point that these words are precisely those which accompany the sign of the cross, the Christian symbol par excellence, and condense in themselves the whole of Christian identity.

"The word comes over the element and becomes sacrament."[11] This formula, which was current in all the textbooks of the Middle Ages, has become a true adage. It must be understood on three levels:

---

11. "*Accedit verbum ad elementum et fit sacramentum.*" The "word" is the grammatical subject of the two verbs in the sentence, rather than the subject of only the first one, according to the rather frequent translation, "The word comes to the element and here is [or 'and thus is made'] the sacrament." The whole tenor of Augustine's sacramental theology favors our translation,

(a) first, the Christological level since the Word, which through the Spirit comes over the element of bread or water, is Christ himself, the Word of God; (b) then, the liturgical level since this risen Christ who is always the same, comes "in-formed" by the liturgy or the color of the day, color that differs depending on the time one is in, Lent, Eastertide, Ordinary Sundays; (c) last, the properly sacramental level where the sacramental word, pronounced in faith by the priest in the capacity of minister, that is, pronounced "in the name of Christ,"[12] is recognized as the word of Christ himself. Indeed, as Augustine had underscored against the Donatists, who held that the reality of the sacrament depended on the personal dignity of the minister who confers it, it is always Christ who baptizes, even through an unworthy minister. . . .

. . . [I]t is clear theologically that every sacrament is a sacrament of the word, or to say it differently, *the word itself mediated under the ritual mode, different from the mode of Scripture.* Although the distinction between word and sacrament is a legitimate one, their dichotomy has had disastrous results. Initiated by the Reformers of the sixteenth century in the context of excessive sacramentalism, against which a reaction in favor of returning to the word is easily understandable, this reaction, recently reconfigured by the ideological opposition between "faith" and "religion," ended by establishing a true competition between the two.[13] The word, source of the "true" faith, would be endowed with all virtues of "authenticity," "responsibility," "commitment," Christian "adulthood" or "maturity" finally reached, whereas sacraments would be suspected of bordering on magic, of fostering the most dubious anthropological and social archaism, of encouraging dependency among believers, and so on. Such reasoning shows forgetfulness of two things: first, that the word also reaches us only through the mediation of a body of writings which is as liable to manipulation as anything else and which is subject to highly ritualized uses even in the most spare liturgies; second, that the sacraments, obviously exposed to pitfalls because of their ritual character . . . are nothing but a particular modality of the word. . . .

. . . It is always *as word* that Christ gives himself to be eaten in the Eucharist. It is impossible to receive communion fruitfully without having "eaten the book" (see Ezek 2–3; Rev 10:9–10), ruminated the word in the Spirit. Here again, nothing is more traditional. Thus

---

12. This is the translation of the formula *"in persona Christi."*

13. The distinction between "faith" and "religion" is precious when it is used to stress the originality of the act of faith. But it is tendentious, even untenable, when it is applied to categories of persons, as sometimes happened in the 1970s.

Ambrose in the fourth century, speaking of the Scriptures: "Eat this food first, in order to be able to come afterward to the food of the body of Christ"; or Augustine: "Sisters and brothers, see that you eat the heavenly bread in a spiritual sense . . . so that all this may help us, beloved, not to eat the flesh and blood of Christ merely in the sacrament, as many of the wicked do, but to eat and drink in order to participate in the Spirit."[14]

What we just said is important. Important of course with regard to the nature of the sacraments: they have no more magical efficacy than the word of God transmitted through the mediation of the Scriptures, since they too are sacraments of the same word. Important also with regard to the understanding of their mode of efficacy: it is the path of the word, in human communication, and not the path of the efficacy of the "instrument" as in classical theology. . . .

---

14. Ambrose, *Expositio in Psalmum 118*, in PL 15:1197–1526; Augustine, *Homilies on the Gospel of John* 26.11; 27.11; *NPNF¹* 7:171 and 178.

CHAPTER 2

Liturgical Theology

The discipline known as "liturgical theology" is a relatively recent development in the theological curriculum. But if the discipline itself is new, the appeal to liturgy as a *locus theologicus*, that is, as a theological source of doctrine and faith, has a long history. This chapter begins with Athanasius of Alexandria and Basil of Caesarea in the fourth century, appealing to the theology of the Holy Spirit's divinity as implied in the baptismal rite, against the denial of that divinity among the semi-Arians. Early reference to Mary as Theotokos ("God-bearer") is documented in a mid-third-century hymn from Egypt (*sub tuum praesidium*). Theodore of Mopsuestia represents the beginnings of allegorical commentary on the eucharistic liturgy and Prosper of Aquitaine, writing against the semi-Pelagian heresy, articulates the classic phrase that contemporary liturgical theology has made its hallmark: *ut legem credendi lex statuat supplicandi* (literally, "that the law of supplicating might constitute the law of believing"), often abbreviated by the Latin tag *lex orandi, lex credendi.*

The medieval section of this chapter includes selections of the great liturgical commentaries by Germanus of Constantinople and Nicholas Cabasilas in the Christian East and Amalarius of Metz and Pope Innocent III for the West. Luther's biting critique of the liturgical theology of sacrifice he saw implied in the Roman *canon missae* and the attempt to curb late medieval abuses by the Council of Trent make up the next section. Pope Pius IX's reference to the *lex orandi* in support of his nineteenth-century promulgation of the dogma of the immaculate conception of the Blessed Virgin Mary lead to the twentieth- and twenty-first-century development of the discipline of liturgical theology itself. This final section reads like an ecumenical "Who's Who" of contemporary liturgical theologians. Included here are discussions of the Christian mystery and the relationship between the "law of prayer" and the "law of belief" (e.g., Odo Casel, Peter Brunner, Alexander Schmemann, Geoffrey Wainwright, Aidan Kavanagh, Edward Kilmartin, Gordon Lathrop, David W. Fagerberg, and Michael B. Aune), liturgical lament (David N. Power), liturgical enculturation (Lutheran World Federation), liturgical aesthetics (Don E. Saliers), free-church "liturgical" theology (Melanie Ross), feminist (Teresa Berger), Hispanic-Latino (Virgil Elizondo), and postmodern approaches (Nathan D. Mitchell) to the subject.

|

Early Christian Authors

|

EGYPT

Athanasius of Alexandria

As early as the Arian controversy in the fourth century, appeal is made to the liturgy in defense of orthodox Trinitarian teaching, in this case to the theology implied in the rite of baptism.

Athanasius of Alexandria, *Four Discourses against the Arians*,
II.41–42 and IV.21; trans. *NPNF²* 4:370–71, 441.

II.41. But let the other heresies and the Manichees also know that the Father of the Christ is One, and is Lord and Maker of the creation through His proper Word. And let the Ariomaniacs know in particular, that the Word of God is One, being the only Son proper and genuine from His Essence, and having with His Father the oneness of Godhead indivisible, as we said many times, being taught it by the Saviour Himself. Since, were it not so, wherefore through Him does the Father create, and in Him reveal Himself to whom He will, and illuminate them? or why too in the baptismal consecration is the Son named together with the Father? For if they say that the Father is not all-sufficient, then their answer is irreligious, but if He be, for this it is right to say, what is the need of the Son for framing the worlds, or for the holy laver? For what fellowship is there between creature and Creator? or why is a thing made classed with the Maker in the consecration of all of us? or why, as you hold, is faith in one Creator and in one creature delivered to us? for if it was that we might be joined to the Godhead, what need of the creature? but if that we might be united to the Son a creature, superfluous, according to you, is this naming of the Son in Baptism, for God who made Him a Son is able to make us sons also. Besides, if the Son be a creature, the nature of rational creatures being one, no help will come to creatures from a creature, since all need grace from God. We said a few words just now on the fitness that all things should be made by Him; but since the course of the discussion has led us also to mention holy Baptism, it is necessary to state, as I think and believe, that the Son is named with the Father, not as if the Father were not all-sufficient, not without meaning, and by accident; but, since He is God's Word and own Wisdom, and being His Radiance, is ever with the Father, therefore it is impossible, if the Father bestows grace, that He should not give it in the Son, for the Son is in the Father as the radiance in the light. For, not as if in need, but as a Father in His own Wisdom hath God rounded the earth, and made all things in the Word which is from Him, and in the Son confirms the Holy Laver. For where the Father is, there is the Son, and where the light, there the radiance; and as what the Father worketh, He worketh through the Son, and the Lord Himself says, "What I see the Father do, that do I also"; so also when baptism is given, whom the Father baptizes, him the Son baptizes; and whom the Son baptizes, he is consecrated in the Holy Ghost. And again as when the sun shines, one might say that the radiance illuminates, for the light is one and indivisible, nor can be detached, so where the Father is or is named, there plainly is the Son also; and is the Father named in Baptism? then must the Son be named with Him.

II. 42. . . . And these too hazard the fulness of the mystery, I mean Baptism; for if the consecration is given to us into the Name of Father and Son, and they do not confess a true Father, because they deny what is from Him and like His Essence, and deny also the true Son, and name another of their own framing as created out of nothing, is not the rite administered by them altogether empty and unprofitable, making a show, but in reality being no help towards religion? For the Arians do not baptize into Father and Son, but into Creator and creature, and into Maker and work. And as a creature is other than the Son, so the Baptism, which is supposed to be given by them, is other than the truth, though they pretend to name the Name of the Father and the Son, because of the words of Scripture, For not he who simply says, "O Lord," gives Baptism; but he who with the Name has also the right faith. On this account therefore our Saviour also did not simply command to baptize, but first says, "Teach"; then thus: "Baptize into the Name of Father, and Son, and Holy Ghost"; that the right faith might follow upon learning, and together with faith might come the consecration of Baptism.

IV. 21. And what more does the Word contribute to our salvation than the Son, if, as they hold, the Son is one, and the Word another? for the command is that we should believe, not in the Word, but in the Son. For John says, "He that believeth on the Son, hath everlasting life; but he that believeth not the Son, shall not see life." And Holy Baptism, in which the substance of the whole faith is lodged, is administered not in the Word, but in Father, Son, and Holy Ghost. If then, as they hold, the Word is one and the Son another, and the

Word is not the Son, Baptism has no connection with the Word. How then are they able to hold that the Word is with the Father, when He is not with Him in the giving of Baptism? But perhaps they will say, that in the Father's Name the Word is included? Wherefore then not the Spirit also? or is the Spirit external to the Father? and the Man indeed (if the Word is not Son) is named after the Father, but the Spirit after the Man? and then the Monad, instead of dilating into a Triad, dilates according to them into a Tetrad, Father, Word, Son, and Holy Ghost. Being brought to shame on this ground, they have recourse to another, and say that not the Man by Himself whom the Lord bore, but both together, the Word and the Man, are the Son; for both joined together are named Son, as they say. Which then is cause of which? and which has made which a Son? or, to speak more clearly, is the Word a Son because of the flesh? or is the flesh called Son because of the Word? or is neither the cause, but the concurrence of the two? If then the Word be a Son because of the flesh, of necessity the flesh is Son, and all those absurdities follow which have been already drawn from saying that the Man is Son. But if the flesh is called Son because of the Word, then even before the flesh the Word certainly, being such, was Son. For how could a being make other sons, not being himself a son, especially when there was a father? If then He makes sons for Himself, then is He Himself Father; but if for the Father, then must He be Son, or rather that Son, by reason of Whom the rest are made sons.

Sub Tuum Praesidium

Even Marian theology, expressed at the Council of Ephesus (431) by the term "Theotokos," appears to have had its origin in devotion and liturgical hymnody.

> *Sub Tuum Praesidium* (third century, Egypt); trans. Kilian McDonnell,
> in "The Marian Liturgical Tradition," in Maxwell E. Johnson, ed.,
> *Between Memory and Hope: Readings on the Liturgical Year*
> (Collegeville, MN: Liturgical Press, Pueblo, 2000), 387.

To your protection we flee, holy Mother of God (Theotokos):
do not despise our prayers in [our] needs,
but deliver us from all dangers,
glorious and blessed Virgin.

CAPPADOCIA

Basil of Caesarea

Like Athanasius, Basil of Caesarea appeals to the rite of baptism in defense of the divinity of the Holy Spirit, as well as provides a Trinitarian theology based on the doxology.

Basil of Caesarea, *De Spiritu Sancto*, I.3, XII.28, and
XXVII.67–68, trans. *NPNF²* 4:3, 18, and 43.

I.3. Lately when praying with the people, and using the full doxology to God the Father in both forms, at one time with the Son together with the Holy Ghost, and at another through the Son in the Holy Ghost, I was attacked by some of those present on the ground that I was introducing novel and at the same time mutually contradictory terms. You, however, chiefly with the view of benefiting them, or, if they are wholly incurable, for the security of such as may fall in with them, have expressed the opinion that some clear instruction ought to be published concerning the force underlying the syllables employed. I will therefore write as concisely as possible, in the endeavour to lay down some admitted principle for the discussion.

XII.28. Let no one be misled by the fact of the apostle's frequently omitting the name of the Father and of the Holy Spirit when making mention of baptism, or on this account imagine that the invocation of the names is not observed. "As many of you," he says, "as were baptized into Christ have put on Christ"; and again, "As many of you as were baptized into Christ were baptized into his death." For the naming of Christ is the confession of the whole, showing forth as it does the God who gave, the Son who received, and the Spirit who is, the unction. So we have learned from Peter, in the Acts, of "Jesus of Nazareth whom God anointed with the Holy Ghost" [Acts 10:38]; and in Isaiah, "The Spirit of the Lord is upon me, because the Lord has anointed me" [Isaiah 60:1]; and the Psalmist, "Therefore God, even your God, has anointed you with the oil of gladness above your fellows." Scripture, however, in the case of baptism, sometimes plainly mentions the Spirit alone.

"For into one Spirit," it says, "we were all baptized in one body." And in harmony with this are the passages: "You shall be baptized with the Holy Ghost" [Acts 1:5]; and "He shall baptize you with the Holy Ghost" [Luke 3:16]. But no one on this account would be justified in calling that baptism a perfect baptism wherein only the name of the Spirit was invoked. For the tradition that has been given us by the quickening grace must remain for ever inviolate. He who redeemed our life from destruction gave us power of renewal, whereof the cause is ineffable and hidden in mystery, but bringing great salvation to our souls, so that to add or to take away anything involves manifestly a falling away from the life everlasting. If then in baptism the separation of the Spirit from the Father and the Son is perilous to the baptizer, and of no advantage to the baptized, how can the rending asunder of the Spirit from Father and from Son be safe for us? Faith and baptism are two kindred and inseparable ways of salvation: faith is perfected through baptism, baptism is established through faith, and both are completed by the same names. For as we believe in the Father and the Son and the Holy Ghost, so are we also baptized in the name of the Father and of the Son and of the Holy Ghost; first comes the confession, introducing us to salvation, and baptism follows, setting the seal upon our assent.

XXVII. 67. Time will fail me if I attempt to recount the unwritten mysteries of the Church. Of the rest I say nothing; but of the very confession of our faith in Father, Son, and Holy Ghost, what is the written source? If it be granted that, as we are baptized, so also under the obligation to believe, we make our confession in like terms as our baptism, in accordance with the tradition of our baptism and in conformity with the principles of true religion, let our opponents grant us too the right to be as consistent in our ascription of glory as in our confession of faith. If they deprecate our doxology on the ground that it lacks written authority, let them give us the written evidence for the confession of our faith and the other matters which we have enumerated. While the unwritten traditions are so many, and their bearing on the "mystery of godliness" [1 Timothy 3:16] is so important, can they refuse to allow us a single word which has come down to us from the Fathers;—which we found, derived from untutored custom, abiding in unperverted churches;—a word for which the arguments are strong, and which contributes in no small degree to the completeness of the force of the mystery?

68. The force of both expressions has now been explained. I will proceed to state once more wherein they agree and wherein they differ from one another;—not that they are opposed in mutual antagonism, but that each contributes its own meaning to true religion. The preposition "in" states the truth rather relatively to ourselves; while "with" proclaims the fellowship of the Spirit with God.

Wherefore we use both words, by the one expressing the dignity of the Spirit; by the other announcing the grace that is with us. Thus we ascribe glory to God both "in" the Spirit, and "with" the Spirit; and herein it is not our word that we use, but we follow the teaching of the Lord as we might a fixed rule, and transfer His word to things connected and closely related, and of which the conjunction in the mysteries is necessary. We have deemed ourselves under a necessary obligation to combine in our confession of the faith Him who is numbered with Them at Baptism, and we have treated the confession of the faith as the origin and parent of the doxology. What, then, is to be done? They must now instruct us either not to baptize as we have received, or not to believe as we were baptized, or not to ascribe glory as we have believed. Let any man prove if he can that the relation of sequence in these acts is not necessary and unbroken; or let any man deny if he can that innovation here must mean ruin everywhere. Yet they never stop dinning in our ears that the ascription of glory "with" the Holy Spirit is unauthorized and unscriptural and the like. We have stated that so far as the sense goes it is the same to say "glory be to the Father and to the Son and to the Holy Ghost," and "glory be to the Father and to the Son with the Holy Ghost." It is impossible for any one to reject or cancel the syllable "and," which is derived from the very words of our Lord, and there is nothing to hinder the acceptance of its equivalent. What amount of difference and similarity there is between the two we have already shown. And our argument is confirmed by the fact that the Apostle uses either word indifferently,— saying at one time "in the name of the Lord Jesus and by the Spirit of our God" [1 Corinthians 6:11]; at another "when you are gathered together, and my Spirit, with the power of our Lord Jesus" [1 Corinthians 5:4], with no idea that it makes any difference to the connection of the names whether he use the conjunction or the preposition.

SYRIA

Theodore of Mopsuestia

Theodore of Mopsuestia (+428) (northern Syria) offers the beginnings of a theolog of the liturgy, based on the acts and gestures of the eucharistic liturgy itself. His representative or allegorical approach to the liturgy as portraying events in the life of Christ and his passion will become common both in East and West in the Middle Ages.

Theodore of Mopsuestia, "Homily 15." 24ff., trans. A Mingana, in *Commentary of Theodore of Mopsuestia on the Lord's Prayer and on the Sacraments of Baptism and the Eucharist*, Woodbrooke Studies 8 (Cambridge: W. Heffer and Sons, Ltd., 1933), 85–89; as adapted by Robert Taft, *The Great Entrance*, 2nd ed., OCA, 35.

It is the deacons who bring out this oblation . . . which they arrange and place on the awe-inspiring altar, a vision . . . awe-inspiring even to the onlookers. By means of the symbols we must see Christ who is now being led out and going forth to his passion, and who, in another moment, is laid out for us on the altar. . . . And when the offering that is about to be presented is brought out in the sacred vessels, the patens and chalices, you must think that Christ our Lord is coming out, led to his passion . . . by the invisible hosts of ministers . . . who were also present when the passion of salvation was being accomplished. . . . And when they bring it out, they place it on the holy altar to represent fully the passion. Thus we may think of him placed on the altar as if henceforth in a sort of sepulcher, and as having already undergone the passion. That is why the deacons who spread linens on the altar represent by this the figure of the linen cloths of the burial. . . . [And afterwards] they stand on both sides and fan the air [aer] above the holy body so that nothing will fall upon it. They show by this ritual the greatness of the body lying there . . . which is holy, awe-inspiring, and far from all corruption . . . a body that will soon rise to an immortal nature. . . .

GAUL

Prosper of Aquitaine

In the context of the semi-Pelagian controversy, and in his defense of the need for divine grace in salvation, Prosper refers to the church's liturgical supplication for grace and, in so doing, expresses the principle *ut legem credendi lex statuat supplicandi*, which has come to express the relationship between liturgy and theology.

Prosper of Aquitaine, *Capitula Coelestini* 8 (Migne, *Patrologia Latina* 51, 205–12), trans. Geoffrey Wainwright, in *Doxology* (London: Epworth Press; New York: Oxford University Press, 1980), 225–26.

In inviolable decrees of the blessed apostolic see, our holy fathers have cast down the pride of this pestiferous novelty and taught us to ascribe to the grace of Christ the very beginnings of good will, the growth of noble efforts, and the perseverance in them to the end. In addition, let us look at the sacred testimony of priestly intercessions which have been transmitted from the apostles and which are uniformly celebrated throughout the world and in every catholic church; so that the law of prayer may establish a law for belief [*ut legem credendi lex statuat supplicandi*]. For when the presidents of the holy congregations perform their duties, they plead the cause of the human race before the divine clemency and, joined by the sighs of the whole church, they beg and pray that grace may be given to unbelievers; that idolaters may be freed from the errors of their impiety; that the Jews may have the veil removed from their hearts and that the light of truth may shine on them; that heretics may recover through acceptance of the catholic faith; that schismatics may receive afresh the spirit of charity; that the lapsed may be granted the remedy of penitence; and finally that the catechumens may be brought to the sacrament of regeneration and have the court of the heavenly mercy opened to them.

Medieval Authors in East and West

EAST

Germanus (+733) and Nicholas continue the type of liturgical commentary begun by Theodore of Mopsuestia.

Germanus of Constantinople

Germanus of Constantinople, "On the Great Entrance,"
from *On the Divine Liturgy,* 37–41, trans. Paul Meyendorff,
in *St. Germanus of Constantinople: On the Divine Liturgy*
(Crestwood, NJ: St. Vladimir's Seminary Press, 1984), 87–89.

37. By means of the procession of the deacons and the representation of the fans, which are in the likeness of the seraphim, the Cherubic Hymn signifies the entrance of all the saints and righteous ahead of the cherubic powers and the angelic host, who run invisibly in advance of the great king, Christ, who is proceeding to the mystical sacrifice, borne aloft by material hands. Together with them comes the Holy Spirit in the unbloody and reasonable sacrifice. The Spirit is seen spiritually in the fire, incense, smoke, and fragrant air: for the fire points to His divinity, and the fragrant

smoke to His coming invisibly and filling us with good fragrance through the mystical, living, and unbloody service and sacrifice of burnt-offering. In addition, the spiritual powers and the choirs of angels, who have seen His dispensation fulfilled through the cross and death of Christ, the victory over death which has taken place, the descent into hell and the resurrection on the third day, with us exclaim the alleluia.

It is also in imitation of the burial of Christ, when Joseph took down the body from the cross, wrapped it in clean linen, anointed it with spices and ointment, carried it with Nicodemus, and placed it in a new tomb hewn out of a rock. The altar is an image of the holy tomb, and the divine table is the sepulcher in which, of course, the undefiled and all-holy body was placed.

38. The discos [= paten] represents the hands of Joseph and Nicodemus, who buried Christ. The discos on which Christ is carried is also interpreted as the sphere of heaven, manifesting to us in miniature the spiritual sun, Christ, and containing Him visibly in the bread.

39. The chalice corresponds to the vessel, which received the mixture, which poured out from the bloodied, undefiled side and from the hands and feet of Christ. . . .

40. The cover on the discos corresponds to the cloth which was on Christ's head and which covered His face in the tomb.

41. The veil, or the aer, corresponds to the stone which Joseph placed against the tomb and which the guards of Pilate sealed. . . .

. . . Thus Christ is crucified, life is buried, the tomb is secured, the stone is sealed. In the company of the angelic powers, the priest approaches, standing no longer as on earth, but attending at the heavenly altar, before the altar of the throne of God, and he contemplates the great, ineffable, and unsearchable mystery of God. . . .

Nicholas Cabasilas

Nicholas Cabasilas (fourteenth century), *A Commentary on the Divine Liturgy*, trans. J. M. Hussey and P. A. McNulty (London: SPCK, 1960), 26–28.

There is another way in which these forms, like all the ceremonies of the Holy Sacrifice, sanctify us. It consists in this: that in them Christ and the deeds he accomplished and the sufferings he endured for our sakes are represented. Indeed, it is the whole scheme of the work of redemption which is signified in the psalms and readings, as in all the actions of the priest throughout the liturgy; the first ceremonies of the service represent the beginnings of this work; the next, the sequel; and the last, its results. Thus, those who are present at these ceremonies have before their eyes all these divine things. The consecration of the elements—the sacrifice itself—commemorates the death, resurrection, and ascension of the Saviour, since it transforms these precious gifts into the very Body of the Lord, that Body which was the central figure in all these mysteries, which was crucified, which rose from the dead, which ascended into heaven. The ceremonies which precede the act of sacrifice symbolize the events which occurred before the death of Christ: his coming on earth, his first appearance and his perfect manifestation. Those which follow the act of sacrifice recall "The promise of the Father," as the Saviour himself called it: that is, the descent of the Holy Spirit upon the apostles, the conversion of the nations which they brought about, and their divine society. The whole celebration of the mystery is like a unique portrayal of a single body, which is the work of the Saviour; it places before us the several members of this body, from beginning to end, in their order and harmony. That is why the psalmody, as well as the opening chants, and before them all that is done at the preparation of the offerings, symbolize the first period of the scheme of redemption. That which comes after the psalms—readings from Holy Scriptures and so on—symbolizes the period which follows. . . .

. . . Because the Holy Scriptures contain divinely-inspired words and praises of God, and because they incite to virtue, they sanctify those who read or chant them. But, because of the selection, which has been made, and the order in which the passages are arranged, they have another function: they signify the coming of Christ and his work. Not only the chants and readings but the very actions themselves have this part to play; each has its own immediate purpose and usefulness. But at the same time each symbolizes some part of the works of Christ, his deeds or his sufferings. For example, we have the bringing of the Gospel to the altar, then the bringing of the offerings. Each is done for a purpose, the one that the Gospel may be read, the other that the sacrifice may be performed; besides this, however, one represents the appearance and the other the manifestation of the Saviour; the first obscure and imperfect, at the beginning of his life; the second, the perfect and supreme manifestation. There are even certain ceremonies, which fulfill no practical purpose, but have only a figurative meaning; such as the action of piercing the Host, and tracing thereon the pattern of a cross, or again the fact that the metal instrument used for the perforation is shaped like a lance; there is also the ceremony which takes place near the end, of mixing a little warm water with the wine. . . .

. . . As far as the ceremonies performed in the eucharistic liturgy are concerned, they all have some connection with the scheme of the work of redemption. Their purpose is to set before us the Divine plan, that by looking upon it our souls may be sanctified, and thus we may be made fit to receive these sacred gifts.

WEST

Liturgical symbolism and its interpretation in the West become also an allegorical or representative symbolism imposed on the words, acts, and gestures of the rites.

Amalarius of Metz

Amalarius of Metz (ca. 780–851), *Liber officialis*, III,
chap. 18, trans. Robert Cabié, in *History of the Mass*
(Portland: Pastoral Press, 1992), 72–73.

The deacon goes to the altar where he picks up the gospel book from which he will read. The altar can stand for Jerusalem since, according to the Scriptures, the proclamation of the Gospel comes from this city: "For from Zion will come the Law, and from Jerusalem the word of the Lord" (Is 2:3). The altar can also stand for the body of the Lord himself, in whom are the words of the Gospel, namely, the Good News. It is Christ who ordered the apostles to preach the Gospel to every creature; it is Christ who said: "my words are spirit and life" (Is 6:64). His words are contained in the Gospel. The deacon who carries the book is, as it were, the feet of Christ. He carries the book upon his right shoulder; this evokes the life of this world in which the Gospel must be announced.

When the deacon greets the people, it is fitting that all turn toward him. The priest and the people are in fact facing the East till the moment when the Lord speaks through the deacon, and they sign themselves on their foreheads. . . . And why on this particular part of the body? The reason is that the forehead is the seat of shame. If the Jews were ashamed to believe in the one whom they desired to crucify, as the Apostle says—"We proclaim Christ crucified, a stumbling block to the Jews" (1 Cor 1:23)—we believe that we are saved by the Crucified One. The Jews were ashamed of his name, whereas we believe that this name protects us. This is why we make the sign of the cross on the forehead, which is the seat of shame, as we have said.

. . . The two candles carried before the gospel book stand for the Law and the Prophets which preceded the gospel teaching. The censer evokes all the virtues that flow from the life of Christ. The censer-bearer ascends the ambo before the gospel so as to spread the odor of perfume, thus showing that Christ did good before announcing the Gospel, as Luke in the Acts of the Apostles attests: "All that Jesus did and taught" (Acts 1:1). He first acted and then taught.

The elevated place from which the Gospel is read shows the superiority of the teaching of the Gospel and its great authority of judgment. The location of the candles shows that the Law and the Prophets are inferior to the Gospel. And when the book, after the reading, is returned to its place, the candles are extinguished since it is the preaching of the Gospel that continues, the Law and the Prophets speaking no longer. . . .

The rites before the gospel stand for Christ's preaching up to the hour of his passion as well as that of those who preach to the end of the world and beyond. The rites after the gospel reveal what has been brought about by Christ's passion, resurrection, and ascension into heaven, and likewise the sacrifice, mortification, and resurrection of his disciples who profess the faith. . . .

Innocent III

Innocent III (1198), *De sacro altaris mysterio*, liber III, 1–3, trans. Robert Cabié, in *History of the Mass*, 82.

The Eucharistic Prayer. The sacred words must not be profaned. If everyone knows these words because all have heard them, then these words can be repeated in public and in profane places. This is why the church has decreed that the priest is to say the prayer secretly, a prayer having the appearance of a mystery. It is said that some shepherds, at a time before this custom was established, repeated these words in the fields and thus were struck down by God.

In the Mysteries we make memory of the passion, namely, of what occurred during the week before the Passover, from the tenth day of the first lunar month when Jesus entered Jerusalem, till the seventeenth day when he was raised from the dead. This is why most sacramentaries contain a picture of Christ's image between the preface and the canon; we are not merely to understand the text but also to contemplate the image, which inspires the memory of the Lord's passion. Perhaps it is the result more of providence than of human art that the Canon begins with the letter T, a letter whose form is that of a cross and which symbolizes a cross. In fact, the T recalls the mystery of the cross since God says through the prophet: "Mark with a tau the foreheads of those who lament and cry" (Ez 9:4).

Te igitur clementissime Pater. The true Lamb entered Jerusalem on the very day when the crowds acclaimed Christ. This was the tenth day of the first lunar month, the day when the Law called for Hebrews to take into their homes the symbolic lamb. Spied upon by those men, full of hate, men who stirred up the people, he was threatened by the snares intended to cause his death. There were three who handed Christ over: God, Judas, and the Jew. . . .To express this the priest makes three crosses over the gifts as he says: *Haec dona, haec munera, haec sancta sacrificia illibata.* He was handed over by God like a gift, by Judas on behalf of those who were present, by the Jew as a sacrifice without stain. It was unto "death, death on a cross" (Phil 2:8) that he was handed over by each of the three. . . .

|

The Protestant and Catholic Reformations

|

PROTESTANT REFORMATION

Martin Luther

In his biting line-by-line critique of the Roman canon of the Mass, Luther attempts to demonstrate what he considers the erroneous and blasphemous liturgical theology expressed by the canon.

Martin Luther, *The Abomination of the Secret Mass* (1525),
trans. Abdel Ross Wentz, in LW 36:320, 322.

See, here the canon comes again to the offering, for now the bread has become the body of Christ. The canon calls it a holy bread and a cup of salvation. How foolishly it does talk of the matter! But we want to do it the honor of giving the best interpretation and not make it too wicked. The priest offers up once again the Lord Christ, who offered himself only once [Heb. 9:25–26], just as he died only once and cannot die again or be offered up again [Rom. 6:9–10]. For through his one death and sacrifice he has taken away and swallowed up all sins. Yet they go ahead and every day offer him up more than a hundred thousand times throughout the world. They thereby deny, both with their deeds and in their hearts, that Christ has washed sin away and has died and risen again. This is such an abomination that I don't believe it could be sufficiently punished on earth if it rained pure fire from heaven [Luke 9:54]. The blasphemy is so great that it must simply wait for eternal hell-fire [Matt. 18:8–9]. . . .

. . . Here again the priest prays for the offering, that God should be gracious to his Son and be pleased with him. And so a miserable man becomes a mediator between God and Christ, his dear Son. O what an abomination!

Now the priest comes again to the dead. This part is worth money, so that they do not say mass in vain. He prays for these who repose in the sleep of peace and rest in Christ and have the sign of faith. If that is true, why should you pray for them? Are you not a madman and a fool? If they have rest and peace, why or how should the priest refresh them and give them peace? So they of necessity contradict themselves, talking out of both sides of their mouth at the same time. They have no idea what they are saying or what they are talking about.

CATHOLIC REFORMATION

The Council of Trent

Because the liturgy is formative of the faith and understanding of the church, the Council of Trent attempts to curb numerous late medieval Mass abuses.

> The Council of Trent, Session 22, "Decree concerning the Things to Be Observed and Avoided in the Celebration of Mass" (1562), trans. H. Schroeder, in *The Canons and Decrees of the Council of Trent* (St. Louis: Herder, 1941), 151–52.

[T]he holy council decrees that local ordinaries shall be zealously concerned and be bound to prohibit and abolish all those things which either covetousness, which is a serving of idols, or irreverence, which can scarcely be separated from ungodliness, or superstition, a false imitation of true piety, have introduced.

And that many things may be summed up in a few, they shall in the first place, as regards avarice, absolutely forbid conditions of compensations of whatever kind, bargains, and whatever is given for the celebration of new masses; also those importunate and unbecoming demands, rather than requests, for alms and other things of this kind which border on simoniacal taint or certainly savor of filthy lucre.

In the second place, that irreverence may be avoided, each in his own diocese shall forbid that any wandering or unknown priest be permitted to celebrate mass. Furthermore, they shall permit no one who is publicly and notoriously wicked either to minister at the altar or to be present at the sacred services; nor suffer the holy sacrifice to be celebrated by any seculars and regulars whatsoever in private houses or entirely outside the church and the oratories dedicated solely to divine worship and to be designated and visited by the same ordinaries; or unless those present have first shown by their outward disposition and appearance that they are there not in body only but also in mind and devout affection of the heart. They shall also banish from the churches all such music which, whether by the organ or in the singing, contains things that are lascivious or impure; likewise all worldly conduct, vain and profane conversations, wandering around, noise and clamor, so that the house of God may be seen to be and may be truly called a house of prayer.

Finally, that no room may be given to superstition, they shall by ordinance and prescribed penalties provide that priests do not celebrate at other than the proper hours; or make use of rites or ceremonies and prayers in the celebration of masses other than those that have been approved by the Church and have been received through frequent and praiseworthy usage. They shall completely banish from the Church the practice of any fixed number of masses and candles, which has its origin in superstitious worship rather than in true religion; and they shall instruct the people as to what the very precious and heavenly fruit of this most holy sacrifice is and whence especially it is derived. They shall also admonish their people to go frequently to their own parish churches, at least on Sundays and the greater feast days.

The Nineteenth Century

Pope Pius IX

In his promulgation of the dogma of the immaculate conception, Pope Pius IX makes explicit reference to the principle of Prosper of Aquitaine, *ut legem credendi lex statuat supplicandi.*

Pope Pius IX, *Apostolic Constitution, Ineffabilis Deus*, December 8, 1854, trans. *Our Lady*, Papal Teaching Series (Boston: Daughters of St. Paul, n.d.), 4–6.

The Catholic Church, directed by the Holy Spirit of God, is the pillar and base of truth and has ever held as divinely revealed and as contained in the deposit of heavenly revelation this doctrine concerning the original innocence of the august Virgin—a doctrine which is so perfectly in harmony with her wonderful sanctity and preeminent dignity as Mother of God—and thus has never ceased to explain, to teach and to foster this doctrine age after age in many ways and by solemn acts. From this very doctrine, flourishing and wondrously propagated in the Catholic world through the efforts and zeal of the bishops, was made very clear by the Church when she did not hesitate to present for the public devotion and veneration of the faithful the Feast of the Conception of the Blessed Virgin. By this most significant fact, the Church made it clear indeed that the conception of Mary is to be venerated as something extraordinary, wonderful, eminently holy, and different from the conception of all other human beings—for the Church celebrates only the feast days of the saints.

And hence the very words with which the Sacred Scriptures speak of Uncreated Wisdom and set forth his eternal origin, the Church, both in its ecclesiastical offices and in its liturgy, has been wont to apply likewise to the origin of the Blessed Virgin, inasmuch as God, by one and the same decree, had established the origin of Mary and the Incarnation of Divine Wisdom.

These truths, so generally accepted and put into practice by the faithful, indicate how zealously the Roman Church, mother and teacher of all Churches, has continued to teach this doctrine of the Immaculate Conception of the Virgin. Yet the more important actions of the Church deserve to be mentioned in detail. For such dignity and authority belong to the Church that she alone is the center of truth and of Catholic unity. It is the Church in which alone religion has been inviolably preserved and from which all other Churches must receive the tradition of the Faith.

The same Roman Church, therefore, desired nothing more than by the most persuasive means to state, to protect, to promote and to defend the doctrine of the Immaculate Conception. This fact is most clearly shown to the whole world by numerous and significant acts of the Roman Pontiffs, our predecessors. To them, in the person of the Prince of the Apostles, were divinely entrusted by Christ our Lord, the charge and supreme care and the power of feeding the lambs and sheep; in particular, of confirming their brethren, and of ruling and governing the universal Church.

Our predecessors, indeed, by virtue of their apostolic authority, gloried in instituting the Feast of the Conception in the Roman Church. They did so to enhance its importance and dignity by a suitable Office and Mass, whereby the prerogative of the Virgin, her exception from the hereditary taint, was most distinctly affirmed. As to the homage already instituted, they spared no effort to promote and to extend it either by the granting of indulgences, or by allowing cities, provinces and kingdoms to choose as their patroness God's own Mother, under the title of "The Immaculate Conception." Again, our predecessors approved confraternities, congregations and religious communities founded in honor of the Immaculate Conception, monasteries, hospitals, altars, or churches; they praised persons who vowed to uphold with all their ability the doctrine of the Immaculate Conception of the Mother of God. Besides, it afforded the greatest joy to our predecessors to ordain that the Feast of the Conception should be celebrated in every church with the very same honor as the Feast of the Nativity; that it should be celebrated with an octave by the whole Church; that it should be reverently and generally observed as a holy day of obligation; and that a pontifical Capella should be held in our Liberian pontifical basilica on the day dedicated to the conception of the Virgin. Finally, in their desire to impress this doctrine of the Immaculate Conception of the Mother of God upon the hearts of the faithful, and to intensify the people's piety and enthusiasm for the homage and the veneration of the Virgin conceived without the stain of original sin, they delighted to grant, with the greatest pleasure, permission to proclaim the Immaculate Conception of the Virgin in the Litany of Loreto, and in the Preface of the Mass, so that *the rule of prayer might thus serve to illustrate the rule of belief.* Therefore, we ourselves, following the procedure of our predecessors, have not only approved and accepted what had already been established, but bearing in mind, moreover, the decree of Sixtus IV, have confirmed by our authority a proper Office in honor of the Immaculate Conception, and have with exceeding joy extended its use to the universal Church.

Contemporary Liturgical Theologians

TWENTIETH-CENTURY APPROACHES

Odo Casel

The modern recovery of the popular term "paschal mystery" as a way to describe the center of Christian worship is due to the influence of, more than anyone else, Dom Odo Casel (+1948), a monk of Maria Laach Abbey, through his *Mysterienlehre* (Mystery Theology).

Odo Casel, *The Mystery of Christian Worship and Other Writings*, ed. Burkhard Neunheuser (London: Darton, Longman & Todd, 1962), 12–13, 34–35, 49, 61.

The content of the mystery of Christ is . . . the person of the God-man and his saving deed for the church; the church, in turn, enters the mystery through this deed. For Paul, Peter, and John, the heart of faith is not the teachings of Christ, not the deeds of his ministry, but the acts by which he saved us. . . . The Christian thing . . . in its full and primitive meaning of God's good Word, or Christ's, is not as it were a philosophy of life with religious background music, nor a moral or theological training; it is a *mysterium* as St. Paul means the word, a revelation made by God to man through acts of god-manhood, full of life and power; it is mankind's way to God made possible by this revelation and the grace of it communicating the solemn entry of the redeemed Church into the presence of the everlasting Father through sacrifice, through perfect devotion; it is the glory that blossoms out of it. At the mid-point of the Christian religion, therefore, stands the sacred *Pasch*, the passage which the Son of God who appeared in the flesh of sin, makes to the Father. The pasch is a sacrifice with the consecration of that person that flows from it; it is the sacrifice of the God-man in death on the cross, and his resurrection to glory; it is the Church's sacrifice in communion with and by the power of the crucified God-man, and the wonderful joining to God which is its effect. . . . The church . . . is drawn into this sacrifice of his; as he sacrificed for her, she now takes an active part in his sacrifice, makes it her own, and is raised thereby with him from the world to God, glorified. Thus Christ becomes the saviour of the body, and the head of the Church. . . .

. . . From the peace of Constantine, the church's triumph over paganism, the language of the ancient mysteries was used even more unhesitatingly to express the unfathomable content of what she herself possessed, as far as this was possible at all; indeed, many ancient forms and customs were taken over to enrich and adorn Christian simplicity. . . . Christianity is of its own very essence . . . a mystery religion, and the mystery language its own most rightful possession. The ancient church lived in mystery, and needed to construct no theory about it. . . . The symbolic, strength-giving rites of the mysteries were real for the ancients; when the church of Christ entered the world she did not end, but rather fulfilled their way of thinking. . . . The Christianity of the ancient world appears to us as the fulfillment and glorification of what Greco-Roman antiquity was.

. . . Christ's mystery is God's revelation in the saving action of his incarnate Son and the redemption and healing of the church. It continues after the glorified God-man has returned to his Father, until the full number of the church's members is complete; the mystery of Christ is carried on and made actual in the mystery of worship. Here Christ performs his saving work, invisible, but present in Spirit and acting upon all men of good-will. It is the Lord himself who acts this mystery; not as he did the primaeval mystery of the Cross, alone, but with his bride, which he won there, his church; to her he has now given all his treasures; she is to hand them on to the children she has got of him. Whoever has God for his Father must, since the incarnation, have the church for his mother [Cyprian, *de Unitate Ecclesiae* 5]. As the woman was formed in paradise from the side of the first Adam, to be a helpmate, like to him [Gen. 2:18], the church is formed from the side of Christ fallen asleep on the cross to be his companion and helper in the work of redemption. At the same time, the fathers teach us the mysteries flow in water and blood from the Lord's side; the church was born from Christ's death-blood and the mystery with it; church and mystery are inseparable. This is the last ground for the fact that they mystery of worship becomes liturgy....

... The sacred mystery is the visible expression, and at the same time the highest living activity of the mystical body of Christ: head and members are one in the sacrifice to the Father, to whom all honour goes up through the Son in the Holy Spirit, and from whom all grace and blessing come down through the same Word and Spirit. So ever deeper knowledge, and life sharing in the mystery become the central theme of the sacrifice to God which pleases him....

... The best of the ancient world did service to Christendom. The service was extremely desirable; in Christianity the mystery-type gained a wholly new meaning. The sacrificial service of the old alliance was done away with, or better, fulfilled with the sacrifice of Christ. With this came the new age: the old was past. In the Church of the new alliance there could only be one sacrifice, the sacrifice of Christ. If it was to act through the centuries, it could only do so by its mystical presence in the sacrament, *in mysterio*, in the worship of the Church which the new alliance had made. In the mystery, Christ lives in the Church, acts in her and with her, preserves and enlivens her. In the mystery we too already breathe the air of the coming age of God's Kingdom and have our conversation in humble faith. For the mystery is the mystery of faith; faith alone grasps the *virtus sacramenti*, the grace contained in the mystery. When faith passes over into vision, the veil of the mystery will fall and we shall see the godhead it contains.

The sacred rites belong to this veil. Antiquity shared in its creation, and so has deserved of Christ; without the form there would be no knowledge of its content. Thus, Hellenism wins a God-given meaning for the whole history of the world.

Jean Cardinal Daniélou

The centrality of the one mystery of Christ is expressed also by Daniélou in this short description.

Jean Cardinal Daniélou, "Le symbolisme des rites baptismaux," in *Dieu vivant* 1 (1948): 17; trans. Robert Taft, "Toward a Theology of Christian Feast," in Taft, *Beyond East and West,* 2nd rev. and enlarged ed. (Rome: Edizioni Christiana Analecta, 1997), 28–29.

The Christian faith has only one object, the mystery of Christ dead and risen. But this unique mystery subsists under different modes: it is prefigured in the Old Testament, it is accomplished historically in the earthly life of Christ, it is contained in mystery in the sacraments, it is lived mystically in souls, it is accomplished socially in the Church, it is consummated eschatologically in the heavenly kingdom. Thus the Christian has at his disposition several registers, a multi-dimensional symbolism, to express this unique reality. The whole of Christian culture consists in grasping the links that exist between Bible and liturgy, Gospel and eschatology, mysticism and liturgy. The application of this method to scripture is called exegesis; applied to liturgy it is called mystagogy. This consists in reading in the rites the mystery of Christ, and in contemplating beneath the symbols the invisible reality.

Peter Brunner

In his development of a systematic theology of Christian worship, Lutheran theologian Peter Brunner offers several theses relating the church's historical and eschatological worship to that of Christ's own *leitourgia* before the heavenly throne.

Peter Brunner, *Worship in the Name of Jesus,* trans. M. H. Bertram (St. Louis: Concordia Publishing House, 1968), 78–83.

1. The worship of the church stands at the end of the road which God has taken with humankind for the realization of salvation. This end appeared in Jesus' cross and resurrection.

2. Like the church itself, worship is an eschatological phenomenon. In the act of worship the Messianic congregation of the last days, set off from the world and already integrated into Christ's body, is gathered as it awaits the return of its Lord. But in the interval between the Lord's ascension and His return, the church, through the mediation of the apostolic Word, has Jesus Himself, His very

body, really present in the Pneuma, in the Baptism-event, and in Holy Communion, so that this body of Jesus becomes manifest in the church itself and is again and again actualized and integrated through its worship activity by virtue of the instituted means.

3. The worship of the church has its place in the heavenly sanctuary, which was opened by Jesus' self-sacrifice; it has its place in the opened access to the Father. The worship of the church is freed for the performance of the celestial liturgy before God's throne. . . . Because the worship of the church takes place in the Pneuma, it takes place in Christ. Consequently, the worship of the church is a participation in the one world-redeeming, never ending worship of the crucified and exalted Christ before God's throne.

4. What happened in Jesus' body on Good Friday and Easter Sunday is now carried out in the individual in a sacramentally hidden but sacramentally real manner. In crossing the threshold of Baptism, man dies with Christ and is again raised up with Christ. Thus he is integrated as an individual in his historical existence into the one crucified body of Jesus.

5. What happened to the individual in crossing the threshold of Baptism imparts its essential content to the earthly worship of the entire body. . . . Especially in Holy Communion is the once-effected establishment of the members as the body of Christ ever and again renewed through the reception of Christ's sacrificial body. By virtue of the Pentecostal epiphany of Jesus' body to the individual at his baptism, the epiphany of Jesus' body, enduring to the Last Day, takes place in Holy Communion for the congregation partaking of the Meal.

6. Thus the worship of the church has its place where the world is already in the process of passing away and the new world of God is already dawning. . . .

7. In worship, the church awaits the last epiphany of its Lord and His body on the Last Day. The real presence of Jesus, vouchsafed ever anew by the Word-bound Pneuma and by Holy Communion, stimulates the expectation of that real presence of Jesus' body, which is already materialized before God's throne. . . . Thus the place of worship is the interim in which the church yearns for the eschatological *transitus*. Sustained by the Word-bound Pneuma and the Word-bound sacrament, the church hastens toward this last epiphany of the Lord and his body. This hastening-toward is carried out principally in its worship.

8. . . . [T]he worship of the church encompasses the entire past of God's plan of salvation. The worship which God implanted in man in creation begins to shine forth again in the worship of the church. . . . In the worship of the church, the salvation-event, which took place

once for all in the body of Jesus on Golgotha and is now eternally valid before God's throne, is really present. For in the worship of the church the pneumatic epiphany of Jesus' one body is carried out through the Word-bound Pneuma and the Word-bound sacrament.

9. But the worship of the church also encompasses, in a peculiar, preliminary way, the future of God's plan of salvation. The Pneuma epiphany of Jesus' body is already the actual beginning of the kingdom of God in this world. In the worship of the church the coming kingdom of God is manifested in advance through the Pneuma and its gifts. Especially in the Lord's Supper do we find an advance manifestation of the eschatological table fellowship of Jesus with His followers in the kingdom of God. In all of this the worship of the church on earth already reflects something of its ultimate form in heaven.

10. But withal the plan-of-salvation's "not yet," implicit in the church's worship on earth still remains. The reality of the future of the kingdom of God and of its worship, which is still to come, is not extinguished. . . . The plan-of-salvation character of the present, in which the church's worship is placed, is constituted by its relationship to the past and to the future of God's plan of salvation. Christologically formulated, this present is described in the Second Article of the Apostles' Creed as "sitting on the right hand of God the Father Almighty." Pneumatologically formulated, this present is described as the eon of the Spirit pentecostally poured out. Therefore this present may be defined "theologically" as the dawn of the eschatological transition, in which God, the Creator of heaven and earth, already placed this heaven and earth, through the Pneuma-presence of His Son's body on earth, under the sign of that end which ushers in the new heaven and the new earth.

Alexander Schmemann

The influential Russian Orthodox liturgical theologian Alexander Schmemann (+1983) offers a justification of the place of the study of liturgy in the theological curriculum and provides a critique of the "mystery" approach of Odo Casel. For Schmemann, Christianity is "saving faith and not . . . a saving cult."

Alexander Schmemann, *Introduction to Liturgical Theology* (London: Faith Press, 1966), 14–16, 23, 82–86.

As its name indicates, liturgical theology is the elucidation of the meaning of worship. . . . it ought to be the elucidation of its theological meaning. Theology is above all explanation, "the search for words appropriate to the nature of God" (Θεοπρεπεῖς λόγοι), i.e., for a system of concepts corresponding as much as possible to the faith and experience of the Church. Therefore the task of liturgical theology consists in giving a theological basis to the explanation of worship and the whole liturgical tradition of the Church. This means, first, to find and define the concepts and categories which are capable of expressing as fully as possible the essential nature of the liturgical experience of the Church; second, to connect these ideas with that system of concepts which theology uses to expound the faith and doctrine of the Church; and third, to present the separate data of liturgical experience as a connected whole, as, in the last analysis, the "rule of prayer" dwelling within the Church and determining her "rule of faith."

If liturgical theology stems from an understanding of worship as the public act of the Church, then its final goal will be to clarify and explain the connection between this act and the Church, i.e., to explain how the Church expresses and fulfills herself in this act.

The accepted doctrine of the Church sees in the "tradition of sacraments and sacred rites" an inviolable element of Tradition, and thus also one of the sources which theology must utilize if it seeks to expound fully the faith and life of the Church. The neglect of this source in scholastic theology is explained by a narrowing down of the concepts both of Tradition and the Church. But the early Church firmly confessed the principle *lex orandi lex est credendi*. Therefore the science of liturgics cannot fail to be a theological science by its very character and purpose; and theology as a whole cannot do without the science of liturgics. . . .

. . . [I]t is only right that liturgical theology should occupy a special, independent place in the general system of theological disciplines. For without an appropriate theological systematization and interpretation, the liturgical tradition does not "arrive" at dogmatic consciousness, and there is a danger either of its complete neglect, or of its haphazard and improper use.

Liturgical theology is therefore an independent theological discipline with its own special subject—the liturgical tradition of the Church, and requiring its own corresponding and special method, distinct from the methods of other theological disciplines. Without liturgical theology our understanding of the Church's faith and doctrine is bound to be incomplete. . . .

. . . Christian worship, by its nature, structure and content, is the revelation and realization by the Church of her own real nature. And this nature is the new life in Christ—union in Christ with God the

Holy Spirit, knowledge of the Truth, unity, love, grace, peace salvation. . . . In this sense the Church cannot be equated or merged with "cult"; it is not the Church which exists for the "cult," but the cult for the Church, for her welfare, for her growth into the full measure of the "stature of Christ" (Eph. 4:13). Christ did not establish a society for the observance of worship, a "cultic society," but rather the Church as the way of salvation, as the new life of re-created mankind. This does not mean that worship is secondary to the Church. On the contrary, it is inseparable from the Church and without it there is no Church. But this is because its purpose is to express, form, or realize the Church—to be the source of that grace which always makes the Church the Church, the people, the Body of Christ, "a chosen race and a royal priesthood" (1 Peter 2:9). . . .

. . . [Odo Casel's] *Mysterienlehre* was the beginning of an extraordinary rehabilitation of the connection between Christianity and the mysteries, of its acceptance . . . as a norm innate in the Christian cult. In the literature of the contemporary liturgical movement there is no more popular term than *mysterion*. The explanation of Christian worship begins and ends with this word, and it is advanced as the most adequate term for the definition of its essence. According to Casel's theory *mysterion* is the necessary and organic form of cult in general, and therefore also of the Christian cult; and the latter, even though genetically independent of the pagan mysteries, was first of all, a mystery in its form and essence and, second, the natural and complete "fulfillment" of those beliefs and expectations and that spirituality which found expression in the Hellenistic mysteries.

While not denying Casel's great services in the task of reviving the liturgical question, or the depth and truth of many of his views, we must nevertheless regard his basic assertion—concerning the mysteriological nature of the Christian cult—as mistaken. We feel rather that the early Church openly and consciously set herself and her cult in opposition to the "mysteries," and that much of her strength was devoted to a struggle with this mysteriological piety in the first and decisive period of her confrontation with the Graeco-Roman world. . . .

. . . Christianity was preached as a saving faith and not as a saving cult. In it the cult was not an object of faith but its result. Historians have not sufficiently emphasized the fact that cult had no place in the preaching of Christianity, that it is not even mentioned in its *kerygma*. This is so because at the centre of the Christian *kerygma* there is a proclamation of the fact of the coming of the Messiah and a call to believe in this fact as having saving significance. A New Aeon is entering into the world as a result of this fact, is being revealed in the world: faith is what brings man into this New Aeon. The cult is only the realization, the actualization of what the believer has already attained by faith, and its whole significance is in the fact that it leads in the Church, the new people of God, created and brought into being by faith. . . .

. . . [I]n Christianity the cult establishes the reality of the Church. Its purpose is not the individual sanctification of its members but the creation of the people of God as the Body of Christ, the manifestation of the Church as new life in the New Aeon. It is not an end, but a means. . . . it is to be now the revelation of the eschatological fullness of the Kingdom in anticipation of the "Day of the Lord." This difference in the function of the cult and its interrelation with the faith and life of the society performing it also determines its difference in content from the mysteriological cults. The mysteriological cult is symbolic in so far as the myth depicted in it is void of historical authenticity; it is only in the cult that the myth becomes a reality at all. Hence the necessity to reproduce it in all detail, to portray the saving drama, to repeat it in the cult. The drama is conceived of as efficacious and saving only in this repetition. The Christian cult, on the contrary, is not experienced as a repetition of the saving fact in which it is rooted, since this fact was unique and unrepeatable. The Christian cult is the proclamation of the saving nature of this fact and also the realization and revelation, the actualization of its eternal efficacy, of the saving reality created by it. "To proclaim the Lord's death, to confess His resurrection"—this is not the same thing as repetition or portrayal. It is quite evident historically that the early Church knew nothing about the later "symbolical" explanation of her ceremonies of worship. . . .

. . . The early Christian cult not only did not have the main features of a mysteriological cult, but the Church consciously and openly set herself in opposition to mysteriological piety and the cults of the mysteries. . . . The radical newness of the Christian *lex orandi* and of the "liturgical piety" determined by it . . . provides us with a vantage point from which we may understand the changes in the Church's worship which came as a result of the peace of Constantine.

Geoffrey Wainwright

British Methodist Geoffrey Wainwright's approach to liturgical theology, based on Prosper of Aquitaine's statement, is concerned with the precise relationship between liturgy and doctrine in an ecumenical context.

Geoffrey Wainwright, *Doxology: The Praise of God in Worship, Doctrine, and Life: A Systematic Theology* (New York: Oxford University Press, 1990), 218, 251–52.

The Latin tag *lex orandi, lex credendi* may be construed in two ways. The more usual way makes the rule of prayer a norm for belief: what is prayed indicates what may and must be believed. But from the grammatical point of view it is equally possible to reverse subject and predicate and so take the tag as meaning that the rule of faith is the norm for prayer: what must be believed governs what may and should be prayed. The linguistic ambiguity of the Latin tag corresponds to a material interplay which in fact takes place between worship and doctrine in Christian practice: worship influences doctrine, and doctrine worship. . . .

. . . Roman Catholicism characteristically appeals to existing liturgical practice for proof in matters of doctrine. There *lex orandi, lex credendi* is most readily taken to make the (descriptive) pattern of prayer a (prescriptive) norm for belief, so that what is prayed indicates what may and must be believed. Protestantism characteristically emphasizes the primacy of doctrine over the liturgy. The phrase *lex orandi, lex credendi* is not well known among Protestants, but they would most easily take the dogmatic norm of belief as setting a rule for prayer, so that what must be believed governs what may and should be prayed. . . . Although such a distinction can properly be made between the directions in which Catholicism and Protestantism characteristically see the relations between worship and doctrine, yet Catholicism and Protestantism each know also the reverse relationship between the two. Catholicism also seeks to control the liturgy doctrinally. . . . Nor is it unknown that Protestants—in a way which runs counter to their more characteristic view of the relations between worship and doctrine—should turn to the liturgy to illustrate, and perhaps even to reinforce, an item of doctrine. Nevertheless the differences remain. It is rare that the Roman Catholic church prunes its liturgy in any doctrinally substantial way. On the other hand, the origins of Protestantism lie in a critical confrontation with existing liturgy and doctrine, and the original Protestant search for purity of worship and belief is prolonged in the notion of *ecclesia semper reformanda*. . . . The agreement and the difference may be put as follows. Both Catholicism and Protestantism consider that there is properly a complementary and harmonious relation between worship and doctrine to express the Christian truth. They tend to differ on the question of which of the two, doctrine or worship, should set the pace, and they differ profoundly on the question of whether either or both—the Church's worship or its doctrine—may fall into error.

David N. Power

In liturgical memory, thanksgiving, and lament, ethics and witness are grounded.

David N. Power, *Unsearchable Riches: The Symbolic Nature of Liturgy* (New York: Pueblo, 1984), 163–66, 208–9.

The cross stands at the heart of Jesus' relationship with God and of the relationship in which the church expresses its desire to participate in addressing God as "Father." While the cross is the pattern of human relationship with God, it is also the pattern for relationship with human persons and societies. In the crucifixion, Jesus stood firm in his solidarity with the marginal, the poor, and the oppressed. More and more we recognize that the friends and disciples of Jesus, those for whom he gave his life, were those to whom religious, political, and cultural institutions denied independence and the free possibilities for a full human existence. They were those to whom humanity denied the free gift of God. In this sense Jesus died so that human persons might be allowed those religious and cultural conditions necessary for a fully personal relationship with God. He died giving testimony for God and against any human construction which would curtail the gift of life that God gives in covenant and freedom. Paradoxically, the symbolism of Father is a contradiction of all that we associate with paternalism and patriarchy, totalitarianism and tyranny. Addressing God as "Abba" in the memorial of Jesus' death in worship involves us in the human enterprise which engages God's people in giving witness to the promise of the kingdom. . . .

. . . [T]he specific way in which the church appropriates this testimony in liturgy is the prayer of lamentation and thanksgiving. It is in these two ways that—receiving and responding to God's testimony—the community's own experience and self-expression are formulated verbally and in the formulation transformed. They become the ground of that ethic and witness which is in turn expressed in the liturgy's ritual actions or shared table and care.

Lamentation expresses the community's perception of its own and of humanity's sin and of the shackles which are placed on human freedom and on God's word and gift. Griefs which have been suppressed and hopes which have been stilled are allowed expression. In this act, the community remembers the questions to which the gospel speaks instead of stilling them. . . .

. . . Chaos, senselessness, and meaninglessness are part and parcel of human experience. They can be so massive, so terrifying, that societies are built on the capacity to forget. It has been remarked often enough of our own age that senseless death is so daily, so much the fruit of our way of life, so imminent and so global, so prone to reduce thousands to a living death, that peoples ignore it and suppress its remembrance in what they choose to honor. Keeping memory of Jesus can make room for expression of fears, terror, emptiness, and blindness, of the offense and the cruelty that mark our way of being and our social institutions. . . .

. . . [T]he church has no power except in the memory of Jesus Christ, in the remembrance of his suffering and death, of his solidarity with all victims, and of the great power of compassion, of which his death was the climax and witness. To receive the power of that memory, to give freedom to the Spirit that is given, the liturgy constantly retells the story and sings the hymns which celebrate how God's mercy takes our very boundedness as the place of the revelation of power and love. This is the power of the one who said "blessed are the poor," "blessed are the persecuted," "blessed are those who hunger and thirst after justice." One cannot remember Jesus, nor share in the power of God, without remembering those who have become victims of domination and those who in a greater hope protest by their lives this unholy distribution of power. In liturgy, the church remembers all who are dominated, all of nature's loveliness that is suppressed, all who resist, and all who testify. It is thus that it touches God's presence and power in the world.

Aidan Kavanagh

Aidan Kavanagh (+2006), monk of Saint Meinrad's Archabbey, offers a highly influential interpretation of liturgical theology as *theologia prima*, theology in the first instance, as well as insisting that the verb *statuo* be used and correctly interpreted in the Latin phrase *ut legem credendi lex statuat supplicandi*: it is the law of supplicating that establishes the law of believing, not the other way around.

Aidan Kavanagh, *On Liturgical Theology*
(New York: Pueblo, 1984), 76–78, 91–92, 134, 136–37.

The worshiping assembly never comes away from such an experience unchanged, and the assembly's continuing adjustment to that change is not merely a theological datum but theology itself. Theology on this primordial level is thus a sustained dialectic. Its *thesis* is the assembly as it enters into the liturgical act; its *antithesis* is the assembly's changed condition as it comes away from its liturgical encounter with the living God in Word and sacrament. Its *synthesis* is the assembly's adjustment in faith and works to that encounter. The adjustment comprises whole sets of acts both great and small, conscious and unconscious, all of which add up to necessarily critical and reflective theology which is architectonic for the content and significance of the assembly's address to reality itself—both inside and outside church, on the first day and throughout all other days of the week as well. . . .

. . . [T]he adjustment which the assembly undertakes in response to the God-induced change it suffers in its liturgical events is a dynamic, critical, reflective, and sustained act of theology in the first instance, of *theologia prima*. And I maintain that our fall from this into *theologia secunda* has imperceptibly rendered us aphasic and inept in regard to it. For this reason, it is far easier for us to write and react to theologies *of* the liturgy than to perceive theology as it occurs and factor its results wisely for the life of the world.

Our aphasic ineptitude with liturgical theology as *theologia prima* may also be why our pastoral theology is often so remotely pastoral and so genially untheological, quite unlike the theology practiced by the Church fathers, a theology which was with few exceptions thoroughly pastoral. It was a theology preached from within or in close connection with the liturgy rather than taught systematically in classrooms. And, finally, our aphasia concerning *theologia prima* seems to be the reason why we struggle so hard for such modest results in our ecumenical dialogues with certain Eastern Christian churches in which *theologia prima* remains the basic way of doing theology. They speak primary theology to us, we speak secondary theology to them, and we both slide past each other making cordial gestures which are finally equivocal. . . .

. . . If theology as a whole is critical reflection upon the communion between God and our race, the peculiarly graced representative and servant of the cosmic order created by God and restored in Christ, then scrutiny of the precise point at which this communion is most overtly deliberated upon and celebrated by us under God's judgment and in God's presence would seem to be crucial to the whole enterprise.

Belief is always consequent upon encounter with the Source of the grace of faith. Therefore Christians do not worship because they believe. They believe because the One in whose gift faith lies is regularly met in the act of communal worship—not because the assembly conjures up God, but because the initiative lies with the God who has promised to be there always. The *lex credendi* is thus subordinated to the *lex supplicandi* because both standards exist and function only within the worshipping assembly's own subordination of itself to its ever-present Judge, Savior, and unifying Spirit.

Lex supplicandi is something much more specific than the broad and fuzzy notion of the "practice of the Church." . . . It is a law of supplicatory prayer—not prayer or worship in general, but of prayer which petitions God for the whole range of human needs in specific, a law of euchological petition. This is the nub of the reason why the *lex supplicandi* founds and constitutes the *lex credendi* and is therefore primary for Christian theology. The way Christians believe is, somehow, constituted and supported by how Christians petition God for their human needs in worship.

The liturgical dialectic of encounter, change, and adjustment to change amounts to a reflective and lived theology which is native to all the members of the faithful assembly. This is *theologia* which is constant, regular, and inevitable as these people encounter God in worship and adjust to the changes God visits upon them. The liturgical assembly is thus a theological corporation and each of its members a theologian. . . . Mrs. Murphy and her pastor are primary theologians whose discourse in faith is carried on . . . in the vastly complex vocabulary of experiences had, prayers said, sights seen, smells smelled, words said and heard and responded to, emotions controlled and released, sins committed and repented, children born and loved ones buried, and in many other ways. . . . [Their] vocabulary is not precise, concise, or scientific. It is symbolic, aesthetic, and sapiential. . . . Nowhere else can that primary body of perceived data be read so well as in the living tradition of Christian worship.

Edward Kilmartin

Jesuit liturgist Edward Kilmartin returns to the notion of the mutual interplay between the *lex orandi* and *lex credendi*.

Edward Kilmartin, *Christian Liturgy I. Theology*
(Kansas City, MO: Sheed & Ward, 1988), 97.

The slogan "law of prayer-law of belief" leaves in suspense which magnitude might be the subject, and which the predicate, in particular instances. Consequently, it seems legitimate to state the axiom in this way: *the law of prayer is the law of belief, and vice versa.* . . . On the one hand, the law of prayer implies a comprehensive, and, in some measure a pre-reflective, perception of the life of faith. On the other hand, the law of belief must be introduced because the question of the value of a particular liturgical tradition requires the employment of theoretical discourse. One must reckon with the limits of the liturgy as lived practice of the faith. History has taught us that forms of liturgical prayer and ritual activity, however orthodox, often had to be dropped or changed to avoid heretical misunderstanding. Moreover, in new historical and cultural situations, the question of the correspondence between the community's understanding of Christian truth, and its expression in the liturgy and that of the authentic whole tradition, must continually be placed. To respond responsibly to this problem, other sources of theology must be introduced along with the liturgical-practical grounding of the knowledge of faith.

Gordon Lathrop

Influential Lutheran liturgist Gordon Lathrop provides an ecumenical list and discussion of the essentials of Christian worship, which elsewhere he refers to as the Ordo.

Gordon Lathrop, *Open Questions in Worship,*
vol. 1: *What Are the Essentials of Christian Worship?*
(Minneapolis: Augsburg Fortress, 1994), 22–23.

So these are the essentials of Christian worship. A community *gathers in prayer* around the scriptures *read* and proclaimed. This community of the word then tastes the meaning of that word by keeping the meal of Christ, *giving thanks* over bread and cup and *eating* and drinking. It is this word-table community, the body of Christ, which gathers other people to its number, continually *teaching* both itself and these newcomers the mercy and mystery of God and *washing* them in the name of that God. All of these essential things urge the community toward the world—toward prayer for the world, sharing with the hungry of the world, caring for the world, giving witness to the world.

Around these central things, which will be most evident in Sunday and festival worship, other gatherings of Christians may also take place. *Like the planets around the sun, these other gatherings will reflect the light of the central Sunday gathering.* They will do so mostly by repeating and echoing the readings, the songs, the prayers, and the blessings of the Sunday assembly. Or these other gatherings will be intended to help inquirers, newcomers, and candidates for baptism to come more deeply into the mystery which is at the heart of the Sunday assembly: reading and discussing the scriptures with them, praying for them. Both sorts of Christian gatherings—daily prayer and "seeker services" or "catechumenal gatherings"—will come to their purpose most clearly as they are turned toward the full Christian assembly around these essential things.

There are certain dangers in talking about the *essentials* of Christian worship. For one thing, people may forget what they are *for*, *why* they are essential. A church may begin to think that simply to read the scripture and have a sermon is enough, for *whatever* purpose these are done: ideological training, self-realization, the attempt to please God. Or a community may begin to give formal thanks and do the eating and drinking for a variety of skewed reasons: to ensure a good crop, to sanctify a government, to heighten the solidarity of a particular racial or sexual or economic group. Or the washing and naming of God may take place simply to mark a birth as a rite of passage. Or any one of these things may be forced on people, in ways utterly devoid of the love to which the things themselves bear witness.

No. The *reasons* for these essential things belong to their essential character. Word, table, and bath occur at the heart of a participating community so that all people may freely encounter God's mercy in Christ, that they may come to faith again and again, that they may be formed into a community of faith, that they may be brought to the possibility of love for God's world. When these reasons are not manifest in the exercise of the central actions themselves, the deep meaning of the essential things is obscured and betrayed. Even so, God acts in these things. Where we have kept the holy things most dead and deadly, fire can still leap out into the hearts and lives of the assembly. The combination of the liberating words of scripture with the gracious actions given by Christ can yield faith.

The other great danger of speaking about the *essentials* of Christian worship is that we will take such speech as minimalist counsel: Do only such things as will barely count to meet the "essential" requirements. No. The word *essential* here is intended to mean just the opposite. *Let these things be central.* Let them stand at the center, large and full, influencing and determining all else we do. Let the scripture reading be done as if it were clearly the first reason we have come together at all. Let the preaching be more serious, more profound, more gracious. Let the prayers be truly intercessions, the real naming of human need. Let the meal be held every Sunday. Let the food be clearly food. Let the hungry be always remembered. Let the thanksgiving be beautiful and strong. Let the whole assembly eat and drink. Let both the font and the name be "unshrunk." . . .

. . . The very centrality of bath, word, and table, and the very reasons for their centrality . . . do begin to give us some characteristics of the mode of our celebration. These characteristics . . . are

corollaries which ought not be easily ignored. A list of such characteristics should include *ritual focus*, a *music which serves*, the importance of *Sunday* and other festivals, a *participating community, many
ministries*, and a *recognized presider* who is in communion with the
churches.

Lutheran World Federation

Influenced greatly by Gordon Lathrop's approach to the Ordo of Christian
worship, as well as by the approach to liturgical inculturation of Anscar
Chupungco, OSB, this document provides a way to think theologically
about liturgy and diverse cultural contexts.

Lutheran World Federation, *Nairobi Statement on Worship and Culture*
(Geneva: Lutheran World Federation, 1996).

1. Introduction
1.1. Worship is the heart and pulse of the Christian Church. In
worship we celebrate together God's gracious gifts of creation and
salvation, and are strengthened to live in response to God's grace.
Worship always involves actions, not merely words. To consider
worship is to consider music, art, and architecture, as well as liturgy
and preaching.

1.2. The reality that Christian worship is always celebrated in
a given local cultural setting draws our attention to the dynamics
between worship and the world's many local cultures.

1.3 Christian worship relates dynamically to culture in at least
four ways. First, it is transcultural, the same substance for everyone everywhere, beyond culture. Second, it is contextual, varying
according to the local situation (both nature and culture). Third, it
is counter-cultural, challenging what is contrary to the Gospel in a
given culture. Fourth, it is cross-cultural, making possible sharing
between different local cultures. In all four dynamics, there are helpful principles which can be identified.

2. Worship as Transcultural
2.1. The resurrected Christ whom we worship, and through whom
by the power of the Holy Spirit we know the grace of the Triune
God, transcends and indeed is beyond all cultures. In the mystery
of his resurrection is the source of the transcultural nature of Christian worship. Baptism and Eucharist, the sacraments of Christ's
death and resurrection, were given by God for all the world. There
is one Bible, translated into many tongues, and biblical preaching of

Christ's death and resurrection has been sent into all the world. The fundamental shape of the principal Sunday act of Christian worship, the Eucharist or Holy Communion, is shared across cultures: the people gather, the Word of God is proclaimed, the people intercede for the needs of the Church and the world, the eucharistic meal is shared, and the people are sent out into the world for mission. The great narratives of Christ's birth, death, resurrection, and sending of the Spirit, and our Baptism into him, provide the central meanings of the transcultural times of the church's year: especially Lent/Easter/Pentecost, and, to a lesser extent, Advent/Christmas/Epiphany. The ways in which the shapes of the Sunday Eucharist and the church year are expressed vary by culture, but their meanings and fundamental structure are shared around the globe. There is one Lord, one faith, one Baptism, one Eucharist.

2.2. Several specific elements of Christian liturgy are also transcultural, e.g., readings from the Bible (although of course the translations vary), the ecumenical creeds and the Our Father, and Baptism in water in the Triune Name.

2.3. The use of this shared core liturgical structure and these shared liturgical elements in local congregational worship—as well as the shared act of people assembling together, and the shared provision of diverse leadership in that assembly (although the space for the assembly and the manner of the leadership vary)—are expressions of Christian unity across time, space, culture, and confession. The recovery in each congregation of the clear centrality of these transcultural and ecumenical elements renews the sense of this Christian unity and gives all churches a solid basis for authentic contextualization.

3. Worship as Contextual

3.1. Jesus whom we worship was born into a specific culture of the world. In the mystery of his incarnation are the model and the mandate for the contextualization of Christian worship. God can be and is encountered in the local cultures of our world. A given culture's values and patterns, insofar as they are consonant with the values of the Gospel, can be used to express the meaning and purpose of Christian worship. Contextualization is a necessary task for the Church's mission in the world, so that the Gospel can be ever more deeply rooted in diverse local cultures.

3.2. Among the various methods of contextualization, that of dynamic equivalence is particularly useful. It involves re-expressing components of Christian worship with something from a local culture that has an equal meaning, value, and function. Dynamic equivalence goes far beyond mere translation; it involves understanding the fundamental meanings both of elements of worship and of the local culture, and enabling the meanings and actions of worship to be "encoded" and re-expressed in the language of local culture.

3.3. In applying the method of dynamic equivalence, the following procedure may be followed. First, the liturgical ordo (basic shape) should be examined with regard to its theology, history, basic elements, and cultural backgrounds. Second, those elements of the ordo that can be subjected to dynamic equivalence without prejudice to their meaning should be determined. Third, those components of culture that are able to re-express the Gospel and the liturgical ordo in an adequate manner should be studied. Fourth, the spiritual and pastoral benefits our people will derive from the changes should be considered.

3.4. Local churches might also consider the method of creative assimilation. This consists of adding pertinent components of local culture to the liturgical ordo in order to enrich its original core. The baptismal ordo of "washing with water and the Word", for example, was gradually elaborated by the assimilation of such cultural practices as the giving of white vestments and lighted candles to the neophytes of ancient mystery religions. Unlike dynamic equivalence, creative assimilation enriches the liturgical ordo—not by culturally re-expressing its elements, but by adding to it new elements from local culture.

3.5. In contextualization the fundamental values and meanings of both Christianity and of local cultures must be respected.

3.6. An important criterion for dynamic equivalence and creative assimilation is that sound or accepted liturgical traditions are preserved in order to keep unity with the universal Church's tradition of worship, while progress inspired by pastoral needs is encouraged. On the side of culture, it is understood that not everything can be integrated with Christian worship, but only those elements that are connatural to (that is, of the same nature as) the liturgical ordo. Elements borrowed from local culture should always undergo critique and purification, which can be achieved through the use of biblical typology.

4. Worship as Counter-cultural

4.1. Jesus Christ came to transform all people and all cultures, and calls us not to conform to the world, but to be transformed with it (Romans 12:2). In the mystery of his passage from death to eternal life is the model for transformation, and thus for the counter-cultural nature of Christian worship. Some components of every culture in the world are sinful, dehumanizing, and contradictory to the values of the Gospel. From the perspective of the Gospel, they need critique and transformation. Contextualization of Christian faith and worship necessarily involves challenging of all types of oppression and social injustice wherever they exist in earthly cultures.

4.2. It also involves the transformation of cultural patterns which idolize the self or the local group at the expense of a wider humanity, or which give central place to the acquisition of wealth at the expense of the care of the earth and its poor. The tools of the counter-cultural in Christian worship may also include the deliberate maintenance or recovery of patterns of action which differ intentionally from prevailing cultural models. These patterns may arise from a recovered sense of Christian history, or from the wisdom of other cultures.

5. Worship as Cross-cultural

5.1. Jesus came to be the Savior of all people. He welcomes the treasures of earthly cultures into the city of God. By virtue of Baptism, there is one Church; and one means of living in faithful response to Baptism is to manifest ever more deeply the unity of the Church. The sharing of hymns and art and other elements of worship across cultural barriers helps enrich the whole Church and strengthen the sense of the communio of the Church. This sharing can be ecumenical as well as cross-cultural, as a witness to the unity of the Church and the oneness of Baptism. Cross-cultural sharing is possible for every church, but is especially needed in multicultural congregations and member churches.

5.2. Care should be taken that the music, art, architecture, gestures and postures, and other elements of different cultures are understood and respected when they are used by churches elsewhere in the world. The criteria for contextualization (above, sections 3.5 and 3.6) should be observed.

Don E. Saliers

United Methodist liturgical theologian Don Saliers underscores the importance of aesthetics in Christian worship under the topic of "The Aesthetics of the Holy."

> Don E. Saliers, *Worship as Theology: Foretaste of Glory Divine*
> (Nashville: Abingdon Press, 1994), 211–12.

Christian liturgy in its whole range . . . possesses formative and expressive power for human imagination, emotion, thought, and volition. This power is for good or for ill. When liturgy is thoughtlessly performed, without affection and life-connection, it will far less awaken us to the realities of biblical faith much less to the holy things signified. At its worst, Christian liturgy has formed communities in deep hatred, as against the Jews, or has created and sustained social indifference and privatization of faith. But this is not inherent in the aesthetics of liturgical celebration. Respect for the aesthetic power and cultural embeddedness of language can liberate the multiple ranges of meaning accumulated in the primary symbols, sign-actions, and the texts. Rediscovery of the deep humanity of the sacraments in our own time of reform and renewal requires attentiveness to the permanent tension of which we have spoken. We can discern when liturgies violate the glory of God. Here the new "literalism" born of various ideologies simply cannot serve as our framework of interpretation for the polysemantic character of liturgical action. The library called the Holy Bible presents us with too much richness for literalist reduction to help us. Attending to this very richness and to the complexity of symbol in relation to suffering and hope can inform a liberating style of celebration. The continual juxtaposition of the readings with song, variable prayers, and the fixed and variable structures of symbol and sacramental action is generative of ever-fresh insight.

Classical definitions of liturgy speak of the glorification of God and the sanctification of our humanity. This may be best understood as a simultaneous ongoing process. For only when the art of liturgy simultaneously takes us into the mystery of God's own being and action *and* into the depths of our humanity will its holiness be revealed. If Jesus Christ is by virtue of the animating power of God's Holy Spirit, at the center of our assemblies, then the image of the humanity of God "at full stretch" is always before us. Healing, reconciling, feeding, in prophetic cries, in weeping over Jerusalem or Lazarus, or in arms outstretched in blessing and forgiveness, this offer of grace is extended. At the heart of God's mercy, justice, and love is the free offer to us of our own true humanity. This is what St. Irenaeus meant in claiming that the glory of God is the living human being. . . .

. . . The art of it all may be summed up: Christian liturgy is symbolic, parabolic, and metaphoric. It is an epiphany of the divine self-communication in and through the created order's sensible signs. Thus the arts that serve, the art of common prayer, and ritual action must lead to sharing what theology cannot finally explain in rational categories. It is for liturgy to allow us to apprehend in wonder, gratitude, and adoration what theology tries to say is holy. St. Augustine reminded us long ago that when we receive the Eucharist, it is our own mystery we receive.

Like Jesus' own parables, good liturgy disturbs, breaks open, and discloses a new world. The aesthetic—that is, the perceptual power—of liturgy pulls together, even "throws together" (*symbolein*) words, signs, and acts to reveal. Liturgy is metaphoric—it carries us across the border of our own consciousness, across the border of our own common-sense world of cause and effect. It is epiphanic: a shining forth of what the eye does not yet see. In these ways liturgy has aesthetic range, and this has to do with the well-formed, the beautiful, and the sensate activities of how we come to know God through the created order. All of these artful features of liturgical celebration led Romano Guardini to define Christian liturgy as "Holy Play"—a wondrous set of improvisations on the *cantus firmus*: the song of creation, incarnation, resurrection, and consummation. This is hidden in every "Glory to God in the highest," and is made explicit in "Maranatha." Advent discerns the end and thus becomes an ever-new beginning: "Come, O Come, Emmanuel."

Robert Taft

The Eastern Catholic Jesuit liturgiologist Robert Taft articulates a liturgical theology that is simultaneously a liturgical spirituality.

Robert Taft, "What Does Liturgy Do? Toward a Soteriology of Liturgical Celebration: Some Theses," *Worship* 66, no. 3 (1992): 207–11.

[W]e see a water bath but believe in another greater cleansing; we see bread and wine but believe in a higher food, the body and blood of Christ. In so doing we believe in Jesus' "for-us," which is the basis of our "for one another" in him, as our only possible *Antwort* to him, which is, in turn, the basis of all Christian life. This, then, is what I think the Catholic Church means when it says that liturgy is the work of the whole Christ, head and members. And it is faith that makes the concrete fact transparent in its true reality. As such, liturgy is eschatological, for what is present is the final fulfillment of humanity, the eschaton, to which Christ has already broken through, bringing us with him inchoatively. Indeed, as Patrick Regan has well said, it is not so much an *eschaton*, a final *thing*, but the *eschatos*, the final *person*, Jesus Christ himself, whose life is in us through the Spirit, which is the final age toward whose perfection we ever strive in faith.[1]

1. Patrick Regan, "Pneumatological and Eschatological Aspects of Liturgical Celebration," *Worship* 51 (1977): 346–47.

It is only thus, in his Body, that is, in *us*, that the Risen Christ is *visibly* present in the world. And it is only in its liturgical celebration that the Church is constituted as the eschatological People of God among the nations of the world. For in the teaching of St Paul as well as in that of Vatican II, liturgy and life in Christ are one.

Hence liturgy is not just ritual, not just a cult, not just the worship we offer God. It is first of all God's coming to us in Christ. Nor is it individual, or narcissistic, for it is also a ministry of each one of us to one another. It is only through our faith that Christ can be visibly present to others in the present dispensation. The commonly heard contemporary complaint, "I don't go to church because I don't *get* anything out of it," the summit of a selfish narcissism suitably expressive of our age, shows how little this is understood, this gift of Christ only we can bring to one another by the shining forth of the intensity of our faith in the life of the assembly! As Gerhard Delling has said: "Worship is the self-portrayal of religion. In worship the sources by which religion lives are made visible, its expectations and hopes are expressed, and the forces which sustain it are made known. In many respects the essence of a religion is more directly intelligible in its worship than in statement of its basic principles or even in descriptions of its sentiments."[2] What Delling says here of the phenomenological/epistemological level is even more true on the existential: not only in worship is religion *known*; it is through worship that it is *fed and lives*. . . .

. . . This has ever been the testimony of the Orthodox/Catholic Christendom, East and West: it is through the liturgy that Christ feeds us, and we live. An Eastern expression of it can be savored in one of my favorite anecdotes, the answer given by an old Russian Orthodox village priest to the Western interlocutor who was badgering him, trying to tell him that what was important was conversion, confession, catechetical education, prayer—beside which the overdone liturgical rites in which his Orthodox tradition was immersed were totally secondary. The Russian priest replied, "Among you it is indeed secondary. Among us Orthodox (and at these words he blessed himself) it is not so. The liturgy is our common prayer, it initiates our faithful into the mystery of Christ better than all your catechism. It passes before our eyes the life of our Christ, the Russian Christ, and that can be understood only in common, at our holy rites, in the mystery of our icons. When one sins, one sins alone. But to understand the mystery of the Risen Christ, neither your books nor your sermons are of any help. For that, one must have lived with

---

2. Gerhard Delling, *Worship in the New Testament* (London, 1961), xi.

the Orthodox Church the joyous Night (Easter). And he blessed himself again."[3]

But the East has no monopoly on truth. And so the same teaching can be seen equally well, if less dramatically expressed, in what Pius XII said about the liturgical year in his 1947 encyclical *Mediator Dei* (no. 165): "[It] is not a cold and lifeless representation of the events of the past, or a simple and bare record of a former age. It is rather Christ himself who is ever-living in his Church."

And since *we* are that Church in whom Christ lives, the liturgy, as the common celebration of our salvation in him, is the most perfect expression and realization of the spirituality of the Church. If there are different "schools" of spirituality in East and West, they are but variant local accents of the same spiritual vernacular, the one spirituality of the Church. And the spirituality of the Church is a biblical and liturgical spirituality. . . .

. . . The mystery that is Christ is the center of Christian life, and it is this mystery and nothing else that the Church, through the Spirit, preaches in the Word and renews sacramentally in the liturgy so that we might be drawn into it ever more deeply. When we leave the assembly to return to our mundane tasks, we have only to assimilate what we have experienced, and realize this mystery in our lives: in a word, to become other Christs. For the liturgy is like an active prophecy. Its purpose is to reproduce in our lives what the Church exemplifies for us in its public worship. The spiritual life is just another word for a personal relationship with God, and the liturgy is nothing more than the common expression of the Mystical Body's personal relationship to God, which in turn is simply the relationship of the man Jesus to his Father, given as his Spirit, his gift to us.

The value of such a liturgical spirituality is the unity it effects and manifests between the public ministry and worship of the Church and the no less important hidden spiritual life of unceasing prayer and charity carried out in faith and hope by individual members of Christ's Body. The putative tension between public and private, objective and subjective, liturgical and personal piety, is an illusion, a false dichotomy. For in public worship it is precisely this work of spiritual formation that the Church, as the Body of Christ, head and members, carries on.

That's what liturgy does, that's what liturgy means. But unless we encounter this total Christ, head and members, not just Christ in himself, but also in others, in faith, hope, and charity, it will not do or mean what it's supposed to for us.

---

3. Recounted by Charles Bourgeois, SJ, "Chez les paysans de la Podlachie et du nord-est de la Pologne. Mai 1924–Décember 1925," *Études* 191 (1927): 585.

MORE RECENT APPROACHES

David W. Fagerberg

David W. Fagerberg, *Theologia Prima: What Is Liturgical Theology?* 2nd ed. (Chicago: Liturgy Training Publications; Mundelein, IL: Hillenbrand Books, 2004), ix–x, 41–42, 96.

Liturgical theology is normative for the larger theological enterprise because it is the trysting place where the sources of theology function precisely as sources. Liturgical theology is furthermore normative for liturgical renewal because such efforts should arise out of the tradition of the Church and not our individual preferences. The subject matter of theology is God, humanity, and creation, and the vortex in which these three existentially entangle is liturgy.

My working definition of liturgical theology continues to be owed to Alexander Schmemann, Aidan Kavanagh, and Robert Taft. I take the term to mean the theological work of the liturgical assembly, not the work done by an academic upon liturgical material. It may seem easier to approach the idea as theology considered in the light of liturgy, or liturgy considered in the light of theology, but I consider this approach misleading because it leaves the impression that there are two subjects (liturgy and theology) instead of one subject (liturgical theology). The simple aim of this book remains the same: to gain some clarity in understanding about the shape and deployment of the term "liturgical theology" by proposing a distinction between it and other ways theologians treat worship. Rather than saying liturgical theology occurs wherever theology places liturgy upon its list of discussion topics, or wherever piety leaves the church to enter the scholar's study, I propose two defining attributes of liturgical theology: it is *theologia prima* and it is found in the structure of the rite, in its *lex orandi*. It recognizes that the liturgical community does genuine theology, although admittedly of a primary and not secondary kind, and it recognizes that the law of prayer establishes the Church's law of belief. Liturgical theology is the faith of the Church in ritual motion, as Kavanagh was fond of saying; a genuine theology, but one manifested and preserved in the rite as *lex orandi* even before it is parsed systematically.

Christianity involves liturgy, theology, and asceticism the way a pancake involves flour, milk, and eggs: they are ingredients to the end result. Leave one out and you don't have exactly the same thing anymore. Liturgy is a substantially theological enterprise; asceticism is a product of and prerequisite for Christian liturgy; liturgy and theology integrate by ascetical means. I do not see myself trying to coordinate two dyads (liturgical theology and liturgical asceticism), but I see myself trying to understand how the terms in one triad (liturgy-theology-asceticism) relate to each other. The horizontal base line of the triangle is liturgy. "Seek the reason why God created," Maximus the Confessor counseled, "for that is knowledge." This wisdom is possessed by the liturgical theologian, and liturgical asceticism is the price of its possession.

The definition of liturgical theology being proposed therefore rests upon two crucial affirmations about the theology done by the liturgical community: 1) it is genuine theology, although it is *theologia prima* and not *theologia secunda*, 2) and it is *lex orandi*. It must be said that academic theology is a species within the genus theology, but it is not the whole genus. It is true that the theological outcome of a liturgy is quite different in form and purpose from the theological outcome of an academic study, but I deny that theology is only really done when one crosses the threshold out of liturgy into the academy. The liturgical rite is the ontological condition for what is itself a genuine theology, albeit of a different kind: it is primary theology and not secondary theology. It can be translated into secondary theology for certain purposes, but it is not necessary to do so in order to have real theology instead of the mere rudiments of theology. Regarding the second point, a premier role for liturgical theology is established because as *lex orandi* the liturgy is where human words about God are grounded in the Word of God. Liturgical theology is normative for the larger theological enterprise because it alone, of all the activities that make up the family of theological games, is the place where the sources of theology function precisely as sources.

Both liturgy and theology suffer a distortion when they are severed from one another. The goal of the liturgical theologian is not to insinuate liturgy into theology, or to persuade the theological community to include more sacramentaries in its bibliography pages, or urge that a more doxological spin be placed on our language. The goal of liturgical theology is to gainsay the presupposed dichotomy insofar as it exists at all. Since liturgical theology apprehends the faith of the Church as it is epiphanized in liturgical structure, therefore the first methodological step is to look at the deep structures of the rite. Unfortunately, there has been a three-way rupture between cult, theology, and piety. Liturgical cult is no longer the expression and norm of either reasonable faith (theology) or affective faith (piety). I am seeking to gain recognition for liturgy as theology, find a home for it in the current taxonomy of the field of theology, and discover its normative quality.

Teresa Berger

Teresa Berger provides a feminist theological interpretation of various feasts and seasons of the liturgical year, in this case, the focus on the passion during Holy Week.

Teresa Berger, *Fragments of Real Presence: Liturgical Traditions in the Hands of Women* (New York: Herder & Herder, 2005), 186–87 and 189–91.

Tuesday of Holy Week: Passion Devotion (long before the film). I spend much of the day reading about late-medieval passion devotions. The sheer ubiquity, bloodstained intensity, and devotional multiplicity of these devotions—including calculations of the number of strokes and of the drops of Jesus' blood as well as the length of his side wound—put Mel Gibson's *Passion of the Christ* in historical context. A fifteenth-century Flemish image of the Crucified, for example, has Jesus' body oozing streams of blood from his head, arms, torso, side, legs, and feet. An indulgence of eighty thousand years was the reward for gazing at this image and praying. There was also, in late medieval England, a fervent devotion to the Three Nails. We have not come far with the contemporary sale of Passion Nail Pendants, Nail Zipper Pulls, and Nail Key Rings. But in the late Middle Ages, there was also a peculiar fascination with the side wound of Christ, and this wound could be seen as feminine.[4] Visually, its pointed oval flesh resembled female genitalia. Moreover, the side wound of Christ did as women do: it bled, birthed new life, offered itself as a breast at which to suckle, and, finally, invited penetration. A crucial image of mystic union, after all, was that of entering Christ's wound. Nothing in our current fascination with the passion of Christ allows for this kind of gender ambiguity or invites the destabilization of binary gender stereotypes in quite the same way. Might this be a loss? Obviously, the medieval responses to the image of the Crucified are foreign to most of us and cannot simply be resurrected. But are our own binary gender stereotypes really constructive for the journey through Holy Week and beyond?

Good Friday; The Real Presence of Women. . . . Maybe the real presence of women at the cross is not all there is, important as this real presence surely was. Maybe the women who were there, in the

---

4. See further Flora Lewis, "The Wound in Christ's Side and the Instruments of the Passion: Gendered Experience and Response," in *Women and the Book: Assessing the Visual Evidence*, ed. Lesley Smith and Jane H. M. Taylor, Library Studies in Medieval Culture (London: British Library, 1997), 204–29.

midst of that agony, also rendered present a knowledge born from within their own female bodies. The knowledge is this: that unimaginable pain searing through a body, and water breaking forth, and flesh being torn, and blood flowing profusely are not signs of death alone. They are also signs of a woman laboring to birth new life. Will any of the women, maybe Mary, his mother, have wondered about the similarity?

The thought of Jesus' death as a form of birthing is not as far-fetched as it might seem at first. This was especially true in Jesus' time when the experiences of childbirth and of dying were clearly linked. Maternal mortality was high. A womb and a tomb were not strangers to each other. Jesus himself evoked the image of a woman in labor in childbirth on the night before he died: "When a woman is in labor, she has pain, because her hour has come. But when her child is born, she no longer remembers the anguish. . ." (John 16:21). Indeed, Jesus' approaching death came to be described with the very same words: "When Jesus knew that his hour had come . . ." (John 13:1). . . .

. . . For some medieval writers, it was this imagery of birthing in connection with Jesus' agony on the cross that captured their imagination. Anselm of Canterbury (ca. 1033–1109), for example, meditated: "Truly, Lord, you are a mother; . . . It is by your death that they [your children] have been born."[5] A century after Anselm, the Cistercian monk Aelred of Rievaulx wrote about the crucifix to his confreres that it will "bring before your mind his Passion for you to imitate, his outspread arms will invite you to embrace him, his naked breasts will feed you with the milk of sweetness to console you."[6] And another hundred years later, the Carthusian mystic, Marguerite d'Oingt prayed thus: "Are you not my mother and more than the mother? . . . when the hour of birth came you were placed on the hard bed of the cross where you could not move or turn around or stretch your limbs as someone who suffers such great pain should be able to do. . . . And surely it was no wonder that your veins were broken when you gave birth to the world all in one day."[7]

Not only medieval mystics cherished the image of Jesus on the cross as maternal labor, however. The sixteenth-century Protestant

5. Anselm of Canterbury, "Prayer to St. Paul," in *The Prayers and Meditations of St. Anselm with the Proslogion*, trans. Sister Benedicta Ward, Penguin Classics (Harmondsworth: Penguin, 1973), 153ff.

6. Quoted in Caroline Walker Bynum, "'. . . And Women His Humanity': Female Imagery in the Religious Writing of the Later Middle Ages," in *Fragmentation and Redemption: Essays on Gender and the Human Body in Medieval Religion*, 3rd ed. (New York: Zone Books, 1994), 158ff.

7. *The Writings of Margaret of Oingt*, Medieval Prioress and Mystic, trans. with an introduction, essay, and notes by Renate Blumenfeld-Kosinski, Focus Library of Medieval Women (Newburyport, MA: Focus Information Group, 1990), 31.

lay reformer Katharina Schütz Zell put it thus: "[Christ] gives the analogy of bitter labor and says; 'A women when she bears a child has anguish and sorrow' [John 16:21] and He applies all of this to His suffering, in which He so hard and bitterly bore us, nourished us and made us alive, gave us to drink from His breast and side with water and blood, as a mother nurses her child."[8]

As I go forward on this particular Good Friday, at the solemn Veneration of the Cross, I venerate the body of Christ and all its labored pain, I venerate and adore the body of a God who passionately labors to birth new life, amidst searing pain, breaking water, and much blood.

Michael B. Aune

Michael Aune critiques much of modern liturgical theology and argues that the starting point must be not ecclesiology or the liturgical assembly's actions but God and God's salvific activity.

Michael B. Aune, "Liturgy and Theology: Rethinking the Relationship," Part 2, *Worship* 81, no. 2 (2007): 156–57.

Liturgical questions and liturgical matters are ... *theological* because their object is God and they are seen with their origin and orientation towards God. While sooner or later God's gracious self-communication in liturgy and in Christian life will need to be understood in its anthropological context, humankind's receptivity for the One revealed and how it expresses and incarnates a heart-felt commitment to God of an existence in faith, for now the reference is back to this self-communication of God.

Yet the nearly unquestioned starting-point for liturgical theology or for considering the relationship between liturgy and theology has been "church," "assembly," because in its use of the "holy things" of word, bath, and table, "it is called to faith in the triune God."[9] Similarly, baptismal ecclesiologies or persons-in-communion ecclesiologies are seen as the proper framework for understanding and appropriating just what the activity of worship is and does. While

8. Quoted in Elsie Anne McKee, "Katharina Schütz Zell and the 'Our Father,'" in *Oratio: Das Gebet in patristischer und reformatorischer Sicht*, ed. Emidio Campi et al., Forschungen zur Kirchen- und Dogmengeschichte 76 (Göttingen: Vandenhoeck & Ruprecht, 1999), 242f.

9. Gordon Lathrop, *Holy People: A Liturgical Ecclesiology* (Minneapolis: Fortress Press, 1999), 14.

God is presumed to be the enabler of such activity, the emphasis in the long run is that liturgy is an action, the *Vollzug* of the church.

In my judgment, the greater need in liturgical theology is not for an *ecclesiology*—liturgical or otherwise—that can sustain or undergird what happens in and among worshipers around word, bath, and/or table, but rather for a *theology* which, by implication, is a way of speaking of God by speaking to God. For some traditions such as Lutheranism or Calvinism, the primary action is always God's. Moreover, the question of where the emphasis is to be placed has always been, at least until the past generation, an important part of Lutheran theology. To shift the emphasis toward "church" and/ or "assembly" can leave one vulnerable or susceptible to a different kind of theology where God no longer appears to be the initiator of the action of worship. A consequence of such a shift is to operate with a different set of "normative" ideas of what liturgical celebration is. With the great deal of talk about "presiders" and "assemblies" or the "creative planning" of individuals, one could begin to wonder, as Pope Benedict XVI has done, whether God is less and less in the picture. More and more important is what is done by human beings who have come together for worship and do not like to be subjected to a "pre-determined pattern."

. . . Pope Benedict's comments . . . are germane to the considerations of a more appropriate starting point for liturgical theology or for the unfolding of the liturgy-theology relationship. . . . The question is whether it is better theologically to inaugurate such considerations from within the framework provided by ecclesiology—baptismal, eucharistic, communio, or otherwise—or somewhere else; say, something even more fundamental and basic that can be called *theology* in the sense of thinking, praying, praising, celebrating what God is doing, has done, and will do on humankind's behalf that somehow gets it across that this is *saving*.

Hence, the usual "tack" of either abstracting or sliding over what *theology* is will no longer do. Work needs to continue toward greater clarity about what *theology* is. And once that occurs, then the subjective side of *theology* as "recognition" or "acknowledgment" can begin to be worked out more fully—how the Christian expresses his or her response to God's gracious self-communication in the conditions of earthly life and history and *worship*—made possible the ongoing revelation and action of God. This basic dynamic of divine initiative and answering human response indicates that worship is dialogical—a dynamic that is central to the articulation of a *theological* concept of liturgy. . . .

Melanie Ross

Melanie Ross offers a liturgical theology for nonliturgical churches of the free-church traditions.

Melanie Ross, "Joseph's Britches Revisited: Reflections on Method in Liturgical Theology," *Worship* 80, no. 6 (2006): 528–50.

In 1998, Gordon Lathrop wrote an article entitled "New Pentecost or Joseph's Britches? Reflections on the History and Meaning of the Worship Ordo in the Megachurches." Lathrop's intention in the article was twofold. First, he wished to temper claims that mega-churches had produced a new liturgical movement or a reformation. Drawing on James White's description of worship in the Frontier tradition, Lathrop demonstrated that the threefold service order lauded as a "new" liturgical development by megachurches was in fact a much older pattern which had originated with Charles Finney. Lathrop's second intention was more contentious: "to reintroduce a good and widespread discussion of the old and apparently unresolved issue which is at the center of the disagreement between the megachurches and classic, ecumenical Christianity: the question of means, or what Finney called measures."[10]

... Upon reading "Joseph's Britches," I repeatedly heard the claim, "This is what worship means to you." The only problem is, it isn't. There is a gaping chasm between the "not wrong" of Lathrop's article (Finney's historical legacy in American worship) and the "not right" (my own experience worshiping in this context does not match Lathrop's conclusions), and my article will attempt to build a reconciliatory bridge through a discussion of methodology. . . . I suggest that a change in optic lens is needed—hermeneutics, not structuralism, best plays to the analytic strengths of the Free Church. A hermeneutic methodology brings three significant strengths to liturgical theology: it emphasizes the event nature of worship; it focuses on meaning in the context of relationship; and it values the interpreter's "lived experience."

[1. Event Nature of Worship.] For a scholar interpreting a tradition with a highly structured order of worship—one in which "the meaning of the liturgy resides first of all in the liturgy itself"[11]— [Lathrop's] structuralism is a logical methodological choice. This

---

10. Gordon Lathrop, "New Pentecost or Joseph's Britches? Reflections on the History and Meaning of the Worship Ordo in Megachurches," *Worship* 72 (1998): 533.

11. Gordon Lathrop, *Holy Things: A Liturgical Theology* (Minneapolis: Fortress Press, 1993), 35.

method insists that "structural analysis must come first in order to ground an adequate understanding of the meaning of the text."[12] . . . However, structuralism is less compatible with a Free Church approach to worship since, as Christopher Ellis explains, structure and ordo are not the logical starting points in Free Church liturgical theology:

> Tradition does not carry for the Free Churches the burden of author-ity which it would carry in Roman Catholic or Orthodox churches. Authority is found elsewhere—in Scripture, the missionary imperative, pastoral need and common sense rationalism. Thus the ordo, or under-lying principles, of evolving worship cannot carry the *lex credendi* . . . because the patterning of worship is subservient to other theological authorities.[13]

I do not mean to imply that Free Church services are devoid of order. Thomas Long has noted that congregations which resist being restrained by fixed liturgies nevertheless have structure; other authors, including David Newman, have correctly identified the fact that Free Churches are as likely to fall into ruts as any other tradi-tion.[14] I simply wish to emphasize the fact that Free Churches do not flag structure as the methodological starting point in their own theological self-understanding. . . .

[2. "Meaning" in the context of relationship.] [W]hen writing about the catechumenate process, Lathrop suggests that "each of those who accompany the people coming to baptism may best do so like . . . one of two guests who have been given the freedom of the house assuring the other that the house is not strange. . . ."[15] The focal point of hospitality is a floor plan, a blueprint—in short, on becoming comfortable within a structure. . . . I chose this passage from *Holy Things* because of its strong contrast with the following excerpt from Sally Morgenthaler's *Worship Evangelism*. Both authors address how congregations might best offer liturgical hospitality, yet the difference in their approaches is striking. Morgenthaler asserts,

> . . . great musical performances, thought-provoking drama, touching testimonies, relevant messages, and apologetics about God and faith are wonderful tools God can use to touch the seeker's mind and heart. Notice, however, that their operation does not hinge on any movement or response from those in attendance. They are all examples of presen-tation, and presentation does not require people to give back anything

---

12. Brian Kovacs, "Philosophical foundations for structuralism," *Semeia* 10 (1978): 104.

13. Christopher Ellis, *The Gathering: A Theology and Spirituality of Worship in Free Church Tradi-tion* (London: SCM Press, 2004), 67.

14. Thomas G. Long, *Beyond the Worship Wars* (Bethesda: Alban Institute, 2001), 46, and David Newman, "Observations on Method in Liturgical Theology," *Worship* 57 (1983): 380.

15. Lathrop, *Holy Things*, 123.

of themselves to God. It does not involve the listener or observer in any of the expression of worship: heartfelt praise, adoration, reverence, thanksgiving, repentance, confession, or commitment.[16]

For Lathrop, "worship evangelism" means making the symbols of the meeting large and accessible; for Morgenthaler, worship evangelism means drawing unbelievers into a dynamic relationship with God. This points to the second major difference between structuralist and hermeneutic methodologies: whereas structuralism focuses on "meaning of" (meaning in the context of inter-textual and intratextual relationships), hermeneutics focuses on "meaning for" (meaning in the context of the text-reader relationship).[17] . . . . Free Churches cannot settle for the structuralist liturgical list which offers our world a sanctuary of meaning because a hermeneutical approach insists that meaning is "irrevocably dialogical in character."[18]

[3. Value of "lived experience."] . . . In *Holy Things*, Lathrop speaks of a "third thing" which emerges from the juxtaposition of two elements of the ordo. For example:

> Scripture and preaching lead to intercessory prayer, concretely naming before God the needs of those who suffer. . . . Thanksgiving and receiving food lead to the distribution of food to the poor . . . the two things of baptism—teaching and the bath—yield a third: always coming to the meeting. . . . In each case, the name of this third thing is not good deeds or even social action. It is faith.[19]

In his study of worship in a Baptist congregation, Martin Stringer also employs the concept of a "third thing." Note, however, that there are clear differences in the ways Lathrop and Stringer employ the notion of "thirdness":

> When a story that we sense in worship "speaks" to us, we find ourselves at a point in time in which two stories, our own and the liturgical, are instantaneously superimposed in such a way as to allow a flow of meaning or emotion between them. . . . The two stories are not only bridged at the moment of interaction, but they become one, they merge, and the story that results, the story of the interaction, becomes a third, completely new story, one which is related to both the other two

16. Sally Morgenthaler, *Worship Evangelism: Inviting Unbelievers into the Presence of God* (Grand Rapids: Zondervan, 1995), 48.

17. Elizabeth Struthers Malbon, "Structuralism, Hermeneutics, and Contextual Meaning," *Journal of the American Academy of Religion* 51 (1983): 207–30, here at 222.

18. Graham Hughes, *Worship as Meaning: A Liturgical Theology for Late Modernity* (New York: Cambridge University Press, 2003), 66.

19. Lathrop, *Holy Things*, 213.

and yet different in form from either. . . . The interaction bridges, and so merges, two stories, creating in its turn a third and transforming the other two. . . .[20]

Whereas Lathrop suggests a juxtaposition of liturgical elements, Stringer suggests a juxtaposition of personal and liturgical stories. Christopher Ellis best pinpoints the difference between the two accounts: "For Free Church worship, [relationships within the ordo] are not primarily the 'liturgical co-efficients' within a service, but the interaction of the values which shape the worship and provide it with theological coherence."[21]

. . . I conclude by expressing my fundamental agreement with Lathrop's initial thesis: liturgical theology could indeed benefit from a good and widespread discussion of old and unresolved issues between Free Churches and other denominations. Before such a discussion can take place, however, significant methodological work remains to be done. The researcher in liturgy "will have to develop an ability to make careful, disinterested observations. . . not *a priori* judgments as to whether this liturgy or solemn play is apt or inept by historical or contemporary standards. We will have to learn to listen to participants on various levels of sophistication tell, as best they can, why they did this and not that."[22] Furthermore, we must allow these primary theologians to speak for themselves, offering words of critique at the points where secondary theology needs to be refined.

Virgil Elizondo

Liturgical theology in a Hispanic-Latino context finds one of its major sources in the actual lived faith expressions of the people in what is often referred to as *religiosidad popular*, that is, "popular religion."

Virgil Elizondo, "The Treasure of Hispanic Faith," in *Mestizo Worship*, ed. Virgil Elizondo and Timothy Matovina (Collegeville, MN: Liturgical Press, 1998), 75-79.

[T]he Hispanic church has much to contribute to the entire community of believers. The popular faith expressions are the most beloved treasure of our people. They are also concrete manifestations of the

---

20. Martin Stringer, *On the Perception of Worship* (Birmingham: University of Birmingham Press, 1999), 104.

21. Ellis, *The Gathering*, 73.

22. Mary Collins, "Liturgical Methodology and the Cultural Evolution of Worship in the United States," *Worship* 49 (1975): 101

church's tradition as it has been interiorized in the hearts of the faithful by the Spirit. These expressions begin to accomplish the goal of evangelization as the transformation not only of human hearts and the various strata of society, but even culture itself. Hence it should not be surprising that Paul VI told the Hispanic Catholics of the United States that we should not put aside our legitimate religious practices, nor that he told the entire world that popular piety manifests a thirst for God which only the simple and the poor can know.[23]

If you will listen to our prayer forms, take part in our processions, devotions, and liturgical fiestas, listen to our ordinary first names, and see the decorations in our neighborhoods, homes, and even on our bodies, you will quickly discover that faith for us is not an abstract formula or merely a Sunday affair, but the fundamental living reality of our lives. In our devotion to the saints, the doctrines of our church are personalized and become human stories.

We meet *Papacito Dios* (Daddy God) from the earliest days of our lives and God remains a constant source of support throughout life. We communicate easily and in a very personal way with God as Father, with Mary as our mother, with Jesus as our Lord and brother, and with the saints and souls in purgatory as members of our extended family. We argue with them, we ask them favors, we tell them jokes, we include them in our popular songs, we visit and converse easily with them.[24] We keep pictures or images of them alongside the portraits of the family and best friends. We do not consider them graven images but rather simple expressions of our dearest friends. Their friendship is one of our deepest treasures and has enabled us to withstand the rejection of society without deep scars and to endure the suffering of oppression without giving up hope.

Yet our intimacy with them cannot be reduced to an opium which will drug us so as to keep us oppressed. The banner of Our Lady of Guadalupe has led all our struggles for justice—from the first struggles for independence to the present day movements of the farm workers. She has been our leader and our strength. Mary has been our banner, the rosary has been our marching cadence, and the religious songs have been our invincible spirit.

Like Mary, we treasure in our hearts the revelations of Jesus as we have experienced him in the annual reenactment of the journey to Bethlehem in the *posadas,* the birth of Jesus, the visit of the shepherds and later on of the astrologers, the day of earth on Ash

---

23. *Evangelii Nuntiandi* 20, 48; Paul VI, Radio Message to the Hispanic People, 18 August 1977. It is likewise interesting to note that popular religion has become an important *locus theologicus* for U.S. Latino theology.

24. For an example of such intimacy with God, Mary, and the saints, see the conversations of Doña Margarita, in Victor Villaseñor, *Rain of Gold* (Houston: Arte Publico, 1991), 423–25, 474–75.

Wednesday, the *Semana Santa* (Holy Week) with the procession of palms, the washing of feet, the agony in the garden, the passion and death of Jesus, the *siete palabras* (seven last words), his burial and the *pésame* (condolences) to his mother, the *Sabado de Gloria* (Saturday of Glory) with the dramatic reenactment of the resurrection, May, the month of Mary, June of the Sacred Heart and Corpus Christi, October of the rosary, November of the communion of saints, all culminating with the great feast of Christ the King.

The first missioners, who planted the seeds of our *sensus fidelium*, were aware of the need to experience the fundamental elements of the mystery of Christ in a living way. For experience of Christ is the beginning of faith.

In these experiences of the historical events upon which the Creed is based, the people spontaneously intuit much of Christianity's deepest meaning. They may not be able to express it through the doctrinal formulation or theological discourse of the educated elite, but as you hear them speaking about what it means to them in their lives, as many of us experienced in the Cursillo movement, there is certainly no doubt whatsoever that they truly intuit the deepest meaning of our faith.[25]

These living experiences give us a simple and very enjoyable way of not just hearing explanations about the mystery of Christ, but actually living them out. Sermons and catechetical classes we forget easily, but those things that we have experienced together with the other believers and have deeply marked our minds and hearts will never be forgotten.

This type of evangelization and catechesis has great advantages:

1. These celebrations and devotions are easily accessible not just to a few but to the masses of the people. It is through these practices that the church can best fulfill her mandate of universality and truly reach the hearts of the masses.[26]

2. They are enjoyed by all and in various ways they touch everyone—from the youngest to the oldest, from the frivolous to the pious, from the sober to the drunk, from the intellectuals to the illiterate, from the mystics to the unbelievers. No one is left untouched when he or she has participated in one of these reenactments of Christ's life. Through these celebrations the faithful come to appreciate the spiritual signification of the things that they experience together.

3. Because we take part in them from birth, they become the core symbols of our life and the deepest treasures of our heart. Some

---

25. John Paul II, Address to Latin American Bishops at Puebla, 28 January 1979.

26. *Evangelii Nuntiandi* 57; Conclusions of the Third General Conference of Latin American Bishops (Puebla), 449.

among the community will conceptualize and investigate the explicit meaning and message to these mysteries and their full implications in daily life, but even for those who cannot explain them rationally, they will still be of ultimate and transcendental signification.

Where these expressions of the Catholic faith are missing from the churches, the Hispanics will likewise be missing. They will seek them out wherever they are being celebrated and celebrate them on their own if they cannot be found. They are our way of incarnating and making fully alive the presence of Jesus, his way, and his church.

In all the beauty of our tradition there was one element missing that we are quickly discovering with great joy: direct contact with the Scriptures. Once introduced to it, Hispanics have a great love for the Bible and enjoy discussing it and studying it seriously. It is the study and celebration of the Scriptures that is bringing out the deeper meaning which is encased in the various expressions of our tradition.

The renewal of Vatican II has emphasized the question of meaning, but the tragedy is that much of the western church often continues to reduce meaning to conceptual and verbal knowledge, and thus to lose sight of that knowledge of the heart which human reason itself cannot understand. This is not because it is irrational, but because it is transrational!

Advertisers certainly know this well, for in order to sell products they appeal to the inner yearnings of the heart and not to rational discourse. Let me state it clearly. We are not in any way denying the need for serious intellectual study, but stating that no amount of knowledge alone can replace or substitute for the treasures of the heart, for it is in the hearts of the faithful that the Spirit dwells as in a temple.[27] It is from the treasures of the heart that study and contemplation must begin.

But these expressions are not mere externals. They reflect a life of deep faith not just in God but in the kingdom of God, which means God's way for humanity. They are both the signs of the way of life and the ongoing sources for this way of life.

Among the Hispanic poor people, there are many living gospel values which are expressed through our culture that I hope will not die out as we enter into a highly individualistic and technological society. The strong emphasis is on the extended family and family values, a Christian sense of suffering with resignation and hope, spontaneous hospitality and generosity, our humor and way of life, a deep and unquestioned sense of the providence of God, a warm

---

27. 1 Cor. 3:16; 6:19; Vatican II: *Dogmatic Constitution on the Church*, 4.

and personal sense of faith, and respect and love of children and old people, who are the kings and queens of the home.

There is an entire way of life that is embodied and expressed in our religious symbols. Since life and symbol are intimately linked one to another, as one disappears so will the other.

Today our popular expressions of the faith should not be merely tolerated or, even worse, ridiculed. Rather, they should be joyously welcomed into the total life of the United States church. The religious treasures we carry in our hearts are the greatest gift that we bring to the life of the church in this country.

Catholics in our country are hungry for visible expressions of our Catholic heritage. They are tired of the polarizations of the left and the right. Incorporating the faith expressions of the poor and the marginated into the life of the church will be not only a powerful source of unity, but also a clear witness that the Gospel is being lived and proclaimed in fidelity to the way of Jesus and the church.

But Christ also carried out this proclamation by innumerable signs . . . and among all these signs there is the one to which he attaches great importance: the humble and the poor are evangelized, become his disciples and gather together "in his name" in the great community of these who believe in him.[28]

Nathan D. Mitchell

Nathan D. Mitchell, "The Amen Corner: Being Good and Being Beautiful,"
Worship 74, no. 6 (November 2000): 557–58.

Liturgy is God's work for us, not our work for God. Only God can show us how to worship God—fittingly, beautifully. Liturgy is not something beautiful we do for God, but something beautiful God does for us and among us. Public worship is neither our work nor our possession; as the Rule of St Benedict reminds us, it is *opus Dei*, God's work. Our work is to feed the hungry, to refresh the thirsty, to clothe the naked, to care for the sick, to shelter the homeless; to visit the imprisoned; to welcome the stranger; to open our hands and hearts to the vulnerable and the needy. If we are doing those things well, liturgy and the Catholic identity it rehearses will very likely take care of themselves. Liturgical art is our public gratitude that God is doing for us what we cannot do for ourselves. And there, perhaps, is where ethics and aesthetics together can begin to change the face of worship.

---

28. *Evangelii Nuntiandi*, 12.

Nathan D. Mitchell, *Meeting Mystery: Liturgy, Worship, and Sacraments*
(Maryknoll, NY: Orbis Books, 2006), 38–40, 223–25.

I am arguing, then, that Christian ritual is best understood as tablature or musical score—and that liturgical scores are "rhizomal, nomadic," limitlessly multiple in meaning and internally "indeterminate," that is, capable of verification only through the *exteriority* of ethical action.[29] Christian liturgy begins as ritual practice but ends as ethical performance. Liturgy of the neighbor verifies liturgy of the church, much as a composer's score makes *music* only through the risk of performance.

Hence, the ancient, binary formula *lex orandi, lex credendi* ("the rule of prayer is the rule of faith")—though often invoked to assert the priority of doxology over doctrine[30]—is in fact something of a red herring. The formula is flawed from the get-go, because its reasoning is circular: "We *believe*," it asserts, "that the church's public prayer shapes what (and how?) we believe." But such a statement *already expresses* fundamental *convictions—beliefs*—about the nature of both Christ and church, beliefs that make liturgy possible (and obligatory) in the first place. There is a sense, of course, in which it is quite true to say that liturgy is where theology is born—where the church is "caught in the act of being most overtly itself as it stands faithfully in the presence of the One who is both object and source" of its faith—and hence that liturgy alone deserves the moniker *theologia prima*.[31] Still, the *lex orandi, lex credendi* formula suffers from the same limitations that beset all such closed-circuit, binary oppositions. If doxology checks doctrine, might not the reverse be true as well, viz., that doctrine checks doxology?

[. . .]

The slogan *lex orandi, lex credendi* does not, then, offer as much

---

29. I use the term "ritual" here and throughout this book in much the way Ronald Grimes understands it. Ritual, Grimes argues, is the "general idea," the formal "definition or characterization," while rites are what people actually enact (see Ronald Grimes, "Emerging Ritual," in *Proceedings of the North American Academy of Liturgy* [Valparaiso, IN: NAAL, 1990], 16). The term "ritual" is thus broader; it implies a "convergence of several kinds [of action] we normally think of as distinct. It is an 'impure' genre. Like opera, which includes other genres—for example, singing, drama, and sometimes even dancing—a ritual may include all these and more" (see Ronald Grimes, *Ritual Criticism* [Columbia: University of South Carolina Press, 1990], 192). For a detailed and technical discussion of ritual as a fusion of thought and action, theory and culture—as well as of the relation between definitions of ritual and understandings of culture—see two books by Catherine Bell: *Ritual Theory, Ritual Practice* (New York: Oxford University Press, 1992) and *Ritual: Perspectives and Dimensions* (New York: Oxford University Press, 1997).

30. See, e.g., Aidan Kavanagh, *On Liturgical Theology* (Collegeville, MN: Liturgical Press/A Pueblo Book, 1984/1992), 3: "Worship conceived broadly is what gives rise to theological reflection, rather than the other way around."

31. Ibid., 74, 75.

light as it may seem to promise. In spite of the tension between them, doxology and doctrine remain a cozy *ménage à deux,* each partner in the pair defining itself in terms of the other. But the deeper question is not whether faith controls worship, or vice versa, but whether either of them can be verified in the absence of a *lex agendi* (a rule of action or behavior), an ethical imperative that flows from the Christian's encounter with a God who is radically "un-God-like," a God who, in the cross of Jesus and in the bodies of the "poor, the hungry, the thirsty, the naked, the imprisoned," has become everything we believe a God is *not.* The ethical imperative implied by the phrase *lex agendi* breaks apart our comfortable "faith and worship" duo by introducing that subversive element of *indeterminacy.*

Christian liturgy, moreover, gives this indeterminacy an unsettling theological twist. Indeterminacy destabilizes; it de-centers— and that is salutary, even if discomfiting. The God who is "beyond all forms of being, of wisdom, and of power," the God who acquires a Self only through those "little ones who do not exist" (i.e., the marginalized have-nots whose poverty, hunger, and misery count for nothing in the world's eyes) can be met and worshiped only within the "body of the world and of humanity"—more specifically, of suffering humanity. Christian liturgy always speaks the Word of the cross, and it is "a rupturing Word."[32]

Are we postmoderns still capable of learning how to speak "liturgy," or is it, like Latin, a dead language? . . . postmodern thought is typically "rhizomal," characterized by an endless multiplicity of connections. In contrast, liturgy's speech—if it is "the words of the Word," as [Jean-Luc] Marion suggests—seems flat and one-dimensional, terminally boring. Moreover, while *modernity* in the West was defined by the *emergence* of Descartes' autonomous self, with its preference for rigorous scientific method and "clear and distinct ideas," the complex polyphony of *postmodernism* is much more difficult to decode. Some prefer to distinguish *postmodernity* (as a term describing culture) from *postmodernism* (a dominant philosophy, theology, or worldview). But many would agree with Michel de Certeau, that capitalist conquering Western cultures have become *"recited societies,"* that is, societies defined by their *stories,* especially those fables repeated by marketers, spin doctors, and peddlers of information technology—stories cited and *recited* as "gospel truth," especially in the media. As Graham Ward puts it, people in recited societies "believe what they *see,* and what they see is *produced for*

---

32. Stanislas Breton, *The Word and the Cross,* trans. Jacquelyn Porter (New York: Fordham University Press, 2002), 120–22.

them," largely through televised images.[33] And because ours is a world of technologized images; because our images are produced on screens; and because there is not necessarily any "original" behind or beyond those screens, it is very difficult for us to distinguish fiction from fact (hence that oxymoronic phenomenon known as "reality TV"). We install "authorities" (news anchors, politicians, radio talk-show hosts, Internet blogs) to tell us the difference. The challenges "recited societies" pose for the metaphoric logic of liturgical language are fairly obvious. Meeting them will require at least two distinct strategies. First, liturgy needs to retrieve its native tongue, its primary speech—which is *the language of the body itself.* The "words of the Word" are the words of the *Word made flesh,* the words of a Word whose body is a *human* body—a body that, even on the other side of Easter, does not lose its links to history and the world. This, of course, is a hard saying for us "Cartesian Christians," who tend to privilege mind over matter and thought over action. And yet Christian worship will have a future only if it can find its way back to the body as the premier site of ritual, of liturgical celebration. The ancient Christian ritual instinct was, I suspect, the right one: *our bodies make our prayers.* We pray as a body through the gestures, postures, and shared exertions of singing, responding, processing, lifting, moving, touching, tasting, saying, seeing, hearing. If liturgy is the church's gossip; our bodies are the church's best and most reliable grapevine. After all, the mind will say anything one wants to hear; the body never lies. Liturgy speaks a language whose primary story—whose native narrative or *text*—is the *body itself.* Our bodies, moreover, are not images but *icons.* Images invite voyeurism (they beg to be looked at). But icons are different. We do not look at icons; they look at us. It is significant that the Letter to the Colossians celebrates Jesus as *eikōn tou Theou aoratou,* "the image of the invisible God, firstborn of all creation . . . head of the body, the church . . . the beginning . . . the firstborn from the dead" (Col 1:15–18).

How do we go about learning the body's iconic language? A good place to begin might be Ivan Illich's fascinating commentary on Hugh of St. Victor's *Didascalion.* Illich notes that throughout much of the first millennium, Christian readers experienced written pages as tablature, notation, a performance piece, a musical *score* for mumblers. The words painted on a page were meant to be *mouthed, read aloud,* their meanings *tasted* and absorbed by the body.[34] That is why

---

33. Graham Ward, "Introduction," in *The Blackwell Companion to Postmodern Theology,* ed. Graham Ward (Oxford: Blackwell, 2001), xxii.

34. Ivan Illich, *In the Vineyard of the Text: A Commentary to Hugh's Didascalion* (Chicago: University of Chicago Press, 1993), 2.

Augustine was amazed (and perhaps annoyed) to see his mentor, Bishop Ambrose of Milan, reading *with his eyes only*. In the ancient world, reading was done "out loud," by munching the words, by a devout chewing that made *the body itself* the principal text, interpreter, and language of the liturgy. Liturgical reading was emphatically not the self's withdrawal into Cartesian "interiority." The book was a body, the body a book. Hence, in the liturgy, both bodies and the written pages of Gospel books were encircled by light and bathed in smoky fragrance. Reading and chanting *aloud* kept alive the *critical social connection* that bound the reader's *body* to God's Word, that linked person to person in a democracy of reading that created a community of devout "munchers" who understood that human speech is, above all, a desire to touch, to connect; that mouth and tongue embody "the innate imperfection of [all] human [striving] . . . ambition, and anxiety."[35] To read aloud was to feel in one's flesh both the wonder and the woundedness of words.

Liturgical assemblies might thus be called "recited societies" in reverse, where reading is not the assertion of a controlling autonomy (by the interiorized self), but a *kenotic* experience in which God's Word, painted on pages and chanted in human speech and song, is reinscribed onto human bodies. Liturgy is never a homemade celebrity spectacle, nor is it a self-indulgent celebration of a closed community's interests, power, or prestige. On the contrary, liturgy *embodies* emptiness, powerlessness—that *"absence"* in human life where *God's* Word and *ours* are surrendered into mutual presence that creates *communion* without suffering *confinement*. Worship is inescapably embodied and iconic; it makes us—we don't make it. Why? Because liturgy is the moment when God's own Word places itself at the mercy of the body, at the mercy of human flesh. In liturgy, God's Word surrenders to world, to history, and to bodies. That is what is [sic] means to say that "God *names us*" in the act of Christian worship.

35. W. S. Merwin, *The Ends of the Earth* (Washington, DC: Shoemaker & Hoard, 2004), 151.

Sacraments and Rites of Christian Initiation

The study of the sacraments and rites of Christian initiation—namely, baptism and its accompanying rites, called either "confirmation," "chrismation," or simply, depending on locale, prebaptismal or postbaptismal rites—is best done not only chronologically but geographically, since differing regions, especially in the first few centuries, had both distinct rites and theological interpretations of those rites that differed from other areas. So, for example, after looking at various biblical models and images, the first section provides a glimpse of various texts from the early Semitic-based Syrian tradition, which has as its overall theological focus the "new birth in water and the Holy Spirit" emphasis of John 3:5 and the "washing of the renewal in the Holy Spirit" of Titus 3:5. This is contrasted with the West in the first three centuries, where documents like the treatise on baptism by Tertullian in North Africa display a theology closely related to the death-and-burial symbolism of Paul in Romans 6 and a developing preference for baptism at Easter.

In the second section, dealing with the time span of the fourth, fifth, and sixth centuries, samples of the great mystagogues, the great expounders of the "mysteries" of Christian initiation to the catechumens and neophytes of both East and West, are provided. Here the catecheses and mystagogical catecheses of such notables as John Chrysostom, Cyril of Jerusalem, and Ambrose of Milan are presented, together with other authors and documents (e.g., *Apostolic Constitutions*, Sarapion of Thmuis, Augustine of Hippo [especially on a developing theology of original sin], conciliar texts from Spain and Gaul on episcopal ratification of irregular baptisms, Innocent I's *Letter to Decentius of Gubbio*, the *Verona Sacramentary*, John the Deacon, and Pope Gregory I), thus providing as far as possible in limited space, an overview of the most important documents of this period that have been highly influential in the modern reform of Christian initiation rites. Here as well we see a theological synthesis of baptism as birth, adoption, death, and resurrection coming to the fore in most traditions, together with a theological preference for baptism at Easter, rather than on other feasts, which might have been more compatible with other theological approaches (e.g., Epiphany, viewed as the feast of the baptism of Jesus).

The medieval section begins with three representative Eastern Christian rites, the Maronite (Syria), the Coptic (Egypt), and the Byzantine (Constantinople). All three of these rites are celebrated today by various Eastern Orthodox, Oriental Orthodox, and Eastern Catholic churches. For the Roman West, selections from the rites of Christian initiation in the *Gelasian Sacramentary, Ordo Romanus XI,* and the rite of confirmation from *The Pontifical of William Durandus* are offered, with the non-Roman West represented by an eighth-century missal from northern France. Theological interpretation of baptism, together with justification of confirmation as a separate sacrament, is provided by Thomas Aquinas, the famous "Decree for the Armenians," and by several other authors.

The section concerned with the Protestant and Catholic Reformations includes selections from Martin Luther and the Lutheran confessional writings, from the challenges of the Anabaptists, from the Reformed tradition (especially Ulrich Zwingli, John Calvin, and Martin Bucer), from the Church of England's 1549 and 1552 editions of *The Book of Common Prayer,* from the canons and decrees of the Council of Trent, and from early Methodism in England.

In the final section, texts are offered from the post–Vatican II reform of the rites of Christian initiation, especially regarding the restoration of the adult catechumenate in what is known as the Rite of Christian Initiation of Adults. In light of a renewed perspective on adult initiation as reflected in this restoration, the question of infant baptism, an important issue since the time of Augustine of Hippo, has generated a great deal of contemporary discussion and debate. Selections from the pertinent writings of Karl Barth, Aidan Kavanagh, Edmund Schlink, Mark Searle, and the 1982 ecumenically convergent Faith and Order paper of the World Council of Churches, *Baptism, Eucharist, and Ministry,* provide a starting point for this ongoing topic.

The First Three Centuries

THE NEW TESTAMENT

The New Testament presents a variety of images to illustrate the rich and varied experience of Christian baptism.

Select Texts

The baptism of Jesus: Mark 1:9–11 (see also
Matt. 3:13–17; Luke 3:21–22; John 1:29–34).

In those days Jesus came from Nazareth of Galilee and was baptized by John in the Jordan. And just as he was coming up out of the water, he saw the heavens torn apart and the Spirit descending like a dove on him. And a voice came from heaven, "You are my Son, the Beloved; with you I am well pleased."

Romans 6:3–5.

Do you not know that all of us who have been baptized into Christ Jesus were baptized into his death? Therefore we have been buried with him by baptism into death, so that, just as Christ was raised from the dead by the glory of the Father, so we too might walk in newness of life. For if we have been united with him in a death like his, we will certainly be united with him in a resurrection like his.

1 Corinthians 12:13 (see also Gal. 3:27–28).

For in the one Spirit we were all baptized into one body—Jews or Greeks, slaves or free—and we were all made to drink of one Spirit.

Acts 2:38 (see also Acts 22:16).

Peter said to them [at Pentecost], "Repent, and be baptized every one of you in the name of Jesus Christ so that your sins may be forgiven; and you will receive the gift of the Holy Spirit."

John 3:5 (see also Titus 3:5).

Jesus answered, "Very truly, I tell you, no one can enter the kingdom of God without being born of water and Spirit."

Acts 8:36–38.

As they were going along the road, they came to some water; and the eunuch said, "Look, here is water! What is to prevent me from being baptized? [And Philip said, "If you believe with all your heart, you may." And he replied, "I believe that Jesus Christ is the Son of God."] He commanded the chariot to stop, and both of them, Philip and the eunuch, went down into the water, and Philip baptized him.

Acts 8:15–17 (but see also Acts 10:47 and 19:2–6).

The two went down [to Samaria] and prayed for them that they might receive the Holy Spirit (for as yet the Spirit had not come upon any of them; they had only been baptized in the name of the Lord Jesus). Then Peter and John laid their hands on them, and they received the Holy Spirit.

Acts 10:48 (see also Acts 2:38; 8:12, 16; 19:5; and 22:16).

So he ordered them to be baptized in the name of Jesus Christ.

Matthew 28:19.

Go therefore and make disciples of all nations, baptizing them in the name of the Father and of the Son and of the Holy Spirit.

Titus 3:4–5.

But when the goodness and loving kindness of God our Savior appeared, he saved us, not because of any works of righteousness that we had done, but according to his mercy, through the water of rebirth and renewal by the Holy Spirit.

1 Peter 3:21–22.

And baptism, which this [the flood] prefigured, now saves you— not as a removal of dirt from the body, but as an appeal to God for a good conscience, through the resurrection of Jesus Christ, who has gone into heaven and is at the right hand of God, with angels, authorities, and powers made subject to him.

SYRIA

The early Syrian Christian tradition offers examples of initiatory practice and theology rooted in a Semitic Christian context wherein an interpretation of baptism as new birth and regeneration (John 3:5 and Titus 3:5) appears as the dominant paradigm.

The Didache

The Didache, VII (late first or early second cent.),
trans. Cyril C. Richardson, in LCC 1:174.

Now about baptism: this is how to baptize. Give public instruction on all these points, and then "baptize" in running water, "in the name of the Father and of the Son and of the Holy Spirit." If you do not have running water, baptize in some other. If you cannot in cold, then in warm. If you have neither, then pour water on the head three times "in the name of the Father, Son, and Holy Spirit." Before the baptism, moreover, the one who baptizes and the one being baptized must fast, and any others who can. And you must tell the one being baptized to fast for one or two days beforehand.

Justin Martyr

Justin Martyr, *First Apology*, LXI, LXV (ca. 155), trans.
Edward Rochie Hardy, in LCC 1:282–83, 285–86.

61. How we dedicated ourselves to God when we were made new through Christ I will explain, since it might seem to be unfair if I left this out from my exposition. Those who are persuaded and believe that the things we teach and say are true, and promise that they can live accordingly, are instructed to pray and beseech God with fasting for the remission of their past sins, while we pray and fast along with them. Then they are brought by us where there is water, and are reborn by the same manner of rebirth by which we ourselves were reborn; for they are then washed in the water in the name of God the Father and Master of all, and of our Saviour Jesus Christ, and of the Holy Spirit. . . . There is named at the water, over him who has chosen to be born again and has repented of his sinful acts, the name of God the Father and Master of all. Those who lead to the washing the one who is to be washed call on [God by] this term only. For no one may give a proper name to the ineffable God, and if anyone should dare to say that there is one, he is hopelessly insane. This

washing is called illumination, since those who learn these things are illumined within. The illuminand is also washed in the name of Jesus Christ, who was crucified under Pontius Pilate, and in the name of the Holy Spirit, who through the prophets foretold everything about Jesus. . . .

65. We, however, after thus washing the one who has been convinced and signified his assent, lead him to those who are called brethren, where they are assembled. They then earnestly offer common prayers for themselves and the one who has been illuminated and all others everywhere, that we may be made worthy, having learned the truth, to be found in deed good citizens and keepers of what is commanded, so that we may be saved with eternal salvation. On finishing the prayers we greet each other with a kiss.

Justin Martyr, *Dialogue with Trypho,* 88, trans. *DBL*, 3–4.

[W]hen Jesus had gone to the river Jordan, where John was baptizing, and when he had stepped into the water, a fire was kindled in the Jordan; and when He came out of the water, the Holy Spirit lighted on Him like a dove, [as] the apostles of this very Christ of ours wrote. Now, we know that he did not go to the river because He stood in need of baptism, or of the descent of the Holy Spirit like a dove; . . . but . . . the Holy Spirit . . . for humanity's sake . . . lighted on Him in the form of a dove, and there came at the same instant from the heavens a voice . . . "You are my Son; this day I have begotten You"; [the Father] saying that His generation would take place for all people, at the time when they would become acquainted with Him: "You are my Son; this day I have begotten You."

In this early Syrian community, women deacons were required for baptismal administration, especially in the case of women candidates.

Didascalia Apostolorum

Didascalia Apostolorum, XVI (ca. 250), trans. R. Hugh Connolly
(Oxford: Clarendon Press, 1969), 146–47.

In many other matters the office of a woman deacon is required. In the first place, when women go down into the water, those who go down into the water ought to be anointed by a deaconess with the oil of anointing; and where there is no woman at hand, and especially no deaconess, he who baptizes must of necessity anoint her who is being baptized. But where there is a woman, and especially a deaconess, it is not fitting that women should be seen by men: but with the imposition of hands do thou anoint the head only. As of old the priests and kings were anointed in Israel, do thou in like manner with the imposition of the hand, anoint the head of those who receive baptism, whether of men or women. . . . Let a woman deacon, as we have already said, anoint the women. But let a man pronounce over them the invocation of the divine Names in the water. And when she who is being baptized has come up from the water, let the deaconess receive her, and teach and instruct her how the seal of baptism ought to be (kept) unbroken in purity and holiness.

The Acts of Judas Thomas

The Acts of Judas Thomas: "The Baptism of Gundaphorus," trans. *DBL*, 16–17.

Chapters 25–27 (Syriac): And they begged of him that they might receive the sign, and said to him: "Our souls are turned to God to receive the sign for we have heard that all the sheep of that God whom you preach are known to him by the sign." Judas said to them: "I too rejoice, and I ask of you to partake of the Eucharist and of the blessing of this Messiah whom I preach." And the king gave orders that the bath should be closed for seven days, and that no man should bathe in it. And when the seven days were done, on the eighth day the three of them entered into the bath by night that Judas might baptize them. And many lamps were lighted in the bath. And when they had entered into the bath-house, Judas went in before them. And our Lord appeared to them, and said to them: "Peace be with you, my brothers." And they heard the voice only, but the form they did not see, whose it was, for until now they had not been baptized. And Judas went up and stood upon the edge of the cistern, and poured oil upon their heads, and said: " Come, holy name of the Messiah; come, power of grace from on high: come, perfect mercy; come, exalted gift; come, sharer of the blessing; come, revealer of hidden mysteries; come, mother of seven houses, whose rest was in the eighth house; come, messenger of reconciliation, and communicate with the minds of these youths; come Spirit of holiness, and purify their reins and their hearts." And he baptized them in the Name of the Father and of the Son and of the Spirit of holiness. And when they had come up out of the water, a youth appeared to them, and he was holding a lighted taper; and the light of the lamps became pale through its light. And when they had departed, he became invisible to them; and the Apostle said: "We were not even able to bear Your light, because it is too great for our vision." And when dawn came and was morning, he broke the Eucharist.

The Acts of Judas Thomas: "The Baptism of Sifur," trans. *DBL*, 17–18.

(*Chapters 132–133, Syriac*): And Sifur the general said to him: "I and my daughter and my wife will henceforth live purely, in one mind and in one love; and we beg that we may receive the sign [of ownership] from your hands." . . . And he [Judas] began to speak of baptism, and said: "This is the baptism of the remission of sins; this is the bringer forth of new men; this is the restorer of understandings, and the mingler of soul and body, and the establisher of the new man in the Trinity, and which becomes a participation in the remission of sins. Glory to you, hidden power of baptism. Glory to you, hidden power, that communicates with us in baptism. Glory to you, power visible in baptism. Glory to you, you new creatures, who are renewed through baptism, who draw nigh to it in love." And when he had said these things; he cast oil upon their heads and said: "Glory to you, beloved [olive] fruit. Glory to you, name of the Messiah. Glory to you, hidden power that dwells in the Messiah [or, oil]." And he spoke, and they brought a large vat, and he baptized them in the Name of the Father and the Son and the Spirit of holiness. And when they were baptized and had put on their clothes, he brought bread and wine

EGYPT

The early Egyptian tradition displays some close parallels with that of Syria in initiation theology and rite.

Clement of Alexandria

Clement of Alexandria, *The Teacher*, I, vi, 25–26 (ca. 200), in *DBL*, 247.

25. But do not find fault with me for claiming that I have such knowledge of God. This claim was rightfully made by the Word, and he is outspoken. *When the Lord was baptized, a voice loudly sounded from heaven, as a witness to him who was beloved: "You are my beloved Son; this day have I begotten you."*

26. This is what happens with us, whose model the Lord made himself. When we are baptized, we are *enlightened*; being *enlightened*, we become *adopted sons* [see Gal 4:5]; becoming *adopted sons*, we are made perfect; and becoming perfect, we are made divine. "I have said," it is written, "you are gods and all the sons of the Most High" [Ps 81:6]. This ceremony is often called "free gift" [Rom 5:2, 15; 7:24], "enlightenment" [Heb 6:4; 10:32], "perfection" [Jas 1:7; Heb 7:11], and "cleansing" [Titus 3:5; Eph 5:26]—"cleansing,"

because through it we are completely purified of our sins; "free gift," because by it punishments due to our sins are remitted; "enlightenment," since by it we behold the wonderful holy light of salvation, that is, it enables us to see God clearly; finally, we call it "perfection" as needing nothing further, for what more does he need who possesses the knowledge of God?

NORTH AFRICA

Latin-speaking North Africa favors a rite based on a Romans 6 death-and-burial theology, with the gift of the Holy Spirit associated with postbaptismal imposition of hands. Easter also begins to emerge as a preferred occasion for Christian initiation in the West.

Tertullian

Tertullian, *On Baptism* (ca. 200), trans. Ernest Evans, in *Tertullian's Homily on Baptism* (London: SPCK, 1964), 11, 17, 31, 35, 39, 41.

4. Therefore, in consequence of that ancient original privilege, all waters, when God is invoked, acquire the sacred significance of conveying sanctity: for at once the Spirit comes down from heaven and stays upon the waters, sanctifying them from within himself, and when thus sanctified they absorb the power of sanctifying. . . . Thus when the waters have in some sense acquired healing power by an angel's intervention, the spirit is in those waters corporally washed, while the flesh is in those same waters spiritually cleansed. . . .

7. After that we come up from the washing and are anointed with the blessed unction, following that ancient practice by which, ever since Aaron was anointed by Moses, there was a custom of anointing them for priesthood with oil out of a horn. That is why [the high priest] is called a christ, from "chrism" which is [the Greek for] "anointing": and from this also our Lord obtained his title, though it had become a spiritual anointing, in that he was anointed with the Spirit of God the Father. . . .

8. Next follows the imposition of the hand in benediction, inviting and welcoming the Holy Spirit. . . .

13. For there has been imposed a law of baptizing, and its form prescribed: *"Go,"* he says, *"teach the nations, baptizing them in the Name of the Father and the Son and the Holy Ghost"* [Matt. 28:19]. . . .

17. It remains for me to advise you of the rules to be observed in giving and receiving baptism. The supreme right of giving it belongs to the high priest, which is the bishop: after him, to the presbyters and

deacons, yet not without commission from the bishop, on account of the Church's dignity: for when this is safe, peace is safe. Except for that, even laymen have the right: "for that which is received on equal terms can be given on equal terms." . . .

18. It follows that deferment of baptism is more profitable, in accordance with each person's character and attitude, and even age: and especially so as regards children. For what need is there, if there really is no need, for even their sponsors to be brought into peril, seeing they may possibly themselves fail of their promises by death, or be deceived by the subsequent development of an evil disposition? It is true our Lord says, *"Forbid them not to come to me"* [Matt. 19:14]. So let them come when they are growing up, when they are learning, when they are being taught what they are coming to: let them be made Christians when they have become competent to know Christ. Why should innocent infancy come with haste to the remission of sins? Shall we take less cautious action in this than we take in worldly matters? Shall one who is not trusted with earthly property be entrusted with heavenly? Let them first learn how to ask for salvation, so that you may be seen to have given to one that asketh. With no less reason ought the unmarried also to be delayed until they either marry or are firmly established in continence. . . .

19. The Passover provides the day of most solemnity for baptism, for then was accomplished our Lord's passion, and into it we are baptized. . . . After that, Pentecost is a most auspicious period for arranging baptisms, for during it our Lord's resurrection was several times made known among the disciples, and the grace of the Holy Spirit first given. . . . For all that, every day is a Lord's day: any hour, any season, is suitable for baptism. If there is a difference of solemnity, it makes no difference to the grace. . . .

20. Those who are at the point of entering upon baptism ought to pray, with frequent prayers, fastings, bendings of the knee and all-night vigils, along with the confession of all their sins, so as to make a copy of the baptism of John.

Tertullian, *Of the Crown* (ca. 211), xxiii.

In short, to begin with baptism, when on the point of coming to the water we then and there, as also somewhat earlier in church under the bishop's control, affirm that we renounce the devil and his pomp and his angels. After this we are thrice immersed, while we answer interrogations rather more extensive than our Lord has prescribed in the gospel. Made welcome then [into the assembly] we partake of a compound of milk and honey, and from that day for a whole week we abstain from our daily bath.

ROME

The following document, the so-called *Apostolic Tradition,* ascribed to Hippolytus of Rome, ca. 217, appears here in this early context only because of traditional attributions both to Rome and to Hippolytus, as well as because of its influence in contemporary liturgical reform. Recent scholarship would question its provenance, authorship, date, and certainly its claim of apostolicity.

The Apostolic Tradition

While the core of the rite described in the following may fall within the second or third centuries, the earliest manuscript (Latin) is from the fifth century, with several lacunae in this particular section, and likely reflects a composite rite no earlier than the fourth century.

The Apostolic Tradition, XV–XXI (ca. 217), trans. Geoffrey J. Cuming, in *Hippolytus: A Text for Students* (Bramcote, Notts.: Grove Books, 1976), 15–21.

Of Newcomers to the Faith

15. Those who come forward for the first time to hear the word shall first be brought to the teachers before all the people arrive, and shall be questioned about their reason for coming to the faith. And those who have brought them shall bear witness about them, whether they are capable of hearing the word. They shall be questioned about their state of life: Has he a wife? Is he the slave of a believer? Does his master allow him? Let him hear the word. If his master does not bear witness about him that he is a good man, he shall be rejected. If his master is a heathen, teach him to please his master, that there be no scandal. If any man has a wife or a woman a husband, they shall be taught to be contented, the man with his wife and the woman with her husband. But if any man is not living with a wife, he shall be instructed not to fornicate, but to take a wife lawfully or remain as he is. If anyone is possessed by a demon, he shall not hear the word of teaching until he is pure.

Of Crafts and Professions

16. Inquiry shall be made about the crafts and professions of those who are brought for instruction. If a man is a brothel-keeper, let him cease or be rejected. If anyone is a sculptor or a painter, let them be instructed not to make idols; let them cease or be rejected. If anyone is an actor or gives theatrical performances, let him cease or be rejected. He who teaches children had best cease; but if he has no craft, let him have permission.

Similarly, a charioteer who competes in the games, or goes to them, let him cease or be rejected. One who is a gladiator or teaches gladiators to fight, or one who fights with beasts in the games, or a public official employed on gladiatorial business, let him cease or be rejected.

If anyone is a priest, or keeper, of idols, let him cease or be rejected.

A soldier under authority shall not kill a man. If he is ordered to, he shall not carry out the order; nor shall he take the oath. If he is unwilling, let him be rejected. He who has the power of the sword, or is a magistrate of a city who wears the purple, let him cease or be rejected. A catechumen or believer who want to become soldiers should be rejected, because they have despised God.

A prostitute, a profligate, a eunuch, or anyone else who does things of which it is a shame to speak, let them be rejected, for they are impure. Neither shall a magician be brought for examination. A charmer, an astrologer, a diviner, an interpreter of dreams, a mountebank, a cutter of fringes of clothes, or a maker of phylacteries, let them be rejected.

A man's concubine, if she is his slave and has reared her children and remained faithful to him alone, may be a hearer; otherwise, let her be rejected. Let any man who has a concubine cease, and take a wife lawfully; but if he is unwilling, let him be rejected.

If we have left anything out, the facts themselves will teach you; for we all have the Spirit of God.

Of the Time of Hearing the Word after (Examination of) Crafts and Professions
17. Catechumens shall continue to hear the word for three years. But if a man is keen, and perseveres well in the matter, the time shall not be judged, but only his conduct.

Of the Prayer of Those Who Hear the Word
18. When the teacher has finished giving instruction, let the catechumens pray by themselves, separated from the faithful; and let the women, whether faithful or catechumens, stand by themselves in some place in the church when they pray. And when they have finished praying, they shall not give the Peace, for their kiss is not yet holy. But let only the faithful greet one another, men with men and women with women; but the men shall not greet the women. And let all the women cover their heads with a hood, but (not) just with a piece of linen, for that is no veil.

Of Laying Hands on the Catechumens
19. After their prayer, when the teacher has laid hands on the

catechumens, he shall pray and dismiss them. Whether the teacher is a cleric or a layman, let him act thus.

If a catechumen is arrested for the name of the Lord, let him not be in two minds about his witness. For if he suffers violence and is killed (before he has received baptism) for the forgiveness of his sins, he will be justified, for he has received baptism in his blood.

Of Those Who Will Receive Baptism

20. And when those who are to receive baptism are chosen, let their life be examined: have they lived good lives when they were catechumens? Have they honoured the widows? Have they visited the sick? Have they done every kind of good work? And when those who brought them bear witness to each: "He has," let them hear the gospel.

From the time they were set apart, let hands be laid on them daily while they are exorcized. And when the day of their baptism approaches, the bishop shall exorcize each one of them, in order that he may know whether he is pure. And if anyone is not good or not pure, let him be put aside, because he has not heard the word with faith, for it is impossible that the Alien should hide himself for ever.

Those who are to be baptized should be instructed to bathe and wash themselves on the Thursday. And if a woman is in her period, let her be put aside, and receive baptism another day. Those who are to receive baptism shall fast on the Friday. On the Saturday those who are to receive baptism shall be gathered in one place at the bishop's decision. They shall all be told to pray and kneel. And he shall lay his hand on them and exorcize all alien spirits, that they may flee out of them and never return into them. And when he has finished exorcizing them, he shall breathe on their faces; and when he has signed their foreheads, ears, and noses, he shall raise them up.

And they shall spend the whole night in vigil; they shall be read to and instructed. Those who are to be baptized shall not bring with them any other thing, except what each brings for the eucharist. For it is suitable that he who has been made worthy should offer an offering then.

Of the Conferring of Holy Baptism

21. At the time when the cock crows. First let prayer be made over the water. Let the water be flowing in the font or poured over it.

Let it be thus unless there is some necessity; if the necessity is permanent and urgent, use what water you can find. They shall take off their clothes. Baptize the little ones [*parvulos*] first. All those who can speak for themselves shall do so. As for those who cannot speak for themselves, their parents or someone from their family shall speak for them. Then baptize the men, and lastly the women, who shall have loosened all their hair, and laid down the gold and silver ornaments which they have on them. Let no one take any alien object down into the water.

And at the time fixed for baptizing, the bishop shall give thanks over the oil, which he puts in a vessel: one calls it "oil of thanksgiving." And he shall also take other oil and exorcize it: one calls it "oil of exorcism." And a deacon takes the oil of exorcism and stands on the priest's left; and another deacon takes the oil of thanksgiving and stands on the priest's right. And when the priest takes each one of those who are to receive baptism, he shall bid him renounce, saying:

> I renounce you, Satan, and all your service and all your works.

And when each one has renounced all this, he shall anoint him with the oil of exorcism, saying to him:

> Let every spirit depart far from you.

And in this way, he shall hand him over naked to the bishop or the priest who stands by the water to baptize. In the same way a deacon shall descend with him into the water and say, helping him to say:

> I believe in one God, the Father almighty . . .

And he who receives shall say according to all this:

> I believe in this way.

And the giver, having his hand placed on his head, shall baptize him once. And then he shall say:

> Do you believe in Christ Jesus, the Son of God, who was born from the holy Spirit from the Virgin Mary, and was crucified under Pontius Pilate, and died, and rose again on the third day alive from the dead, and ascended into heaven, and sits at the right hand of the Father, and will come to judge the living and the dead?

And when he has said, "I believe," he shall be baptized again. And he shall say again:

> Do you believe in the holy Spirit and the holy Church and the resurrection of the flesh?

Then he who is being baptized shall say, "I believe," and thus he shall be baptized a third time.

And then, when he has come up, he shall be anointed from the oil of thanksgiving by the presbyter, who says:

> I anoint you with holy oil in the name of Jesus Christ.

And so each of them shall wipe themselves and put on their clothes, and then they shall enter into the church.

And the bishop shall lay his hands on them and invoke, saying:

Lord God, you have made them worthy to receive remission of sins through the laver of regeneration of the holy Spirit: send upon them your grace, that they may serve you according to your will; for to you is glory, to Father and Son with the holy Spirit in the holy Church, both now and to the ages of ages. Amen.

Then, pouring the oil of thanksgiving from his hand and placing it on his head, he shall say:

I anoint you with holy oil in God the Father almighty and Christ Jesus and the holy Spirit.

And having signed him on the forehead, he shall give him a kiss and say:

The Lord be with you.

And he who has been signed shall say:

And with your spirit.

So let him do with each one. And then they shall pray together with all the people: they do not pray with the faithful until they have carried out all these things. And when they have prayed, they shall give the kiss of peace.

The Fourth, Fifth, and Sixth Centuries

ANTIOCHIA

The region of Antioch in the middle to the late fourth century shows signs of a ritual and theological development in which the rites are becoming more elaborate, and theological reflection on the rites themselves comes to the fore in catechesis.

John Chrysostom

John Chrysostom, *Baptismal Instructions* (ca. 390), Stavronikita Series No. 2, trans. *DBL*, 45–47, adapted from Paul W. Harkins, *St. John Chrysostom: Baptismal Instructions* (Westminster, MD: Newman Press, 1963).

2. 18. [T]he priest approaches each in turn and demands your contracts and confessions and instructs each one to pronounce those fearful and awesome words: *I renounce you, Satan.*

20. . . . The priest then instructs you to say, *I renounce you, Satan, your pomp, your worship and your works.* There is great power in

these few words. For the angels who are present and the invisible powers rejoice at your conversion. . . .

21. Have you seen the terms of the contract? After the renunciation of the Evil One and all the works he delights in, the priest instructs you to speak again as follows: *And I pledge myself Christ, to you.*

22. Then once you have made this covenant, this renunciation and contract, since you have confessed his sovereignty over you and pronounced the words by which you pledge yourself to Christ, you are now a soldier and have signed on for a spiritual contest. Accordingly the bishop anoints you on the forehead with spiritual myron, placing a seal on your head and saying: *N. is anointed in the name of the Father, the Son and the Holy Spirit.*

23. Now the bishop knows that the Enemy is enraged and is sharpening his teeth going around like a roaring lion, seeing that the former victims of his tyranny have suddenly defected. Renouncing him, they have changed their allegiance and publicly enlisted with Christ. It is for this reason that the bishop anoints you on your forehead and marks you with the seal, to make the devil turn away his eyes. He does not dare to look at you directly because he sees the light blazing from your head and blinding his eyes. From that day onwards you will confront him in battle, and this is why the bishop anoints you as athletes of Christ before leading you into the spiritual arena.

24. Then after this at the appointed hour of the night, he strips you of all your clothes, and as if he were about to lead you into heaven itself by means of these rites, he prepares to anoint your whole body with this spiritual oil so that his unction may armor all your limbs and make them invulnerable to any weapons the Enemy may hurl.

25. After this anointing he takes you down into the sacred waters, at the same time burying the old nature and raising "the new creature, which is being renewed after the image of the creator." Then by the words of the priest and by his hand the presence of the Holy Spirit flies down upon you and another man comes up out of the font, one washed from all the stain of his sins, who has put off the old garment of sin and is clothed in the royal robe.

26. To give you a further lesson that the substance of the Father, the Son and the Spirit is one, baptism is conferred in this form. As the priest pronounced the words, *N. is baptized in the name of the Father and of the Son and of the Holy Spirit,* he plunges your head into the water and lifts it up again three times, by this sacred rite preparing you to receive the descent of the Holy Spirit. For the priest is

not the only one who touches your head; Christ also touches it with his right hand. This is shown by the actual words of the one who baptizes you. He does not say, "I baptize N.," but rather, "N. is baptized." This shows that he is only the minister of the grace and merely lends his hand since he has been ordained for this by the Spirit. It is the Father, Son and Holy Spirit, the indivisible Trinity, who bring the whole rite to completion. It is faith in the Trinity that bestows the grace of remission of sin, and the confession of the Trinity that grants us the adoption of sons.

27. As soon as they come up from those sacred waters all present embrace them, greet them, kiss them, congratulate and rejoice with them, because those who before were slaves and prisoners have all at once become free men and sons who are invited to the royal table. For as soon as they come up from the font, they are led to the awesome table, which is laden with all good things. They taste the body and blood of the Lord and become the dwelling place of the Spirit; since they have put on Christ, they go about appearing everywhere like angels on earth and shining as brightly as the rays of the sun.

Apostolic Constitutions

Unlike in Chrysostom's rite, we see here the presence of a postbaptismal anointing, even though, as in early Syria, the Holy Spirit is associated with the prebaptismal anointing.

Apostolic Constitutions, VII (ca. 380), trans. James Donaldson, in *ANF* 7:477.

22. Now concerning baptism, O bishop, or presbyter, we have already given direction, and we now say, that thou shalt so baptize as the Lord commanded us, saying: "Go ye, and teach all nations, baptizing them in the name of the Father, and of the Son, and of the Holy Ghost (teaching them to observe all things whatsoever I have commanded you" [Matt. 28:19]: of the Father who sent, of Christ who came, of the Comforter who testified. But thou shalt beforehand anoint the person with holy oil, and afterward baptize him with water, and in the conclusion shalt seal him with the ointment; that the anointing with oil may be a participation of the Holy Spirit, and the water, a symbol of the death *of Christ*, and the ointment the seal of the covenants. But if there be neither oil nor ointment, water is sufficient both for the anointing, and for the seal, and for the confession of him that is dead, or indeed is dying together *with Christ*. But before baptism, let him that is to be baptized fast. . . .

43. Him [the Father], therefore, let the priest even now call upon in baptism, and let him say: Look down from heaven and sanctify this water, and give it grace and power, that so he that is to be baptized, according to the command of Thy Christ, may be crucified with Him, and may die with Him, and may be buried with Him, and may rise with Him to the adoption which is in Him, that he may be dead to sin, and live to righteousness.

Pseudo-Dionysius the Areopagite

Pseudo-Dionysius the Areopagite, *Ecclesiastical Hierarchy*, 2.7, trans. *DBL*, 61.

7. When the ministers have entirely unclothed him, the priests bring the holy oil of the anointing. Then he begins the anointing with a threefold sealing, and for the rest assigns the man to the priests for the anointing of his whole body, while he himself advances to the mother of filial adoption, and when he has purified the water within it by the holy invocations and perfected it by three cruciform effusions of the most pure Chrism and by the same number of injections of the most holy Chrism, and has invoked the sacred melody of the inspiration of the God-absorbed prophets, he orders the man to be brought forward; and when one of the priests from the register has announced him and his guarantor, the priests conduct him near to the water and lead him by the hand to the hand of the Hierarch. Then the Hierarch stands down [in the water] and when the priests have again called aloud to him in the water the name of him that is being perfected, the Hierarch dips him three times, invoking the threefold Subsistence of the Divine Blessedness, at the three immersions and emersions of him that is being perfected. The priests then take him and entrust him to the sponsor and guide of his introduction: and when they, with his help, have cast appropriate clothing over him who is being perfected; they lead him again to the Hierarch, who when he has sealed the man with the most divinely operating Chrism pronounces him to be from now on a partaker of the most divinely perfecting Eucharist.

JERUSALEM

Thanks to both Cyril (or John) of Jerusalem and the Gallician pilgrim Egeria, the contents and interpretation of the late-fourth–century, highly influential Christian initiation rites of Jerusalem can be easily reconstructed.

Cyril of Jerusalem

Cyril of Jerusalem, *Catechetical Lectures* (ca. 350), trans.
William Telfer, in LCC 4:64–65, 68, 71, 80.

Procatechesis 1. Already the savour of bliss is upon you, who have come to be enlightened [those to be baptized at the end of Lent]; you have begun to pluck spiritual flowers with which to weave heavenly crowns. Already are you redolent of the fragrance of the Holy Spirit. You have reached the royal vestibule. O may the King himself conduct you within.

Lo, now the trees are in blossom; and grant the fruit be duly gathered.

So far, your names have been enrolled, and you have been called up for service. . . .

4. You have a long period of grace, forty days for repentance. . . .

11. Let this be your solemn charge; learn the things that are told you, and keep them for ever. . . .

Lecture 1. 4. You were a catechumen till now but now you are to be called believer. Henceforth you are transplanted among the olives of that paradise: or are being grafted on a good olive tree being taken from a wild olive.

Cyril of Jerusalem, *Mystagogical Catechesis* (ca. 348), trans.
R. W. Church, in *St. Cyril of Jerusalem's Lectures on the Christian Sacraments*,
ed. Frank Leslie Cross (London: SPCK, 1960), 53, 55, 60, 61, 64.

Catechesis I. 1. Let us now teach you exactly about these things that ye may know the deep meaning to you-ward of what was done on that evening of your baptism.

2. First, ye entered into the outer hall of the Baptistery, and there facing towards the West, ye heard the command to stretch forth your hand, and as in the presence of Satan ye renounced him. . . .

4. What then did each of you standing up say? "I renounce thee, Satan, thou wicked and most cruel tyrant!" meaning, "I fear thy might no longer; for Christ hath overthrown it."

9. Then wast thou told to say, *I believe in the Father and in the Son and in the Holy Ghost and in one Baptism of repentance.* Of which things we spoke at length in the former lectures, as God's grace allowed us.

Catechesis II. 3. Then, when ye were stripped, ye were anointed with exorcized oil, from the very hairs of your head to your feet, and were made partakers of the good olive tree, Jesus Christ. . . .

4. After these things, ye were led to the holy pool of Divine Baptism, as Christ was carried from the Cross to the Sepulchre which is

before our eyes [in Jerusalem]. And each of you was asked, whether he believed in the name of the Father, and of the Son, and of the Holy Ghost, and ye made that saving confession, and descended three times into the water, and ascended again, here also covertly pointing by a figure at the three-days of burial of Christ. . . .

5. O strange and inconceivable thing! we did not really die, we were not really buried, we were not really crucified and raised again, but our imitation was but in a figure [*mimēsis*], while our salvation is in reality.

Catechesis III. 3. In the same manner to you also, after you had come up from the pool of the sacred streams, was given the Unction, the emblem [*antitypon*] of that wherewith Christ was anointed; and this is the Holy Ghost.

4. And ye were first anointed on your forehead. . . . Then on your ears. . . . Then on your nostrils. . . . Then on your breast.

5. When ye are counted worthy of this holy chrism, ye are called Christians, verifying also the name by your new birth.

Egeria

Egeria (ca. 384), *Egeria's Travels*, trans. John Wilkinson
(London: SPCK, 1971), 143–46.

45.1 1 feel I should add something about the way they instruct those who are to be baptized at Easter. Names must be given in before the first day of Lent, which means that a presbyter takes down all the names before the start of the eight weeks for which Lent lasts here, as I have told you. Once the priest has all the names, on the second day of Lent at the start of the eight weeks, the bishop's chair is placed in the middle of the Great Church, the Martyrium, the presbyters sit in chairs on either side of him, and all the clergy stand. Then one by one those seeking baptism are brought up, men coming with their fathers and women with their mothers. As they come in one by one, the bishop asks their neighbours questions about them: "Is this person leading a good life?" . . . And if his inquiries show him that someone has not committed any of these misdeeds, he himself puts down his name. . . .

They have here the custom that those who are preparing for baptism during the season of the Lenten fast go to be exorcized by the clergy first thing in the morning. . . . All those to be baptized, the men and the women, sit round him [bishop] in a circle. . . . though not catechumens, who do not come in while the bishop is teaching.

His subject is God's Law; during the forty days he goes through the whole Bible, beginning with Genesis, and first relating the literal meaning of each passage, then interpreting its spiritual meaning. He also teaches them at this time all about the resurrection and the faith. And this is called *catechesis*. After five weeks' teaching they receive the Creed, whose content he explains article by article in the same way as he explained the Scriptures, first literally and then spiritually. . . . all through Lent, three hours' catechesis a day. . . .

[During Holy Week] the candidates go up to the bishop, men with their fathers and women with their mothers, and repeat the Creed to him. When they have done so, the bishop speaks to them all as follows: "During these seven weeks you have received instruction in the whole biblical Law. You have heard about the faith, and the resurrection of the body. You have also learned all you can as catechumens of the content of the Creed. But the teaching about baptism itself is a deeper mystery, and you have not the right to hear it while you remain catechumens. Do not think it will never be explained; you will hear it all during the eight days of Easter after you have been baptized. But so long as you are catechumens you cannot be told God's deep mysteries." . . .

[After Easter, the bishop] interprets all that takes place in Baptism. . . . Indeed the way he expounds the mysteries and interprets them cannot fail to move his hearers.

EGYPT

Unique among early Christian liturgical documents, the mid-fourth-century Prayers of Sarapion, Bishop of Thmuis in northern Egypt, witness to a consecration of the baptismal waters by an invocation of the Logos, in reference to the baptism of Jesus in the Jordan. These prayers may also be the first witness to the introduction of a postbaptismal anointing in the Egyptian liturgical tradition.

The Prayers of Sarapion of Thmuis

The Prayers of Sarapion of Thmuis, trans. Maxwell E. Johnson,
Prayer 7: "Sanctification of Waters," in *The Prayers of Sarapion of Thmuis:
A Literary, Liturgical, and Theological Analysis*, OCA 249
(Rome: Pontifical Oriental Institute, 1995), 55–.

King and Lord of all and creator of all, through the descent of your only-begotten Jesus Christ you have graciously given salvation to all created nature. Through the coming of your inexpressible word you have redeemed that which is formed, having been created by you. Look now from heaven and gaze upon these waters and fill them with holy Spirit. Let your inexpressible word come to be in them. Let it change their operation and make them generative, being filled with your grace, so that the mystery now being accomplished may not be found empty in those being born again, but may fill with divine grace all those who go down and are baptized. Lover of humanity, benefactor: spare that which is made by you, save the creature which was made by your right hand, and mold all who are born again of your divine and inexpressible form, so that through being formed and born again they may be able to be saved and be made worthy of your kingdom. And as your only-begotten word, when he descended upon the waters of the Jordan made them holy, so also now let him descend into these. Let him make them holy and spiritual in order that those who are baptized may no longer be flesh and blood but spiritual and able to give worship to you, the uncreated Father through Jesus Christ in holy Spirit, through whom (be) to you the glory and the power both now and unto all the ages of ages. Amen.

The Prayers of Sarapion of Thmuis, Prayer 15:
"Prayer for the Oil of Those Being Baptized."

Master, lover of humanity and lover of souls, compassionate and merciful, God of truth, we call upon you, following and obeying the promises of your only-begotten, who has said, "if you forgive the sins of any they are forgiven them." And we anoint with this oil those who approach this divine rebirth, imploring that our Lord Christ Jesus may work in it and reveal healing and strength-producing power through this oil [or, imploring that healing and strength-producing power may work in it and reveal our Lord Christ Jesus through this oil], and may heal their soul, body, spirit from every sign of sin and lawlessness or satanic taint, and by his own grace may grant forgiveness to them so that, having no part in sin, they will live in righteousness. And, when they have been molded again through this oil and purified through the bath and renewed in the Spirit, they will be strong enough to conquer against other opposing works and deceits of this life which come near them, and so be bound and united to the flock of our Lord and Savior Jesus Christ and inherit the promises to the saints. For through him (be) to you the glory and the power in holy Spirit unto all the ages of ages. Amen.

The Prayers of Sarapion of Thmuis, Prayer 16: "Prayer for the
Chrism with Which the Baptized Are Anointed."

God of powers, the helper of every soul who turns to you and comes
under the powerful hand of your only-begotten, we implore you
that, through the divine and inexpressible power of our Lord and
Savior Jesus Christ, divine and heavenly energy may work in this
chrism, so that those who have been baptized and are anointed by
it, with the impression of the sign of the saving cross of the only-
begotten, the cross through which Satan and all opposing powers
were overthrown and triumphed over, as those having been reborn
and renewed through the washing of regeneration, they may also
become sharers of the gift of the Holy Spirit and, having been sealed
in this seal, may remain firm and immovable, without harm and safe
from violence, free from insult and unassailable, dwelling in the faith
and knowledge of the truth until the end, expecting the heavenly
hopes of life and the eternal promises of our Lord and Savior Jesus
Christ, through whom (be) to you the glory and the power in holy
Spirit both now and forever. Amen.

NORTH ITALY

Ambrose of Milan witnesses to a baptismal rite that includes a postbaptismal *pedilavium* (foot washing), related to a developing theology of original
sin. Ambrose's reference to something called the "spiritual seal," if any gesture was intended or used, may be a postbaptismal rite of the imposition
of hands on the head of the newly baptized.

Ambrose of Milan

Ambrose of Milan, *On the Sacraments,* Books I.2, 4; II.20; and III.1, 4, 5, 8
(ca. 390), trans. T. Thompson, in *St. Ambrose "On the Mysteries" and the
Treatise "On the Sacraments"* (London: SPCK, 1919; rev. ed., 1950).

Book I.2. Therefore, what did we do on the Saturday? What but the
"opening"? Which mysteries of "opening" were performed, when the
priest touched thine ears and nostrils? It is this which our Lord Jesus
Christ indicates in the gospel when a *deaf and dumb* [Mark 7.32]
man was brought to him, and he touched his ears and mouth.

4. We came to the font; thou didst enter. . . . A levite met thee, a
presbyter met thee. Thou wast anointed as Christ's athlete; as about
to wrestle in the fight of this world, thou didst profess the objects of
thy wrestling. . . .

Book II.20. Thou wast asked, "Dost thou believe in God the Father Almighty?" Thou saidest, "I believe," and didst dip, that is, thou wast buried. Again thou wast asked, "Dost thou believe in our Lord Jesus Christ, and in his cross?" Thou saidest, "I believe," and didst dip: therefore thou wast also *buried with Christ* [Rom. 6.4; Col. 2.12]: for he who is buried with Christ rises again with Christ. A third time thou wast asked, "Dost thou believe also in the Holy Ghost?" Thou saidest, "I believe," and didst dip a third time, that the triple confession might absolve the fall of thy former life.

Book III.1. Yesterday we discoursed on the font, whose appearance is somewhat like that of a tomb in shape; into which, believing in the Father and the Son and the Holy Ghost, we are received, and plunged, and emerge, that is, we are raised up. Moreover thou receivest *myron,* that is *ointment upon the head.* . . .

4. Thou camest up out of the font. What followed? [T]he high priest . . . was girt up and washed thy feet. . . .

5. We are not ignorant that the Roman Church has not this custom. Her type and form we follow in all things; however, she has not this custom of washing the feet. See then, perhaps she has declined it on account of the numbers. There are, however, some who say and try to urge that this ought to be done, not as a sacrament, not at baptism, not at the regeneration; but only as we should wash the feet of a guest. The latter is an act of humility, the former a work of sanctification. Accordingly, learn how it is a sacrament and a means of sanctification. *"Unless I wash thy feet, thou wilt have no part with me"* [John 13:8]. This I say, not to find fault with others, but to recommend my own usage. In all things I desire to follow the Roman Church. Yet we too are not without discernment; and what other places have done well to retain, we too, do well to maintain. . . .

8. There follows the spiritual seal, which you have heard mentioned in the lesson today. For after the font, it remains for the "perfecting" to take place, when, at the invocation of the priest, the Holy Spirit is bestowed, *"the spirit of wisdom and understanding, the spirit of counsel and strength, the spirit of knowledge and godliness, the spirit of holy fear"* [Isa. 11:2–3], as it were the seven virtues of the Spirit.

NORTH AFRICA

Although the initiation rites for adults in North Africa were similar to those elsewhere in the West—indeed, Augustine of Hippo was baptized in Milan by Ambrose in 387—the question of infant initiation, thanks to Pelagianism, was of particular concern to Augustine in his episcopacy.

Augustine of Hippo

Augustine of Hippo, *Enchiridion*, XIII (421), trans. Albert C. Outler, in LCC 7:365–67.

42. This is the meaning of the great sacrament of baptism, which is celebrated among us. All who attain to this grace die thereby to sin—as he himself is said to have died to sin because he died in the flesh, that is, "in the likeness of sin"—and they are thereby alive by being reborn in the baptismal font, just as he rose again from the sepulcher. This is the case no matter what the age of the body.

43. For whether it be a newborn infant or a decrepit old man—since no one should be barred from baptism—just so, there is no one who does not die to sin in baptism. Infants die to original sin only; adults, to all those sins which they have added, through their evil living, to the burden they brought with them at birth. . . .

45. Still, even in that one sin—which "entered into the world by one man and so spread to all men" [Rom. 5:12], and on account of which infants are baptized—one can recognize a plurality of sins, if that single sin is divided, so to say, into its separate elements. . . .

46. It is also said—and not without support—that infants are involved in the sins of their parents, not only of the first pair, but even of their own, of whom they were born. . . .

This is why each one of them must be born again, so that he may thereby be absolved of whatever sin was in him at the time of birth. For the sins committed by evil-doing after birth can be healed by repentance—as, indeed, we see it happen even after baptism. For the new birth [*regeneratio*] would not have been instituted except for the fact that the first birth [*generatio*] was tainted.

SPAIN AND GAUL

Texts from local Spanish and Gallican councils demonstrate a concern for episcopal ratification of baptisms performed in what may be called irregular or emergency contexts. Terms like "perfection" or "confirmation" become attached to this ratification, which, in some cases at least, included an imposition of hands.

Local Conciliar Texts from Spain

The Council of Elvira (305), in *DBL*, 154–55.

Canon 38. That in cases of necessity, even the faithful [fideles] may baptize.

[It was agreed] that a faithful man, who has held fast to his baptism and is not bigamous may baptize a sick catechumen at sea, or where there is no church at hand: provided that if he survives he shall bring him to a bishop so that he may be perfected [*perfici*] through the laying on of a hand.

Canon 77. Concerning baptized people who die before they have been confirmed.

It was agreed that when a deacon who has charge of faithful people [*regens plebem*] baptizes some of them in the absence of a bishop or presbyter, it shall be the duty of the bishop to perfect [*perficere*] them: but if any depart this life before confirmation, he will be justified by virtue of the faith in which he has believed.

The First Council of Toledo (398), in *DBL*, 155.

Canon 20. Although the custom is almost everywhere preserved, that none but the bishop blesses chrism, yet because in some places or provinces the presbyters are said to bless chrism, it was agreed that none but the bishop shall henceforth bless chrism: and he shall send it into his diocese in such fashion that deacons and subdeacons shall be sent from each church to the bishop before Easter, so that the chrism which the bishop has blessed shall arrive in time for Easter. While the bishops have the undoubted right to bless chrism at any time, presbyters may do nothing without the knowledge of the bishop: it is decreed that the deacon may not give chrism but the presbyter may do so in the absence of the bishop, or in his presence if he commands.

A Local Conciliar Text from Gaul

The First Council of Orange (441), trans. *DBL*, 256.

(*Canon 2*): By no means should *any minister* who accepts the duty of baptizing proceed without chrism, because it is agreed among us to be *chrismated once*. However, at confirmation [*in confirmatione*], the priest [*sacerdos*, i.e., bishop] will be reminded about those who were not chrismated in baptism, when some necessity appeared. For among certain ministers of this chrism, it is nothing but a blessing [or, *chrism can only confer its blessing once*], not to foreshadow anything, *but that a repeated chrismation not be held necessary.*

ROME

Roman documents witness to a development of the roles of various ministers in the initiation rites, particularly with regard to Rome's unique postbaptismal structure of a presbyteral anointing, followed by a laying on of
hands and another anointing, both of which become reserved to the ministry of bishops.

The Letter of Pope Innocent I to Decentius of Gubbio

The Letter of Pope Innocent I to Decentius of Gubbio, 3, trans. Martin Connell,
in *Church and Worship in Fifth-Century Rome: The Letter of Innocent I to
Decentius of Gubbio*, AGLS 52 (Cambridge: Grove Books, 2002), 28.

3. Regarding the signing of infants, this clearly cannot be done val-
idly by anyone other than the Bishop. For even though presbyters
are priests, none of them holds the office of pontiff. For not only is
it ecclesiastical custom that shows this should be done only by pontiffs—in other words, that they alone would sign or give the comforting Spirit—but there is also that reading in the Acts of the Apostles
that describes Peter and John being ordered to give the Holy Spirit to
those who had already been baptized. For whether the Bishop is present or not, presbyters are allowed to anoint the baptized with chrism.
But they are not allowed to sign the forehead with the same oil consecrated by the Bishop, for that is used by the bishops only when they
give the Spirit, the Paraclete. I cannot reveal the words themselves,
lest I seem to betray more than is needed to respond to your inquiry.

The Verona [Leonine] Sacramentary

An early Roman collection of Mass prayers, this sacramentary, or presider's book, demonstrates not only that Pentecost was a baptismal day in the
early Roman liturgy, but that a theology of baptism based on John 3:5 and
Titus 3:5 was also a characteristic Roman baptismal theology.

The Verona [Leonine] Sacramentary. Sacramentarium Veronense, ed. L. C. Mohlberg,
in *Rerum Ecclesiasticarum Documenta* (Rome: Herder, 1956), trans. DBL, 1:207–8.

At Pentecost, for those that come up from the Font

[The Collect]
O ineffable and merciful God, grant that the children of adoption

whom your Holy Spirit has called unto itself [*id ipsum*] may harbour nothing earthly in their joy, nothing alien in their faith; through.

[In the Canon]
We ask you graciously to accept this oblation which we offer to you for these whom you have deemed worthy to regenerate by water and the Holy Spirit, granting them remission of all their sins; and command their names to be written in *the book of the living* [Ps. 69.28]; through.

[A Blessing of Water, Honey, and Milk]
Bless also we ask you, O Lord, these your creatures of water, honey, and milk, and give your servants drink of this fount of water of everlasting life, which is the spirit of truth, and nourish them with this milk and honey according as you promised to our fathers, Abraham, Isaac, and Jacob, to lead them into the land of promise, a land flowing with honey and milk. Therefore, O Lord, unite your servants to the Holy Spirit, as this honey and milk is united, wherein is signified the union of heavenly and earthly substance [*substantia*] in Christ Jesus our Lord, through whom all these, *etc.*

The Blessing of the Font
We offer you [this] prayer, O Lord, the eternal begetter of [all] things, Almighty God, whose *Spirit was borne upon the waters* [Gen. 1.3 Vulg.], whose eyes looked down from on high upon Jordan's stream when John was baptizing [*tingeret*] those who in penitence confessed their sins: and therefore we pray your holy glory that your hand may be laid upon this water that you may cleanse and purify the lesser man who shall be baptized in it: and that he, putting aside all that is deathly, may be reborn and brought to life again through the new man reborn in Christ Jesus, with whom you live and reign in the unity of the Holy Spirit, unto the ages of ages.

John the Deacon

This famous Letter to Senarius offers valuable information on the catechumenate and its rites at Rome, even if by this date it is now something performed primarily on infants.

John the Deacon (ca. 500), *Letter to Senarius* 3–6, 7, 12, trans. *DBL*, 211–12.

3. . . . There cannot therefore be any doubt that before a man is reborn in Christ he is held close in the power of the devil: and unless he is extricated from the devil's toils, renouncing him among the first

beginnings of faith with a true confession, he cannot approach the grace of the saving laver. And therefore he must first enter the classroom of the catechumens. *Catechesis* is the Greek word for instruction. He is instructed through the Church's ministry, by the blessing of one laying his hand [upon his head], that he may know who he is and who he shall be. . . . He receives therefore exsufflation and exorcism, in order that the devil may be put to flight and an entrance prepared for Christ our God: so that being delivered from the power of darkness he may be *translated to the kingdom* [Col. 1.13] of the glory of the love of God. . . . The catechumen receives blessed salt also, to signify that just as all flesh is kept healthy by salt, so the mind which is drenched and weakened by the waves of this world is held steady by the salt of wisdom and of the preaching of the word of God. . . .

4. And so by the efforts of himself and others the man who recently had received exsufflation and had renounced the toils and the pomps of the devil is next permitted to receive the words of the Creed [*symbolum*] which was handed down by the Apostles: so that he who a short time before was called simply a catechumen may now be called a competent, or elect. . . . Then follow those occasions which according to the Church's custom are commonly called scrutinies. For we scrutinize their hearts through faith, to ascertain whether since the renunciation of the devil the sacred words have fastened themselves on his mind: whether they acknowledge the future grace of the Redeemer: whether they confess that they believe in God the Father Almighty. . . . [T]heir ears are touched with the oil of sanctification, and their nostrils also are touched: the ears because through them faith enters the mind, according as the apostle says: *Faith comes by hearing, and hearing by the word of God* [Rom. 10.17]. . . .

5. . . .The unction of the nostrils signifies . . . that since the oil is blessed in the Name of the Saviour, they may be led unto his spiritual odour by the inner perception of a certain ineffable sweetness, so that in delight they may sing: *Your Name is as ointment poured forth: we shall run after the savour of your ointments* [Cant. 1.3].

6. Next the oil of consecration is used to anoint their breast, in which is the seat and dwelling place of the heart; so that they may understand that they promise with a firm mind and a pure heart eagerly to follow after the commandments of Christ, now that the devil has been driven out. They are commanded to go in naked even down to their feet. . . . And then when the elect or catechumen has advanced in faith by these spiritual conveyances, so to speak, it is necessary to be consecrated in the baptism of the one laver, in which sacrament his baptism is effected by a threefold immersion. And rightly so: for whoever comes to be baptized in the Name of the Trinity must signify that Trinity in a threefold immersion, and must

acknowledge his debt to the bounty of him who upon the third day rose from the dead. He is next arrayed in white vesture, and his head anointed with the unction of the sacred chrism: that the baptized person may understand that in his person a kingdom and a priestly mystery have met. For priests and princes used to be anointed with the oil of chrism, priests that they might offer sacrifices to God, princes that they might rule their people. . . . All the neophytes are arrayed in white vesture to symbolize the resurgent Church, just as our Lord and Saviour himself in the sight of certain disciples and prophets was thus transfigured on the mount, so that it was said: *His face shone as the sun: his raiment was made white as snow* [Matt. 17.2]. This prefigured for the future the splendour of the resurgent Church, of which it is written: *Who is this that riseth up* [Cant. 3.6; 8.5] all in white? And so they wear white raiment so that though the ragged dress of ancient error has darkened the infancy of their first birth, the costume of their second birth should display the raiment of glory, so that clad in a wedding garment he may approach the table of the heavenly bridegroom as a new man.

7. I must say plainly and at once, in case I seem to have overlooked the point that all these things are done even to infants, who by reason of their youth understand nothing. And by this you may know that when they are presented by their parents or others, it is necessary that their salvation should come through other people's profession, since their damnation came by another's fault. . . .

12. You ask why milk and honey are placed in a most sacred cup and offered with the sacrifice at the Paschal Sabbath. The reason is that it is written in the Old Testament and in a figure promised to the New People: *I shall lead you into a land of promise, a land flowing with milk and honey* [Lev. 20.24]. The land of promise, then, is the land of resurrection to everlasting bliss, it is nothing else than the land of our body, which in the resurrection of the dead shall attain to the glory of incorruption and peace. This kind of sacrament, then, is offered to the newly-baptized so that they may realize that no others but they, who partake of the Body and Blood of the Lord, shall receive the land of promise: and as they start upon the journey thither, they are nourished like little children with milk and honey, so that they may sing: *How sweet are your words unto my mouth, O Lord, sweeter than honey and the honeycomb* [Ps. 119.103; 19.11].

Pope Gregory I

In spite of Innocent's insistence on the right of the bishop to anoint the forehead with chrism in baptism, Gregory's letter reveals that in the late sixth century the unity of the rites of Christian initiation, including what will come to be called "confirmation," is more important than the physical presence of the bishop.

Pope Gregory I, *Letter 26 to Januarius* (594), trans. Paul Turner, in *Sources of Confirmation: From the Fathers through the Reformers* (Collegeville, MN: Liturgical Press, 1993), 58.

It has also come to our attention that some people were scandalized that we prohibited presbyters to anoint those who have been baptized with chrism. And, indeed, we have done this according to the ancient custom of our Church. But if any are troubled at all by this, we concede that where bishops are absent, even presbyters ought to anoint the baptized with chrism on their foreheads.

The Medieval Period in East and West

THE CHRISTIAN EAST

Of the seven living liturgical rites of the Christian East (Armenian, Byzantine, Coptic, East Syrian, Ethiopic, Maronite, and West Syrian), the following three rites provide a glimpse of how Christian initiation developed in Syria (Maronite), Egypt (Coptic), and Constantinople (Byzantine).

The Syriac-Maronite Rite

The Syriac-Maronite Rite, trans. adapted from *DBL*, 104-7.

19. Doxology
The celebrant makes the sign of the cross over the baptismal water saying: Glory be to the Father and to the Son and to the Holy Spirit, who sanctifies these waters through the Mystery of the Glorious Trinity, now and forever. Amen.

20. Prayer of the Anaphora
The celebrant breathes upon the waters saying: Look, O Lord, upon these waters placed before You. Drive away, O Lord, all evil spirits and their powers from this water and place, and from all who will enter into it to be baptized. Give them the strength of the Holy Spirit. As the womb of our mother Eve gave birth to mortal children

subject to corruption, let this Baptism become a womb, which will give birth to spiritual and immortal children. As the Holy Spirit hovered over the waters at the creation and gave life to animals of every kind, let Him hover over this Baptism, dwell within it and sanctify it. Let it change the earthly Adam into a spiritual one. Let all who enter it receive spiritual strength in place of the weakness of the flesh. Together with this natural life let them receive a spiritual one, and in addition to this visible world, let them receive a participation in the invisible one, and in place of a weak spirit let Your life-giving Spirit dwell within them.

R. Amen.

21. Epiclesis

The celebrant makes a profound bow, saying: Hear me, O Lord, hear me, O Lord, hear me, O Lord. Let the Holy Spirit descend upon this water and sanctify it. Let Him fill it with unfailing strength, let Him bless it. Let it become as the water that flowed from the side of Your only Son upon the cross, so that it may purify and cleanse all who are baptized in it. May it clothe each one with the robe of heavenly justice and with the armor of faith against the attacks of the evil one.

The celebrant stands upright saying: They will rise up from this water purified and sanctified, wearing the armor of salvation. Then will they give glory and thanksgiving to the Glorious Trinity, Father, Son and Holy Spirit, to Him is glory forever, Amen.

22. Blessing of the Water with Myron (Chrism)

The celebrant mixes four drops of sacred Myron in the water in the form of a cross. The Assembly says: Alleluia *before the first, second and third drops.*

R. Alleluia.

(First Drop) We sign these waters with sacred Myron (Chrism) in the name of the Father, life of the living,

R. Alleluia.

(Second Drop) And in the name of His Only Son, who like Him is life of the living,

R. Alleluia.

(Third and Fourth Drops) And in the name of the Holy Spirit, the beginning and end of all things, and the sanctifier and restorer of all life.

Blessed are You, O Glorious Trinity, who purified and sanctified these waters with Your power that they may become a new womb, giving birth to spiritual children. To You be glory forever. Amen.

23. Diaconal Proclamation

Bow your heads before the merciful God, and before this life-giving Baptism and receive blessings from the Lord.

Let N. be signed as a member of Your church and let him be counted among Your spiritual flock and enter into Your fold. Let him mingle with Your sheep and become Yours. Preserve him from all evil and let him be sanctified with the seal of the glorious Trinity that he may sing praise and thanksgiving to You, now and forever. Amen.

24. Anointing with the Oil of Catechumens

The celebrant stands facing West, while the candidate faces East. Dipping his right thumb in the Oil of the catechumens the celebrant anoints the candidate by making the sign of the cross + upon his fore-head, saying: N. is signed a member of the Christian community with the holy life-giving oil [or, "is anointed as a member of the flock of Christ with the living oil of the divine anointing"] in the name of the Father + and of the Son, and of the Holy Spirit.

R. Amen.

25. Baptismal Formula

The celebrant baptizes the candidate by pouring water on his head in the following manner: either one, or both sponsors present or carry the candidate to the baptismal font, his face toward the East. The celebrant takes the candidate with his left hand, and pours water with his right hand three times over the head of the candidate. The celebrant may baptize by immersion only if the candidate is an infant.

Pouring the first time, the celebrant says: N. is baptized a member of the Christian community [or, "a lamb in the flock of Christ"], in the name of the Father,

R. Amen.

Pouring the second time: And of the Son,

R. Amen.

Pouring the third time: And of the Holy Spirit for everlasting life.

R. Amen.

After the Baptism, the celebrant presents the candidate to the god-parents who receive him over the baptismal font. The candidate is then vested by the godparents in a white garment.

26. Concluding Prayer

May God who granted that you should bear His life-giving sign enable you to keep it pure for the life of your soul so that you may worthily call the Father *Our Father.* As He made you worthy of this Holy Baptism, may He grant you to lead a true Christian life worthy of His Kingdom.

27. Chrismation Formula

The celebrant dips his right thumb into the Holy Myron and marks the candidate on the forehead three times in the form of a cross, saying: With this Holy Myron (Chrism) of Jesus Christ, symbol of the true faith, the seal and fullness of the gifts of the Holy Spirit, this servant of God, N., is signed in the name of the Father + and of the Son + and of the Holy Spirit. +

R. Amen.

28. Concluding Prayer for Chrismation

N., you have been clothed by the Father, you have received the Son, you have put on the Holy Spirit, you have been given the glorious robe which Adam lost.

The Coptic Rite

The Coptic Rite, in *DBL*, 136–39.

[L]et him who is to be baptized be stripped: and let him look towards the west, with his right hand outstretched, and let him say thus as follows. But if he is a child, let his father or his mother or his sponsor say on his behalf thus: I renounce you, Satan, and all your unclean works, and all your wicked angels and all your evil demons, and all your power and all your abominable service, and all your evil cunning and error, and all your host, and all your authority, and all the rest of your impieties.

And he shall say three times: I deny you.

Let the priest breathe into the face of him who is to be baptized, and say three times: Come out, you unclean spirit.

After this they shall be turned to the east, with both their hands uplifted, saying thus: I profess you, O Christ my God, and all your saving laws, and all your reviving service, and all your lifegiving works.

Again he shall bid them to confess the faith, saying: I believe in one God, God the Father Almighty, and his Only-Begotten Son, Jesus Christ our Lord, and the holy lifegiving Spirit, and the resurrection of the flesh, and the one only catholic apostolic Church. Amen.

And you shall ask him three times, saying: Do you believe?

And he shall say: I believe.

. . . After this take the agallielaion of the oil of exorcism. Anoint him who is to be baptized on his breast and his arms and over his heart behind and between his two hands in the sign of the cross, saying: You are anointed, child of N. with the oil of gladness, availing against all the workings of the adversary, unto your grafting into the sweet olive tree of the holy catholic Church of God. Amen.

. . . And the deacon leads him that is to be baptized from the west and brings him to the east over against the Jordan (the font), to the left hand of the priest. And the priest asks him his name, and immerses him three times; and at each immersion he raises him up and breathes in his face.

At the first immersion he shall say: I baptize you, son of *N.* in the Name of the Father.

The second time: And of the Son.

The third time: And of the Holy Spirit. Amen.

And if the person that shall be baptized be a female, he shall say: I baptize you, daughter of *N.*

After he has baptized all the children, he shall pour water over his hands in the Jordan, and shall wash the surroundings of the Jordan and the cross. . . .

. . . Then take the Holy Chrism and pray over it, saying: O Lord who alone are mighty, who works all marvels, and nothing is impossible with you, O Lord, but by your will your power works in all things; give the Holy Spirit in the pouring out of the Holy Chrism. Let it be a living seal and a confirmation to your servants. Through your Only-Begotten Son, Jesus Christ our Lord. Through whom.

And after this the priest shall begin to anoint the children with the holy unction in the sign of the cross, each one with thirty six crosses.

[He anoints the candidates at about thirty different parts of the body, as he says:] In the Name of the Father and of the Son and of the Holy Spirit.

An unction of the grace of the Holy Spirit.

An unction of the pledge of the kingdom of heaven.

An unction of participation in eternal and immortal life.

A holy unction of Christ our God, and a seal that shall not be loosed. The perfection of the grace of the Holy Spirit, and the breastplate of the faith and the truth.

You are anointed, son/daughter of *N.* with holy oil, in the Name of the Father and of the Son and of the Holy Spirit. *Amen.*

And when the signing of each of the children is finished, he shall lay his hand on him and say: May you be blessed with the blessing of the heavenly ones, and the blessing of the angels. May the Lord Jesus Christ bless you: and in his name (*here he shall breathe in the face of him that has been baptized and say*), receive the Holy Spirit and be a purified vessel; through Jesus Christ our Lord, whose is the glory, with his good Father and the Holy Spirit, now and ever.

After this he shall clothe him that has been baptized in a white garment, and he shall say: A garment of eternal and immortal life. Amen.

After he has finished the signing and the breathing on all the children, he shall say over them this prayer: The deacon says: Let us ask the Lord.

The priest says: Master, Lord God Almighty, who alone are eternal, the Father of our Lord and our God and our Saviour Jesus Christ; who commanded that your servants should be born through the laver of the new birth, and has bestowed upon them forgiveness of their sins and the garment of incorruption and the grace of sonship. Now again, O our Master, send down upon them the grace of your Holy Spirit the Paraclete; make them partakers of life eternal and immortality, in order that, according as your Only-Begotten Son, our Lord and our God and our Saviour Jesus Christ promised, being born again by water and spirit, they may be able to enter into the kingdom of heaven. Through the Name and the power and the grace of your Only-Begotten Son Jesus Christ our Lord. Through whom.

After that he has clothed them with the rest of their clothing, he shall say this prayer over the crowns: Lord God Almighty, the Father of our Lord and our God and our Saviour Jesus Christ, who placed crowns upon your holy apostles and your prophets and your martyrs who pleased you, crowns unfading: now again now bless these crowns which we have prepared to place upon your servants who have received holy baptism that they may be to them crowns of glory and honour. *Amen.*

Crowns of blessing and glory. *Amen.*

Crowns of virtue and righteousness. *Amen.*

Crowns of wisdom and understanding. *Amen.*

Give them strength to fulfil your commandments and your ordinances, that they may attain unto the benefits of the kingdom of heaven. Through Christ our Lord. Through whom.

The priest girds each one of them with a girdle in the form of a cross, and sets the crown on the head of each one of them. . . .

. . . After this, give them of the Holy Mysteries.

The Byzantine Rite

The Byzantine Rite, in *DBL*, 121–23.

[T]he candidate is stripped and his shoes removed, and the priest turns him to the west. The candidate's hands being raised, the priest says three times: I renounce Satan, and all his works and all his service and all his angels and all his pomp.

And the candidate or his sponsor answers each time.

And again the priest asks, saying: Have you renounced Satan?

And he replies: We have renounced.

And the priest says: Then blow upon him.

And the priest turns him to the east, his hands being lowered, and says: And I adhere to Christ, and I believe in one God, the Father Almighty, *and the rest.*

And when the priest has spoken three times, again he asks them: And have you adhered to Christ?

And they answer: We have adhered.

And the priest says: Worship him. . . .

. . . A prayer which the priest makes before he baptizes. . . .

. . . We confess your love, we tell forth your mercy, we do not hide the goodness of your works. You have set free the children of our race. You sanctified a virgin's womb by your birth: the whole creation hymns your appearing. For you, our God, looked upon the earth and dwelt among men. For you sanctified the waves of Jordan, you sent down your Holy Spirit from heaven and crushed down the heads of the serpents that lurked there. Therefore, our loving king, be present now in the visitation of your Holy Spirit and sanctify this water. Give it the grace of redemption, the blessing of Jordan. Make it a fount of purity, a gift of sanctification, a way of deliverance from sins, a protection against disease, a destruction to demons, unapproachable to the power of the enemy, filled with angelic power. Let all who seek the overthrow of this your child flee away from it, that we may praise your name, O Lord, which is wondrous and glorious and fearful to the enemy.

And he breathes into the water three times and signs it with his finger three times, and says: May all the enemy powers be crushed down by the sign of the type of the cross of your Christ. May all aerial and unseen shapes depart from us, may no dark demon lie hidden in this water: and, we pray you, Lord, let no evil spirit go down with him at his baptism to bring darkness of counsel and confusion of mind. But, maker of all things, declare this water to be a water of rest, water of redemption, water of sanctification, a cleansing of the pollution of the body and soul, a loosening of chains, forgiveness of sins, enlightenment of souls, washing of rebirth, grace of adoption, raiment of immortality, renewal of spirit, fount of life. For you, Lord, have said, *Wash yourselves and make yourselves clean* [Isa. 1.16]. Take away the wickedness from our souls. You have given us the new birth from above by water and Spirit. Be present, Lord, in this water and grant that those who are baptized therein may be refashioned, so that they may *put off the old man, which is corrupt according to the deceitful lusts* [Eph. 4.22], and put on the new man, who is restored after the image of him that created him: that being *planted together in the likeness of the death* [Rom. 6.5] of your Only-Begotten Son, through baptism, they may share also in his resurrection: and guarding the gift of your Holy Spirit, and increasing the store of grace, they may receive the *prize of the high calling* [Phil. 3.14] and be numbered among *the first-born who are written in heaven* [Heb. 12.23] in Christ Jesus our Lord, for with him and the all-holy and good and life-giving Spirit the glory and the power are yours, now and for ever and unto all ages. Amen.

And after the Amen the priest says: Peace be to you all.

The deacon: Let us bow our heads to the Lord.

The priest bows his head towards the vessel of olive oil which is held up by the deacon, and breathes upon it three times and seals it three times, and says: O Master, Lord God of our fathers, who sent to those who were in Noah's ark a dove bearing a twig of olive in its mouth, to be a symbol of reconciliation and of salvation from the flood, and thereby prefigured the mystery of grace: who has furnished the fruit of the olive unto the fulfilment of your holy mysteries, and thereby filled with the Holy Spirit those who are under the law, and perfected those who live in grace: bless even this oil with the power and operation and indwelling of your Holy Spirit, so that it may be a chrism of incorruption, a shield of righteousness, a renewal of soul and body, turning away every work of the devil, unto deliverance from all evil for those who are anointed in faith and partake of it: unto your glory, and the glory of your Only-Begotten Son, and of your holy and good and life-giving Spirit, now, etc.

And after the Amen, the deacon says: Let us attend.

And the priest takes the bowl of holy oil and makes three crosses with it in the water: and he sings Alleluia three times with the congregation, and after this puts the bowl aside. Blessed be God that *enlightens* and sanctifies *every man that comes into the world* [John 1.9], now and always and unto all ages. Amen.

And he that is to be baptized is brought to the priest: and the priest takes holy oil on his finger, and makes the sign of the cross upon the forehead and breast and back of him that is to be baptized, and says: Such a one is anointed with the oil of gladness, in the Name of the Father and of the Son and of the Holy Spirit, etc.

And then his whole body is anointed by the deacon, and after that the priest baptizes him, saying: Such a one is baptized in the name, etc.

And after he is baptized, the singer begins: Blessed are they whose iniquities have been forgiven [Ps. 32.1].

And after this, while the deacon recites a prayer, the priest says this prayer: Blessed are you, O Lord God, the Almighty, the fount of good things, *the sun of righteousness* [Mal. 4.2], who has raised up a light of salvation to those in darkness, through the epiphany of your Only Begotten Son our God, and to us unworthy given the blessed cleansing of his holy water and divine sanctification in the life-giving chrism: who even at this moment has been pleased to give new birth to these your servants newly enlightened, by water and Spirit, and has bestowed upon them forgiveness of their sins, both willingly and unwillingly committed: therefore, Master most benevolent, give to them also the seal of the gift of your holy and all-powerful and worshipful Spirit, and the communion of the Holy Body and Precious Blood of your Christ. Guard them in your sanctification: strengthen them in the right faith: deliver them from the evil one and from all his ways, and by your saving fear keep their souls in holiness and righteousness that being well-pleasing to you in every work and word, they may become sons and inheritors of your heavenly kingdom. (*Aloud*) For you are our God, whose property is to have mercy and to save, and to you we send up our praise, to the Father and the Son, *etc.*

And after this prayer he says: As many as are baptized in Christ have put on Christ [Gal. 3.27].

And the priest anoints those that have been baptized with the holy oil, making the sign of the cross on the forehead and eyes and nostrils and mouth and both ears, saying: The seal of the gift of the Holy Spirit.

And he retires, saying: Blessed are they whose iniquities are forgiven and whose sins are covered [Ps. 32.1].

And the priest approaches the entrance [i.e., the door through the screen between chancel and sanctuary] with the neophytes, and the divine liturgy begins.

THE CHRISTIAN WEST

The Gelasian Sacramentary (Rome)

This seventh-century sacramentary, that is, book of prayers for the celebration of the Eucharist and other sacraments, offers a picture of the Roman rite of Christian initiation that, with some changes over the centuries, will become standard at Rome. For a more complete picture, it should be compared with the document, that immediately follows, *Ordo Romanus XI*.

The Gelasian Sacramentary: Liber Sacramentorum Romanae Aeclesiae ordinnis anni circuli, ed. L. C. Mohlberg, in *Rerum Ecclesiasticarum Documenta*, vol. 4 (Rome: Herder, 1960), in DBL, 233–36.

The Blessing of the Font

Almighty everlasting God, be present at the mysteries of your great goodness, be present at your sacraments, and for the creation of the new people which the fount of baptism brings forth to you send down the Spirit of adoption [Rom. 8.5]: that those things which our lowly ministry performs may be perfected by the operation of your power. Through . . .

The Consecration of the Font

God, who by your invisible power wonderfully effects your sacraments: although we are not worthy to perform so great mysteries, yet do not forsake the gifts of your grace, but incline the ears of your goodness to our prayers. God whose Spirit at the beginning of the world was borne upon the waters [Gen. 1.2], that even the nature of water might conceive the power of sanctification: God who by the outpouring of the flood signified a type of regeneration, when you by water washed away the sins of a wicked world, so that by the mystery of one and the same element there should be both an end of sin and a beginning of virtue: look down, O Lord, upon your Church and multiply in her your generations, you who makes glad your city with the rush of the flood [Ps. 46.5] of your grace: open the fount of baptism for the renewal of all nations of the world, that by the command of your majesty it may receive the grace of your Only-Begotten by the Holy Spirit: let your Holy Spirit by the secret admixture of his light give fruitfulness to this water prepared for human regeneration, so that, sanctification being conceived therein, there may come forth from the unspotted womb of the divine font a heavenly offspring, reborn unto a new creature: that grace may be a mother to people of every age and sex, who are brought forth into a common infancy. Therefore, O Lord, at your command let every unclean spirit depart far away, let all the wickedness of the wiles of the devil stand far off, let him not fly about to lay his snares, let him not creep secretly in, let him not corrupt with his infection. May this holy and innocent creature be free from every assault of the enemy and purified by the departure of all wickedness. May the fount be alive, the water regenerating, the wave purifying, so that all who shall be washed in this saving laver by the operation of the Holy Spirit within them may be brought to the mercy of perfect cleansing.

Here you sign [the water].

Wherefore I bless you, O creature of water, through God the living, through God the holy, through God who in the beginning separated you by his word from the dry land and commanded you in four rivers to water the whole earth, who in the desert gave sweetness to your bitterness that men might drink you, and for a thirsty people brought you forth from the rock. I bless you also through Jesus Christ his only Son our Lord, who in Cana of Galilee by his power in a wonderful sign did change you into wine, who walked upon you with his feet, and was baptized in you by John in Jordan, who shed you forth from his side with his blood, and commanded his disciples that believers should be baptized in you, saying *Go, teach all nations, baptizing them in the Name of the Father and of the Son and of the Holy Spirit* [Matt. 28.19].

Here you shall change [the pitch of] your voice.

Almighty God, be present of your favour among us as we observe your commands: graciously inspire us. Bless with your mouth these simple waters, that besides their natural purity which fits them for the washing of men's bodies they may have the power to purify their minds. May the power of your Holy Spirit descend into all the water of this font and make the whole substance of this water fruitful with regenerating power. Here may the stains of all sins be blotted out. Here may the nature which was founded upon your image be restored to the honour of its origin and cleansed from the filth of age, that every one who enters this sacrament of regeneration may be reborn in a new infancy of true innocence. Through our Lord Jesus Christ your Son, who shall come in the Holy Spirit to judge the living and the dead and this world by fire.

Then when the font is blessed you baptize each one in order, and ask these questions:

Do you believe in God the Father Almighty? *R.* I believe.

And do you believe in Jesus Christ his only Son our Lord, who was born and suffered? *R.* I believe.

And do you believe in the Holy Spirit; the holy Church; the remission of sins; the resurrection of the flesh? *R.* I believe.

Then by single turns you dip him three times in the water. [Deinde per singulas vices mergis eum tertio in aqua.]

Then when the infant has gone up from the font he is signed on the head with chrism by the presbyter, with these words: The Almighty God, the Father of our Lord Jesus Christ, who has made you to be regenerated *of water and the Holy Spirit* [John 3.5], and has given you remission of all your sins, himself anoints you with the chrism of salvation in Christ Jesus unto eternal life. *R.* Amen.

Then the sevenfold Spirit is given to them by the bishop. To seal them [ad consignandum], *he lays his hand upon them with these words:* Almighty God, Father of our Lord Jesus Christ, who has made your servants to be regenerated of *water and the Holy Spirit* [John 3.5], and has given them remission of all their sins, Lord, send upon them your Holy Spirit the Paraclete, and give them the *spirit of wisdom and understanding, the spirit of counsel and might, the spirit of knowledge and godliness, and fill them with the spirit of fear* [Isa. 11.2f] of God, in the Name of our Lord Jesus Christ with whom you live and reign ever God with the Holy Spirit, throughout all ages of ages. Amen.

Then he signs them on the forehead with chrism, saying: The sign of Christ unto life eternal.

R. Amen.

Peace be with you.

R. And with your spirit.

Then, while a litany is chanted, he goes up to his throne, and says: Glory be to God on high.

Ordo Romanus XI (Rome)

The *Ordines Romani* contain rubrical guides for the use of prayers provided in a sacramentary so that the rite could be celebrated in the Roman manner even outside of Rome. *Ordo Romanus XI* accompanies the prayers of the *Gelasian Sacramentary*, the selection preceding this one.

"Ordo Romanus XI," in *Les Ordines Romani du Haut Moyen-Age,* ed. M. Andrieu, vol. 2 (Louvain: "Spicilegium Sacrum Lovanense" bureaux, 1948), trans. *DBL,* 250–51.

81. It is to be so ordered that from the first scrutiny which begins in the third week of Lent to the vigil of the Pascha on Holy Saturday there shall be seven scrutinies, corresponding to the seven gifts of the Holy Spirit, so that when the sevenfold number is completed there may be given to them the sevenfold grace of the Spirit.

82. And the presbyter announces that on Holy Saturday at the third hour they are to return to church and are then catechized and make return of the Creed and are baptized and their sevenfold oblations completed.

83. The order in which they are catechized is as follows.

After the third hour of the Sabbath, they go to the church and are arranged in the order in which their names are written down, males on the right side, females on the left.

84. And the priest makes the sign of the cross on the forehead of each and places his hand on the head of each and says: *Be not deceived, Satan.*

85. When that is done, the presbyter touches the nostrils and ears of each with spittle from his mouth and says in the ears of each one: *Effeta, that is be opened, unto the odour of sweetness,* and the rest.

86. When this is done, he walks around them, placing a hand on their heads and chanting in a loud voice: *I believe in one God,* and the rest. He turns to the females and does likewise.

87. Then the archdeacon says to them: *Pray, you elect. Bow the knee. Complete your prayers together and say Amen.* And all reply *Amen.*

88. Again they are admonished by the archdeacon in these words: *Let the catechumens go.*

If anyone is a catechumen, let him go.

Let all the catechumens go outside and await the hour when the grace of God shall be able to enfold you.

89. Then the blessing of the candle is performed. Then follow the lessons belonging to the day, each with its canticle.

90. When this is done, the pontiff and all the priests go in procession from the church until they come to the fonts, singing the litany, that is *Kyrieleison*: the notaries go before the pontiff, holding on high two lighted candles the height of a man, with censers and incense, and they begin the litany which follows: *O Christ, hear us,* and the rest.

91. When the litany is finished, the whole clergy and people stand round about the font, and when silence has been made the pontiff says: *The Lord be with you.* And all the people reply: *And with your spirit.*

92. And he says: *Let us pray,* and recites the blessing: *Almighty, everlasting God.*

93. Another: *God, who by your invisible power,* and the rest.

94. When all this is done, he pours chrism from a golden vessel over the water into the fonts in the manner of a cross. With his hand he stirs the chrism and the water, and sprinkles all the font and the people standing about.

95. When this is done, and before the children are baptized, everyone who wishes shall receive a blessing, each taking some of the water in his own vessel, for sprinkling in their houses or vineyards or fields or orchards.

96. Then the pontiff baptizes one or two of the infants, or as many as he wishes, and the rest are baptized by a deacon whom he shall appoint.

97. Raising the infants in their hands, they offer them to one presbyter. The presbyter makes the sign of the cross with chrism upon the crown of their heads with his thumb, saying: *Almighty God, the Father of our Lord Jesus Christ,* and the rest.

98. And those who are to receive them are ready with towels in their hands and accept them from the pontiff or the deacons who baptize them.

99. The pontiff goes from the font and sits in his throne which is placed ready in the church, wherever he wishes. And the infants are carried down before him and he gives to each a stole and over garment [*stola, casula*] and chrismal cloth and ten coins, and they are robed.

100. And being vested, they are arranged in order as their names are written, in a circle, and the pontiff makes a prayer over them,

confirming them with an invocation of the sevenfold grace of the Holy Spirit.

101. When the prayer has been said, he makes the sign of the cross with his thumb and chrism on the forehead of each one saying: *In the Name of the Father and of the Son and of the Holy Spirit. Peace be to you.* And they reply: *Amen.*

102. Great care must be taken that this is not neglected, because it is at that point that every baptism is confirmed and justification made for the name of Christianity.

103. After this they go in to Mass and all the infants receive communion. Care is to be taken lest after they have been baptized they receive any food or suckling before they communicate.

104. Afterwards let them come to Mass every day for the whole week of the Pascha and let their parents make oblations for them.

105. This foregoing order of baptism is to be observed in just the same way on the Sabbath of Pentecost as on the holy Sabbath of the Pascha.

Confirmation in the Pontifical of William Durandus (Rome)

Pontificals are bishops' books for the conferring of various sacraments (e.g., confirmation and holy orders). This thirteenth-century document reveals the development of confirmation, which will remain in the Roman Catholic Church until the modern revision of the rite of confirmation in 1971, called for by the Second Vatican Council.

> *Confirmation in the Pontifical of William Durandus:*
> *Le Pontifical Romain au Moyen-Age,* III, ed. Michel Andrieu, Studi e Testi 88
> (Vatican City: Bibloteca apostolica vaticana, 1940), 333–35; trans. adapted
> from Turner, *Sources of Confirmation,* in *DBL,* 252–53.

The bishop intending to chrismate children on the forehead, prepared with alb, stole, white chasuble, and mitre, sends out a reminder as it may be called in the Notice concerning parishes needing to be visited. Then, after the thumb of his right hand has been washed and dried, while those to be confirmed are kneeling down with their hands joined before their heart, the bishop, standing, his mitre removed, similarly with hands joined before his heart says, May the Holy Spirit come upon you and the power of the Most High keep you from your sins.

All respond, Amen.

Then he says Our help is in the name of the Lord. Lord, hear my prayer. The Lord be with you. And with your spirit. Let us pray.

And then, after his hands have been raised and extended over those to be confirmed, he says, Almighty eternal God, who deigned to give rebirth to these your servants out of *water and the Holy Spirit* [John 3.5], send upon them the sevenfold Holy Spirit, your Paraclete, from the heavens, the *Spirit of wisdom and understanding, the Spirit of counsel and fortitude, the Spirit of knowledge and piety, fill them with the spirit of fear* [Isa. 11.2f] of you and consign them with the sign of the cross of Christ in gracious eternal life. Through Christ our Lord. *All respond,* Amen.

Then, as the bishop sits on the faldstool before the altar or prepared in another place, those needing to be consigned are presented to him by the sponsor after the name of each one has been requested one by one. After the tip of the thumb of his right hand has been dipped in chrism, the bishop makes the cross on each one's forehead, saying, John, or Mary, or with whatever other name, I sign you with the sign of the cross and I confirm you with the chrism of salvation. In the name of the Father and of the Son, and of the Holy Spirit, that you may be filled with the same Holy Spirit and have eternal life.

Each responds, Amen.

And while saying In the name of the Father and of the Son and of the Holy Spirit, *he draws the sign of the cross on each one's face.*

And then he lightly delivers a slap on the cheek, saying, Peace be with you.

When all have been thus consigned, he dries his thumb with a bit of bread or a linen cloth and washes it with water over some tin cup or basin. The water of washing with the linen cloth or bread is thrown in the fonts or the pool. And again the antiphon is sung, Confirm, O God, what you have worked in us from your holy temple, which is in Jerusalem. *The versicle is* Glory be to the Father. As it was in the beginning. *And then the antiphon* Confirm *is repeated....*

... After confirmation has thus unfolded, the bishop announces to the confirmed or chrismated that in honor of the Holy Trinity, they should wear the chrism band on their forheads for three days, and on the third day the priest will wash their foreheads and burn the bands upon the fonts or they may make a taper from them for use of the altar. Then he announces to the sponsors that they should instruct and form their godchildren in good morals and deeds, that they may flee from evil things and do good. They should also teach them the Creed, the Our Father, and the Hail Mary, since they oblige themselves to this, as is contained more full in our "Synodal Constitutions."

The Missale Gothicum (Gaul)

The liturgical rites of Gaul—like those of Milan and Spain—display profound differences from the Roman rite, especially with regard to postbaptismal actions and gestures wherein no real equivalent to Roman confirmation appears.

Missale Gothicum, ed. L. C. Mohlberg, in *Rerum Ecclesiasticarum Documenta*, vol. 5 (Rome: Herder, 1961), trans. *DBL*, 260–62.

Dearly beloved brothers, you stand by the shore of a life-giving fount, you are to lead new voyagers to embark and ply their trade upon a new sea. They set sail with the cross for their mast, with heavenly desire to guide them, with no staff but the sacrament. The place indeed is small, but full of grace: the Holy Spirit has brought them on a fair course. Let us therefore pray our Lord God to bless this font, that to all who go down into it it may be a laver of rebirth unto the remission of all their sins. Through the Lord . . .

This collect follows: O God, who for the salvation of human souls sanctified the waters of Jordan, may there descend upon these waters the angel of your blessing, that your servants over whom it has been poured may receive remission of their sins, and being *born again of water and the Holy Spirit* [John 3.5] may serve you faithfully for ever. Through the Lord . . .

Contestatio

It is meet and right, O Lord holy, Father Almighty, everlasting God, the author and Father of holy chrisms, who through your only Son our Lord and God gave us a new sacrament, who before the beginning of the world bestowed your Holy Spirit upon the waters which supported him, who by your angel of healing watched over the waters of Bethsaida, who by the condescension of Christ your Son sanctified the bath of Jordan: look down, O Lord, upon these waters which are made ready to blot out men's sins; may the angel of your goodness be present in these sacred fonts, to wash away the stains of the former life and to sanctify a little dwelling for you: so that the souls of those who are reborn may flourish unto eternal life and may truly be renewed by the newness of baptism. O Lord our God, bless this creature of water, may your power descend upon it, pour down from on high your Holy Spirit the Comforter, the Angel of truth, sanctify O Lord the waves of this flood as you sanctified the stream of Jordan, so that all who go down into this font in the Name of the Father and the Son and the Holy Spirit shall be counted worthy to receive the pardon of their sins and the infusion of the Holy Spirit, through Jesus Christ our Lord, who with the Father and the Holy Spirit is blessed throughout all the ages of the ages.

Then you make a cross with the chrism and say: I exorcize you, creature of water, I exorcize you, all you armies of the devil, all you shades and demons, in the Name of our Lord Jesus Christ of Nazareth, who was incarnate in the Virgin Mary, to whom the Father *has put all things in subjection* [1 Cor. 15:27] both in heaven and earth. Do you fear and tremble, you and all your wickedness, give place to the Holy Spirit, so that for all who go down to this font it may be a laver of the baptism of regeneration, unto the remission of all their sins, through Jesus Christ our Lord who shall come *in the throne of his* Father's *glory* [Matt. 19:28] with his holy angels to judge you, you enemy, and this world, by fire unto the ages of ages.

Then you breathe three times upon the water and pour in chrism in the form of a cross, and say: The infusion of the saving chrism of our Lord Jesus Christ, that to all who descend therein it may be a *well of water springing up unto everlasting life* [John 4:14]. Amen.

While you baptize him you question him and say: I baptize you, N., in the Name of the Father and of the Son and of the Holy Spirit, unto the remission of sins, that you may have eternal life. Amen.

While you touch him with chrism you say: I anoint you with the chrism of holiness, the garment of immortality [cf. Gel. 60], which our Lord Jesus Christ first received from the Father, that you may bear it entire and spotless before the judgement seat of Christ and live unto all eternity.

While you wash his feet, you say: I wash your feet as our Lord Jesus Christ did to his disciples. So may you also do unto pilgrims and strangers, that you may have eternal life.

While you place the robe upon him, you say: Receive the white robe, and bear it spotless before the judgement seat of our Lord Jesus Christ. Amen.

A Collect

Dearly beloved brothers, let us pray to our Lord and God for his neophytes who are now baptized, that when the Saviour shall come in his majesty he may clothe with the garments of eternal salvation those whom he has regenerated with water and the Holy Spirit. Through the Lord.

Another Collect

For those who are baptized, who seek the chrism, who are crowned in Christ, to whom our Lord has been pleased to grant a new birth, let us ask Almighty God that they may bear the baptism which they have received spotless unto the end. Through the Lord.

WESTERN MEDIEVAL
THEOLOGICAL INTERPRETATIONS

The following documents are all concerned with specific theological issues involving either baptism or the interpretation of confirmation within a context where the postbaptismal rites, now called confirmation, have been separated from baptism proper.

Eusebius Gallicanus or Faustus of Riez

This homily, possibly from the fifth century, had a high degree of influence in the development of the theology of confirmation as a sacrament of strength and increase in grace. Assumed to have been delivered by a pope, the fictional Melchiades, it was viewed as an authoritative text by Thomas Aquinas and others.

Eusebius Gallicanus (seventh century)
or Faustus of Riez (fifth century), "Homily 29, On Pentecost," 1–2,
trans. Turner, in *Sources of Confirmation*, 35–36.

What the imposition of the hand bestows in confirming individual neophytes, the descent of the Holy Spirit gave people then in the world of believers. . . . the Holy Spirit, who descends upon the waters of baptism by a salvific falling, bestows on the font a *fullness toward innocence*, and presents *in confirmation an increase for grace*. And because in this world we who will be prevailing must walk in every age between invisible enemies and dangers, *we are reborn in baptism for life*, and we are confirmed after baptism for the strife. *In baptism we are washed; after baptism we are strengthened*. And although the benefits of rebirth suffice immediately for those about to die, nevertheless the helps of confirmation are necessary for those who will prevail. Rebirth in itself immediately saves those needing to be received in the peace of the blessed age. Confirmation arms and supplies those needing to be preserved for the struggles and battles of this world. But the one who arrives at death after baptism, unstained with acquired innocence, is confirmed by death because one can no longer sin after death.

Pope Innocent III

Pope Innocent III now interprets the confirmation anointing as symbolizing the apostolic imposition of hands.

Pope Innocent III (pope 1198–1216), *"When He Had Come,"* 2 (1204),
trans from Turner, *Sources of Confirmation*, 81, emphasis added.

[T]he imposition of the hand is *represented* by the chrismation of
the forehead. It is called "confirmation" by another name, because
through it the Holy Spirit is given for growth and strength. For this
reason, although a simple priest or presbyter may produce other
oils, only the high priest, that is the bishop, ought to confer this one,
because it is told concerning the apostles alone, whose successors are
the bishops, that they gave the Holy Spirit through the imposition of
the hand, as a reading of the Acts of the Apostles shows.

Thomas Aquinas

With Thomas, baptism and confirmation reach their classic Western theological synthesis.

Thomas Aquinas, "Effects of Baptism," in *Summa Theologiae*, Q. 69, art. 2, Reply, p. 127, in
Summa Theologiae, 3a. 66–72, trans. *St. Thomas Aquinas: Summa Theologiae*, vol. 57: *Baptism
and Confirmation* (3a. 33–72), ed. J. J. Cunningham (New York: McGraw Hill, 1975).

A person is incorporated into the passion and death of Christ
through baptism: *If we have died with Christ, we believe we shall also
live with him.* It is clear from this that to every one baptized the passion of Christ is communicated for his healing just as he himself had
suffered and died. But the passion of Christ . . . is sufficient satisfaction for the sins of all [people]. Therefore the one who is baptized is
freed from the debt of all punishment due to him for his sins, just as
if he himself had sufficiently made satisfaction for all his sins.

Hence: 1. Since the one baptized, inasmuch as he becomes a
member of Christ, participates in the pain of the passion of Christ
just as if he himself suffered that pain, his sins are thus set in order
by the pain of Christ's passion.

2. Water not only washes but it also refreshes. So its refreshing
quality signifies the removal of the debt of punishment just as the
cleansing aspect signifies the washing away of sin.

Thomas Aquinas, "Effects of Baptism," in *Summa Theologiae*,
Q. 69, art. 5, Reply, p. 137.

By baptism a person is reborn in the life of the spirit, which is proper
to the faithful of Christ, as St. Paul says, *The life I now live in the flesh
I live by faith in the Son of God.* But there is no life if the members are

not united to the head from which they receive feeling and motion. Thus it is necessary that a person be incorporated by baptism into Christ as a member of his. But as feeling and motion flow from the natural head to the members, so from the spiritual head, which is Christ, there flow to his members spiritual feeling, which is the knowledge of truth, and spiritual motion, which results from the impulse of grace. Thus *John* says: *We have beheld him full of grace and truth, and of his fullness we have all received.* It follows then that the baptized are enlightened by Christ in the knowledge of truth, and made fruitful by him in the fruitfulness of good works by the infusion of grace.

Thomas Aquinas, "On the Baptism of Infants," in *Summa Theologiae,*
Q. 68, art. 9, Reply, pp. 109–10.

As St. Paul says, *If, because of one man's trespass death reigned through that one man*, namely Adam, *much more will those who receive the abundance of grace and the free gift of righteousness reign in life through the one man, Jesus Christ.* But infants contract original sin from the sin of Adam, as is clear from the fact that they are subject to mortality which through the sin of the first man *spread to all men*, as St Paul states in the same place. Much more, therefore, can infants receive grace through Christ in order to reign in eternal life. But the Lord himself says, *Unless a man be born of water and the Holy Spirit he cannot enter the kingdom of God.* Therefore it became necessary to baptize infants that, since by birth they incurred damnation through Adam, so by rebirth they might attain salvation through Christ.

Indeed, it became fitting for infants to be baptized that, nourished from infancy in the things, which pertain to Christian living, they may more strongly persevere in the same. . . .

Hence: 1. Spiritual rebirth which takes place through baptism is in some ways similar to physical birth, in this respect that, as the infant in the mother's womb does not receive independent nourishment but is sustained by the nourishment of the mother, so also children not having the use of reason, as if in the womb of Mother Church, receive salvation not independently but through the activity of the Church. . . .

. . . 3. Just as the infant when he is baptized believes not of himself but through others, so he is not questioned himself but through others, and these profess the faith of the Church on behalf of the child who is joined to the same by the *sacrament of faith.* The infant acquires thereby a good conscience for himself, not indeed in act, but as a habit, through sanctifying grace.

Thomas Aquinas, "On What Is Necessary in the Administration of Baptism,"
in *Summa Theologiae*, Q. 66, art. 10, Reply, pp. 45–46.

In baptism certain things are done which are *necessary* for the sacrament and certain others which pertain to the *solemnity* of the sacrament. *Necessary* for the sacrament are the form which designates the principal cause of the sacrament, the minister who is the instrumental cause, and the use of the matter, viz, washing with water which designates the principal effect of the sacrament. The other things, which the Church observes in the baptismal rite all pertain to the solemnity of the sacrament.

Three reasons can be given for the use of these things in sacramental administration. First of all, to arouse the devotion of the faithful and reverence for the sacrament. . . . Secondly, to instruct the faithful. . . . Thirdly, because the devil's power to impede the effect of the sacrament is held in check through the prayers, blessings and the like. . . .

. . . The things which belong to the solemnity of the sacrament, though not essential, cannot be considered superfluous because they pertain to the good (*bene esse*) of the sacrament.

Thomas Aquinas, "Confirmation," in *Summa Theologiae*,
Q. 72, art. 1, Reply, p. 189.

[P]eople also receive a spiritual life through baptism, which is spiritual regeneration. But in confirmation people receive as it were a certain mature age of spiritual life. For this reason, Pope Melchiades says, "The Holy Spirit who descends upon the waters of baptism in a salvific falling bestows on the font a fullness toward innocence. In confirmation it presents an increase for grace. In baptism we are reborn for life. After baptism we are strengthened." And therefore it is clear that confirmation is a special sacrament.

Council of Florence

Council of Florence, "The Decree for the Armenians" (1439), trans. from
Enchiridion Symbolorum Definitionum et Declarationum, ed. Henry Denzinger and
Adolf Schönmetzer, 33rd ed. (Freiburg: Herder, 1965), 333–34.

Holy baptism holds the first place of all the sacraments, which is the doorway to the life of the spirit, and through it we are made members of Christ and his body, the Church. And since with the first man death entered the world, unless we are reborn of water and the Spirit, we are not able, as Truth says, to enter the kingdom of heaven. The matter of this sacrament is water, pure and natural: it does not matter if it be cold or warm.

The form is: "I baptize you in the name of the Father and of the Son and of the Holy Spirit." We do not deny, however, that at the words, "So and so, the servant of Christ, is baptized in the name of the Father and of the Son and of the Holy Spirit," or "So and so is baptized by my hands in the name of the Father and of the Son and of the Holy Spirit," baptism is truly conferred, seeing that the sacrament is conferred if the chief cause from which baptism receives its power, the holy Trinity, [is invoked] by the minister or the instrument who passes on the external sacrament, that is, if the power is expressed through which he works, namely, by the invocation of the holy Trinity.

The minister of this sacrament is a priest, who from his office is competent to baptize. In the case of necessity, however, not only a priest but a deacon, or even a lay man or woman, or indeed even a pagan or heretic, is able to baptize, as long as he uses the form of the Church, and intends to do what the Church does.

The effect of this sacrament is the remission of all sin, original and actual, and all punishment which is due for this guilt. On account of this, no satisfaction for previous sin is imposed on those being baptized; but if they die before they commit another sin, they attain immediately the kingdom of heaven and the vision of God.

The second sacrament is confirmation. The matter is chrism, made from oil whose glow suggests conscience and balsam whose odor signifies a good reputation. The chrism is blessed by the bishop. The form is: "I sign you in the sign of the cross, and confirm you with the chrism of salvation, in the name of the Father and of the Son and of the Holy Spirit."

The ordinary minister is the bishop. And although for other anointings a simple priest suffices; this ought not be conferred except by a bishop: because of the Apostles alone (whose place the bishops hold) is it written, that they gave the Holy Spirit by the imposition of hands, in which manner the Acts of the Apostles manifests: When the Apostles who were in Jerusalem had heard that Samaria had received the word of God, they sent Peter and John to them. They, when they had come, prayed for them, that they might receive the Holy Spirit: for it had not yet come on them, but they had been baptized in the name of the Lord Jesus. Then they laid hands on them and they received the Holy Spirit [Acts 8:14–17]. The place of this imposition of hands is given to confirmation in the Church. It is also appointed that on occasion, through the Apostolic See, for reasonable and urgent needs, a dispensation is given to simple priests to administer the sacrament of confirmation with chrism blessed by a bishop.

The effect of this sacrament is that through it the Holy Spirit is given to strengthen those to whom it is given, as it was given to the Apostles in the day of Pentecost, namely that the Christian might boldly confess the name of Christ. Thus the confirmand is anointed, on the forehead, where the seat of shame is, that he may never blush to confess the name of Christ especially his cross, which is a scandal to the Jews and folly to the Gentiles according to the Apostle; on account of which he is signed with the sign of the cross.

The Protestant and Catholic Reformations

THE LUTHERAN REFORMATION

Martin Luther

Martin Luther seeks minimal changes in baptismal rites but a renewed appreciation for baptism, as the following texts demonstrate.

Martin Luther, *The Holy and Blessed Sacrament of Baptism* (1519), trans. Charles M. Jacobs and E. Theodore Bachmann, in LW 35:29, 30, 34, 36, 42.

1. Although in many places it is no longer customary to thrust and dip infants into the font, but only with the hand to pour the baptismal water upon them out of the font, nevertheless the former is what should be done. . . .

3. The significance of baptism is a blessed dying unto sin and a resurrection in the grace of God, so that the old man, conceived and born in sin, is there drowned, and a new man, born in grace, comes forth and rises. . . .

11. There is no greater comfort on earth than baptism. . . .

12. For this reason we must boldly and without fear hold fast to our baptism, and set it high against all sins and terrors of conscience. We must humbly admit, "I know full well that I cannot do a single thing that is pure. But I am baptized, and through my baptism God, who cannot lie, has bound himself in a covenant with me. He will not count my sin against me, but will slay it and blot it out." . . .

19. If, then, the holy sacrament of baptism is a matter so great, gracious, and full of comfort, we should diligently see to it that we ceaselessly, joyfully, and from the heart thank, praise, and honor God for it.

Martin Luther, *On the Babylonian Captivity of the Church* (1520), trans. A. T. W. Steinhäuser, Frederick C. Ahrens, and Abdel Ross Wentz, in LW 36:59.

This message should have been impressed upon the people untiringly, and this promise should have been dinned into their ears without ceasing. Their baptism should have been called to their minds again and again, and their faith constantly awakened and nourished. For just as the truth of this divine promise, once pronounced over us, continues until death, so our faith in it ought never to cease, but to be nourished and strengthened until death by the continual remembrance of this promise made to us in baptism.

Luther's famous *Sindflutgebet* (Deluge of Flood Prayer) was influential in the reform of baptismal rites carried out by several Protestant Reformers.

Martin Luther, "Flood Prayer," in *The Order of Baptism Newly Revised* (1526), trans. Paul Zeller Strodach and Ulrich S. Leupold, in LW 53:107–8.

Almighty eternal God, who according to thy righteous judgment didst condemn the unbelieving world through the flood and in thy great mercy didst preserve believing Noah and his family, and who didst drown hardhearted Pharaoh with all his host in the Red Sea and didst lead thy people Israel through the same on dry ground, thereby prefiguring this bath of thy baptism, and who through the baptism of thy dear Child, our Lord Jesus Christ, hast consecrated and set apart the Jordan and all water as a salutary flood and a rich and full washing away of sins: We pray through the same thy groundless mercy that thou wilt graciously behold this N. and bless him with true faith in the spirit so that by means of this saving flood all that has been born in him from Adam and which he himself has added thereto may be drowned in him and engulfed, and that he may be sundered from the number of the unbelieving, preserved dry and secure in the holy ark of Christendom, serve thy name at all times fervent in spirit and joyful in hope, so that with all believers he may be made worthy to attain eternal life according to thy promise; through Jesus Christ our Lord. Amen.

Martin Luther, *Large Catechism* (1529),
trans. Theodore G. Tappert, in *The Book of Concord*
(Philadelphia: Fortress Press, 1959), 444.

We do the same in infant Baptism. We bring the child with the purpose and hope that he may believe, and we pray God to grant him
faith. But we do not baptize him on that account, but solely on the
command of God. Why? Because we know that God does not lie. My
neighbor and I—in short, all men—may err and deceive, but God's
Word cannot err.

Martin Luther, Confirmation, in *On the Babylonian Captivity of the
Church* (1520), from Turner, *Sources of Confirmation*, 43.

[W]e seek sacraments divinely instituted, among which we find no
reason that we should number confirmation. Indeed, for the constitution of a sacrament there is required above all things a word of
divine promise, by which faith may be exercised. But we read that
Christ promised nothing anywhere about confirmation. . . . This is
why it is enough to have confirmation as a certain ecclesiastical rite
or sacramental ceremony, similar to other ceremonies of consecrating water and other things.

Confirmation as the bishops want it should not be bothered with.
Nevertheless we do not fault any pastor who might scrutinize the
faith from children. If it be good and sincere, he may impose hands
and confirm.

THE ANABAPTISTS

Menno Simons

The Anabaptists protest against infant baptism, arguing that baptism is for
believers only.

Menno Simons, *Foundation of Christian Doctrine* (1539), trans. Leonard Verduin, in *The
Complete Writings of Menno Simons* (Scottdale, PA: Herald Press, 1956), 120, 126–27.

Christ, after His resurrection, commanded His apostles saying, Go
ye therefore, and teach all nations, baptizing them in the name of the
Father, and of the Son, and the Holy Ghost; teaching them to observe
all things whatsoever I have commanded you; and, lo, I am with you
always, even unto the end of the world. Amen [Matt. 28:19].

Here we have the Lord's commandment concerning baptism, as

to when according to the ordinance of God it shall be administered and received; namely, that the Gospel must first be preached, and then those baptized who believe it, as Christ says: Go ye into all the world, and preach the gospel to every creature; he that believeth and is baptized shall be saved, but he that believeth not, shall be damned [Mark 16:16]. Thus has the Lord commanded and ordained; therefore, no other baptism may be taught or practiced forever. The Word of God abideth forever.

Young children are without understanding and unteachable; therefore baptism cannot be administered to them without perverting the ordinance of the Lord, misusing His exalted name, and doing violence to His holy Word. In the New Testament no ceremonies for infants are enjoined, for it treats both in doctrines and sacraments with those who have ears to hear and hearts to understand. Even as Christ commanded, so the holy apostles also taught and practiced, as may be plainly perceived in many parts of the New Testament. Peter said, Repent and be baptized every one of you in the name of Jesus Christ for the remission of sins, and ye shall receive the gift of the Holy Ghost [Acts 2:38]. And Philip said to the eunuch, If thou believest with all thine heart, thou mayest [Acts 8:37]. Faith does not follow from baptism, but baptism follows from faith. . . .

Luther writes that children should be baptized in view of their own faith and adds, if children had no faith, then their baptism would be blaspheming the sacrament. It appears to me to be a great error in this learned man, through whose writings at the outset the Lord effected no little good, that he holds that children without knowledge and understanding have faith, whereas the Scriptures teach so plainly that they know neither good nor evil, that they cannot discern right from wrong. Luther says that faith is dormant and lies hidden in children, even as in a believing person who is asleep, until they come to years of understanding. If Luther writes this as his sincere opinion, then he proves that he has written in vain a great deal concerning faith and its power. But if he writes this to please men, may God have mercy on him, for I know of a truth that it is only human reason and invention of men. It shall not make the Word and ordinance of the Lord to fall. We do not read in Scripture that the apostles baptized a single believer while he was asleep. They baptized those who were awake, and not sleeping ones. Why then do they baptize their children before their sleeping faith awakes and is confessed by them?

Bucer does not follow this explanation, but he defends infant baptism in a different way, namely, not that children have faith, but that they by baptism are incorporated in the church of the Lord so that they may be instructed in His Word. He admits that infant baptism is not expressly commanded by the Lord; nevertheless he maintains that it is proper. . . .

Since we have not a single command in the Scriptures that infants are to be baptized, or that the apostles practiced it, therefore we confess with good sense that infant baptism is nothing but human invention and notion, a perversion of the ordinances of Christ, a manifold abomination standing in the holy place where it ought not to stand.

REFORMED PROTESTANTISM

Ulrich Zwingli

Ulrich Zwingli responds to the Anabaptist challenge to infant baptism.

Ulrich Zwingli, *Of Baptism* (1525), trans.
G. W. Bromiley, in LCC 24:138, 145–46, 156.

And in Genesis 17 God himself makes it quite clear that circumcision is not a sign for the confirmation of faith but a covenant sign: "This is my covenant, which ye shall keep, between me and you and thy seed after thee; every man child among you shall be circumcised." Note that God calls it a contract or covenant. Similarly, the feast of the paschal lamb was a covenant, as we read in Exodus 12: "And ye shall observe this thing for an ordinance to thee and to thy sons for ever." Note that the paschal lamb was a covenant sign. . . . Similarly, baptism in the New Testament is a covenant sign. It does not justify the one who is baptized, nor does it confirm his faith, for it is not possible for an external thing to confirm faith. For faith does not proceed from external things. . . .

Hence the meaning of the words "baptizing them" is this: with this external sign you are to dedicate and pledge them to the name of the Father, the Son and the Holy Ghost, and to teach them to observe all the things that I have committed to you. . . .

All that I am now claiming is this: I have proved that baptism is an initiatory sign, and that those who receive it are dedicated and pledged to the Lord God. I am not basing the baptism of infants upon this fact. I am simply following up my main argument or thesis, which is to prove from the words of Christ himself and of all the disciples that baptism is simply a mark or pledge by which those who receive it are dedicated to God. And in the dispute concerning Christ's words in Matthew 28 I claim only that we cannot use those words to disallow infant baptism. . . .

But it is clear that the external baptism of water cannot effect spiritual cleansing. Hence water-baptism is nothing but an external ceremony, that is, an outward sign that we are incorporated and engrafted into the Lord Jesus Christ and pledged to live to him and to follow him. And as in Jesus Christ neither circumcision nor uncircumcision avails anything, but a new creature, the living of a new life (Gal. 6), so it is not baptism which saves us, but a new life. Therefore one of the good results of the controversy has been to teach us that baptism cannot save or purify. Yet I cannot but think that in other respects the Anabaptists themselves set too great store by the baptism of water, and for that reason they err just as much on the one side as the papists do on the other. For though the whole world were arrayed against it, it is clear and indisputable that no external element or action can purify the soul.

John Calvin

John Calvin shows a very high esteem for baptism and its public celebration.

> John Calvin, *Institutes of the Christian Religion*, IV (1559),
> trans. Ford Lewis Battles, in LCC 21:1303–4, 1323, 1325.

XV.1. Baptism is the sign of the initiation by which we are received into the society of the church, in order that, engrafted in Christ, we may be reckoned among God's children. Now baptism was given to us by God for these ends (which I have taught to be common to all sacraments): first, to serve our faith before him; secondly, to serve our confession before men. We shall treat in order the reasons for each aspect of its institution. Baptism brings three things to our faith which we must deal with individually.

The first thing that the Lord sets out for us is that baptism should be a token and proof of our cleansing; or (the better to explain what I mean) it is like a sealed document to confirm to us that all our sins are so abolished, remitted, and effaced that they can never come to his sight, be recalled, or charged against us. For he wills that all who believe be baptized for the remission of sins [Matt. 28:19; Acts 2:38].

Accordingly, they who regarded baptism as nothing but a token and mark by which we confess our religion before men, as soldiers bear the insignia of their commander as a mark of their profession, have not weighed what was the chief point of baptism. It is to receive baptism with this promise: "He who believes and is baptized will be saved" [Mark 16:16]. . . .

22. But this principle will easily and immediately settle the controversy: infants are not barred from the Kingdom of Heaven just because they happen to depart the present life before they have been immersed in water. Yet we have already seen that serious injustice is done to God's covenant if we do not assent to it, as if it were weak of itself, since its effect depends neither upon baptism nor upon any additions. Afterward, a sort of seal is added to the sacrament, not to confer efficacy upon God's promise as if it were invalid of itself, but only to confirm it to us. From this it follows that the children of believers are baptized not in order that they who were previously strangers to the church may then for the first time become children of God, but rather that, because by the blessing of the promise they already belonged to the body of Christ, they are received into the church with this solemn sign.

Accordingly, if, when the sign is omitted, this is neither from sloth nor contempt nor negligence, we are safe from all danger. It is, therefore, much more holy to revere God's ordinance, namely, that we should seek the sacraments from those only to whom the Lord has committed them. When we cannot receive them from the church, the grace of God is not so bound to them but that we may obtain it by faith from the Word of the Lord. . . .

XVI.2. It therefore now remains for us, from the promises given in baptism, to inquire what its force and nature are. Scripture declares that baptism first points to the cleansing of our sins, which we obtain from Christ's blood; then to the mortification of our flesh, which rests upon participation in his death and through which believers are reborn into newness of life and into the fellowship of Christ. All that is taught in the Scriptures concerning baptism can be referred to this summary, except that baptism is also a symbol for bearing witness to our religion before men.

John Calvin, *Draft Ecclesiastical Ordinances* (1541),
trans. J. K. S. Reid, in LCC 22:66.

Baptism is to take place at the time of Sermon, and should be administered only by ministers or coadjutors. The names of children with those of their parents are to be registered, that, if any be found a bastard, the magistrate may be informed.

The stone or baptismal font is to be near the pulpit, in order that there be better hearing for the recitation of this mystery and practice of baptism.

Only such strangers as are men of faith and of our communion are to be accepted as godparents, since others are not capable of making the promise to the Church of instructing the children as is proper.

Calvin's critique of confirmation is even stronger than Luther's.

John Calvin, "Confirmation," in *Tracts containing Antidote to the Council of Trent; Antidote to the Canons on Confirmation*, trans. J. D. C. Fisher, in *Christian Initiation: The Reformation Period* (London: SPCK, 1970; repr. Chicago: Liturgy Training Publications, 2007), 254.

I hasten to declare that I am certainly not of the number of those who think that confirmation, as observed under the Roman papacy, is an idle ceremony, inasmuch as I regard it as one of the most deadly wiles of Satan. Let us remember that this pretended sacrament is nowhere recommended in Scripture, either under this name or with this ritual, or this signification. . . . Let the Romanists produce the word, if they wish us to contemplate in the oil anything beyond the oil itself. . . . [E]ven if they could prove themselves to imitate the apostles in the imposition of hands , . . whence do they derive their oil, which they call the oil of salvation? Who has taught them to seek salvation in oil? Who has taught them to attribute to it the property of imparting spiritual strength? . . . And with this they joined detestable blasphemy, because they said that sins were only forgiven by baptism, and that the Spirit of regeneration is given by that rotten oil which they presumed to bring in without the word of God.

This was once the custom, that the children of Christians after they had grown up were stood up before the bishop that they might fulfill that duty which was required of those adults who were offering them for baptism. . . . Therefore, those who had been initiated at baptism as infants, because they had not then performed a confession of faith before the Church towards the end of childhood—or as adolescence was beginning—were again presented by the parents, were examined by the bishop according to a formula of catechism which people held definite and universal. But so that this action, which otherwise deservedly ought to have been weighty and holy, might have all the more of reverence and dignity, the ceremony of the imposition of hands was also being used.

THE ENGLISH REFORMATION

The Church of England retains much of the traditional rites of Christian initiation but ties confirmation and first communion to a process of catechizing.

First and Second Prayer Books of Edward VI

"Exhortations in the Rite of Baptism," from *The Booke of Common Prayer*, 1549
and 1552, in Fisher, *Christian Initiation*, 91–93, 94–95; 107–8; 111.

Friends, you hear in this gospel [Mark 10] the words of our Saviour Christ, that he commanded the children to be brought to him, how he blamed those that would have kept them from him, how he exhorteth all men to follow their innocency. Ye perceive how by this outward gesture and deed he declared his good will toward them. For he embraced them in his arms, he laid his hands upon them, and blessed them: *Doubt ye not,* therefore, but earnestly believe, *that he will likewise favourably receive these present infants, that he will embrace them with the arms of his mercy, that he will give unto them the blessing of eternal life: and make them partakers of his everlasting kingdom.* Wherefore we being thus persuaded of the good will of our heavenly Father toward these infants, declared by his Son Jesus Christ, and nothing doubting but that he favourably alloweth *this charitable work of ours,* in bringing these children to his holy baptism, let us faithfully and devoutly give thanks unto him, and say the prayer which the Lord himself taught. And in declaration of our faith, let us also recite the articles contained in our creed. . . .

. . . Well beloved friends, ye have brought these children here to be baptized, ye have prayed for them that our Lord Jesus Christ would vouchsafe to receive them, to lay his hand upon them, to bless them, to release them of their sins, to give them the kingdom of heaven, and everlasting life. Ye have heard also that our Lord Jesus Christ hath promised in his gospel to grant all these thing that ye have prayed for: which promise he for his part will most surely keep and perform. Wherefore, after this promise made by Christ, these infants must also faithfully for their part promise by you that be their sureties, that they will forsake the devil and all his works, and constantly believe God's holy word and obediently keep his commandments. . . .

. . . Forasmuch as these children have promised by you to forsake the devil and all his works, to believe in God and to serve him, you must remember that it is your parts and duty to see that these infants be taught, so soon as they shall be able to learn, what a solemn vow, promise and profession they have made by you. And that they may know these things the better, ye shall call upon them to hear sermons, and chiefly you shall provide that they may learn the creed, the Lord's prayer and the ten commandments in the English tongue, and all other things which a Christian ought to know and believe to his soul's heath, and that these children may be virtuously brought up to lead a godly and Christian life, remembering always that baptism doth represent unto us our profession which is to follow the example of our Saviour Christ, and to be made like unto him, that as he died and rose again for us, so should we which are baptized die from sin, and rise again unto righteousness, continually mortifying all our evil and corrupt affections, and daily proceeding in all virtue and godliness of living. . . .

. . . The minister shall command . . . that the children be brought to the bishop to be confirmed of him, so soon as they can say in their vulgar tongue the articles of the faith, the Lord's prayer and the ten commandments, and be further instructed in the catechism, set forth for that purpose, accordingly as it is there expressed.

Bucer underscores the role of godparents in the responsibilities and duties they undertake on behalf of the baptized.

> Martin Bucer, *Censura* (1551), in Fisher, *Christian Initiation*, 103.

I would wish . . . that all those questions in this catechism [the renunciation of Satan and profession of faith] . . . should be addressed to the godfathers and godmothers themselves, in some such manner as this: Will you for your part faithfully undertake that this infant, when he is of an age, shall learn the catechism of our religion, and, having learnt that, shall renounce Satan and profess his belief in God the Father and the Son, etc.? If this alteration of this passage found favor, it should thus be altered: and the following exhortation to the godfathers and godmothers, as it is most godly and vitally necessary, ought therefore not to be read as it were in passing by the ministers, but be commended with the utmost seriousness to the sponsors and enjoined upon them. . . . But it ought to be thought sufficient if they from their heart promise all possible diligence in this matter. For these things are done in the sight of God, and these promises are made to God.

The rite of confirmation here is the late medieval rite of Sarum (Salisbury) in English, though with the use of chrism abolished.

> "Confirmation," in *The Book of Common Prayer* (1549),
> in Fisher, *Christian Initiation*, 241–42.

Almighty and everliving God, who hast vouchsafed to regenerate these they servants of water and the Holy Ghost, and hast given unto them forgiveness of all their sins, send down from heaven, we beseech thee, O Lord, upon them thy Holy Ghost, the Comforter, with the manifold gifts of grace, the spirit of wisdom and understanding, the spirit of counsel and ghostly strength, the spirit of knowledge and true godliness, and fulfil them, O Lord, with the spirit of thy holy fear.

Answer: Amen.

Minister: Sign them, O Lord, and mark them to be thine for ever, by the virtue of thy holy cross and passion. Confirm and strength them with the inward unction of thy Holy Ghost, mercifully unto everlasting life. Amen.

Then the bishop shall cross them in the forehead, and lay his hands upon their heads, saying: N., I sign thee with the sign of the cross, and lay my hand upon thee, in the name of the Father and of the Son and of the Holy Ghost. Amen.

And thus shall he do to every child one after another. And when he hath laid his hand upon every child, then he shall say: The peace of the Lord abide with you.

Answer: And with thy spirit.

Bucer, the "father of Protestant confirmation," underscores the necessity of catechesis leading to confirmation.

Martin Bucer, *Censura* (1551), trans. E. C. Whitaker, in *Martin Bucer and the Book of Common Prayer* (London: Alcuin Club, 1974), in ACC 55:112, 114.

Such an occasion [bishop's visitation], when the churches are thus visited and renewed in the religion of Christ would be particularly suitable for the solemn administration of confirmation to those who had reached that stage in the catechizing of our faith. Such care on the part of the bishops would go a long way to arouse the people to make progress in all true and effective knowledge of Christ. The men of old time, true bishops, gave care of this kind to their churches with the greatest zeal, and in Germany the superintendents, who commonly perform the function of bishops in our church, have carefully followed their example.

The last of this series of instruction is a warning that no-one is to be admitted to Holy Communion unless he has been confirmed. This instruction will be very wholesome if only those are confirmed who have confirmed the confession of their mouth with a manner of life consistent with it and from whose conduct it can be discerned that they make profession of their own faith and not another's.

In this revision, which remains today as the confirmation prayer in the Church of England, the Holy Spirit is no longer requested to be sent down from heaven upon the confirmands but now only to continue to strengthen them.

"Confirmation," in *The Book of Common Prayer* (1552),
in Fisher, *Christian Initiation*, 251–52.

Almighty and everliving God, who hast vouchsafed to regenerate these thy servants of water and the Holy Ghost, and hast given unto them forgiveness of all their sins, strengthen them, we beseech thee, O Lord, with the Holy Ghost, the Comforter, and daily increase in them thy manifold gifts of grace, the spirit of wisdom and understanding, the spirit of counsel and ghostly strength, the spirit of knowledge and true godliness, and fulfil them, O Lord, with the spirit of thy holy fear. Amen.

Then the bishop shall lay his hand upon every child severally, saying:

Defend, O Lord, this child with thy heavenly grace, that he may continue thine for ever, and daily increase in thy Holy Spirit more and more, until he come unto thy everlasting kingdom. Amen....

... The blessing of God almighty, the Father, the Son and the Holy Ghost, be upon you, and remain with you for ever. Amen.

THE CATHOLIC (COUNTER) REFORMATION

The Council of Trent reaffirms Roman Catholic positions on baptism and confirmation against those asserted by various Protestant Reformers. With regard to the rites themselves, the medieval texts and rubrics of both baptism and confirmation are standardized in the *Rituale Romanum* of 1614 and the *Pontificale Romanum* of 1596.

The Council of Trent

"Canons on Baptism," in H. Schroeder, trans., *The Canons and Decrees
of the Council of Trent* (St. Louis: Herder, 1941), 53–55.

Canon 1. If anyone says that the baptism of John had the same effect as the baptism of Christ, let him be anathema.

Can. 5. If anyone says that baptism is optional, that is, not necessary for salvation, let him be anathema.

Can. 7. If anyone says that those baptized are by baptism made debtors only to faith alone, but not to the observance of the whole law of Christ, let him be anathema.

Can. 12. If anyone says that no one is to be baptized except at that age at which Christ was baptized, or when on the point of death, let him be anathema.

Can. 13. If anyone says that children, because they have not the act of believing, are not after having received baptism to be numbered among the faithful, and that for this reason are to be rebaptized when they have reached the years of discretion; or that it is better that the baptism of such be omitted than that, while not believing by their own act, they should be baptized in the faith of the Church alone, let him be anathema.

"Canons on Confirmation," in Schroeder, *The Canons and Decrees of the Council of Trent*, 54–56.

Canon 1. If anyone says that the confirmation of those baptized is a empty ceremony and not a true and proper sacrament; or that of old it was nothing more than a sort of instruction, whereby those approaching adolescence gave an account of their faith to the Church, let him be anathema.

Can. 2. If anyone says that those who ascribe any power to the holy chrism of confirmation, offer insults to the Holy Ghost, let him be anathema.

Can. 3. If anyone says that the ordinary minister of holy confirmation is not the bishop alone, but any simple priest, let him be anathema.

METHODISM

John Wesley

John Wesley wrestles with problems of the relationship of baptism to conversion.

John Wesley, *Articles of Religion* (1784); Article XXVII revised in John Wesley, *Sunday Service* (Nashville: United Methodist Publishing House, 1984), 312.

XVII. Of Baptism
Baptism is not only a sign of profession, and mark of difference, whereby Christians are distinguished from others that are not baptized; but it is also a sign of regeneration, or the new birth. The baptism of young children is to be retained in the church.

John Wesley, "The New Birth" (1760), in *Sermons on Several Occasions* (London: Epworth Press, 1956), 519–20, 523.

II, 5. From hence it manifestly appears, what is the nature of the new birth. It is that great change which God works in the soul when He brings it into life; when He raises it from the death of sin to the life of righteousness. . . .

IV, 2. From the preceding reflections we may, secondly, observe, that as the new birth is not the same thing with baptism, so it does not always accompany baptism: they do not constantly go together. A man may possibly be "born of water," and yet not be "born of the Spirit." There may sometimes be the outward sign, where there is not the inward grace. I do not now speak with regard to infants: it is certain our Church [of England] supposes that all who are baptized in their infancy are at the same time born again; and it is allowed that the whole Office for the Baptism of Infants proceeds upon this supposition. Nor is it an objection of any weight against this, that we cannot comprehend how this work can be wrought in infants. For neither can we comprehend how it is wrought in a person of riper years. But whatever be the case with infants, it is sure all of riper years who are baptized are not at the same time born again. "The tree is known by its fruits." And hereby it appears too plain to be denied, that divers of those who were children of the devil before they were baptized continue the same after baptism: "for the works of their father they do": they continue servants of sin, without any pretence either to inward or outward holiness.

|

Modern Developments

|

POST-VATICAN II ROMAN CATHOLICISM

The reform of Christian initiation rites called for in the Constitution on the Sacred Liturgy 64–7 (1963) leads to a restoration of the adult catechumenate, a restoration followed by many other churches in the late twentieth and early twenty-first centuries.

Rite of Christian Initiation of Adults

Rite of Christian Initiation of Adults (1972), in *The Rites of the Catholic Church* (New York: Pueblo Publishing Co., 1988) 1:36–37.

4. The initiation of catechumens is a gradual process that takes place within the community of the faithful. By joining the catechumens in reflecting on the value of the paschal mystery and by renewing their own conversion, the faithful provide an example that will help the catechumens to obey the Holy Spirit more generously.

5. The rite of initiation is suited to a spiritual journey of adults that varies according to the many forms of God's grace, the free cooperation of the individuals, the action of the Church, and the circumstances of time and place.

6. This journey includes not only the periods for making inquiry and for maturing, . . . but also the steps marking the catechumens' progress, as they pass, so to speak, through another doorway or ascend to the next level.

1. The first step: reaching the point of initial conversion and wishing to become Christians, they are accepted as catechumens, by the church.
2. The second step: having progressed in faith and nearly completed the catechumenate, they are accepted into a more intense preparation for the sacraments of initiation.
3. The third step: having completed their spiritual preparation, they receive the sacraments of Christian initiation.

These three steps are to be regarded as the major, more intense moments of initiation and are marked by three liturgical rites: the first by the rite of acceptance into the order of catechumens; . . . the second by the rite of election or enrollment of names; . . . and the third by the celebration of the sacraments of Christian initiation.

Modern Roman Catholic thinking on Christian initiation has led to a profound awareness of the inseparable connection between baptism and confirmation.

Rite of Christian Initiation of Adults (1972), in *The Rites of the Catholic Church*, 1:146–47.

215. The conjunction of the two celebrations [baptism and confirmation] signifies the unity of the paschal mystery, the close link between the mission of the Son and the outpouring of the Holy Spirit, and the connection between the two sacraments through which the Son and the Holy Spirit come with the Father to those who are baptized.

THEOLOGICAL ISSUES RELATED TO THE
CHRISTIAN INITIATION OF INFANTS

Karl Barth

In a classic and influential statement Karl Barth argues against infant baptism.

Karl Barth, *The Teaching of the Church regarding Baptism* (1943), trans. Ernest A. Payne (London: SCM Press, 1948), 9, 14, 27, 29, 33, 40–41, 49.

Christian baptism is in essence the representation (*Abbild*) of a man's renewal through his participation by means of the power of the Holy Spirit in the death and resurrection of Jesus Christ, and therewith the representation of man's association with Christ, with the covenant of grace which is concluded and realised in Him, and with the fellowship of His Church. . . .

Baptism testifies to a man that this event is not his fancy but is objective reality which no power on earth can alter and which God has pledged Himself to maintain in all circumstances. . . . Baptism then is a picture in which, man, it is true, is not the most important figure but is certainly the second most important. . . .

In baptism we have to do not with the *causa* but with the *cognitio salutis*. If one confounds *causa* and *cognitio*, at once and inevitably one overlooks and mistakes the peculiarity of the purpose which baptism serves (and also that of faith!). . . .

The sacramental happening in which a real gift comes to man from Jesus Christ Himself is not in fact any less genuine a happening, because Christ's word and work on this occasion in this dimension and form, and Christ's power on this occasion, have not a causative or generative, but a cognitive aim. . . .

The experience to which a man is subjected in baptism consists in being made sure with divine certainty and being placed under obligation by divine authority. . . .

Baptism without the willingness and readiness of the baptized is true, effectual and effective baptism, but it is not correct; it is not done in obedience, it is not administered according to proper order, and therefore it is necessarily clouded baptism. It must and ought not to be repeated. It is, however, a wound in the body of the Church and a weakness for the baptized, which can certainly be cured but which are so dangerous that another question presents itself to the Church: how long is she prepared to be guilty of the occasioning of this wounding and weakening through a baptismal practice which is, from this standpoint, arbitrary and despotic?

We have in mind here the custom of the baptism of children. . . .

From the standpoint of a doctrine of baptism, infant-baptism can hardly be preserved without exegetical and practical artifices and sophisms—the proof to the contrary has yet to be supplied! One wants to preserve it only if one is resolved to do so on grounds, which lie outside the biblical passages on baptism and outside the thing itself. The determination to defend it on extraneous grounds has certainly found expression from century to century.

Aidan Kavanagh

Roman Catholic liturgical scholar Aidan Kavanagh underscores adult initiation as the "norm" for baptism, confirmation, and first communion.

Aidan Kavanagh, "Christian Initiation in Post-Conciliar
Catholicism: A Brief Report," in *LWSS*, 5–6.

[T]he days of baptism in infancy and confirmation in adolescence as our norm are numbered; that the days of evangelization by initiating youths into "appropriate" civil structures are numbered; that the days of catechizing solely in school classrooms are numbered; that the days in which we regard a man's or woman's entry into novitiate or seminary as their "entry into the Church" are numbered; that the days of our practical equation of Church and civil society are over.

I may be wrong about this but I do not think so. For as I have traveled my own hemisphere speaking with a variety of Christian groups, I find recurring quite across denominational lines a growing concern for Christian identity as individuals and as churches. The questions "Who am I as a Christian?" and "Who are we as a Church?" must be regarded as initiatory questions if Tertullian was right when he said *Fiat non nascuntur Christiani*. The answers begin in the "making" of Christians—from the first stirrings of belief, through the catechumenate (a catechumen is a type of Christian already endowed with sacramental rights to Christian marriage, the liturgy of the Word, and Christian burial), to the united sacramental process of baptism-confirmation-eucharist which constitutes the assembly of the *fideles*, and beyond that into the continuing conversion which is ecclesial life together. The Roman rites view all this, both in whole and in each of its parts, as a sustained and closely articulated process rather than as a series of separate and discrete events. It is a ". . . *transitus, secum trahens progressivam sensus et morum immutationem, cum suis socialibus consectariius manifestus fieri et tempore . . . paulatim evolvi debet*" [". . . transition that brings with it a progressive change in outlook and style of life which should become evident by a gradual evolution over a period of time"].

Here we may see something of the sense of "economic dynamism" restored to a sacramental theology *ad robur*. This implies that no single single sacrament discloses its root-meaning in isolation from those that precede and succeed it within the continuing conversion that is ecclesial life. Concretely put, conversion leading into baptism-confirmation can now more fertilely be seen as the compound way in which the eucharist begins, and the eucharist can be seen as the mode in which that compound way is sustained in the Church's annual round of life, especially through Lent and the paschal vigil. Among other things, this perspective throws light on how penance, for example, might be more adequately grasped in theory and employed in pastoral practice: rather less as an ecclesiastical technique for alleviating guilt similar to that of psychological analysis; rather more as an act of worship by which the baptismal conversion in faith is strengthened and eucharistic communion in faith is sustained. For the sacrament of reconciliation is not primarily about guilt; it is about a life of faith shared—as, indeed, are all the sacraments.

Edmund Schlink

Reacting in part to Karl Barth, Lutheran theologian Edmund Schlink offers several theses in support of infant baptism.

Edmund Schlink. *The Doctrine of Baptism*, trans. Herbert J. A. Bouman (St. Louis: Concordia Publishing House, 1972) 157–60.

1. Although there is no explicit word of the Lord or of an apostle which commands or forbids infant Baptism, the question of infant Baptism is by no means left to the arbitrary decision of the church. On the contrary, the church may baptize children only if she is certain that in this way she is acting in the obedience of faith to the divine task assigned to her.

2. In baptizing the children that will grow up in her midst—whether they were born to members of the church or whether they are brought along at the Baptism of their parents—the church acknowledges that all . . . are born under the dominion of sin and of death. Even though the infants have not rebelled against God by their own decision and are different from adult sinners in this respect, they cannot by their decision rid themselves of the dominion of sin as they grow up. . . .

3. In baptizing children the church acknowledges the revealed saving will of God that all . . . are saved by Jesus Christ and the power of the Holy Spirit. . . .

4. The church baptizes children in the conviction that through Baptism God assigns them to Jesus Christ, crucified and risen for all the world, as the Lord. The church believes that through Baptism God embraces the entire subsequent life of the child in a saving way by giving it into Christ's death in order that it might participate in His resurrection life.

5. The church baptizes children in the conviction that through Baptism God gives them the Holy Spirit who leads into all truth. . . . The beginning of the Spirit's activity in [a person] is not bound to the precondition of human recognition and confession, but the Holy Spirit is the gift by means of which alone [one] can be awakened to the knowledge of faith.

6. The church baptizes her children in the conviction that through Baptism God makes them members of the church, of the body of Christ and of the prophetic, priestly, and royal people of God. . . .

7. In baptizing children the church is confident that God will hear the prayers with which the children are brought to Baptism and by which their growing up is surrounded. . . .

8. In baptizing children the church is confident that God will prove himself powerful by means of the Gospel with which the church will accompany the life of the baptized children. . . . With a view to the children growing up in her midst the church may have the confidence that through assurance, admonition, and instruction, as well as through absolution, Lord's Supper, and blessing Christ will prove to be their Lord and Savior and that the Holy Spirit will enrich them with His gifts and guide them.

9. In baptizing children the church acknowledges that not only the salvation of the believers but also the origin and preservation of their faith are God's deed which He accomplishes through the Gospel and the sacraments in the power of the Holy Spirit. . . . Not only the salvation received by faith is a gift of grace, but also the believing reception itself.

10. In baptizing children the church acknowledges that faith and Baptism belong together. The church baptizes the children that will grow up in her midst, and she does so by faith in the saving activity of God who by means of Baptism assigns them to Jesus Christ. . . .

11. In baptizing children the church knows that the temporal sequence of faith and Baptism has been relativized by God's eschatological activity. . . . The baptized has in Christ already experienced his future death, and the life of the one risen from the dead has rightly been opened for him. In this eschatological bracketing the

question whether the faith of the person to be baptized must necessarily precede Baptism fades away, and the temporal sequence of faith and Baptism cannot be made the norm of validity. But the connection between faith and Baptism which encompasses the course of life is decisive: Whoever does not believe will not participate in salvation in spite of Baptism which he received. Since faith and Baptism belong together, the church baptizes only those children who will grow up under the witness of faith.

12. Thus, the church, in baptizing children born and growing up in her midst, is certain that she is acting in the obedience of faith. . . . In baptizing children before they can know and confess Christ themselves, the church is not neglecting their decision of faith but is rather helping them to come to the Yea of faith. The church is not violating their freedom but helping them to attain to the freedom of faith. Thus the church acts as the mother of believers and by means of no other act confesses so unmistakably that it is God alone who saves [humankind]. For by means of infant Baptism the person is received into the kingdom of God without any contribution of his own. Just as the resurrection of the dead occurs without the assistance of the dead, so also the new creation of [humanity] whose life is forfeit to sin and death is accomplished through Baptism.

Mark Searle

Mark Searle suggests strongly that infant initiation is not so much a problem to be solved as an opportunity to be grasped.

Mark Searle, "Infant Baptism Reconsidered," in *LWSS*, 408–9.

Adult baptism, the economy of the "twice born," tends to draw to itself the vocabulary of regeneration as opposed to generation; of brothers and sisters rather than sons and daughters; of voluntary decision rather than divine vocation; of change rather than faithfulness; of breaking with the past rather than growth towards the future; of death and resurrection rather than adoption and filiation. The language of infant initiation, on the other hand, is inclined to speak in terms of the womb rather than the tomb, of election rather than choice, of loyalty rather than commitment, of the preconscious operations of grace rather than of personal convictions, of nurturing the life of faith rather than of passing from unbelief to belief. In Jungian terms, a regime which attaches importance to infant initiation gives a larger role to the "feminine" aspects of Christianity, while adult initiation displays the more "masculine" elements of Christian imagery.

While there are many other and stronger reasons for upholding the baptism of infants, this would seem a further argument for retaining it. At a time when the Church is so intent on rescuing the humane values of Christianity and is concerned to do greater justice to the role of the family and to the Christian vision of sexuality, and at a time when the role of the nonrational and prerational dimensions of the life of faith is being recovered, perhaps infant initiation ought to be seen less as a problem to be grappled with than as an opportunity to be grasped. Far from barring children from the font, the chrism, and the altar, the Church should welcome their participation in these sacraments as a reminder both of the catholicity of the Church and of the fact that, no matter how informed or committed we might be as adults, when we take part in the sacramental liturgies of the Church we are taking part in more than we know.

Baptism, Eucharist, and Ministry

An ecumenical convergence on the baptism of infants and adults has emerged.

"Baptismal Practice," from World Council of Churches, *Baptism, Eucharist, and Ministry*, Faith and Order Paper No. 111 (Geneva: World Council of Churches, 1982), paragraphs IV.A.12–13; B.14, and Commentary 14.b and c.

IV.A.12. Both the baptism of believers and the baptism of infants take place in the Church as the community of faith. When one who can answer for himself or herself is baptized, a personal confession of faith will be an integral part of the baptismal service. When an infant is baptized, the personal response will be offered at a later moment in life. In both cases, the baptized person will have to grow in the understanding of faith. For those baptized upon their own confession of faith, there is always the constant requirement of a continuing growth of personal response in faith. In the case of infants, personal confession is expected later, and Christian nurture is directed to the eliciting of this confession. All baptism is rooted in and declares Christ's faithfulness unto death. It has its setting within the life and faith of the Church and, through the witness of the whole Church, points to the faithfulness of God, the ground of all life in faith. At every baptism the whole congregation reaffirms its faith in God and pledges itself to provide an environment of witness and service. Baptism should, therefore, always be celebrated and developed in the setting of the Christian community.

Baptism is an unrepeatable act. Any practice, which might be interpreted as "re-baptism" must be avoided.

IV.B.14. In God's work of salvation, the paschal mystery of Christ's death and resurrection is inseparably linked with the pentecostal gift of the Holy Spirit. Similarly, participation in Christ's death and resurrection is inseparably linked with the receiving of the Spirit. Baptism in its full meaning signifies and effects both.

Christians differ in their understanding as to where the sign of the gift of the Spirit is to be found. Different actions have become associated with the giving of the Spirit. For some it is the water rite itself. For others, it is the anointing with chrism and/or the imposition of hands, which many churches call confirmation. For still others it is all three, as they see the Spirit operative throughout the rite. All agree that Christian baptism is in water and the Holy Spirit.

COMMENTARY (14)

(b) If baptism, as incorporation into the body of Christ, points by its very nature to the eucharistic sharing of Christ's body and blood, the question arises as to how a further and separate rite can be interposed between baptism and admission to communion. Those churches which baptize children but refuse them a share in the eucharist before such a rite may wish to ponder whether they have fully appreciated and accepted the consequences of baptism.

(c) Baptism needs to be constantly reaffirmed. The most obvious form of such reaffirmation is the celebration of the eucharist. The renewal of baptismal vows may also take place during such occasions as the annual celebration of the paschal mystery or during the baptism of others.

Federation of Diocesan Liturgical Commissions

"Position Statement on Re-uniting the Three Sacraments of Christian Initiation of the Federation of Diocesan Liturgical Commissions," *FDLC Newsletter* 22, no. 4 (December 1995): 45.

It is the position of the delegates . . . that the Board of Directors of the [FDLC] and the Bishops' Committee on the Liturgy urge the National Conference of Catholic Bishops to take the initiative to propose to the Apostolic See a discussion on the restoration of the ancient practice of celebrating confirmation and communion at the time of baptism, including the baptism of children who have not yet reached catechetical age, so that through connection of these three sacraments, the unity of the Paschal Mystery would be better signified and the eucharist would again assume its proper significance as the culmination of Christian initiation.

CHAPTER 4

The Eucharist

The Eucharist is both the culmination of the sacraments and rites of Christian initiation, surveyed in the previous chapter, and the repeatable sacrament of Christian initiation. In the words of Thomas Aquinas, "the Eucharist is the summit of the spiritual life, and the goal of all the sacraments" (*Summa Theologiae* III, q. 73, a. 3).

This chapter, like the previous one, proceeds historically from the relevant biblical texts through key patristic, medieval, Reformation, and post-Reformation texts up to contemporary discussion and ecumenical liturgical and theological convergence; similarly it presents both liturgical texts and descriptive or interpretative theological texts. Unlike the previous chapter, however, a major concern here is with the developing theology of the Eucharist, especially with regard to the real presence of Christ in the Eucharist and to accompanying theologies of consecration and eucharistic sacrifice. From biblical and early Jewish and Jewish-Christian texts related to the Eucharist; through pre-Nicene texts focusing on the various meanings of the Eucharist in authors such as Ignatius of Antioch, Justin Martyr, Clement of Alexandria, Origen, Tertullian, and Irenaeus of Lyons; to post-Nicene authors such as Cyril of Jerusalem (who taught consecration by the epiclesis of the Holy Spirit), Ambrose of Milan (who argued that such consecration took place through the words of Christ [the *Verba Christi*] in the narrative of institution), and Augustine's focus on the church and the Eucharist; to the medieval eucharistic controversies of the West in the ninth and eleventh centuries and the decree on transubstantiation at the Fourth Lateran Council (1215) and Thomas Aquinas on the meaning of this term; through Reformation critique and defense of the real presence and calls for reform related to the question of eucharistic sacrifice and the sharing of both bread and cup in the eucharistic celebration (see Martin Luther and Archbishop Cranmer below); all the way to contemporary thought (e.g., Edward Schillebeeckx), this chapter gives a succinct presentation on the history of eucharistic thought, especially in the West.

At the same time, since a great deal of eucharistic theology is to be read out of liturgical texts, especially with regard to the question of eucharistic sacrifice and the presence and function even of an institution narrative or epiclesis, an abundance of eucharistic anaphoras (eucharistic prayers) from the pre-Nicene period through the Reformation are provided. Here early prayers (e.g., *The Didache, The Strasbourg Papyrus, The Anaphora of Sts. Addai and Mari*) without a narrative of institution are given, along with the later classic eucharistic prayers of both East and West: the anaphora of the so-called *Apostolic Tradition*, which forms the basis for Eucharistic Prayer II in the modern Mass of the Roman Rite and is used in other modern liturgical revisions by various churches; an early Egyptian example from *The Prayers of Sarapion of Thmuis*; the anaphoras of St. John Chrysostom and Basil, both of which are still used today in the Byzantine Rite; the Roman Canon of the Mass (Eucharistic Prayer I in today's Mass of the Roman Rite); select Gallican (French) and Mozarabic (Spanish) prayers; and Martin Luther's and Thomas Cranmer's approach to eucharistic prayer deletion or revision.

In addition, other documents of a more descriptive nature, such as the famous *Ordo Romanus I*, which gives a detailed account of a papal mass at Rome in the seventh century, as well as catechetical and conciliar texts are also included. The chapter ends with pertinent selections from the 1982 Faith and Order document of the World Council of Churches, *Baptism, Eucharist, and Ministry*, demonstrating the great ecumenical convergence in eucharistic doctrine and liturgical celebration that has taken place in the modern world.

|

The First Three Centuries

|

HEBREW BIBLE AND JEWISH PRAYERS

Select Texts

New Testament texts, especially Mark 14:22–26, Matthew 26:26–30, and Luke 22:14–22, narrate the institution of the Eucharist in relationship to the Jewish Passover.

Exodus 12:6–8, 24–27.

"You shall keep it [the lamb] until the fourteenth day of this month; then the whole assembled congregation of Israel shall slaughter it at twilight. They shall take some of the blood and put it on the two doorposts and the lintel of the houses in which they eat it. They shall eat the lamb that same night; they shall eat it roasted over the fire with unleavened bread and bitter herbs. . . .

"You shall observe this rite as a perpetual ordinance for you and your children. When you come to the land that the LORD will give you, as he has promised, you shall keep this observance. And when your children ask you, 'What do you mean by this observance?' you shall say, 'It is the passover sacrifice to the LORD, for he passed over the houses of the Israelites in Egypt, when he struck down the Egyptians but spared our houses.'" And the people bowed down and worshiped.

The earliest text of this prayer appears in the *Siddur Rav Saadya Gaon* in a tenth-century-CE manuscript. Rav Saadya was a ninth-century president (Gaon) of the Academy in Babylon.

"Birkath ha-mazon" (Blessing over Food), in *PEER*, 10–11.

Blessing of him who nourishes
Blessed are you, Lord our God, King of the universe, for you nourish us and the whole world with goodness, kindness, grace, and mercy. Blessed are you, Lord, for you nourish the universe.

Blessing for the land
We will give thanks to you, Lord our God, because you have given us for our inheritance a desirable land, good and wide, the covenant and the law, life and food. . . .
Blessed are you, Lord, for the land and for food.

Blessing for Jerusalem
Have mercy, Lord our God, on us your people Israel, and your city Jerusalem, on your sanctuary and your dwelling place, on Zion, the habitation of your glory, and the great and holy house over which your name is invoked. Restore the kingdom of the house of David to its place in our days, and speedily build Jerusalem. . . .
Blessed are you, Lord, for you build Jerusalem.

The text of this morning blessing does not appear in this fixed form until many centuries later as well.

"Yotser Berakah" (Blessing for Light), in *PEER*, 11–12.

May you be blessed, our rock, our king, our redeemer, who creates the saints. May your name be glorified for ever, our king who makes the angels. Your angels stand over the world and proclaim aloud, in fear, with one voice the great words of the living God and king of the universe. All beloved, all the chosen, all powers, and all . . . do the will of their creator in fear and trembling; and all open their mouths in holiness and purity, singing melodiously, and bless and glorify and magnify and adore the holy king, the name of God, mighty king, great and terrible: holy is he. And all, one from another, take upon them the yoke of the heavenly kingdom and give each other in turn to proclaim the holy creator with a quiet mind, a bright tongue, and a holy gentleness, all with one mind answering and saying in fear:

Holy, holy, holy (is the) Lord of hosts; the whole earth is full of his glory.

And the wheels and holy living creatures raise themselves with great thunder, give glory from the other side and say:

Blessed be the glory of the Lord from his place. . . .

NEW TESTAMENT

Select Texts

Multiple images of the Eucharist appear in the New Testament.

Mark 14:22–26 (see also Matt. 26:26–30; Luke 22:14–22 and 1 Cor. 11:23–26).

While they were eating, he took a loaf of bread, and after blessing it he broke it, gave it to them, and said, "Take; this is my body." Then he took a cup, and after giving thanks he gave it to them, and all of them drank from it. He said to them, "This is my blood of the [new] covenant, which is poured out for many. Truly I tell you, I will never again drink of the fruit of the vine until that day when I drink it new in the kingdom of God." When they had sung the hymn, they went out to the Mount of Olives.

Luke 24:28–35.

As they came near the village to which they were going, he walked ahead as if he were going on. But they urged him strongly, saying, "Stay with us, because it is almost evening and the day is now nearly over." So he went in to stay with them. When he was at the table with them, he took bread, blessed and broke it, and gave it to them. Then their eyes were opened, and they recognized him; and he vanished from their sight. They said to each other, "Were not our hearts burning within us while he was talking to us on the road, while he was opening the scriptures to us?" That same hour they got up and returned to Jerusalem; and they found the eleven and their companions gathered together. They were saying, "The Lord has risen indeed, and he has appeared to Simon!" Then they told what had happened on the road, and how he had been made known to them in the breaking of the bread.

John 6:51–58.

"I am the living bread that came down from heaven. Whoever eats of this bread will live for ever; and the bread that I will give for the life of the world is my flesh." The Jews then disputed among themselves, saying, "How can this man give us his flesh to eat?" So Jesus said to them, "Very truly, I tell you, unless you eat the flesh of the Son of Man and drink his blood, you have no life in you. Those who eat my flesh and drink my blood have eternal life, and I will raise them up on the last day; for my flesh is true food and my blood is true drink. Those who eat my flesh and drink my blood abide in me, and I in them. Just as the living Father sent me, and I live because of the Father, so whoever eats me will live because of me. This is the bread that came down from heaven, not like that which your ancestors ate, and they died. But the one who eats this bread will live for ever."

1 Corinthians 10:16–17; 21.

The cup of blessing that we bless, is it not a sharing in the blood of Christ? The bread that we break, is it not a sharing in the body of Christ? Because there is one bread, we who are many are one body, for we all partake of the one bread. . . . You cannot drink the cup of the Lord and the cup of demons. You cannot partake of the table of the Lord and the table of demons.

1 Corinthians 11:27–29.

Whoever, therefore, eats the bread or drinks the cup of the Lord in an unworthy manner will be answerable for the body and blood of the Lord. Examine yourselves, and only then eat of the bread and drink of the cup. For all who eat and drink [in an unworthy manner] without discerning the [Lord's] body, eat and drink judgment against themselves.

Acts 2:42, 46.

They devoted themselves to the apostles' teaching and fellowship, to the breaking of bread and the prayers. . . .

Day by day, as they spent much time together in the temple, they broke bread at home and ate their food with glad and generous hearts.

SYRIA

Early Syrian documents provide valuable information on the structure of the eucharistic liturgy, its theology, and some texts for the eucharistic prayer.

The Didache

The Didache, IX–X, XIV (late first or early second century), trans. Cyril C. Richardson, in LCC 1:175–76, 178.

9. Now about the Eucharist: This is how to give thanks: First in connection with the cup:

"We thank you, our Father, for the holy vine of David, your child, which you have revealed through Jesus, your child. To you be glory forever."

Then in connection with the piece [broken off the loaf]:

"We thank you, our Father, for the life and knowledge which you have revealed through Jesus, your child. To you be glory forever.

"As this piece [of bread] was scattered over the hills and then was brought together and made one, so let your Church be brought together from the ends of the earth into your Kingdom. For yours is the glory and the power through Jesus Christ forever."

You must not let anyone eat or drink of your Eucharist except those baptized in the Lord's name. For in reference to this the Lord said, "Do not give what is sacred to dogs."

10. After you have finished your meal, say grace in this way:

"We thank you, holy Father, for your sacred name which you have lodged in our hearts, and for the knowledge and faith and immortality which you have revealed through Jesus, your child. To you be glory forever.

"Almighty Master, 'you have created everything' for the sake of your name, and have given men food and drink to enjoy that they may thank you. But to us you have given spiritual food and drink and eternal life through Jesus, your child.

"Above all, we thank you that you are mighty. To you be glory forever.

"Remember, Lord, your Church, to save it from all evil and to make it perfect by your love. Make it holy, 'and gather' it 'together from the four winds' into your Kingdom which you have made ready for it. For yours is the power and the glory forever."

"Let Grace come and let this world pass away."

"Hosanna to the God of David!"

"If anyone is holy, let him come. If not, let him repent."

"Our Lord, come!"

"Amen."

In the case of prophets, however, you should let them give thanks in their own way. . . .

14. On every Lord's Day—his special day—come together and break bread and give thanks, first confessing your sins so that your sacrifice may be pure. Anyone at variance with his neighbor must not join you, until they are reconciled, lest your sacrifice be defiled. For it was of this sacrifice that the Lord said, "Always and everywhere offer me a pure sacrifice; for I am a great King, says the Lord, and my name is marveled at by the nations."

Letter of Pliny to the Emperor Trajan

Letter of Pliny to the Emperor Trajan (ca. 112),
trans. Henry Bettenson, in *Documents of the Christian Church*
(New York: Oxford University Press, 1947), 6–7.

But they declared that the sum of their guilt or error had amounted only to this, that on the appointed day they had been accustomed to meet before daybreak, and to recite a hymn [*carmen*] antiphonally to Christ, as to a god, and to bind themselves by an oath [*sacramentum*], not for the commission of any crime but to abstain from theft, robbery, adultery, and breach of faith, and not to deny a deposit when it was claimed. After the conclusion of this ceremony it was their custom to depart and meet again to take food; but it was ordinary and harmless food; and they had ceased this practice after my edict in which, in accordance with your orders, I had forbidden secret societies. I thought it the more necessary, therefore, to find out what truth there was in this by applying torture to two maidservants, who were called deaconesses [*ministrae*]. But I found nothing but a depraved and extravagant superstition, and I therefore postponed my examination and had recourse to you for consultation.

Ignatius of Antioch

On his way to martyrdom in Rome during the time of the emperor Trajan, Ignatius presents a theology of the Eucharist as a theology of Christian unity.

Ignatius of Antioch, *Letters* (ca. 115), trans. Cyril C. Richardson, in LCC 1:93, 108–9, 114–15.

To the Ephesians
20. At these meetings you should heed the bishop and presbytery attentively, and break one loaf, which is the medicine of immortality [*pharmakon athanasias*], and the antidote, which wards off death but yields continuous life in union with Jesus Christ.

To the Philadelphians
4. Be careful, then, to observe a single Eucharist. For there is one flesh of our Lord Jesus Christ and one cup of his blood that makes *us* one,[1] and one altar, just as there is one bishop along with the presbytery and the deacons, my fellow slaves. In that way whatever you do is in line with God's will.

To the Smyrnaeans
6. They [Docetists] hold aloof from the Eucharist and from services of prayer, because they refuse to admit that the Eucharist is the flesh of our Saviour Jesus Christ, which suffered for our sins and which, in his goodness, the Father raised [from the dead]. Consequently those who wrangle and dispute God's gift face death. . . .

8. You should regard that Eucharist as valid, which is celebrated either by the bishop or by someone he authorizes. Where the bishop is present, there let the congregation gather, just as where Jesus Christ is, there is the Catholic Church. Without the bishop's supervision, no baptisms or love feasts are permitted.

Justin Martyr

Justin Martyr provides an overall outline of the eucharistic liturgy, which is still discernible in several different rites today.

---

1. The Greek text says "*hen potērion eis henosin tou haimatos autou*," literally, "one cup for union with his blood," not "one cup of his blood."

Justin Martyr, *First Apology* (ca. 155), trans. Edward Rochie Hardy, in LCC 1:285–87.

65. We, however, after thus washing the one who has been convinced and signified his ascent, lead him to those who are called brethren, where they are assembled. They then earnestly offer common prayers for themselves and the one who has been illuminated and all others everywhere, that we may be made worthy, having learned the truth, to be found in deed good citizens and keepers of what is commanded, so that we may be saved with eternal salvation. On finishing the prayers we greet each other with a kiss. Then bread and a cup of water and mixed wine are brought to the president of the brethren and he, taking them, sends up praise and glory to the Father of the universe through the name of the Son and of the Holy Spirit, and offers thanksgiving at some length that we have been deemed worthy to receive these things from him. When he has finished the prayers and the thanksgiving, the whole congregation present assents, saying, "Amen." "Amen" in the Hebrew language means, "So be it." When the president has given thanks and the whole congregation has assented, those whom we call deacons give to each of those present a portion of the consecrated bread and wine and water, and they take it to the absent.

66. This food we call Eucharist, of which no one is allowed to partake except one who believes that the things we teach are true, and has received the washing for forgiveness of sins and for rebirth, and who lives as Christ handed down to us. For we do not receive these things as common bread or common drink; but as Jesus Christ our Saviour being incarnate by God's word took flesh and blood for our salvation, so also we have been taught that the food consecrated by the word of prayer which comes from him, from which our flesh and blood are nourished by transformation, is the flesh and blood of that incarnate Jesus. For the apostles in the memoirs composed by them, which are called Gospels, thus handed down what was commanded them: that Jesus, taking bread and having given thanks, said, "Do this for my memorial, this is my body"; and likewise taking the cup and giving thanks he said, "This is my blood"; and gave it to them alone. This also the wicked demons in imitation handed down as something to be done in the mysteries of Mithra; for bread and a cup of water are brought out in their secret rites of initiation, with certain invocations which you either know or can learn.

67. After these [services] we constantly remind each other of these things. Those who have more come to the aid of those who lack, and we are constantly together. Over all that we receive we bless the Maker of all things through his Son Jesus Christ and through the Holy Spirit. And on the day called Sunday there is a meeting in

one place of those who live in cities or the country, and the memoirs of the apostles or the writings of the prophets are read as long as time permits. When the reader has finished, the president in a discourse urges and invites [us] to the imitation of these noble things. Then we all stand up together and offer prayers. And, as said before, when we have finished the prayer, bread is brought, and wine and water, and the president similarly sends up prayers and thanksgivings to the best of his ability, and the congregation assents, saying the Amen; the distribution, and reception of the consecrated [elements] by each one, takes place and they are sent to the absent by the deacons. Those who prosper, and who so wish, contribute, each one as much as he chooses to. What is collected is deposited with the president, and he takes care of orphans and widows, and those who are in want on account of sickness or any other cause, and those who are in bonds, and the strangers who are sojourners among [us], and, briefly, he is the protector of all those in need. We all hold this common gathering on Sunday. . . .

Justin uses the language of offering and sacrifice to refer to the Eucharist.

Justin Martyr, *Dialogue with Trypho* XLI, in *ANF* 1:215.

The Oblation of Fine Flour Was a Figure of the Eucharist.

"And the offering of fine flour, sirs," I said, "which was prescribed to be presented on behalf of those purified from leprosy, was a type of the bread of the Eucharist, the celebration of which our Lord Jesus Christ prescribed, in remembrance of the suffering which He endured on behalf of those who are purified in soul from all iniquity, in order that we may at the same time thank God for having created the world, with all things therein, for the sake of man, and for delivering us from the evil in which we were, and for utterly overthrowing principalities and powers by Him who suffered according to His will. Hence God speaks by the mouth of Malachi, one of the twelve [prophets], as I said before, about the sacrifices at that time presented by you: 'I have no pleasure in you, saith the Lord; and I will not accept your sacrifices at your hands: for, from the rising of the sun unto the going down of the same, My name has been glorified among the Gentiles, and in every place incense is offered to My name, and a pure offering: for My name is great among the Gentiles, saith the Lord: but ye profane it.' [So] He then speaks of those Gentiles, namely us, who in every place offer sacrifices to Him, i.e., the bread of the Eucharist, and also the cup of the Eucharist, affirming both that we glorify His name, and that you profane [it]."

Didascalia Apostolorum

The Holy Spirit is the one who sanctifies the Eucharist.

> *Didascalia Apostolorum,* 2.58 and 6.21–22, trans. Sebastian Brock
> and Michael Vasey, in *The Liturgical Portions of the Didascalia,*
> AGLS 29 (Cambridge: Grove Books, Ltd., 1982), 16 and 32–33.

2.58. But if a presbyter should come from another congregation, you, the presbyters, should receive him in fellowship into your place. And if he is a bishop, let him sit with the bishop, who should accord to him the honour of his rank, even as himself. And do you, the bishop invite him to give a homily to your people; for the exhortation and admonition of strangers is very helpful, especially as it is written, "There is no prophet that is acceptable in his own place." And when you offer the oblation, let him speak the words; but if he is wise and gives the honour to you, and is unwilling to offer, at least let him speak the words over the cup.

6.21–2. For consider and see that prayer is also heard through the Holy Spirit, and the eucharist is accepted and sanctified through the Holy Spirit, and the Scriptures are the words of the Holy Spirit, and are holy . . . .

[O]ffer an acceptable eucharist, the likeness of the body of the kingdom of Christ, both in your congregations and in your cemeteries and on the departures of those who are fallen asleep; pure bread that is made with fire, and sanctified by means of invocations; and without doubting you should pray and offer for those who have fallen asleep. For those who have believed in God, as it says in the Gospel, even though they should fall asleep, are not dead.

EGYPT

The early Egyptian tradition, as represented by Clement and Origen, expresses a eucharistic theology closely associated with the work of the Logos.

Clement of Alexandria

> Clement of Alexandria, *Paedagogus* I, 6, 43, 2; in *ANF* 2:220.

The flesh figuratively represents to us the Holy Spirit; for the flesh was created by Him. The blood points out to us the Word, for as rich blood the Word has been infused into life; and the union of both is the Lord, the food of babes—the Lord who is Spirit and Word.

Clement of Alexandria, *Paedagogus* II, 2, 19, 4–20, 1, in *ANF* 2:242–43.

The blood of the Lord is twofold. For there is the blood of His flesh, by which we are redeemed from corruption; and the spiritual, that by which we are anointed. And to drink the blood of Jesus, is to become partaker of the Lord's immortality; the Spirit being the energetic principle of the Word, as the blood is of the flesh. . . . Accordingly, as wine is blended with water, so is the Spirit with man. And the one, the mixture of wine and water, nourishes to faith; while the other, the Spirit, conducts to immortality. . . . And the mixture of both—of the drink and of the Word—is called Eucharist, renowned and glorious grace; and they who by faith partake of it are sanctified both in body and soul.

Origen of Alexandria

Origen of Alexandria, *Com. in Matt.* 11:14, in *ANF* 10:443.

And in the case of the bread of the Lord, accordingly, there is advantage to him who uses it, when with undefiled mind and pure conscience he partakes of the bread. And so neither by not eating, I mean by the very fact that we do not eat of the bread, which has been sanctified by the word of God and prayer, are we deprived of any good thing; . . . but in respect of the prayer which comes upon it, according to the proportion of the faith, becomes a benefit and is a means of clear vision to the mind which looks to that which is beneficial, and it is not the material of the bread but the word which is said over it is of advantage to him who eats it not unworthily of the Lord.

Origen of Alexandria, *Contra Celsum*, 8, 33, in *ANF* 4:651–52.

We give thanks to the Creator of all, and, along with thanksgiving and prayer for the blessings we have received, we also eat the bread presented to us; and this bread becomes by prayer a sacred body, which sanctifies those who sincerely partake of it.

Origen of Alexandria, *In Matth. ser.* 85, trans. P. Jacquemont, in Willy Rordorf et al., *The Eucharist of the Early Christians* (New York: Pueblo, 1978), 187–88.

That bread which God the Word (*deus verbum*) owns to be His Body, is the Word which nourishes the soul, the Word which proceeds from God the Word (*verbum de deo verbum procedens*), and that bread from heavenly bread which is placed upon the table. . . . And that drink which saturates and inebriates the hearts of those that drink it, the drink in that cup, of which it is said: How goodly is thy inebriating chalice (Ps. 22). . . . Not that visible bread which He held in His hands, did the Divine Logos call His body, but the word, in the mystery of which the bread was to be broken. Not that visible drink did He call His blood, but the word, in the mystery of which this drink was to be poured out. For the body of the Divine Logos or His blood, what else can they be than the word which nourishes and the word which gladdens the hearts?

Perhaps a complete eucharistic prayer by itself, this tripartite prayer of praise, offering, and intercession presents a theology of the Eucharist as the church's "bloodless service."

The Strasbourg Papyrus (ca. 200), in *PEER*, 53–54.

To bless [you] . . . [night] and day . . .

[you who made] heaven [and] all that is in [it, the earth and what is on earth,] seas and rivers and [all that is] in [them]; [you] who made man [according to your] own image and likeness. You made everything through your wisdom, the light [of?] your true Son, our Lord and Savior Jesus Christ; giving thanks through him to you with him and the Holy Spirit, we offer the reasonable sacrifice and this bloodless service, which all the nations offer you, "from sunrise to sunset," from south to north, [for] your "name is great among all the nations, and in every place incense is offered to your holy name and a pure sacrifice.

Over this sacrifice and offering we pray and beseech you, remember your holy and only Catholic Church, all your peoples and all your flocks. Provide the peace, which is from heaven in all our hearts, and grant us the peace of this life. The . . . of the land peaceful things towards us, and towards your [holy] name, the prefect of the province, the army, the princes, councils . . . (*almost one-third of a page is lacking here, and what survives is in places too fragmentary to be restored.*)

[For seedtime and] harvests . . . preserve, for the poor of [your] people, for all of us who call upon [your] name, for all who hope in you. Give rest to the souls of those who have fallen asleep; remember those of whom we make mention today, both those whose names we say [and] whose we do not say. . . . [Remember] our orthodox fathers and bishops everywhere; and grant to us to have a part and a lot with the fair . . . of your holy prophets, apostles, and martyrs. Receive (?)

[through] their entreaties [these prayers]; grant them through our Lord; through whom be glory to you to the ages of ages.

NORTH AFRICA

Tertullian

Tertullian provides valuable information about developing eucharistic theology and liturgical practice in North Africa.

Tertullian, *Against Marcion* 4, 14, in *ANF* 3:418.

[H]aving taken the bread and given it to His disciples, He made it His own body, by saying, "This is my body," that is the figure (*figura*) of my body. A figure, however, there could not have been, unless there were first a veritable body (*corpus veritatis*).

Tertullian, *De Corona* 3, in *ANF* 3:94.

Then when we are taken up (as new-born children), we taste first of all a mixture of milk and honey, and from that day we refrain from the daily bath for a whole week. We take also, in congregations before daybreak, and from the hand of none but the presidents, the sacrament of the Eucharist, which the Lord both commanded to be eaten at meal-times, and enjoined to be taken by all alike.

Tertullian, *Ad uxorem* 2.5, in *ANF* 4:46.

Shall you escape notice when you sign your bed, (or) your body; when you blow away some impurity? Will you not be thought to be engaged in some work of magic? Will not your husband know what it is which you secretly taste before (taking) any food? And if he knows it to be bread, does he not believe it to be *that* (bread) which it is *said* to be? And will every (husband), ignorant of the reason of these things, simply endure them, without murmuring, without suspicion where it be bread or poison?

Tertullian, *De Oratione* 19, in *ANF* 3:687.

Similarly, too, touching the days of Stations, most think that they must not be present at the sacrificial prayers, on the ground that the Station must be dissolved by reception of the Lord's Body. Does, then, the Eucharist cancel a service devoted to God, or bind it more to God? Will not your Station be more solemn if you have withal stood at God's altar? When the Lord's Body has been received and reserved each point is secured, both the participation of the sacrifice and the discharge of duty. If the "Station" has received its name from the example of military life—for we withal are God's military—of course no gladness or sadness chanting to the camp abolishes the "stations" of the soldiers: for gladness will carry out discipline more willingly, sadness more carefully.

Cyprian

Cyprian of Carthage witnesses to the development and significance of the mixed cup of water and wine in the Eucharist as well as to a developing theology of eucharistic sacrifice related to the death of Christ.

Cyprian, "Letter 62, to Caecilius" (ca. 253), in *ANF* 5:362–63.

13. For because Christ bore us all, in that He also bore our sins, we see that in the water is understood the people, but in the wine is showed the blood of Christ. But when the water is mingled in the cup with wine, the people is made one with Christ, and the assembly of believers is associated and conjoined with Him on whom it believes; which association and conjunction of water and wine is so mingled in the Lord's cup, that the mixture cannot any more be separated. Whence, moreover, nothing can separate the Church—that is, the people established in the Church, faithfully and firmly persevering in that which they have believed—from Christ, in such a way as to prevent their undivided love from always abiding and adhering.

Thus, therefore, in consecrating the cup of the Lord, water alone cannot be offered, even as wine alone cannot be offered. For if any one offer wine only, the blood of Christ is dissociated from us, but if the water be alone, the people are dissociated from Christ; but when both are mingled, and are joined with one another by a close union, there is completed a spiritual and heavenly sacrament. Thus the cup of the Lord is not indeed water alone, nor wine alone, unless each be mingled with the other, just as, on the other hand, the body of the Lord cannot be flour alone or water alone, unless both should be united and joined together and compacted in the mass of one bread; in which very sacrament our people are shown to be made one, so that in like manner as many grains, collected, and ground, and mixed together into one mass, make one bread; so in Christ, who is the heavenly bread, we may know that there is one body, with which our number is joined and united.

14. There is then no reason, dearest brother, for any one to think that the custom of certain persons is to be followed, who have thought in the past that water alone should be offered in the cup of the Lord. For we must inquire whom they themselves have followed. For if in the sacrifice which Christ offered none is to be followed but Christ, assuredly it behooves us to obey and do that which Christ did, and what He commanded to be done, since He Himself says in the Gospel, "If ye do whatsoever I command you, henceforth I call you not servants, but friends." . . . Wherefore, if Christ alone must be heard, we ought not to give heed to what another before us may have thought was to be done, but what Christ, who is before all, first did. . . . But if we may not break even the least of the Lord's commandments, how much rather is it forbidden to infringe such important ones, so great, so pertaining to the very sacrament of our Lord's passion and our own redemption, or to change it by human tradition into anything else than what was divinely appointed! For if Jesus Christ, our Lord and God, is Himself the chief priest of God the Father, and has first offered Himself a sacrifice to the Father, and has commanded this to be done in commemoration of Himself, certainly that priest truly discharges the office of Christ, who imitates that which Christ did; and he then offers a true and full sacrifice in the Church to God the Father, when he proceeds to offer it according to what he sees Christ Himself to have offered.

16. Does any one perchance flatter himself with this notion, that although in the morning, water alone is seen to be offered, yet when we come to supper we offer the mingled cup? But when we sup, we cannot call the people together to our banquet, so as to celebrate the truth of the sacrament in the presence of all the brotherhood. But still it was not in the morning, but after supper, that the Lord offered the mingled cup. Ought we then to celebrate the Lord's cup after supper, that so by continual repetition of the Lord's supper we may offer the mingled cup? It behooved Christ to offer about the evening of the day, that the very hour of sacrifice might show the setting and the evening of the world; as it is written in Exodus, "And all the people of the synagogue of the children of Israel shall kill it in the evening." And again in the Psalms, "Let the lifting up of my hands be an evening sacrifice." But we celebrate the resurrection of the Lord in the morning.

17. And because we make mention of His passion in all sacrifices (for the Lord's passion is the sacrifice which we offer), we ought to do nothing else than what He did. For Scripture says, "For as often as ye eat this bread and drink this cup, ye do show forth the Lord's death till He come." As often, therefore, as we offer the cup in commemoration of the Lord and of His passion, let us do what it is known

the Lord did. And let this conclusion be reached, dearest brother: if from among our predecessors any have either by ignorance or simplicity not observed and kept this which the Lord by His example and teaching has instructed us to do, he may, by the mercy of the Lord, have pardon granted to his simplicity. But we cannot be pardoned who are now admonished and instructed by the Lord to offer the cup of the Lord mingled with wine according to what the Lord offered, and to direct letters to our colleagues also about this, so that the evangelical law and the Lord's tradition may be everywhere kept, and there be no departure from what Christ both taught and did.

GAUL

Irenaeus of Lyons

Irenaeus directs attention to how, through the reception of the Word of God, the bread and wine of the Eucharist become the body and blood of Christ.

Irenaeus of Lyons, *Adversus Haereses*, 4, 17, 5, and 4, 18, 5, in *ANF* 1:486.

4, 17, 5. Again, giving directions to His disciples to offer to God the first-fruits of His own, created things—not as if He stood in need of them, but that they might be themselves neither unfruitful nor ungrateful—He took that created thing, bread, and gave thanks, and said, "This is My body." And the cup likewise, which is part of that creation to which we belong, He confessed to be His blood, and taught the new oblation of the new covenant; which the Church receiving from the apostles, offers to God throughout all the world, to Him who gives us as the means of subsistence the first-fruits of His own gifts in the New Testament, concerning which Malachi, among the twelve prophets, thus spoke beforehand: "I have no pleasure in you, saith the Lord Omnipotent, and I will not accept sacrifice at your hands. For from the rising of the sun, unto the going down [of the same], My name is glorified among the Gentiles, and in every place incense is offered to My name, and a pure sacrifice; for great is My name among the Gentiles, saith the Lord Omnipotent;"—indicating in the plainest manner, by these words, that the former people [the Jews] shall indeed cease to make offerings to God, but that in every place sacrifice shall be offered to Him, and that a pure one; and His name is glorified among the Gentiles.

4, 18, 5. When, therefore, the mingled cup and the manufactured bread receives the Word of God . . . the Eucharist becomes the body and blood of Christ. . . . For as bread from the earth, receiving the invocation of God is no longer common bread but a Eucharist composed of two things, both an earthly and a heavenly one, so also our bodies, partaking of the Eucharist, are no longer corruptible, having the hope of eternal resurrection.

ROME

The Anaphora of *The Apostolic Tradition*

While there may be sections of this prayer that are quite early, the final form is most likely no earlier than the mid- to late fourth century, and so one should be quite cautious about assuming that it is a third-century prayer, or that it represents the liturgical tradition of Rome. It appears here only because traditional scholarship has tended to place it here chronologically and geographically.

The Anaphora of *The Apostolic Tradition*, IV, XXI, trans. Geoffrey J. Cuming, in *Hippolytus: A Text for Students* (Bramcote, Notts.: Grove Books, 1976), 10–11, 21–22.

The Ordination of a Bishop
4. And when he has been made bishop, all shall offer the kiss of peace, greeting him because he has been made worthy. Then the deacons shall present the offering to him; and he, laying his hands on it with all the presbytery, shall give thanks, saying: The Lord be with you; and all shall say: And with your spirit.

Up with your hearts.
We have them with the Lord.
Let us give thanks to the Lord.
It is fitting and right.

And then he shall continue thus: We render thanks to you, O God, through your beloved child Jesus Christ, whom in the last times you sent to us a saviour and redeemer and angel of your will; who is your inseparable Word, through whom you made all things, and in whom you were well pleased. You sent him from heaven into the Virgin's womb; and, conceived in the womb, he was made flesh and was manifested as your Son, being born of the holy Spirit and the Virgin. Fulfilling your will and gaining for you a holy people, he stretched out his hands when he should suffer, that he might release from suffering those who have believed in you.

And when he was betrayed to voluntary suffering that he might destroy death, and break the bonds of the devil, and tread down hell, and shine upon the righteous, and fix a term, and manifest the resurrection, he took bread and gave thanks to you, saying, "Take, eat; this is my body, which shall be broken for you." Likewise also the cup, saying, "This is my blood, which is shed for you; when you do this, you make my remembrance."

Remembering therefore his death and resurrection, we offer to you the bread and the cup, giving you thanks because you have held us worthy to stand before you and minister to you. And we ask that you would send your holy Spirit upon the offering of your holy Church; that, gathering (it) into one, you would grant to all who partake of the holy things (to partake) for the fullness of the holy Spirit for the strengthening of faith in truth, that we may praise and glorify you through your child Jesus Christ, through whom be glory and honour to you with the holy Spirit, in your holy Church, both now and to the ages of ages. Amen.

The Conferring of Holy Baptism
[follows immediately after material on p. 117]
21. And then the offering shall be presented by the deacons to the bishop; and he shall give thanks over the bread for the representation, which the Greeks call "antitype" [*antitypum*], of the body of Christ; and over the cup mixed with wine for the antitype, which the Greeks call "likeness" [*similitudinem*], of the blood which was shed for all who have believed in him; and over milk and honey mixed together in fulfillment of the promise which was made to the fathers, in which he said, "a land flowing with milk and honey," in which also Christ gave his flesh, through which those who believe are nourished like little children, making the bitterness of the heart sweet by the gentleness of his word; and over water, as an offering to signify the washing, that the inner man also, which is the soul, may receive the same things as the body. And the bishop shall give a reason for all these things to those who receive.

And when he breaks the bread, in distributing fragments to each, he shall say: The bread of heaven in Christ Jesus.

And he who receives shall answer: Amen.

And if there are not enough presbyters, the deacons also shall hold the cups, and stand by in good order and reverence: first, he who holds the water; second, the milk; third, the wine. And they who receive shall taste of each thrice, he who gives it saying: In God the Father almighty.

And he who receives shall say: Amen.

And in the Lord Jesus Christ.

(Amen).

And in the holy Spirit and the holy Church.

And he shall say: Amen.

So shall it be done with each one.

When these things have been done, each one shall hasten to do good works and to please God and to conduct himself rightly, being zealous for the Church, doing what he has learnt and advancing in piety.

The Fourth, Fifth, and Sixth Centuries

ANTIOCHIA

The Anaphora of Sts. Addai and Mari

One of the characteristics of this classic, possibly third-century eucharistic prayer, still used by the Ancient Church of the East today in Iraq, Iran, and around the world, is the absence of the words of Christ, the institution narrative.

> *The Anaphora of Sts. Addai and Mari*, trans. adapted from *PEER*, 42–44.

Priest: Peace be with you.
Answer: And with you and your spirit.
Priest: The grace of our Lord . . .
Answer: Amen.
Priest: Up with your minds.
Answer: They are with you, O God.
Priest: The offering is offered to God, the Lord of all.
Answer: It is fitting and right.
The priest . . . : Worthy of glory from every mouth and thanksgiving from every tongue is the adorable and glorious name of the Father and of the Son and of the Holy Spirit. He created the world through his grace and its inhabitants in his compassion; he saved people through his mercy, and gave great grace to mortals.

Your majesty, O Lord, a thousand thousand heavenly beings adore; myriad myriads of angels, and ranks of spiritual beings, seraphim, glorify your name, crying out and glorifying . . . :
People: Holy, holy . . .
The priest . . . : And with these heavenly armies we, also, even we, your lowly, weak, and miserable servants, Lord, give you thanks because you have brought about us a great grace which cannot be

repaid. For you put on our human nature to give us life through your divine nature; you raised us from our lowly state; you restored our Fall; you restored our immortality; you forgave our debts; you justified our sinfulness; you enlightened our intelligence. You, our Lord and our God, conquered our enemies, and made the lowliness of our weak nature to triumph through the abundant mercy of your grace. . . . You, Lord, through your many mercies which cannot be told, be graciously mindful of all the pious and righteous Fathers who were pleasing in your sight, in the commemoration of the body and blood of your Christ, which we offer to you on the pure and holy altar, as you taught us.

And grant us your tranquility and your peace for all the days of this age. . . . That all the inhabitants of the earth may know you, that you sent our Lord Jesus Christ, your beloved Son, and he, our Lord and our God, taught us through his life-giving gospel all the purity and holiness of the prophets, apostles, martyrs, confessors, bishops, priests, deacons, and all children of the holy Catholic Church who have been sealed with the living seal of holy baptism. And we also, Lord, (*thrice*) your lowly, weak, and miserable servants, who have gathered and stand before you, [and] have received through tradition the form which is from you, rejoicing, exalting, commemorating, and celebrating this mystery of the passion, death and resurrection of our Lord Jesus Christ.

May your Holy Spirit, Lord, come and rest on this offering of your servants, and bless and sanctify it, that it may be to us, Lord, for remission of debts, forgiveness of sins, and the great hope of resurrection from the dead, and new life in the kingdom of heaven, with all who have been pleasing in your sight.

And because of all your wonderful dispensation towards us, with open mouths and uncovered faces we give you thanks and glorify you without ceasing in your Church, which has been redeemed by the precious blood of your Christ.

Apostolic Constitutions

This document shows the further development of the prayers in *The Didache* (see pp. 182–83) toward a more explicit celebration of the Eucharist.

Apostolic Constitutions, 7:25–26 (ca. 381), in *ANF* 7:470.

Concerning the eucharistical thanksgiving say thus:

We thank Thee, our Father, for that life which Thou hast made known to us by Jesus Thy Son, by whom Thou madest all things, and takest care of the whole world; whom Thou hast sent to become man for our salvation; whom Thou hast permitted to suffer and to die; whom Thou hast raised up, and been pleased to glorify, and hast set Him down on Thy right hand; by whom Thou hast promised us the resurrection of the dead. Do thou, O Lord Almighty, everlasting God, so gather together Thy Church from the ends of the earth into Thy kingdom, as this corn was once scattered, and is now become one loaf. We also, our Father, thank Thee for the precious blood of Jesus Christ, which was shed for us and for His precious body, whereof we celebrate this representation, as Himself appointed us, "to show forth His death." For through Him glory is to be given to Thee for ever. Amen. Let no one eat of these things that is not initiated; but those only who have been baptized into the death of the Lord. But if any one that is not initiated conceal himself, and partake of the same, "he eats eternal damnation;" because, being not of the faith of Christ, he has partaken of such things as it is not lawful for him to partake of, to his own punishment. But if any one is a partaker through ignorance, instruct him quickly, and initiate him, that he may not go out and despise you.

A Thanksgiving at the Divine Participation.

XXVI. After the participation, give thanks in this manner:

We thank thee, O God and Father of Jesus our Saviour, for Thy holy name, which Thou hast made to inhabit among us; and that knowledge, faith, love, and immortality which Thou hast given us through Thy Son Jesus. Thou, O Almighty Lord, the God of the universe, hast created the world, and the things that are therein, by Him; and hast planted a law in our souls, and beforehand didst prepare things for the convenience of men. O God of our holy and blameless fathers, Abraham, and Isaac, and Jacob, Thy faithful servants; Thou, O God, who art powerful, faithful, and true, and without deceit in Thy promises; who didst send upon earth Jesus Thy Christ to live with men, as a man, when He was God the Word, and man, to take away error by the roots: do Thou even now, through Him, be mindful of this Thy holy Church, which Thou hast purchased with the precious blood of Thy Christ, and deliver it from all evil, and perfect it in Thy love and Thy truth, and gather us all together into Thy kingdom which Thou hast prepared. Let this Thy kingdom come. "Hosanna to the Son of David. Blessed be He that cometh in the name of the Lord"—God the Lord, who was manifested to us in the flesh. If any one be holy, let him draw near; but if any one be not such, let him become such by repentance. Permit also to your presbyters to give thanks.

The Anaphora of St. John Chrysostom

This is the final version of a eucharistic prayer brought from Antioch to Constantinople and quite likely edited by John Chrysostom himself. It is used today regularly in the Byzantine Rite outside of Lent.

The Anaphora of St. John Chrysostom, in PEER, 131–34.

The priest says: The grace of our Lord Jesus Christ, and the love of the God and Father, and the fellowship of the Holy Spirit be with you all.

People: And with your spirit.

Priest: Let us lift up our hearts.

People: We have them with the Lord.

Priest: Let us give thanks to the Lord.

People: It is fitting and right <to worship the Father, the Son, and the Holy Spirit, the consubstantial and undivided Trinity>.

The priest begins the holy anaphora: It is fitting and right to hymn you, <to bless you, to praise you,> to give you thanks, to worship you in all places of your dominion. For you are God, ineffable, inconceivable, invisible, incomprehensible, existing always and in the same way, you and your only-begotten Son and Your Holy Spirit. You brought us out of non-existence into existence; and when we had fallen, you raised us up again, and did not cease to do everything until you had brought us up to heaven, and granted us the kingdom that is to come. For all these things we give thanks to you and to your only-begotten Son and to your Holy Spirit, for all that we know and do not know, your seen and unseen benefits that have come upon us.

We give you thanks also for this ministry; vouchsafe to receive it from our hands, even though thousands of archangels and ten thousands of angels stand before you, cherubim and seraphim, with six wings and many eyes, flying on high, *(aloud)* singing the triumphal hymn <proclaiming, crying, and saying>:

People: Holy, <holy, holy, Lord of Sabaoth; heaven and earth are full of your glory. Hosanna in the highest. Blessed is he who comes in the name of the Lord. Hosanna in the highest>.

The priest, privately: With these powers, Master, lover of man, we also cry and say: holy are you and all-holy, and your only-begotten Son, and your Holy Spirit; holy are you and all-holy and magnificent is your glory; for you so loved the world that you gave your only-begotten Son that all who believe in him may not perish, but have eternal life.

When he had come and fulfilled all the dispensation for us, on the night in which he handed himself over, he took bread in his holy and undefiled and blameless hands, gave thanks, blessed, broke, and gave it to his holy disciples and apostles, saying, *(aloud)* "Take, eat; this is my body, which is <broken> for you <for forgiveness of sins." *People:* Amen>. <*privately*> Likewise the cup also after supper, saying, *(aloud)* "Drink from this, all of you; this is my blood of the new covenant, which is shed for you and for many for the forgiveness of sins."

People: Amen.

The priest, privately: We therefore, remembering this saving commandment and all the things that were done for us: the cross, the tomb, the resurrection on the third day, the ascension into heaven, the session at the right hand, the second and glorious coming again; *(aloud)* offering you your own from your own, in all and for all,

People: we hymn you, <we bless you, we give you thanks, Lord, and pray to you, our God>.

The priest says *privately:* We offer you also this reasonable and bloodless service, and we pray and beseech and entreat you, send down your Holy Spirit on us and on these gifts set forth; and make this bread the precious body of your Christ, [changing it by your Holy Spirit] Amen; and that which is in this cup the precious blood of your Christ, changing it by your Holy Spirit, Amen; so that they may become to those who partake for vigilance of soul, for fellowship with the Holy Spirit, for the fullness of the kingdom (of heaven), for boldness toward you, not for judgement or condemnation.

We offer you this reasonable service also for those who rest in faith, <forefathers,> Fathers, patriarchs, prophets, apostles, preachers, evangelists, martyrs, confessors, ascetics, and all the righteous <spirits> perfected in faith; *(aloud)* especially our all-holy, immaculate, highly glorious, Blessed Lady, Mother of God and ever-Virgin Mary; <*diptychs of the dead;*> Saint John the <prophet,> forerunner, and Baptist, and the holy, <glorious,> and honored Apostles; and this saint whose memorial we are keeping; and all your saints: at their entreaties, look on us, O God.

And remember all those who have fallen asleep in hope of resurrection to eternal life, <*he remembers them by name*> and grant them rest where the light of your own countenance looks upon them.

Again we beseech you, remember, Lord, all the orthodox episcopate who rightly divide the word of your truth, all the priesthood, the diaconate in Christ, and every order of the clergy.

We offer you this reasonable service also for the (whole) world, for the holy, catholic, and apostolic Church, for those who live in a chaste and reverend state, [for those in mountains and in dens and in caves of the earth,] for the most faithful Emperor, the Christ-loving Empress, and all their court and army: grant them, Lord, a peaceful reign, that in their peace we may live a quiet and peaceful life in all godliness and honesty.

Remember, Lord, the city in which we dwell, and all cities and lands, and all who dwell in them in faith.

(aloud) Above all, remember, Lord, our Archbishop N.

<Diptychs of the living.>

Remember, Lord, those at sea, travellers, the sick, those in adversity, prisoners, and their salvation.

Remember, Lord, those who bring forth fruit and do good works in your holy churches and remember the poor; and send out your mercies upon us all, *(aloud)* and grant us with one mouth and one heart to glorify and hymn your all-honorable and magnificent name, the Father, the Son, and the Holy Spirit, <now and always and to the ages of ages>.

People: Amen.

JERUSALEM

Cyril [or John] of Jerusalem

The Mystagogical Catecheses offer a theology of the Eucharist consecrated in relationship to an explicit epiclesis (invocation) of the Holy Spirit and an outline of its celebration in late-fourth-century Jerusalem. Of particular interest is the fact that in this time period the Jerusalem liturgy may not yet have included the words of institution in its eucharistic praying. The description of the eucharistic prayer here will be replaced eventually in Jerusalem by the prayer known as St. James, the name given to the entire Jerusalem liturgy in subsequent history.

Cyril [or John] of Jerusalem, *Mystagogical Catecheses* (ca. 380 or later), trans. R. W. Church, in *St. Cyril of Jerusalem's Lectures on the Christian Sacraments*, ed. Frank Leslie Cross (London: SPCK, 1951), 68, 73–75, 78–79.

IV. 3. Therefore with fullest assurance let us partake as of the Body and Blood of Christ: for in the figure [*typōs*] of Bread is given to thee His Body, and. in the figure [*typōs*] of Wine His Blood; that thou by partaking of the Body and Blood of Christ, mightest be made of the same body and the same blood with Him. For thus we come to bear Christ in us, because His Body and Blood are diffused through our members; thus it is that, according to the blessed Peter, "we become partakers of the divine nature" [2 Pet. 1:4]. . . .

V. 4. . . . The Priest cries aloud, LIFT UP YOUR HEARTS. For truly ought we in that most awful hour to have our heart on high with God. . . . Then ye answer, WE LIFT THEM UP UNTO THE LORD: assenting to him, by your avowal. . . .

5. Then the Priest says, LET US GIVE THANKS TO THE LORD. . . . Then ye say, IT IS MEET AND RIGHT . . . .

6. After this we make mention of heaven, and earth, and sea; of the sun and moon; of the stars and all the creation, rational and irrational, visible and invisible; of Angels, Archangels, Virtues, Dominions, Principalities, Powers, Thrones; of the Cherubim with many faces. . . . We make mention also of the Seraphim, whom Esias by the Holy Ghost beheld encircling the throne of God, and with two of their wings veiling their countenance,[2] and with two their feet, and with two flying, who cried, HOLY, HOLY, HOLY, LORD GOD OF SABAOTH. . . .

7. Then having sanctified ourselves by these spiritual Hymns, we call upon the merciful God to send forth His Holy Spirit upon the gifts lying before Him; that He may make the Bread the Body of Christ, and the Wine the Blood of Christ; for whatsoever the Holy Ghost has touched is sanctified and changed [*metabeblētai*].

8. Then, after the spiritual sacrifice is perfected, the Bloodless Service upon that Sacrifice of Propitiation, we entreat God for the common peace of the Church, for the tranquility of the world; for kings; for soldiers and allies; for the sick; for the afflicted; and, in a word, for all who stand in need of succour we all supplicate and offer this Sacrifice.

9. Then we commemorate also those who have fallen asleep before us, first, Patriarchs, Prophets, Apostles, Martyrs, that their prayers and intervention God would receive our petition. Afterwards also on behalf of the holy Fathers and Bishops who have fallen asleep before us, and in a word of all who in past years have fallen asleep among us. . . .

11. Then, after these things, we say that Prayer which our Saviour delievered to His own disciples, with a pure conscience styling God our Father, and saying, OUR FATHER WHICH ART IN HEAVEN. . . .

20. After this ye hear the chanter, with a sacred melody inviting you to the communion of the Holy Mysteries, and saying, "O taste and see that the Lord is good" [Ps. 34:8]. Trust not the decision to thy bodily palate; no, but to faith unfaltering; for when we taste we are bidden to taste, not bread and wine, but the sign [*antitypon*] of the Body and Blood of Christ.

---

2. The Greek word here is *prosōpon*, singular for "face" or "countenance." Church's translation incorrectly renders this as a plural, "countenances." I have corrected the translation accordingly.

21. Approaching, therefore, come not with thy wrists extended, or thy fingers open; but make thy left hand as if a throne for thy right, which is on the eve of receiving the King. And having hollowed thy palm, receive the Body of Christ, saying after it, Amen.

EGYPT

Bishop Sarapion of Thmuis

Sarapion witnesses to a theology of consecration by the Logos and provides an early example of one type of eucharistic prayer where the Sanctus and epiclesis are closely united. The bread and cup words separated by the quotation from *The Didache* 9 may provide a clue as to how the words of institution became attached to eucharistic praying in Egypt. See also pp. 189–90 for a similar prayer structure, though without the explicit words of institution.

"Prayer of Offering of Bishop Sarapion of Thmuis" (ca. 350), trans. Maxwell E. Johnson, in *The Prayers of Sarapion of Thmuis: A Literary, Liturgical, and Theological Analysis*, OCA 249 (Rome: Pontificio Istituto Orientale, 1995), 47–49.

It is right and just to praise, to hymn, to glorify you, the uncreated Father of the only-begotten Jesus Christ. We praise you uncreated God, incomprehensible, inexpressible, inconceivable to every created substance. We praise you who are known by the only-begotten Son, who through him was spoken and interpreted and made known to created nature. We praise you who know the Son and who reveal to the saints the glories concerning him; you who are known by your begotten Word and known and interpreted to the saints. We praise you, invisible Father, provider of immortality. You are the source of life, the source of light, the source of all grace and truth. Lover of humanity and lover of the poor, you are reconciled to all and draw all to yourself through the coming of your beloved Son.

We pray, make us living people. Give us spirit of light, in order that we may know you the true (God) and Jesus Christ whom you sent. Give us holy Spirit, in order that we may be able to proclaim and describe your inexpressible mysteries. Let the Lord Jesus speak in us and let holy Spirit hymn you through us.

For you are above all rule and authority and power and dominion and every name being named, not only in this age but also in the coming one. Beside you stand a thousand thousands and a myriad myriads of angels, archangels, thrones, dominions, principalities, and powers. Beside you stand the two most-honored six-winged seraphim. With two wings they cover the face, and with two the feet, and with two they fly; sanctifying. With them receive also our sanctification as we say: Holy, holy, holy Lord of Sabaoth; heaven and earth are full of your glory.

Full is heaven and full also is the earth of your majestic glory, Lord of powers. Fill also this sacrifice with your power and with your participation. For to you we offered this living sacrifice, the unbloody offering. To you we offered this bread, the likeness (*homoiōma*) of the body of the only-begotten. This bread is the likeness (*homoiōma*) of the holy body.

For the Lord Jesus Christ, in the night when he was handed over, took bread, broke it, and gave it to his disciples saying: Take and eat, this is my body which is broken for you for the forgiveness of sins. Therefore we also offered the bread making the likeness (*homoiōma*) of the death.

And we implore you through this sacrifice, God of truth; be reconciled to us all and be merciful. And as this bread was scattered over the mountains and, when it was gathered together, became one, so also gather your holy church out of every nation and every region and every city and village and house, and make one living catholic church.

And we also offered the cup, the likeness (*homoiōma*) of the blood. For the Lord Jesus Christ, taking a cup after supper, said to the disciples: take, drink, this is the new covenant, which is my blood poured out for you for the forgiveness of sins. Therefore, we also offered the cup presenting the likeness (*homoiōma*) of blood.

God of truth, let your holy Word come upon this bread in order that the bread may become body of the Word, and upon this cup in order that the cup may become blood of truth. And make all those who partake to receive a medicine of life for the healing of every illness, and for the strengthening of every advancement and virtue, not for condemnation, God of truth, not for testing and reproach.

For we called upon you, the uncreated, through the only-begotten in holy Spirit. Let this people receive mercy. Let them be made worth of advancement. Let angels be present with them for abolishing evil and for establishing the church. And we call out also for all who have fallen asleep, for whom also the memorial (*anamnēsis*) is made. **After the Announcement of the Names:** Sanctify these souls for you know them all. Sanctify all who have fallen asleep in the Lord. Number them with all your holy powers, and give them a place and mansion in your kingdom. And receive also the thanksgiving (*eucharistia*) of the people and bless those who offer their offerings and thanksgivings. Give to this entire people health, wholeness, cheerfulness, and every advancement of soul and body.

Through your only-begotten Jesus Christ in holy Spirit. As it was and is and will be to generations of generations and to all the ages of ages. Amen.

Basil

This early eucharistic prayer was revised to become one of the two major eucharistic prayers of the Byzantine Rite (the other being that of St. John Chrysostom), probably edited in its final form by Basil of Caesarea itself. Still used by the Coptic Orthodox Church today, "Egyptian Basil," as it is sometimes called, is used also by several Protestant churches today and is the model for Eucharistic Prayer IV in the modern Roman Rite.

The Egyptian Anaphora of St. Basil (early fourth century), in *PEER*, 70–72.

The bishop: The Lord be with you all.
People: And with your spirit.
Bishop: Let us lift up our hearts.
People: We have them with the Lord.
Bishop: Let us give thanks to the Lord.
People: It is fitting and right.
Bishop: It is fitting and right, fitting and right, truly it is fitting and right, I AM, truly Lord God, existing before the ages, reigning until the ages; you dwell on high and regard what is low; you made heaven and earth and the sea and all that is in them. Father of our Lord and God and Savior Jesus Christ, through whom you made all things visible and invisible, you sit on the throne of your glory; you are adored by every holy power. Around you stand angels and archangels, principalities and powers, thrones, dominions, and virtues; around you stand the cherubim with many eyes and the seraphim with six wings, forever singing the hymn of glory and saying:
People: Holy, holy, holy Lord (etc.)
Bishop: Holy, holy, holy you are indeed, Lord our God. You formed us and placed us in the paradise of pleasure; and when we had transgressed your commandment through the deceit of the serpent, and had fallen from eternal life, and had been banished from the paradise of pleasure, you did not cast us off for ever, but continually made promises to us through your holy prophets; and in these last days you manifested to us who sat in darkness and the shadow of death your only-begotten Son, our Lord and God and Savior, Jesus Christ. He was made flesh of the Holy Spirit and of the holy Virgin Mary, and became man; he showed us the ways of salvation, granted

us to be reborn from above by water and the Spirit, and made us a people for [his] own possession, sanctifying us by his Holy Spirit. He loved his own who were in the world, and gave himself for our salvation to death who reigned over us and held us down because of our sins.

. . . by his blood [The earliest Coptic text begins here]. From the cross he descended into hell and rose from the dead and the third day, he ascended into heaven and sat at the right hand of the Father; he appointed a day on which to judge the world with justice and render to each according to his works.

And he left us this great mystery of godliness for when he was about to hand himself over to death for the life of the world, he took bread, blessed, sanctified, broke, and gave it to his holy disciples and apostles, saying, "Take and eat from this, all of you; this is my body, which is given for you and for many for forgiveness of your sins. Do this for my remembrance."

Likewise also the cup after supper: he mixed wine and water, blessed, sanctified, gave thanks, and again gave it to them, saying, "Take and drink from it, all of you; this is my blood which shall be shed for you and for many for the forgiveness of your sins. Do this for my remembrance. For as often as you eat this bread and drink this cup, you proclaim my death until I come."

We therefore, remembering his holy sufferings, and his resurrection from the dead, and his ascension into heaven, and his session at the right hand of the Father, and his glorious and fearful coming to us (again), have set forth before you your own from your own gifts, this bread and cup. And we, sinners and unworthy and wretched, pray you, our God, in adoration that in the good pleasure of your goodness your Holy Spirit may descend upon us and upon these gifts that have been set before you, and may sanctify and make them holy of holies.[3]

Make us all worthy to partake of your holy things for sanctification of soul and body, that we may become one body and one spirit, and may have our portion with all the saints who have been pleasing to you from eternity.

---

3. The final version of this prayer, "Byzantine Basil," has this instead: "And having set for the likenesses of the holy body and blood of your Christ, we pray and beseech you, O holy of holies, in the good pleasure of your bounty, that your [all-]Holy Spirit may come upon us and upon these gifts set forth, and bless them and sanctify and make (*he signs the holy gifts with the cross three times, saying:*) this bread the precious body of our Lord and God and Savior Jesus Christ. Amen. And this cup the precious blood of our Lord and God and Savior Jesus Christ, [Amen.] which is shed for the life of the world <and salvation> Amen <*thrice*>" (PEER, 119–20).

Remember, Lord, also your one, holy, catholic, and apostolic Church; give it peace, for you purchased it with the precious blood of Christ; and (remember) all the orthodox bishops in it.

Remember first of all your servant Archbishop Benjamin and his colleague in the ministry holy Bishop Colluthus, and all who with him dispense the word of truth; grant them to feed the holy churches, your orthodox flocks, in peace.

Remember, Lord, the priests and all the deacons who assist, all those in virginity and chastity, and all your faithful people; and have mercy on them all.

Remember, Lord, also this place, and those who live in it in the faith of God.

Remember, Lord, also mildness of climate and the fruits of the earth.

Remember, Lord, those who offer these gifts to you, and those for whom they offered them; and grant them all a heavenly reward.

Since, Master, it is a command of your only-begotten Son that we should share in the commemoration of your saints, vouchsafe to remember, Lord, those of our fathers who have been pleasing to you from eternity: patriarchs, prophets, apostles, martyrs, confessors, preachers, evangelists, and all the righteous perfected in faith; especially at all times the holy and glorious Mary, Mother of God; and by her prayers have mercy on us all, and save us through your holy name which has been invoked upon us.

Remember likewise all those of the priesthood who have already died, and all those of lay rank; and grant them rest in the bosom of Abraham, Isaac, and Jacob, in green pastures, by waters of comfort, in a place whence grief, sorrow, and sighing have fled away.

(*to the deacon*) Read the names. (*The deacon reads the diptychs.*)

Bishop: Give them rest in your presence; preserve in your faith us who live here, guide us to your kingdom, and grant us your peace at all times; through Jesus Christ and the Holy Spirit.

The Father in the Son, the Son in the Father with the Holy Spirit, in your holy, one, catholic, and apostolic Church.

NORTH ITALY

Ambrose of Milan

Ambrose provides here the first witness to the Roman canon of the Mass (see pp. 212–14) and to a theology of eucharistic consecration by the words of institution recited in the canon.

Ambrose of Milan, *On the Sacraments*, IV, 13–14, 21–27; V, 18;
and VI, 24 (ca. 390), in *PEER*, 144–46.

BOOK 4

13. Who therefore is the author of the sacraments, if not Jesus? Those sacraments came from heaven, for all counsel is from heaven. It was a great and divine miracle that God rained manna on the people from heaven, and the people ate without working for it.

14. Perhaps you will say, "My bread is common (bread)." But that bread is bread before the words of the sacraments; when consecration has been applied, from (being) bread it becomes the flesh of Christ. So let us explain how that which is bread can be the body of Christ. And by what words and by whose sayings does consecration take place? The Lord Jesus'. For all the other things which are said in the earlier parts are said by the bishop:[4] praise is offered to God; prayer is made for the people, for kings, for others; when the time comes for the venerated sacrament to be accomplished, the bishop no longer uses his own words, but uses the words of Christ. So the word of Christ accomplishes this sacrament. . . .

21. Do you wish to know how consecration is done with heavenly words? Hear what the words are. The bishop says:

Make for us this offering approved, reasonable, acceptable, because it is the figure of the body and blood of our Lord Jesus Christ; who, the day before he suffered, took bread in his holy hands, looked up to heaven to you, holy Father, almighty, eternal God, gave thanks, blessed, and broke it, and handed it when broken to his apostles and disciples, saying, "Take and eat from this, all of you; for this is my body, which will be broken for many."

22. Notice this. *Likewise after supper, the day before he suffered, he took the cup, looked up to heaven to you, holy Father, almighty, eternal God, gave thanks, blessed, and handed it to his apostles and disciples, saying, "Take and drink from this, all of you; for this is my blood."*

See, all those words up to *"Take,"* whether the body or the blood, are the evangelist's; then they are Christ's words, *"Take and drink from this, all of you; for this is my blood."*

23. Notice these points. He says, *"Who, the day before He suffered, took bread in his holy hands."* Before it is consecrated, it is bread; but when the words of Christ are added, it is the body of Christ. Then hear his words: *"Take and eat from this, all of you; for this is my body."* And before the words of Christ, the cup is full of wine and water; when the words of Christ have been employed, the blood is created which redeems his people. So you see in what ways the word of Christ has power to change everything. Our Lord Jesus himself

---

4. Latin: *sacerdos.*

therefore bore witness that we should receive his body and blood.
Ought we to doubt his faith and witness? . . .

25. So you do not say *"Amen"* to no purpose: you confess in spirit
that you are receiving the body of Christ. When you seek it, the
bishop says to you, *"The body of Christ,"* and you say, *"Amen,"* which
means *"It is true."* What your tongue confesses, let your feelings
retain, so that you may know that this is a sacrament whose likeness
has come first.

26. Next, you must learn how great a sacrament it is. See what he
says: *"As often as you do this, so often you will make remembrance of
me until I come again."*

27. And the bishop says:

*Therefore, remembering his most glorious Passion and resurrection
from the dead, and ascension into heaven, we offer to you this spotless
victim, reasonable victim, bloodless victim, this holy bread and this
cup of eternal life; and we pray and beseech you to receive this offering
on your altar on high by the hands of your angels, as you vouchsafed
to receive the gifts of your righteous servant Abel, and the sacrifice of
our patriarch Abraham, and that which the high priest Melchizedek
offered to you.*

BOOK 5
18. Now what is left but the (Lord's) Prayer? . . .

BOOK 6
24. . . . What follows? Hear what the bishop says:
*Through our Lord Jesus Christ, in whom and with whom honor, praise,
glory, magnificence, and power are yours, with the Holy Spirit, from
the ages, and now, and always, and to all the ages of ages. Amen.*

NORTH AFRICA

Augustine of Hippo

Augustine's classic theology of the Eucharist focuses on the connection
between the Eucharist and the community that celebrates and receives it.

Augustine of Hippo, *Treatise on the Gospel of St. John*, XXVI
(ca. 416), trans. Darwell Stone, in *A History of the Doctrine of the Holy
Eucharist* (London: Longmans, Green & Co., 1909), 1:93–94.

He explains how it is that what He speaks of happens, and the meaning of eating His Body and drinking His blood. "He that eateth My
flesh and drinketh My blood abideth in Me, and I in Him" [John

6:56]. This then is to eat that food and to drink that drink, to abide in Christ, and to have Him abiding in oneself. And in this way he who does not abide in Christ, and in whom Christ does not abide, without doubt neither eats His flesh nor drinks His blood, but rather to His own judgement eats and drinks the Sacrament of so great a thing.

Augustine of Hippo, *Sermon 272* (ca. 415), trans. Darwell Stone, in
A History of the Doctrine of the Holy Eucharist, 1: 95–96.

If you wish to understand the body of Christ, hear the Apostle speaking to the faithful, "Now ye are the body and members of Christ" [I Cor. 12:27]. If you then are the body and members of Christ, your mystery is laid on the Table of the Lord, your mystery you receive. To that which you are you answer Amen, and in answering you assent. For you hear the words, The body of Christ; and you answer Amen. Be a member of the body of Christ, that the Amen may be true. Wherefore then in the bread? Let us assert nothing of our own here; let us listen to the reiterated teaching of the Apostle, who when he spoke of this Sacrament said, "We who are many are one bread, one body" [I Cor. 10:17]; understand and rejoice; unity, truth, goodness, love. "One bread." What is that one bread? "Many are one body." Remember that the bread is not made from one grain but from many. When ye were exorcised, ye were so to speak ground. When ye were baptized, ye were so to speak sprinkled. When ye received the fire of the Holy Ghost, ye were so to speak cooked. Be what you see, and receive what you are. . . . Many grapes hang on the cluster, but the juice of the grapes is gathered together in unity. So also the Lord Christ signified us, wished us to belong to Him, consecrated on His Table the mystery of our peace and unity.

Augustine of Hippo, *City of God*, Book X (ca. 420), trans. Darwell Stone,
in *A History of the Doctrine of the Holy Eucharist*, 1:123–24.

6. The whole redeemed City itself, that is the congregation and society of the saints, is offered as a universal sacrifice to God by the High Priest, who offered even Himself in suffering for us in the form of a servant, that we might be the body of so great a Head. For this form of a servant did He offer, in this was He offered: for in this is He mediator and priest and sacrifice. And so when the Apostle exhorted us that we should present our bodies a living sacrifice, holy, pleasing to God, our reasonable service [Rom. 12:1] and that we be not conformed to this world but reformed in the newness of our mind, to prove what is the will of God, that which is good and well-pleasing and complete, which whole sacrifice we ourselves are. . . .

This is the sacrifice of Christians: "the many one body in Christ." Which also the Church celebrates in the Sacrament of the altar, familiar to the faithful, where it is shown to her that in this thing which she offers she herself is offered. . . .

Thus is He priest, Himself offering, Himself also that which is offered. Of this thing He willed the sacrifice of the Church to be the daily Sacrament; and the Church, since she is the body of the Head Himself, learns to offer herself through Him.

The Medieval Period

WESTERN (ROMAN) LITURGICAL TEXTS

For pertinent eucharistic texts from the Christian East used in the Middle Ages, see pp. 196–97; 199–201; 205–7.

The Gregorian Sacramentary

The structure of collect (opening prayer), prayer over the offerings, proper preface, and *ad completa* (post-communion prayer), together with occasional festal inserts into the canon, become the regular structure of the Mass of the Roman Rite.

A complete Mass formulary, from *The Gregorian Sacramentary.*
Le Sacramentaire Grégorien: Ses principales formes d'après les plus anciens manuscrits, ed. Jean Deshusses, Spicilegium Friburgense 16 (Fribourg: Éditions Universitaires Fribourg Suisse, 1971), 99–100; trans. Maxwell E. Johnson.

The Eighth of the Calends of January, that is, the Twenty-fifth Day of the Month of December, the Nativity of the Lord at [the Basilica of] Saint Mary Major.

Collect: God, who have made this most holy night shine with the brightness of the true light, grant we pray that, having known the mysteries of this light on earth, we may be filled fully with its joys in heaven. Through [your Son, Jesus Christ our Lord, who lives and reigns with you and the Holy Spirit, one God, for ever and ever. Amen.]

Super Oblata (Prayer over the Offerings): May the offering of today's feast be acceptable to you, Lord, we ask, so that by the abundance of your grace through this holy exchange, we may be found in his form in Whom our substance is [made one] with you. Through our Lord [Jesus Christ, your Son, who lives and reigns with you and the Holy Spirit, one God, for ever and ever. Amen.]

Preface: It is indeed right and just, equitable and salutary . . . : Because by the mystery of the Word made flesh the light of your glory has shown anew on the eyes of our mind, so that while we perceive the God made visible we may be drawn through this to love [the God] who is invisible. And, therefore, with angels and archangels, with thrones and dominations, and with all of the heavenly host, we sing a hymn to your glory, saying without end: Holy, holy, holy.

Communicantes (Special insert into the Roman Canon for Christmas): Being in communion we celebrate that most holy night in which the spotless virginity of Blessed Mary gave birth to a Savior for the world, and we reverently commemorate, in the first place, the same glorious ever-virgin Mary, Mother of our God and Lord Jesus Christ and also the blessed [Apostles].

Ad Completa: Grant to us, Lord our God, that we who rejoice to celebrate the Nativity of our Lord Jesus Christ, may by a right manner of living merit to share his company. Through [our Lord Jesus Christ, your Son, who lives and reigns with you and the Holy Spirit, one God, for ever and ever. Amen.]

The Roman *Canon Missae*

Witnessed as early as Ambrose of Milan in the late fourth century, the Roman Canon became the singly eucharistic prayer of the Roman Rite until the addition of other eucharistic prayers in the Roman Missal of Paul VI (1970).

The Roman *Canon Missae*, in *PEER*, 163–67.

Priest: The Lord be with you.
People: And with your spirit.
Priest: Up with your hearts.
People: We have them with the Lord.
Priest: Let us give thanks to the Lord our God.
People: It is fitting and right.
Priest: *Vere dignum*—It is truly fitting and right, our duty and our salvation, that we should always and everywhere give you thanks, O Lord, holy Father, almighty eternal God, through Christ our Lord; [*Here a passage proper to the occasion may be inserted.*] through

whom angels praise your majesty, dominions adore, powers fear, the heavens and the heavenly hosts and the blessed seraphim, joining together in exultant celebration. We pray you, bid our voices also to be admitted with theirs, beseeching you, confessing, and saying:

People: Holy, holy, holy, Lord God of Sabaoth. Heaven and earth are full of your glory. Hosanna in the highest. Blessed is he who comes in the name of the Lord. Hosanna in the highest.

Priest: *Te igitur*—We therefore pray and beseech you, most merciful Father, through your Son Jesus Christ our Lord, to accept and bless these gifts, these offerings, these holy and unblemished sacrifices; above all, those which we offer to you for your holy catholic Church; vouchsafe to grant it peace, protection, unity, and guidance throughout the world, together with your servant N. our pope, and N. our bishop, and all orthodox upholders of the catholic and apostolic faith.

Memento Domine—Remember, Lord, your servants, men and women, and all who stand around, whose faith and devotion are known to you, for whom we offer to you, or who offer to you this sacrifice of praise for themselves and for all their own, for the redemption of their souls, for the hope of their salvation and safety, and pay their vows to you, the living, true, and eternal God.

Communicantes—In fellowship with *(here a seasonal clause may follow)* and venerating above all the memory of the glorious ever-Virgin Mary, mother of God and our Lord Jesus Christ, and also of your blessed apostles and martyrs Peter, Paul, Andrew, James, John, Thomas, Philip, Bartholomew, Matthew, Simon and Thaddaeus, Linus, Cletus, Clement, Xystus, Cornelius, Cyprian, Laurence, Chrysogonus, John and Paul, Cosmas and Damian, and all your saints; by their merits and prayers grant us to be defended in all things by the help of your protection; through Christ our Lord.

Hanc igitur—Therefore, Lord, we pray you graciously to accept this offering made by us your servants, and also by your whole family; and to order our days in peace; and to command that we are snatched from eternal damnation and numbered among the flock of your elect; through Christ our Lord.

This paragraph varies according to the occasion.
Quam oblationem—Vouchsafe, we beseech you, O God, to make this offering wholly blessed, approved, ratified, reasonable, and acceptable; that it may become to us the body and blood of your dearly beloved Son Jesus Christ our Lord;

Qui pridie—who, on the day before he suffered, took bread in his holy and reverend hands, lifted up his eyes to heaven to you, O God, his almighty father, gave thanks to you, blessed, broke, and gave it to his disciples, saying, "Take and eat from this, all of you; for this is my body." Likewise after supper, taking also this glorious cup in his holy and reverend hands, again he gave thanks to you, blessed and gave it to his disciples, saying, "Take and drink from it, all of you; for this is the cup of my blood, of the new and eternal covenant, the mystery of faith, which will be shed for you and for many for forgiveness of sins. As often as you do this, you will do it for my remembrance."

Unde et memores—Therefore also, Lord, we your servants, and also your holy people, having in remembrance the blessed Passion of your Son Christ our Lord, likewise his resurrection from the dead, and also his glorious ascension into heaven, do offer to your excellent majesty from your gifts and bounty a pure victim, a holy victim, an unspotted victim, the holy bread of eternal life and the cup of everlasting salvation.

Supra quae—Vouchsafe to look upon them with a favorable and kindly countenance, and accept them as you vouchsafed to accept the gifts of your righteous servant Abel, and the sacrifice of our patriarch Abraham, and that which your high priest Melchizedek offered to you, a holy sacrifice, an unblemished victim.

Supplices te—We humbly beseech you, almighty God, bid these things be borne by the hands of your angel to your altar on high, in the sight of your divine majesty, that all of us who have received the most holy body and blood of your Son by partaking at this altar may be filled with all heavenly blessing and grace; through Christ our Lord.

Memento etiam—Remember also, Lord, the names of those who have gone before us with the sign of faith, and sleep in the sleep of peace. We beseech you to grant to them and to all who rest in Christ a place of restoration, light, and peace; through Christ our Lord.

Nobis quoque—To us sinners your servants also, who trust in the multitude of your mercies, vouchsafe to grant some part and fellowship with your holy Apostles and martyrs, with John, Stephen, Matthias, Barnabas, Ignatius, Alexander, Marcellinus, Peter, Felicity, Perpetua, Agatha, Lucy, Agnes, Cecilia, Anastasia, and all your saints: into whose company we ask that you will admit us, not weighing our merit, but bounteously forgiving; through Christ our Lord.

Here a blessing may follow.
Per quem—Through him, Lord, you ever create, sanctify, quicken, bless, and bestow all these good things upon us. Through him and with him and in him all honor and glory is yours, O God the Father almighty, in the unity of the Holy Spirit, through all the ages of ages. Amen.

Ordo Romanus I

This ordo, giving directions on how to celebrate the Roman eucharistic liturgy, describes a papal liturgy at Rome in the early Middle Ages. Apart from the several papal ceremonies, it is very similar to the Mass in the Roman Missal of Paul VI (1970). The following selection provides only the eucharistic portion of the rite. For the Liturgy of the Word, see pp. 254–56.

Ordo Romanus I, VIII–XXI (ca. 700), trans. E. G. Cuthbert F. Atchley (London: De La More Press, 1905), 129–33, 135, 137, 139, 141, 143, 145, and 147 (altered).

12. The deacon in the meantime returns to the altar, where a collet stands holding a chalice with a corporas lying on it; raising the chalice in his left arm, he offers the corporas to the deacon, who takes it off the chalice and lays it on the right part of the altar, throwing the other end of it over to the second deacon in order to spread it. Then there go up to the throne the chancellor and the secretary, and the chief counsellor, with all the district officials and notaries: but the subdeacon with the empty chalice follows the archdeacon.

[The Offertory.]
13. The pontiff now goes down to the place where the notables sit, the chancellor holding his right hand and the chief counsellor his left: and he receives the loaves of the princes in the order of their "promotion" (?). The archdeacon next receives the flasks of wine, and pours them into the greater chalice which is carried by a district-subdeacon, and a collet follows him holding a bowl outside his planet, into which the chalice when full is emptied. A district-subdeacon takes the loaves from the pontiff and hands them to the subdeacon attendant, who places them in a linen cloth held by two collets. An hebdomadary bishop receives the rest of the loaves after the pontiff, so that he may, with his own hand, put them into the linen cloth which is carried after him. Following him the deacon-attendant receives the flasks of wine, and pours them into the bowl with his own hand, after the archdeacon. Meanwhile the pontiff, before passing over to the women's side, goes down before the Confession, and there receives the loaves of the chancellor, the secretary, and the chief counsellor. For on festivals they offer at the altar after the deacons. In like manner the pontiff goes up to the women's side, and performs there all things in the same order as detailed above. And the presbyters do likewise, should there be need, either after the pontiff or in the presbytery.

[The Lavatory.]

14. After this, the pontiff returns to his throne, the chancellor and the secretary each taking him by the hand, and there washes his hands. The archdeacon stands before the altar and washes his hands at the end of the collection of the offerings. Then he looks the pontiff in the face, signs to him, and, after the pontiff has returned his salutation, approaches the altar.

[The Preparation of the Offering.]

Then the district-subdeacons, taking the loaves from the hand of the subdeacon-attendant, and carrying them in their arms, bring them to the arch-deacon, who arranges them on the altar. The subdeacons, by the bye, bring up the loaves on either side. Having made the altar ready, the archdeacon then takes the pontiff's flask of wine from the subdeacon-oblationer, and pours it through a strainer into the chalice; then the deacons' flasks, and, on festivals, those of the chancellor, the secretary, and the chief counsellor as well. Then the subdeacon-attendant goes down into the choir, receives a ewer of water from the hand of the ruler of the choir and brings it back to the archdeacon, who pours it into the chalice, making a cross as he does so. Then the deacons go up to the pontiff: on seeing which, the chancellor, the secretary; the chief of the district-counsellors *(sic)*, the district-notaries, and the district-counsellors come down from their ranks to stand in their proper places.

[The Offerings of the Clergy.]

15. Then the pontiff, arising from his throne, goes down to the altar and salutes it, and receives the loaves from the hands of the hebdomadary presbyter and the deacons. Then the archdeacon receives the pontiff's loaves from the subdeacon-oblationer, and gives them to the pontiff. And when the latter has placed them on the altar, the archdeacon takes the chalice from the hand of a district-subdeacon and sets it on the altar on the right side of the pontiff's loaf, the offertory-veil being twisted about its handles. Then he lays the veil on the end of the altar, and stands behind the pontiff, and the latter bows slightly to the altar and then turns to the choir and signs to them to stop singing.

16. The offertory being finished, the bishops stand behind the pontiff, the senior in the midst, and the rest in their order; the archdeacon standing on the right of the bishops, the second deacon on their left, and the rest in order arranged in a line. And the district-subdeacons go behind the altar at the end of the offertory and face the pontiff, so that when he says, *For ever and ever,* or, *The Lord be with you,* or, *Lift up your hearts,* or, *Let us give thanks,* they may be there to answer, standing upright, until the time when the choir

begin to sing the angelical hymn, that is, *Holy, holy, holy.* And when
they have finished it, the pontiff rises alone and enters on the canon.

[The Canon.]
The bishops, however, and the deacons, subdeacons, and presbyters
remain in the presbytery, and bow themselves down. Now when the
pontiff says, *To us sinners, also,* the subdeacons rise up, and when he
says, *By whom all these things, O Lord,* the archdeacon arises alone.
When the pontiff says, *By him, and with him,* the archdeacon lifts up
the chalice with the offertory-veil passed through its handles, and,
holding it, raises it towards the pontiff. Then the latter touches the
side of the chalice with the loaves, saying,

[The Sacring.]
By him, and with him, as far as, *For ever and ever. Amen.* Then the
pontiff sets the loaves down again in their place, and the archdeacon
puts the chalice down by them, and removes the offertory-veil from
the handles of the same.

[The removal of the Paten.]
17. We have, by the bye, omitted something about the paten. When
the pontiff begins the canon, a collet comes near, having a linen cloth
thrown around his neck, and holds the paten before his breast on
the right side [of the altar?] until the middle of the canon. Then the
subdeacon-attendant holds it outside his planet, and comes before
the altar, and waits there with it until the district-subdeacon takes
it from him.

18. But at the end of the canon, the district-subdeacon stands
behind the archdeacon with the paten. And when the pontiff says,
And safe from all unquiet, the archdeacon turns round, and after
kissing the paten, takes it and gives it to the second deacon to hold.

[The Sancta; and the Kiss of Peace.]
When the pontiff says, *The peace of the Lord be with you always,*
he makes a cross with his hand thrice over the chalice, and drops a
consecrated fragment [reserved from the last solemn mass] into it.
Meanwhile the archdeacon gives the kiss of peace to the chief hebdomadary bishop, then to the rest of the clergy in order, and then to
the people.

[The Fraction.]
19. Then the pontiff breaks one of the loaves on its right side, and
leaves the fragment which he breaks off upon the altar: but the rest
of his loaves he puts on the paten which the deacon is holding, and
returns to his throne. Immediately the chancellor, the secretary, and

the chief counsellor, with all the district officials and notaries, go up to the altar, and stand in their order on the right and left. [The invitations to breakfast.] The invitationer and the treasurer, and the notary of the papal vicar, when the choir sing *O Lamb of God,* go up and stand facing the pontiff in order that he may sign to them to write down the names of those who are to be invited either to the pontiff's table, by the invitationer, or to the papal vicar's, by his notary: and when the list of names is completed, they go down and deliver the invitations.

The archdeacon now lifts up the chalice and gives it to the district-subdeacon, who holds it near the right corner of the altar. Then the subdeacons-attendant, with the collets, who carry little sacks, draw near to the right and left of the altar: the collets hold out their arms with the little sacks, and the subdeacons-attendant stand in front, in order to make ready the openings of the sacks for the archdeacon to put the loaves into them, first those on the right, and then those on the left. The collets then pass right and left among the bishops around the altar, and the rest [i.e. the subdeacons] go down to the presbyters, in order that they may break the consecrated loaves. [The Fraction continued.] Two district-subdeacons, however, have proceeded to the throne, carrying the paten to the deacons, in order that they may perform the fraction. Meanwhile the latter keep their eyes on the pontiff so that he may sign to them when to begin: and when he has signed to them, after returning the pontiff's salutation, they make the fraction.

The archdeacon, after that the altar has been cleared of the loaves, except the fragment which the pontiff broke off his own loaf and left on the altar (which is done so that, while the solemnities of mass are being celebrated, the altar may never be without a sacrifice), looks at the choir, and signs to them to sing, *O Lamb of God,* and then goes to the paten with the rest. [The Commixture.] The fraction being finished, the second deacon takes the paten from the subdeacon and carries it to the throne to communicate the pontiff: who after partaking, puts a particle which he has bitten off the holy element into the chalice which the archdeacon is holding, making a cross with it thrice, and saying, *May the commixture and consecration of the Body and Blood of our Lord Jesus Christ be to us who receive it for life eternal, Amen. Peace be with thee.* [And he answers] *And with thy spirit.* And then the pontiff is communicated with the chalice by the archdeacon.

[The Communion.]
20. Then the archdeacon comes with the chalice to the corner of the altar, and announces the next station: and after he has poured

a small quantity of the contents of the chalice into the bowl held by the collet, there approach to the throne, so that they may communicate from the pontiff's hand, first the bishops in order, and then the presbyters in like manner, so that they may communicate after them. Then the chief hebdomadary bishop takes the chalice from the hands of the archdeacon, in order to administer the species of wine to the remaining ranks down to the chief counsellor. Then the archdeacon takes the chalice from him, and pours it into the bowl which we mentioned above: he then hands the empty chalice to the district-subdeacon, who gives him the reed wherewith he communicates the people with the species of wine. But the subdeacon-attendant takes the chalice and gives it to the collet, who replaces it in the sacristy. And when the archdeacon has administered the cup to those whom the pope communicated, the pontiff comes down from his throne, with the chancellor and the chief counsellor, who hold his hands, in order to communicate those who are in the places allotted to the magnates, after which the archdeacon communicates them with the cup.

After this the bishops communicate the people, the chancellor signing to them to do so with his hand under his planet, at the pontiff's formal request: and then the deacons administer the cup to them. Next they all pass over to the left side of the church, and do the same there. Moreover, the presbyters, at a sign from the chancellor, by command of the pontiff, communicate the people also, and afterwards administer the cup to them as well.

[The Communion Anthem.] Now as soon as the pontiff began to communicate the magnates, the choir immediately began to sing the communion-anthem by turns with the subdeacons; and they go on singing until, when all the people have communicated, the pontiff signs to them to sing *Glory be to the Father*, and then, after repeating the verse, they cease.

The pontiff, directly after communicating those on the women's side goes back to the throne and communicates the district officials in order, and those who stand in a group, and on festivals twelve of the choir as well. But on other days these communicate in the presbytery. After all these the invitationer, and the treasurer, the collet who holds the paten, he who holds the towel, and he who offers water at the lavatory, communicate at the throne; and after the pontiff has communicated them, the archdeacon administers the cup to them.

21. Then a district-subdeacon stands before the pontiff in order that he may sign to him: but the pontiff first looks at the people to see if they have finished communicating, and then signs to him. Then he goes to the pontiff's shoulder and looks towards the precentor,

making a cross on his forehead as a sign to him to sing *Glory be:* and the precentor returns his salutation, and sings *Glory be to the Father,* etc., *As it was in the beginning,* etc., and the verse. [The Postcommunion.] At the end of the anthem the pontiff rises with the archdeacon and comes before the altar and says the postcommunion collect, facing eastwards. For at this part of the service, when he says, *The Lord be with you,* he does not turn to the people.

[The Dismissal.] At the end of the collect, one of the deacons, appointed by the archdeacon, looks towards the pontiff for him to sign to him, and then says to the people, *Go, [mass] is over!* and they answer, *Thanks be to God.*

Then the seven collets carrying their candlesticks go before the pontiff, and a district-subdeacon with the thurible, to the sacristy. But as he goes down into the presbytery, first the bishops say, *Sir, bid a blessing;* and the pontiff answers, *May the Lord bless us!* and they answer, *Amen.* After the bishops the presbyters say the same, and then the monks, then the choir, then the military banner-bearers, i.e. those who carry standards: after them the bearers, after them the taperers, after them the collets who watch the gate (of the Confession?); after them, but outside the presbytery, those who carry the crosses; then the junior sextons, and this done the pontiff enters the sacristy.

WESTERN (GALLICAN AND MOZARABIC) TEXTS

Unlike the Roman canon of the Mass, where only the preface and occasional festal inserts are variable, the Gallican (French-Germanic) and Mozarabic (Spanish) eucharistic prayers contain several variable sections, determined by feast, and come from an ecclesial world of thought somewhat distinct from that of Rome.

A Gallican Eucharistic Prayer

A Gallican eucharistic prayer, in *PEER*, 3rd ed., 148–50

(Priest:) It is fitting and right, just and right, here and everywhere to give you thanks, Lord, holy Father, eternal God; you snatched us from perpetual death and the last darkness of hell, and gave mortal matter, put together from the liquid mud, to your Son and to eternity. Who is acceptable to tell your praises, who can make a full declaration of your works? Every tongue marvels at you, all priests extol your glory.

When you had overcome chaos and the confused elements and the darkness in which things swam, you gave wonderful forms to the amazed elements: the tender world blushed at the fires of the sun, and the rude earth wondered at the dealings of the moon. And lest no inhabitant should adorn all this, and the sun's orb shine on emptiness, your hands made from clay a more excellent likeness, which a holy fire quickened within, and a lively soul brought to life throughout its idle parts. We may not look, Father, into the inner mysteries. To you alone is known the majesty of your work: what there is in man, that the blood held in the veins washes the fearful limbs and the living earth; that the loose appearances of bodies are held together by tightening nerves, and the individual bones gain strength from the organs within.

But whence comes so great a bounty to miserable men, that we should be formed in the likeness of you and your Son, that an earthly thing should be eternal? We abandoned the commandments of your blessed majesty; we were plunged, mortal once more, into the earth from which we came, and mourned the loss of the eternal comfort of your gift. But your manifold goodness and inestimable majesty sent the saving Word from heaven, that he should be made flesh by taking a human body, and should care for that which the age had lost and the ancient wounds. Therefore all the angels, with the manifold multitude of the saints, praise him with unceasing voice, saying:

SANCTUS
(People:) Holy, holy, [holy, lord God of Sabaoth; heaven and earth are full of your glory. Hosanna in the highest. Blessed is he who comes in the name of the Lord. Hosanna in the highest].

POST-SANCTUS
(Priest:) As the supernal creatures resound on high the praise of your glory, your goodness wished that it should be made known also to your servants; and this proclamation, made in the starry realms, was revealed to your servants by the gift of your magnificence [Or: This proclamation of your magnificence, made in the starry realms, was revealed to your servants by a gift], not only to be known but also to be imitated.

SECRETA (INSTITUTION NARRATIVE)
(privately) Who, the day before he suffered for the salvation of us all, standing in the midst of his disciples the apostles, took bread in his holy hands, looked up to heaven to you, God the Father almighty, gave thanks, blessed, and broke it, and gave it to his apostles, saying, "Take, eat from this, all of you; for this is my body, which shall be broken for the life of the age." Likewise after supper he took the cup in his hands, looked up to heaven to you, God the Father almighty,

gave thanks, blessed, and handed it to his apostles, saying, "Take, drink from this, all of you; for this is the cup of my holy blood, of the new and eternal covenant, which is shed for you and for many for forgiveness of sins." In addition to these words he said to them, "As often as you eat from this bread and drink from this cup, you will do it for my remembrance, showing my Passion to all, (and) you will look for my coming until I come."

POST-SECRETA or POST-MYSTERIUM
(aloud) Therefore, most merciful Father, look upon the commandments of your Son, the mysteries of the Church, (your) gifts to those who believe: they are offered by suppliants, and for suppliants they are to be sought;

DOXOLOGY
through [Jesus Christ your Son, our God and Lord and Savior, who, with you, Lord, and the Holy Spirit, reigns for ever, eternal Godhead, to the ages of ages].
   (People:) Amen.

A Mozarabic Eucharistic Prayer

A Mozarabic eucharistic prayer, in *PEER*, 3rd ed., 152–54.

SURSUM CORDA
   Priest: I will go to the altar of God:
   People: To the God of my joy and gladness.
   Priest: Ears to the Lord.
   People: We have them with the Lord.
   Priest: Up with your hearts.
   People: Let us lift them to the Lord.
   Priest: To our God and Lord Jesus Christ, Son of God, who is in heaven, let us offer fitting praise and fitting thanks.
   People: It is fitting and right.

ILLATIO (PREFACE)
(Priest): It is fitting and right, almighty Father, that we should give you thanks through your Son Jesus Christ, the true and eternal high priest forever, the only priest without spot of sin; for by his blood, which cleanses the hearts of all, we sacrifice to you the propitiatory victim, not only for the sins of the people, but also for our offences, that by the intercession of our high priest for us, every sin committed by the weakness of the flesh may be forgiven; to him rightly all angels cry unceasingly and say,

SANCTUS

(People:) Holy, holy, holy, Lord God of Sabaoth. Heaven and earth are full of the glory of your majesty. Hosanna to the Son of David. Blessed is he who comes in the name of the Lord. Hosanna in the highest.

POST-SANCTUS

(Priest:) Truly holy, truly blessed is your Son, Jesus Christ our Lord, in whose name we offer to you, Lord, these holy offerings, praying that you will be pleased to accept what we offer, and bless it by the outpouring of your Holy Spirit.

SECRETA (INSTITUTION NARRATIVE)

God the Lord and eternal redeemer, who, the day before he suffered, took bread, gave thanks, blessed, and broke it, and gave it to his disciples, saying, "Take and eat; this is my body, which shall be betrayed for you. As often as you eat it, do this for my remembrance."

(People: Amen.)

Likewise the cup also, after supper, saying, "This is the cup of the new covenant in my blood, which shall be shed for you and for many for forgiveness of sins. As often as you drink it, do this for my remembrance."

(People: Amen.)

"As often as you eat this bread and drink this cup, you will proclaim the death of the Lord, until he comes in glory from heaven."

(People:) So we believe, Lord Jesus.

POST-PRIDIE

(Priest): Bless, Lord, this victim that is offered to you in honor of your name, and sanctify the minds and purify the wills of those who partake of it.

(People:) Amen.

By your gift, holy Lord, for you create, sanctify, quicken, bless, and provide for us your unworthy servants all these truly good things, that they may be blessed by you, our God, to the ages of ages.

(People:) Amen.

LITURGICAL COMMENTARIES

For medieval liturgical commentaries on the Eucharist from both East and West, namely, Germanus of Constantinople, Nicholas Cabasilas (East), and Amalarius of Metz, and Innocent III (West) see chapter 2, pp. 51–56.

EUCHARISTIC DOCTRINE

Eucharistic thought in the West, due to several controversies in the ninth and eleventh centuries, came to focus almost exclusively on the issue of real presence. This, in turn, will lead to the development of the terminology of "transubstantiation," as well as to a liturgical practice of drawing greater attention to the elevation of the host at Mass.

Paschasius Radbertus of Corbie

Paschasius Radbertus of Corbie, *The Lord's Body and Blood*, I (ca. 844),
trans. George E. McCracken and Allen Cabaniss, in LCC 9:94.

2. It is . . . clear that nothing is possible outside the will of God or contrary to it, but all things wholly yield to him. Therefore, let no man be moved from this body and blood of Christ which in a mystery are true flesh and true blood since the Creator so willed it: "For all things whatsoever he willed he did in heaven and on earth" [Ps. 115:3], and because he willed, he may remain in the figure of bread and wine. Yet these must be believed to be fully, after the consecration, nothing but Christ's flesh and blood. As the Truth himself said to his disciples: "This is my flesh for the life of the world" [John 6:51], and, to put it in more miraculous terms, nothing different, of course, from what was born of Mary, suffered on the cross, and rose again from the tomb. . . . If our words seem unbelievable to anyone, let him note all the miracles of the Old and New Testaments which, through firm faith, were accomplished by God contrary to natural order, and he will see clearer than day that for God nothing is impossible, since all things that God wills to be, and whatsoever he wills, actually take place.

Ratramnus of Corbie, *Christ's Body and Blood*, X (ca. 845),
trans. George E. McCracken and Allen Cabaniss, in LCC 9:120–21.

The wine also, which through priestly consecration becomes the sacrament of Christ's blood, shows, so far as the surface goes, one thing; inwardly it contains something else. What else is to be seen on the surface than the substance of wine? Taste it, and it has the flavor of wine; smell it, and it has the aroma of wine; look at it, and the wine color is visible. But if you think of it inwardly, it is now to the minds of believers not the liquid of Christ's blood, and when tasted, it has flavor; when looked at, it has appearance; and when smelled, it is proved to be such. Since no one can deny that this is so, it is clear that that bread and wine are Christ's body and blood in a figurative sense. For as to outward appearance, the aspect of flesh is not recognized in that bread, nor in that wine is liquid blood shown, when, however, they are, after the mystical consecration, no longer called bread or wine but Christ's body and blood.

Berengarius

Berengarius, *Recantation* (1059), trans. Darwell Stone,
in *A History of the gDoctrine of the Holy Eucharist*, 1:247.

I, Berengar, an unworthy deacon of the Church of St. Maurice of Angers, acknowledging the true Catholic and Apostolic faith, anathematize every heresy, especially that concerning which I have hitherto been in ill repute, which attempts to affirm that the bread and wine which are placed on the altar are after consecration only a Sacrament and not the real body and blood of our Lord Jesus Christ, and that these cannot be held or broken by the hands of the priests or crushed by the teeth of the faithful with the senses but only by way of sacrament. And I assent to the Holy Roman and Apostolic See, and with mouth and heart I profess that concerning the Sacrament of the Lord's Table I hold the faith which the Lord and venerable Pope Nicholas [II] and this holy synod have by evangelical and apostolic authority delivered to be held and have confirmed to me, namely that the bread and wine which are placed on the altar are after consecration not only a Sacrament but also the real body and blood of our Lord Jesus Christ, and that with the senses [*sensualiter*] not only by way of Sacrament but in reality [*non solum sacramento sed in veritate*] these are held and broken by the hands of the priests and are crushed by the teeth of the faithful.

Fourth Lateran Council

Fourth Lateran Council (1215), trans. from *Enchiridion Symbolorum Definitionum et Declarationum*, ed. Henry Denzinger and Adolf Schönmetzer, 33rd ed. (Freiburg: Herder, 1965), 260.

There is truly one universal Church of the faithful, beyond which no one at all is saved. In it Jesus himself is both priest and sacrifice, whose body and blood are truly contained in the sacrament of the altar under the species of bread and wine by the transubstantiation [*transsubstantiatis*] of bread into body and wine into blood through divine power: that through the perfecting of the mystery of unity we receive of him from himself, that which he received from us. And certainly no one is able to accomplish this sacrament, except a priest, who has been properly ordained, according to the keys of the Church, which Jesus Christ himself gave to the Apostles and their successors. The sacrament of baptism (which is consecrated in water by the invocation of God and the individual members of the Trinity, namely, Father, Son, and Holy Spirit) assists to salvation both infants, as well as adults, when rightly performed in the form of the Church. And, if after the reception of baptism anybody has lapsed into sin, truly he is always able to be restored through penance. Not only virgins and continent ones, but also married persons, through right faith and working good are pleasing to God, and deserve to come to eternal blessedness.

Thomas Aquinas

Thomas Aquinas, *Summa Theologica*, Part III (ca. 1271), trans. Fathers of the English Dominican Province (New York: Benziger Bros., 1947), 11:2447–51.

***Question 75: Art. 2: Whether in This Sacrament the Substance of the Bread and Wine Remains after the Consecration?* . . .**
I answer that, Some have held that the substance of bread and wine remains in this sacrament after consecration. But this opinion cannot stand; first of all, because by such an opinion the truth of this sacrament is destroyed, to which it belongs that Christ's true body exists in this sacrament; which indeed was not there before consecration. . . .

***Art. 4: Whether Bread Can Be Converted into the Body of Christ?* . . .**
I answer that, As stated above (A.2), since Christ's true body is in this sacrament, and since it does not begin to be there by local motion, nor is it contained therein as in a place, as is evident from what was stated above (A.1, ad 2), it must be said then that it begins to be there by conversion of the substance of bread into itself.

Yet the change is not like natural changes, but is entirely supernatural, and effected by God's power alone. . . .

And this is done by Divine power in this sacrament; for the whole substance of the bread is changed into the whole substance of Christ's body, and the whole substance of the wine into the whole substance of Christ's blood. Hence this is not a formal, but a substantial conversion; nor is it a kind of natural movement: but, with a name of its own, it can be called *transubstantiation.* . . .

*Art. 5: Whether the Accidents of the Bread and Wine Remain in
This Sacrament after the Change? . . .*
I answer that, It is evident to sense that all the accidents of the bread
and wine remain after the consecration. And this is reasonably done
by Divine providence. First of all, because it is not customary, but
horrible, for men to eat human flesh, and to drink blood. And therefore Christ's flesh and blood are set before us to be partaken of under
the species of those things which are the more commonly used by
men, namely, bread and wine.

Council of Florence

Council of Florence, "Decree for the Armenians" (1439), trans.
from *Enchiridion Symbolorum Definitionum et Declarationum,* 334–35.

The third is the sacrament of the Eucharist. The matter is wheaten
bread and wine of the grape, which before consecration ought to be
mixed with a little water. The water is mixed, according to the true
testimonies of the holy fathers and doctors of the Church set forth
in former times in disputations. It is believed that the Lord himself
instituted this sacrament with wine mixed with water. This conforms
to the stories of the passion of the Lord. The blessed Pope Alexander
[I] fifth [successor] to the blessed Peter, said: "In the offerings of
sacred things offered to God in the solemnity of masses, bread and
wine mixed with water are offered in sacrifice. For in the chalice of
the Lord not only ought wine alone to be offered nor water, but both
mixed, that is, blood and water, which it is said both flowed from the
side of Christ [John 19:34]."

It agrees with signifying the effect of this sacrament, which is the
union of the Christian people to Christ. The water signifies the people, according to the Apocalypse "many waters, many people" [Rev.
17:15]. And Pope Julius [I], second [successor] after the blessed Syl-
vester said: "The chalice of the Lord, according to canonical teaching; ought to be offered with wine and water mixed, which we see by
the water to mean the people, and the wine shows forth the blood of
Christ." Therefore when wine and water are mixed in the chalice, the
people are united to Christ, and the company of the faithful is joined
to him in whom it believes.

Therefore, since the holy Roman Church, taught by the most
blessed apostles Peter and Paul, with all the other churches of the
Latins and Greeks, in which the light of all holiness and doctrine
have shined, from the beginnings of the Church, have observed this

custom and observe it now. Still, it does not seem appropriate that any region depart from this universal and reasonable practice. We decree, therefore, that the Armenians conform themselves with the entire Christian world, and that their priests mix in the chalice of oblation a little water with the wine, accordingly.

The Protestant and Catholic Reformations

THE LUTHERAN REFORMATION

Martin Luther

Luther condemns what he considers to be Mass abuses in the church of his day but continues to underscore the real presence of Christ in the Eucharist as Christ's gift of himself, his last will and testament.

Martin Luther, *The Babylonian Captivity of the Church* (1520), trans. A. T. W. Steinhäuser, Frederick C. Ahrens, and Abdel Ross Wentz, LW 36:27, 28, 31–33, 35, 51–52.

The first captivity of this sacrament, therefore concerns its substance or completeness, which the tyranny of Rome has wrestled from us. . . . But they are the sinners, who forbid the giving of both kinds [bread and wine] to those who wish to exercise this choice. The fault lies not with the laity, but with the priests. The sacrament does not belong to the priests but to all men. The priests are not lords, but servants in duty bound to administer both kinds to those who desire them, as often as they desire them. . . .

The second captivity of this sacrament [transubstantiation] is less grievous as far as the conscience is concerned, yet the gravest of dangers threatens the man who would attack it, to say nothing of condemning it. . . .

We have to think of real bread and real wine, just as we do of a real cup (for even they do not say that the cup was transubstantiated). Since it is not necessary, therefore, to assume a transubstantiation effected by divine power, it must be regarded as a figment of the human mind, for it rests neither on the Scriptures nor on reason, as we shall see. . . .

And why could not Christ include his body in the substance of the bread just as well as in the accidents? In red-hot iron, for instance, the two substances, fire and iron, are so mingled that every part is both iron and fire. Why is it not even more possible that the body of Christ be contained in every part of the substance of the bread? . . .

What shall we say when Aristotle and the doctrines of men are made to be the arbiters of such lofty and divine matters? Why do we not put aside such curiosity and cling simply to the words of Christ, willing to remain in ignorance of what takes place here and content that the real body of Christ is present by virtue of the words? Or is it necessary to comprehend the manner of the divine working in every detail? . . .

Both natures are simply there in their entirety, and it is truly said: "This man is God; this God is man." Even though philosophy cannot grasp this, faith grasps it nonetheless. And the authority of God's Word is greater than the capacity of our intellect to grasp it. In like manner, it is not necessary in the sacrament that the bread and wine be transubstantiated and that Christ be contained under their accidents in order that the real body and real blood may be present. But both remain there at the same time. . . .

The third captivity of this sacrament is by far the most wicked abuse of all. . . . The holy sacrament has been turned into mere merchandise, a market, and a profit-making business. . . .

It is certain, therefore, that the mass is not a work which may be communicated to others, but the object of faith (as has been said), for the strengthening and nourishing of each one's own faith.

Now there is yet a second stumbling block that must be removed, and this is much greater and the most dangerous of all. It is the common belief that the mass is a sacrifice, which is offered to God. Even the words of the canon seem to imply this, when they speak of "these gifts, these presents, these holy sacrifices," and further on "this offering." Prayer is also made, in so many words, "that the sacrifice may be accepted even as the sacrifice of Abel," etc. Hence Christ is termed "the sacrifice of the altar." Added to these are the sayings of the holy fathers, the great number of examples, and the widespread practice uniformly observed throughout the world.

Over against all these things, firmly entrenched as they are, we must resolutely set the words and example of Christ. For unless we firmly hold that the mass is the promise or testament of Christ, as the words clearly say, we shall lose the whole gospel and all its comfort. Let us permit nothing to prevail against these words—even though an angel from heaven should teach otherwise [Gal. 1:8]—for they contain nothing about a work or a sacrifice. Moreover, we also have the example of Christ on our side. When he instituted this sacrament and established this testament at the Last Supper, Christ did not offer himself to God the Father, nor did he perform a good work on behalf of others, but, sitting at the table, he set this same testament before each one and proffered to him the sign. Now, the more closely our mass resembles that first mass of all, which Christ performed at the Last Supper, the more Christian it will be. But Christ's mass was most simple, without any display of vestments, gestures, chants, or other ceremonies, so that if it had been necessary to offer the mass as a sacrifice, then Christ's institution of it was not complete.

Martin Luther, *The Large Catechism* (1529), trans. Theodore G. Tappert, in *The Book of Concord* (Philadelphia: Fortress Press, 1959), 447.

Now, what is the Sacrament of the Altar? Answer: It is the true body and blood of the Lord Christ in and under the bread and wine, which we Christians are commanded by Christ's word to eat and drink. As we said of Baptism that it is not mere water, so we say here that the sacrament is bread and wine, but not mere bread or wine such as is served at the table. It is bread and wine comprehended in God's Word and connected with it.

Luther's insistence on the Mass as testament and benefit shapes his liturgical reforms in ways that are both conservative in what is retained and radical in what is deleted.

Martin Luther, *Formula Missae et Communionis* for the Church at Wittenberg, 1523, in *PEER*, 3rd ed., 191–95.

That utter abomination follows which forces all that precedes in the Mass into its service and is, therefore, called the offertory. From here on almost everything smacks and savors of sacrifice. And the words of life and salvation (the Words of Institution) are imbedded in the midst of it all, just as the ark of the Lord once stood in the idol's temple next to Dagon. And there was no Israelite who could approach or bring back the ark until it "smote his enemies in the hinder parts, putting them to a perpetual reproach," and forced them to return it—which is a parable of the present time. Let us, therefore, repudiate everything that smacks of sacrifice, together with the entire canon and retain only that which is pure and holy, and so order our mass.

I. After the Creed or after the sermon let bread and wine be made ready for blessing in the customary manner. I have not yet decided whether or not water should be mixed with the wine. I rather incline, however, to favor pure wine without water; for the passage, "Thy wine is mixed with water," in Isaiah 1:22 gives the mixture a bad connotation.

Pure wine beautifully portrays the purity of gospel teaching. Further, the blood of Christ, whom we here commemorate, has been poured out unmixed with ours. Nor can the fancies of those be upheld who say that this is a sign of our union with Christ; for that is not what we commemorate. In fact, we are not united with Christ until he sheds his blood; or else we would be celebrating the shedding of our own blood together with the blood of Christ shed for us. Nonetheless, I have no intention of cramping anyone's freedom or of introducing a law which might again lead to superstition. Christ will not care very much about these matters, nor are they worth arguing about. Enough foolish controversies have been fought on these and many other matters by the Roman and Greek churches. And though some direct attention to the water and blood which flowed from the side of Jesus, they prove nothing. For that water signified something entirely different from what they wish that mixed water to signify. Nor was it mixed with blood. The symbolism does not fit, and the reference is inapplicable. As a human invention, this mixing (of water and wine) cannot, therefore, be considered binding.

II. The bread and wine having been prepared, one may proceed as follows:

The Lord be with you.

Response: *And with thy spirit.*

Lift up your hearts.

Response: *Let us lift them to the Lord.*

Let us give thanks unto the Lord our God.

Response: *It is meet and right.*

It is truly meet and right, just and salutary for us to give thanks to Thee always and everywhere, Holy Lord, Father Almighty, Eternal God, through Christ our Lord . . .

III. Then: *. . . Who the day before he suffered, took bread, and when he had given thanks, brake it, and gave it to his disciples, saying, Take, eat; this is my body, which is given for you.*

After the same manner also the cup, when he had supped, saying, This cup is the New Testament in my blood, which is shed for you and for many, for the remission of sins; this do, as often as ye do it, in remembrance of me.

I wish these words of Christ—with a brief pause after the preface—to be recited in the same tone in which the Lord's Prayer is chanted elsewhere in the canon, so that those who are present may be able to hear them, although the evangelically minded should be free about all these things and may recite these words either silently or audibly.

IV. The blessing ended, let the choir sing the Sanctus. And while the Benedictus is being sung, let the bread and cup be elevated according to the customary rite for the benefit of the weak in faith who might be offended if such an obvious change in this rite of the Mass were suddenly made. This concession can be made especially where through sermons in the vernacular they have been taught what the elevation means.

V. After this, the Lord's Prayer shall be read. Thus, *Let us pray: Taught by thy saving precepts* . . . . The prayer which follows, *Deliver us, we beseech thee* . . . , is to be omitted together with all the signs they were accustomed to make over the host and with the host over the chalice. Nor shall the host be broken or mixed into the chalice. But immediately after the Lord's Prayer shall be said, *The peace of the Lord,* etc., which is, so to speak, a public absolution of the sins of the communicants, the true voice of the gospel announcing remission of sins, and therefore the one and most worthy preparation for the Lord's Table, if faith holds to these words as coming from the mouth of Christ himself. On this account I would like to have it pronounced facing the people, as the bishops are accustomed to do, which is the only custom of the ancient bishops that is left among our bishops.

VI. Then, while the Agnus Dei is sung, let him (the liturgist) communicate, first himself and then the people. But if he should wish to pray the prayer, *O Lord Jesus Christ, Son of the Living God, who according to the will of the Father,* etc., before the communion, he does not pray wrongly, provided he changes the singular *mine* and *me* to the plural *ours* and *us.* The same thing holds for the prayer, *The body of our Lord Jesus Christ preserve my (or thy) soul unto life eternal,* and *The blood of our Lord preserve thy soul unto life eternal.*

VII. If he desires to have the communion sung, let it be sung. But instead of the *complenda* or final collect, because it sounds almost like a sacrifice, let the following prayer be read in the same tone: *What we have taken with our lips, O Lord* . . . The following one may also be read: *May thy body which we have received* . . . (changing to the plural number) . . . *who livest and reignest world without end. The Lord be with you,* etc. In place of the *Ite missa,* let the *Benedicamus domino* be said, adding Alleluia according to its own melodies where and when it is desired. Or the *Benedicamus* may be borrowed from Vespers.

VIII. The customary benediction may be given; or else the one from Numbers 6:24-27, which the Lord himself appointed:

The Lord bless us and keep us. The Lord make his face shine upon us and be gracious unto us. The Lord lift up his countenance upon us, and give us peace.

Or the one from Psalm 67:6–7:

God, even our own God shall bless us. God shall bless us; and all the ends of the earth shall fear him.

I believe Christ used something like this when, ascending into heaven, he blessed his disciples (Luke 24:50-51).

The Augsburg Confession

The Augsburg Confession (1530), Articles X and XXIV,
trans. Tappert, in *The Book of Concord*, 34 and 56.

Art. X. It is taught among us that the true body and blood of Christ are really present in the Supper of our Lord under the form of bread and wine are there distributed and received. The contrary doctrine is therefore rejected.

Art. XXIV. Our churches are falsely accused of abolishing the Mass. Actually, the Mass is retained among us and is celebrated with the greatest reverence. Almost all the customary ceremonies are also retained, except that German hymns are interspersed here and there among the parts sung in Latin.

THE REFORMED TRADITION

Ulrich Zwingli

Ulrich Zwingli's approach to the Eucharist as memorial and representation differs radically from that of Rome and from Luther.

Ulrich Zwingli, *On the Lord's Supper* (1526), trans.
G. W. Bromiley, in LCC 34:195, 213, 234–35.

For it is clear that if they insist upon a literal interpretation of the word "is" in the saying of Christ: "This is my body," they must inevitably maintain that Christ is literally there, and therefore they must also maintain that he is broken, and pressed with the teeth. Even if all the senses dispute it, that is what they must inevitably maintain if the word "is" is taken literally, as we have already shown. Hence they themselves recognize that the word "is" is not to be taken literally. . . .

This [human] nature was a guest in heaven, for no flesh had ever previously ascended up into it. Therefore when we read in Mark 16 that Christ was received up into heaven and sat on the right hand of God we have to refer this to his human nature, for according to his divine nature he is eternally omnipresent, etc. . . . The proper character of each nature must be left intact, and we ought to refer to it only those things which are proper to it. . . . The Ascension can be ascribed properly only to his humanity. . . .

And this he signified by the words: "This is (that is, represents) my body," just as a wife may say: "This is my late husband," when she shows her husband's ring. And when we poor creatures observe this act of thanksgiving amongst ourselves, we all confess that we are of those who believe in the Lord Jesus Christ, and seeing this confession is demanded of us all, all who keep the remembrance or thanksgiving are one body with all other Christians. Therefore if we are the members of his body, it is most necessary that we should live together as Christians, otherwise we are guilty of the body and blood of Christ, as Paul says.

Marburg Colloquy

At and after Marburg, the Protestant Reformation will part ways over the question of the real presence of Christ in the Eucharist.

Luther's comment to Bucer (1529), trans. Martin E. Lehmann, in LW 38:70–71.

"Our spirit is different from yours; it is clear that we do not possess the same spirit."

The Marburg Articles (1529), trans. Martin E. Lehmann, in LW 38:88–89.

Concerning the Sacrament of the Body and Blood of Christ.
Fifteenth, we all believe and hold concerning the Supper of our dear Lord Jesus Christ that both kinds should be used according to the institution by Christ; [also that the mass is not a work with which one can secure grace for someone else, whether he is dead or alive;] also that the Sacrament of the Altar is a sacrament of the true body and blood of Jesus Christ and that the spiritual partaking of the same body and blood is especially necessary for every Christian. Similarly, that the use of the sacrament, like the word, has been given and ordained by God Almighty in order that weak consciences may thereby be excited to faith by the Holy Spirit. And although at this time, we have not reached an agreement as to whether the true body and blood of Christ are bodily present in the bread and wine, nevertheless, each side should show Christian love to the other side insofar as conscience will permit, and both sides should diligently pray to Almighty God that through his Spirit he might confirm us in the right understanding. Amen.

John Calvin

In an attempt to balance the views of Luther and Zwingli, Calvin seeks to refine the issues systematically.

John Calvin, *Short Treatise on the Holy Supper of Our Lord and Only Saviour Jesus Christ* (1541), trans. J. K. S. Reid, in LCC 22:143–44.

We have already seen how Jesus Christ is the only provision by which our souls are nourished. But because it is distributed by the Word of the Lord, which he has appointed as instrument to this end, it is also called bread and water. Now what is said of the Word fitly belongs also to the sacrament of the Supper, by means of which our Lord leads us to communion with Jesus Christ. For seeing we are so foolish, that we cannot receive him with true confidence of heart, when he is presented by simple teaching and preaching, the Father, of his mercy, not at all disdaining to condescend in this matter to our infirmity, has desired to attach to his Word a visible sign, by which he represents the substance of his promises, to confirm and fortify us, and to deliver us from all doubt and uncertainty. Since then it is a mystery so high and incomprehensible, when we say that we have communion with the body and blood of Jesus Christ, and since we on our side are so rude and gross that we cannot understand the smallest things concerning God, it was of consequence that he give us to understand, according as our capacity can bear it.

For this reason, the Lord instituted for us his Supper, in order to sign and seal in our consciences the promises contained in his gospel concerning our being made partakers of his body and blood; and to give us certainty and assurance that in this consists our true spiritual nourishment; so that, having such an earnest, we might entertain a right assurance about salvation. Second, for the purpose of inciting us to recognize his great goodness towards us, so that we praise and magnify it more fully. Third, to exhort us to all sanctity and innocence, seeing that we are members of Jesus Christ, and particularly to unity and brotherly charity, as is specially recommended to us. When we have noted well these three reasons, which our Lord imposed in ordaining his Supper for us, we shall be in a position to understand both what benefits accrue to us from it, and what is our duty in its right use.

John Calvin, *Institutes of the Christian Religion*, IV, 17 (1559),
trans. Ford Lewis Battles, in LCC 21:1364–1404.

5. Now here we ought to guard against two faults. First, we should, not, by too little regard for the signs, divorce them from their mysteries, to which they are so to speak attached. Secondly, we should not, by extolling them immoderately, seem to obscure somewhat the mysteries themselves. . . .

7. Moreover, I am not satisfied with those persons who, recognizing that we have some communion with Christ, when they would show what it is, make us partakers of the Spirit only, omitting mention of flesh and blood. As though all these things were said in vain: that his flesh is truly food, that his blood is truly drink [John 6:55]; that none have life except those who eat his flesh and drink his blood [John 6:53]; and other passages pertaining to the same thing! Therefore, if it is certain that an integral communion of Christ reaches beyond their too narrow description of it, I shall proceed to deal with it briefly, in so far as it is clear and manifest, before I discuss the contrary fault of excess.

For I shall have a longer disputation with the extravagant doctors, who, while in the grossness of their minds they devise an absurd fashion of eating and drinking, also transfigure Christ, stripped of his own flesh, into a phantasm—if one may reduce to words so great a mystery, which I see that I do not even sufficiently comprehend with my mind. I therefore freely admit that no man should measure its sublimity by the little measure of my childishness. Rather, I urge my readers not to confine their mental interest within these too narrow limits, but to strive to rise much higher than I can lead them. For, whenever this matter is discussed, when I have tried to say all, I feel that I have as yet said little in proportion to its worth. And although my mind can think beyond what my tongue can utter, yet even my mind is conquered and overwhelmed by the greatness of the thing. Therefore, nothing remains but to break forth in wonder at this mystery, which plainly neither the mind is able to conceive nor the tongue to express. . . .

10. Even though it seems unbelievable that Christ's flesh, separated from us by such great distance, penetrates to us, so that it becomes our food, let us remember how far the secret power of the Holy Spirit towers above all our senses, and how foolish it is to wish to measure his immeasurableness by our measure. What, then, our mind does not comprehend, let faith conceive: that the Spirit truly unites things separated in space. . . .

19. But when these absurdities have been set aside, I freely accept

whatever can be made to express the true and substantial partaking of the body and blood of the Lord, which is shown to believers under the sacred symbols of the Supper—and so to express it that they may be understood not to receive it solely by imagination or understanding of mind, but to enjoy the thing itself as nourishment of eternal life. . . .

26. Not Aristotle, but the Holy Spirit teaches that the body of Christ from the time of his resurrection was finite, and is contained in heaven even to the Last Day [cf. Acts 3:21]. . . .

30. Unless the body of Christ can be everywhere at once, without limitation of place, it will not be credible that he lies hidden under the bread in the Supper. To meet this necessity, they [Luther] have introduced the monstrous notion of ubiquity. . . .

32. Now, if anyone should ask me how this takes place, I shall not be ashamed to confess that it is a secret too lofty for either my mind to comprehend or my words to declare. And, to speak more plainly, I rather experience than understand it. Therefore, I here embrace without controversy the truth of God in which I may safely rest. He declares his flesh the food of my soul, his blood its drink [John 6:53–56]. I offer my soul to him to be fed with such food. In his Sacred Supper he bids me take, eat, and drink his body and blood under the symbols of bread and wine. I do not doubt that he himself truly presents them, and that I receive them.

THE ANABAPTIST TRADITION

Balthasar Hübmaier

The early Anabaptist understanding of the Eucharist is close to that of Zwingli.

Balthasar Hübmaier, *Summa of the Entire Christian Life* (1525),
trans. H. Wayne Pipkin and John Howard Yoder, in *Balthasar Hübmaier:
Theologian of Anabaptism* (Scottdale, PA: Herald Press, 1989), 88.

From this it follows and is seen clearly that the Supper is nothing other than a memorial of the suffering of Christ who offered his body for our sake and shed his crimson blood on the cross to wash away our sins. But up to the present we have turned this Supper into a bear's mass, with mumbling and growling. We have sold the mass for huge amounts of possessions and money and, be it lamented to God, would gladly henceforth continue with it.

THE COUNCIL OF TRENT

Trent reaffirms the Western medieval concepts and terminology.

The Canons and Decrees of the Council of Trent

Council of Trent, Thirteenth Session, held October 11, 1551, in *The Canons and Decrees of the Council of Trent* (1551, 1562), trans. Philip Schaff, in *The Creeds of Christendom* (Grand Rapids: Baker Book House, n.d.), 2:136–86.

Canon I.—If any one denieth, that in the sacrament of the most Holy Eucharist, are contained truly, really, and substantially, the body and blood together with the soul and divinity of our Lord Jesus Christ, and consequently the whole Christ; but saith that he is only there as in a sign, or in figure, or virtue: let him be anathema.

Canon II.—If any one saith, that in the sacred and holy sacrament of the Eucharist, the substance of the bread and wine remains conjointly with the body and blood of our Lord Jesus Christ, and denieth that wonderful and singular conversion of the whole substance of bread into the body, and of the whole substance of the wine into the blood—the species only of the bread and wine remaining—which conversion indeed the Catholic Church most aptly [*aptissime*] calls Transubstantiation: let him be anathema.

Canon III.—If any one denieth, that, in the venerable sacrament of the Eucharist, the whole Christ is contained under each species, and under every part of each species, when separated: let him be anathema.

Council of Trent, Twenty-first Session, held July 16, 1562, in *The Canons and Decrees of the Council of Trent* (1551, 1562), in *The Creeds of Christendom*, 2:136–86.

Canon I.—If any one saith, that, by the precept of God, or by necessity of salvation, all and each of the faithful of Christ ought to receive both species of the most holy sacrament of the Eucharist: let him be anathema.

Canon II.—If any one saith, that the holy Catholic Church, was not induced by just causes and reasons, to communicate, under the species of bread only, laymen, and also clerics when not consecrating: let him be anathema.

Council of Trent, Twenty-second Session, held September 17, 1562,
in *The Canons and Decrees of the Council of Trent* (1551, 1562),
in *The Creeds of Christendom*, 2:136–86.

Canon I.—If any one saith, that in the mass a true and proper sacrifice is not offered to God; or, that to be offered is nothing else but that Christ is given us to eat: let him be anathema. . . .

Canon III.—If any one saith, that the sacrifice of the mass is only a sacrifice of praise and of thanksgiving; or, that it is a bare commemoration of the sacrifice consummated on the cross, but not a propriatory sacrifice; or, that it profits him only who receives; and that it ought not to be offered for the living and the dead for sins, pains, satisfactions, and other necessities: let him be anathema. . . .

Canon VI.—If any one saith, that the canon of the mass contains errors, and is therefore to be abrogated: let him be anathema.

Canon VII.—If any one saith, that the ceremonies, vestments, and outward signs, which the Catholic Church makes use of in the celebration of masses, are incentives to impiety, rather than offices of piety: let him be anathema.

Canon VIII.—If any one saith, that masses, wherein the priest alone communicates sacramentally, are unlawful, and are, therefore, to be abrogated: let him be anathema.

Canon IX.—If any one saith, that the rite of the Roman Church, according to which a part of the canon and the words of consecration are pronounced in a low tone, is to be condemned; or, that the mass ought to be celebrated in the vulgar tongue only; or, that water ought not to be mixed with the wine that is to be offered in the chalice, for that it is contrary to the institution of Christ: let him be anathema.

Pope Pius V

In *Quo primum*, July 14, 1570, Pius V promulgates the Roman Missal, which will shape Roman Catholic worship until the 1960s.

Pope Pius V, *Quo primum tempore*, trans. R. Cabié, in *History
of the Mass* (Portland, OR: Pastoral Press, 1990), 87.

The Council of Trent reserved to us the publication and correction of the holy books, of the catechism, the missal, and the breviary; once, thanks to God, the catechism for the formation of the people, and the corrected breviary for the celebration of the praise due to

God were published, it appeared necessary for us to consider immediately what remained to be done in this area, namely, the publication of the missal so that it correspond to the breviary, as is right and fitting, just as it is desirable that in the church of God there be one manner of saying the office and one single rite for celebrating Mass. This is why we entrusted this work to men chosen for their learning. They closely compared everything with the ancient manuscripts, corrected and incorrupt, collected from all over; they consulted the writings of those ancient and trustworthy authors who have left us information concerning the holy arrangement of these rites, and they restored the rites of the Mass to the form received from the holy Fathers. Having examined and checked this, and after full consideration, we have ordered that the Missal be published at Rome as soon as possible . . . so that the usages of the holy Roman Church, mother and teacher of all other churches, be adopted and observed by all. . . . We prescribe and order by this declaration, whose force is perpetual, that all the churches relinquish the use of their proper missals . . .; exceptions are made for a rite approved at its origin by the Apostolic See or for a custom faithfully observed by these churches for at least two hundred years for the celebration of Mass; it is not our intention to suppress in any way such a rite or custom.

THE CHURCH OF ENGLAND

The Book of Common Prayer, 1552

Like Luther's *Formula Missae*, 1523, the liturgical reforms of Archbishop Cranmer are conservative and retain a great deal of the classic Western liturgical tradition. Unlike Luther, Cranmer retains a complete eucharistic prayer.

The Book of Common Prayer, 1552, in PEER, 3rd ed., 246–49.

The Order for the Administration of the Lord's Supper
or Holy Communion
the Priest shall proceed, saying, Lift up your hearts.
Answer: We lift them up unto the Lord.
Priest: Let us give thanks unto our Lord God.
Answer: It is meet and right so to do.
Priest: It is very meet, right, and our bounden duty, that we should at all times and in all places, give thanks unto thee, O Lord, holy Father, almighty, everlasting God.

Here shall follow the proper Preface, according to the time, (if there be any especially appointed), or else immediately shall follow,
Therefore with angels, etc.

PROPER PREFACES
Upon Christmas Day, and seven days after
Because thou didst give Jesus Christ . . .

Upon Easter Day, and seven days after
But chiefly are we bound to praise thee . . .

Upon the Ascension Day, and seven days after
Through thy most dearly beloved Son, Jesus Christ . . .

Upon Whit Sunday, and six days after
Through Jesus Christ our Lord, according . . .

Upon the feast of Trinity only
Who art one God, one Lord . . .

After which Preface shall follow immediately
Therefore with angels and archangels, and with all the company of heaven, we laud and magnify thy glorious name, evermore praising thee, and saying,
> Holy, holy, holy, Lord God of hosts, heaven and earth are full
> of thy glory. Glory be to thee, O Lord most high.

PRAYER OF HUMBLE ACCESS
"We do not presume . . . and he in us. Amen."

Then the Priest, standing up, shall say as followeth:
Almighty God, our heavenly Father, which of thy tender mercy didst give thine only Son Jesus Christ to suffer death upon the cross for our redemption; who made there, by his one oblation of himself once offered, a full, perfect, and sufficient sacrifice, oblation, and satisfaction for the sins of the whole world; and did institute, and in his holy gospel command us to continue, a perpetual memory of that his precious death until his coming again; Hear us, O merciful Father, we beseech thee; and grant that we, receiving these thy creatures of bread and wine, according to thy Son our Savior Jesus Christ's holy institution, in remembrance of his death and passion, may be partakers of his most blessed body and blood; who, in the same night that he was betrayed, took bread; and when he had given thanks, he

brake it, and gave it to his disciples, saying, Take, eat; this is my body which is given for you. Do this in remembrance of me. Likewise after supper he took the cup; and when he had given thanks, he gave it to them, saying, Drink ye all of this; for this is my blood of the New Testament, which is shed for you and for many for remission of sins: do this, as oft as ye shall drink it in remembrance of me.

Then shall the Minister first receive the communion in both kinds himself, and next deliver it to other Ministers, if any be there present, that they may help the chief Minister, and after to the people in their hands kneeling. And when he delivereth the bread he shall say,
Take and eat this, in remembrance that Christ died for thee, and feed on him in thy heart by faith with thanksgiving.

And the Minister that delivereth the cup, shall say,
Drink this in remembrance that Christ's blood was shed for thee, and be thankful.

Then shall the Priest say the Lord's Prayer, the people repeating after him every petition.

After shall be said as followeth:
O Lord and heavenly Father, we thy humble servants entirely desire thy fatherly goodness mercifully to accept this our sacrifice of praise and thanksgiving; most humbly beseeching thee to grant, that by the merits and death of thy Son Jesus Christ, and through faith in his blood, we and all thy whole church may obtain remission of our sins, and all other benefits of his passion. And here we offer and present unto thee, O Lord, our selves, our souls and bodies, to be a reasonable, holy, and lively sacrifice unto thee; humbly beseeching thee, that all we which be partakers of this holy communion, may be fulfilled with thy grace and heavenly benediction. And although we be unworthy, through our manifold sins to offer unto thee any sacrifice, yet we beseech thee to accept this our bounden duty and service; not weighing our merits, but pardoning our offences, through Jesus Christ our Lord; by whom, and with whom in the unity of the Holy Ghost, all honour and glory be unto thee, O Father Almighty, world without end. Amen.

Articles of Religion

The Church of England defines its eucharistic doctrine largely in opposition to Trent. Wesley retains the same statements for Methodists.

Church of England, *Articles of Religion* (1563), in *Book of Common Prayer*
(London, 1784); from John Wesley's *Sunday Service* (1784)
(Nashville: United Methodist Publishing House, 1984), 312–13.

XXVIII. *Of the Lord's Supper.* [Methodist XVIII.]

The Supper of the Lord is not only a sign of love that Christians ought to have among themselves one to another; but rather it is a Sacrament of our Redemption by Christ's death: insomuch that to such as rightly, worthily, and with faith, receive the same, the Bread which we break is a partaking of the Body of Christ; and likewise the Cup of Blessing is a partaking of the Blood of Christ.

Transubstantiation, (or the change of the substance of Bread and Wine) in the Supper of the Lord, cannot be proved by Holy Writ; but is repugnant to the plain words of Scripture, overthroweth the nature of a Sacrament, and hath given occasion to many superstitions.

The Body of Christ is given, taken, and eaten, in the Supper, only after an heavenly and spiritual manner. And the mean whereby the Body of Christ is received and eaten in the Supper, is faith.

The Sacrament of the Lord's Supper was not by Christ's ordinance reserved, carried about, lifted up, or worshipped.

XXX. *Of both Kinds.* [Methodist XIX.]

The Cup of the Lord is not to be denied to the Lay-people: for both the parts of the Lord's Sacrament [Methodist: Supper], by Christ's ordinance and commandment, ought to be ministered to all Christian men alike.

XXXI. *Of the one Oblation of Christ finished upon the Cross.* [Methodist XX.]

The Offering of Christ once made is that perfect redemption, propitiation, and satisfaction, for all the sins of the whole world, both original and actual; and there is none other satisfaction for sin, but that alone. Wherefore the sacrifices of Masses, in the which it was commonly said, that the Priest did offer Christ for the quick and the dead, to have remission of pain or guilt, were blasphemous fables, and dangerous deceits.

THE ENLIGHTENMENT

The Enlightenment goes much further from traditional doctrine.

Benjamin Hoadly

Benjamin Hoadly, *A Plain Account of the Nature and End of the Sacrament of the Lord's Supper* (London, 1735), 23–24.

VIII. It appears from these *Passages* that the End for which our Lord instituted this Duty, was the *Remembrance* of Himself; that the *Bread*, to be taken and eaten, was appointed to be the *Memorial* of his *Body* broken; and the *Wine* to be drunk, was ordained to be the *Memorial* of his *Bloud* shed: Or, (according to the express Words of St. *Paul*) That the One was to be eaten, and the Other to be drunk in Remembrance of *Christ*; and this to be continued, until He, who was once *present* with his Disciples, and is now *absent*, shall *come again*.

METHODISM

The Wesleys recapture many early Christian and traditional theological concepts of the Eucharist in their hymns.

John Wesley and Charles Wesley

John Wesley and Charles Wesley, *Hymns on the Lord's Supper* (1745), in *The Eucharistic Hymns of John and Charles Wesley*, ed. J. Ernest Rattenbury (Cleveland: O.S.L. Publications, 1990), H-19, H-23, H-30, H-37.

No. 57
1. O the depth of love Divine,
Th' unfathomable grace!
Who shall say how bread and wine
God into man conveys!
How the bread His flesh imparts,
How the wine transmits His blood,
Fills His faithful people's hearts
with all the life of God!

2. Let the wisest mortal show
How we the grace receive,

Feeble elements bestow
A power not theirs to give.
Who explains the wondrous way
How through these the virtue came?
These the virtue did convey,
Yet still remain the same.

3. How can heavenly spirits rise,
By earthly matter fed,
Drink herewith Divine supplies,
And eat immortal bread?
Ask the Father's Wisdom *how*;
Him that did the means ordain!
Angels round our altars bow
To search it out in vain.

4. Sure and real is the grace,
The manner be unknown;
Only meet us in Thy ways,
And perfect us in one.
Let us taste the heavenly powers;
Lord, we ask for nothing more:
Thine to bless, 'tis only ours
To wonder and adore.

No. 72
1. Come, Holy Ghost, Thine influence shed,
And realize the sign;
Thy life infuse into the bread,
Thy power into the wine.

2. Effectual let the tokens prove,
And made, by heavenly art,
Fit channels to convey Thy love
To every faithful heart.

No. 93
1. Come, let us join with one accord
Who share the supper of the Lord,
Our Lord and Master's praise to sing;
Nourish'd on earth with living bread,
We now are at His table fed,
But wait to see our heavenly King;
To see the great Invisible

Without a sacramental veil,
With all His robes of glory on,
In rapturous joy and love and praise
Him to behold with open face,
High on his everlasting throne!

No. 116
1. Victim Divine, Thy grace we claim
While thus Thy precious death we show;
Once offer'd up, a spotless Lamb,
In Thy great temple here below,
Thou didst for all mankind atone,
And standest now before the throne.

2. Thou standest in the holiest place,
As now for guilty sinners slain;
Thy blood of sprinkling speaks, and prays,
All-prevalent for helpless man;
Thy blood is still our ransom found,
And spreads salvation all around.

THE AMERICAN FRONTIER

The American frontier recovers weekly communion for all and, in accord
with Jacksonian democracy, institutes liturgical democracy.

Alexander Campbell

Alexander Campbell, "Breaking the Loaf," in *The Christian System*, 2nd ed. (1839;
New York: Arno Press and *New York Times*, 1969), 305, 311, 325, 327, 329–31.

*Prop. IV.—All Christians are members of the house or family of God,
are called and constituted a holy and royal priesthood, and may,
therefore, bless God for the Lord's table, its loaf, and cup—approach
it without fear, and partake of it with joy as often as they please, in
remembrance of the death of their Lord and Saviour. . . .*

*Prop. VII.—The breaking of the one loaf, and the joint participation
of the cup of the Lord, in commemoration of the Lord's death, usually
called "the Lord's Supper," is an instituted part of the worship and edification of all Christian congregations in all their stated meetings. . . .*

A cloud of witnesses to the plainness and evidence of the New Testament on the subject of the weekly celebration of the Lord's supper might be adduced. . . . Thus our seventh proposition is sustained by the explicit declarations of the New Testament, by the reasonableness of the thing itself when suggested by the Apostles, by analogy, by the conclusions of the most eminent reformers, and by the concurrent voice of all Christian antiquity. But on the plain sayings of the Lord and his Apostles, we rely for authority and instruction upon *this* and *every other* Christian institution. . . .

The model which we have in our eye of good order and Christian decency in celebrating this institution [is a small church of undisclosed location]. . . .

They had appointed two senior members, of a very grave deportment, to preside in their meetings. These persons were not competent to labor in the word and teaching; but they were qualified to rule well, and to preside with Christian dignity. One of them presided at each meeting. . . .

Thus having spoken, he took a small loaf from the table, and in one or two periods gave thanks for it. After thanksgiving, he raised it in his hand, and significantly brake it, and handed it to the disciples on each side of him, who passed the broken loaf from one to another, until they all partook of it. There was no stiffness, no formality, no pageantry; all was easy, familiar, solemn cheerful. He then took the cup in a similar manner, and returned thanks for it, and handed it to the disciple sitting next to him, who passed it round; each one waiting upon his brother, until all were served. The thanksgiving before the breaking of the loaf, and the distributing of the cup, were as brief and pertinent to the occasion, as the thanks usually presented at a common table for the ordinary blessings of God's bounty. . . .

Nothing appeared to be done in a formal or ceremonious manner. . . . The joy, the affection, and the reverence which appeared in this little assembly was the strongest argument in favor of their order, and the best comment on the excellency of the Christian institution.

The Modern Period

New approaches to the Eucharist dawn.

ROMAN CATHOLIC

Constitution on the Sacred Liturgy

Constitution on the Sacred Liturgy (Collegeville, MN:
Liturgical Press, 1963), 7, 9, 33.

7. To accomplish so great a work, Christ is always present in his Church, especially in her liturgical celebrations. He is present in the sacrifice of the Mass, not only in the person of his minister, the same now offering, through the ministry of priests, who formerly offered himself on the cross, but especially under the eucharistic species. By his power, he is present in the sacraments, so that when a man baptizes it is really Christ himself who baptizes. He is present in his word, since it is he himself who speaks when the holy scriptures are read in the Church. He is present, lastly, when the Church prays and sings, for he promised: "Where two or three are gathered together in my name, there am I in the midst of them" [Matt. 18:20]. . . .

54. In Masses which are celebrated with the people, a suitable place may be allotted to their mother tongue. . . .

55. The dogmatic principles which were laid down by the Council of Trent remaining intact, communion under both kinds may be granted when the bishops think fit, not only to clerics and religious, but also to the laity, in cases to be determined by the Apostolic See.

Edward Schillebeeckx

Edward Schillibeeckx suggests a eucharistic theology of real presence focused on a reciprocity of offer and acceptance.

Edward Schillebeeckx, OP, "Transubstantiation, Transfinalization,
Transignification," *Worship* 40, no. 6 (1966): 336–38.

The "real presence" must be viewed against the background of the saving act of Christ, who in this sacramental bread gives himself to us. Christ remains truly present in the sacred host before being received in communion, but always as an offer. . . . The presence becomes reciprocal—that is to say, presence in the full and completive human sense—only in the acceptance of this offered presence, and in that way it becomes the presence of Christ in our hearts, which is the very purpose of the eucharist. Only a eucharistic presence that is personally *offered and accepted* becomes an altogether

complete presence. The presence of Christ in the tabernacle is therefore real, but as such it is only offered, and in this sense it is secondary in relation to the complete, reciprocal presence to which it is
directed as to its end and perfection. . . .

[I]n the eucharist we ought to be concerned with an interpersonal relationship between Christ and us, an interpersonal relationship in which Christ gives himself to [us] by means of bread and
wine, which by this very gift, have undergone a transfinalization
and an ontological and therefore radical transignification. The bread
and wine have become this real presence offered by Christ, who gave
his life for us on the cross; offered by Christ in order that we might
participate in this sacrifice and in the new covenant which is life for
us all. The chemical, physical, or botanical reality of bread and wine
is not changed; otherwise, Christ would not be present under the
sign of eatable bread and drinkable wine. Eucharistic sacramentality
demands precisely that the physical reality does not change, otherwise there would no longer be a eucharistic sign.

ECUMENICAL CONVERGENCE

The 1982 World Council of Churches Faith and Order Commission document *Baptism, Eucharist, and Ministry* represents not a consensus but a
contemporary convergence in eucharistic theology and liturgical celebration among a variety of distinct Christian communions, Catholic, Protestant, and Orthodox.

Baptism, Eucharist and Ministry

World Council of Churches, *Baptism, Eucharist, and Ministry*, Faith and Order Paper 111
(Geneva: World Council of Churches, 1982), paragraphs II.2; III.27–28.

a. Theology. II. 2. The eucharist is essentially the sacrament of the
gift which God makes to us in Christ through the power of the Holy
Spirit. Every Christian receives this gift of salvation through communion in the body and blood of Christ. In the eucharistic meal,
in the eating and drinking of the bread and wine, Christ grants
communion with himself. God himself acts, giving life to the body
of Christ and renewing each member. In accordance with Christ's
promise, each baptized member of the body of Christ receives in
the eucharist the assurance of the forgiveness of sins (Matt. 26:28)
and the pledge of eternal life (John 6:51–58). Although the eucharist
is essentially one complete act, it will be considered here under the

following aspects: thanksgiving to the Father, memorial of Christ, invocation of the Spirit, communion of the faithful, meal of the Kingdom.

b. III. *The Celebration of the Eucharist*. 27. The eucharistic liturgy is essentially a single whole, consisting historically of the following elements in varying sequence and of diverse importance:

—hymns of praise;

—act of repentance;

—declaration of pardon;

—proclamation of the Word of God, in various forms;

—confession of faith (creed);

—intercession for the whole Church and for the world;

—preparation of the bread and wine;

—thanksgiving to the Father for the marvels of creation, redemption and sanctification (deriving from the Jewish tradition of the *berakah*);

—the words of Christ's institution of the sacrament according to the New Testament tradition;

—the anamnesis or memorial of the great acts of redemption, passion, death, resurrection, ascension and Pentecost, which brought the Church into being;

—the invocation of the Holy Spirit (*epiklesis*) on the community, and the elements of bread and wine (either before the words of institution or after the memorial, or both; or some other reference to the Holy Spirit which adequately expresses the "epikletic" character of the eucharist);

—consecration of the faithful to God;

—reference to the communion of saints;

—prayer for the return of the Lord and the definitive manifestation of his Kingdom;

—the Amen of the whole community;

—the Lord's prayer;

—sign of reconciliation and peace;

—the breaking of the bread;

—eating and drinking in communion with Christ and with each member of the Church;

—final act of praise;

—blessing and sending.

III. 28. The best way towards unity in eucharistic celebration and communion is the renewal of the eucharist itself in the different churches in regard to teaching and liturgy. The churches should test their liturgies in the light of the eucharistic agreement now in the process of attainment.

The liturgical reform movement has brought the churches closer together in the manner of celebrating the Lord's Supper. However, a certain liturgical diversity compatible with our common eucharistic faith is recognized as a healthy and enriching fact. The affirmation of a common eucharistic faith does not imply uniformity in either liturgy or practice.

CHAPTER 5

Liturgies of the Word

Premodern Development

This chapter provides a simple overview with the most basic texts of a variety of different liturgies, sacraments, and services from the New Testament through the patristic, medieval, and Reformation eras to the modern period of ecumenical convergence. While we know of no eucharistic liturgy without some form of a Liturgy or Service of the Word connected with it, there are plenty of examples of Word services throughout history without the Eucharist, including even catechetical gatherings for baptismal formation and teaching services in the early period (see chapter 3 for examples of catechesis and chapter 7 for examples of other daily services). While many of the texts of the Liturgy of the Word presented for the early, medieval, and Reformation periods were part of the eucharistic liturgy, services of the Word without the Eucharist after the Reformation are included as well and became in several places the primary focus of Sunday worship, with the Eucharist becoming itself a kind of occasional service, especially among Protestants.

EARLY ACCOUNTS

Scripture

Luke 4:16–21 (see also Matt. 7:28-29; Mark 1:21–28).

When he came to Nazareth, where he had been brought up, he went to the synagogue on the sabbath day, as was his custom. He stood up to read, and the scroll of the prophet Isaiah was given to him. He unrolled the scroll and found the place where it was written:

"The Spirit of the Lord is upon me,
because he has anointed me to bring good news to the poor.
He has sent me to proclaim release to the captives
and recovery of sight to the blind,

to let the oppressed go free,
to proclaim the year of the Lord's favor."

And he rolled up the scroll, gave it back to the attendant, and sat down. The eyes of all in the synagogue were fixed on him. Then he began to say to them, "Today this scripture has been fulfilled in your hearing."

Acts 13:14–16.

But they went on from Perga and came to Antioch in Pisidia. And on the sabbath day they went into the synagogue and sat down. After the reading of the law and the prophets, the officials of the synagogue sent them a message, saying, "Brothers, if you have any word of exhortation for the people, give it." So Paul stood up and with a gesture began to speak.

Justin Martyr

Justin Martyr, *First Apology*, LXVII (ca. 155), trans. Edward Rochie Hardy, in LCC 1:287.

And on the day called Sunday there is a meeting in one place of those who live in cities or the country, and the memoirs of the apostles or the writings of the prophets are read as long as time permits. When the reader has finished, the president in a discourse urges and invites [us] to the imitation of these noble things. Then we all stand up together and offer prayers.

MEDIEVAL ORDINES

The *Ordines Romani* describe worship in Rome and become the model for high mass in medieval Europe.

Ordo Romanus Primus

Ordo Romanus Primus, VIII–XI (ca. 700), trans. E. G. Cuthbert F. Atchley (London: De La More Press, 1905), 129–33 (altered).

The pope passes between them [bearers of candlesticks] to the upper part of the choir, and bows his head to the altar. He then rises up, and prays, and makes the sign of the cross on his forehead; after which he gives the kiss of peace to one of the hebdomadary bishops [on duty that week], and to the archpresbyter, and to all the deacons.

Then, turning towards the precentor, he signals to him to sing *Gloria Patri* and the precentor bows to the pope, and begins it. Meanwhile the ruler of the choir precedes the pope in order to set his cushion before the altar, if it should be the season for it [Lent or penitential days]: and approaching it, the pope prays there until the repetition of the verse [entry anthem]. Now when "As it was in the beginning" is said, the deacons rise up in order to salute the sides of the altar, first two, and then the rest by twos, and return to the pope. And then, the latter rises, and kisses the book of the gospels and the altar, and, going to his throne, stands there facing eastwards.

Now, after the anthem is finished, the choir begins *Kyrie eleison*. But the precentor keeps his eye on the pope, so that the latter may signal him if he wishes to change the number of the Kyries, and bows to him. When they have finished, the pope turns himself round towards the people, and begins, *Gloria in excelsis Deo*, if it be the season for it [not Lent], and at once turns back again to the east until it is finished. Then, after turning again to the people, he says, *Pax vobis* and once more turning to the east, says *Oremus*, and the collect follows. At the end of it, he sits, and the bishops and presbyters sit in like manner.

Meanwhile, the district subdeacons go up to the altar, and place themselves at the right and left of the altar. Then the pope signals to the bishops and presbyters to sit. Now, as soon as the subdeacon who is going to read perceives that the bishops and presbyters are sitting down after the pope, he goes up into the ambo and reads the epistle. When he has finished reading, a chorister goes up into the same with the book of chants and sings the respond. And then *Alleluia* is sung by another singer, if it should be the season when *Alleluia* is said; if not, a tract [penitential verse]; if when neither one nor the other is appointed, only the respond is sung.

Then the deacon kisses the pope's feet, and the latter says to him in an undertone, "*Dominus sit in corde tuo et in labiis tuis.*" Then the deacon comes before the altar, and after kissing the book of the gospels, takes it up in his hands; and there walk before him [to the ambo] two district-subdeacons, who have taken the censer from the hand of the subdeacon-attendant, diffusing incense. And in front of them they have two acolytes carrying two candlesticks. On coming to the ambo, the acolytes part before it, and the subdeacons and the deacon with the gospel-book pass between them. The subdeacon who is not carrying the censer then turns towards the deacon, and offers him his left arm on which to rest the gospel-book, in order that the former may open it with his right hand at the place where the mark for reading was put: then, slipping his finger into the place where he has to begin, the deacon goes up to read, while the two subdeacons turn back to stand before the step coming down from the ambo. The gospel ended, the pope says *Pax tibi*; and then *Dominus vobiscum*. Answer is made, *Et cum spiritu tuo*; and he says, *Oremus*.

When the deacon is come down from the ambo, the subdeacon who first opened the gospel-book previously, takes it from him and hands it to the subdeacon-attendant, who stands in his rank. Then the latter, holding the book before his breast, outside his planet [chasuble], offers it to be kissed by all who stand [in the choir] in the order of their rank. And after this, an acolyte is ready on the step by the ambo with the case in which the same subdeacon puts the gospel-book so that it may be sealed. But the acolyte of the same district as that to which the subdeacon belongs carries it back to the Lateran.

REFORMATION CHANGES

Martin Luther

Martn Luther's changes in the Liturgy of the Word are conservative.

Martin Luther, *Formula Missae* (1523), trans. Paul Zeller Strodach
and Ulrich S. Leupold, in LW 53:20–25.

We therefore first assert: It is not now nor ever has been our intention to abolish the liturgical service of God completely, but rather to purify the one that is now in use from the wretched accretions which corrupt it and to point out an evangelical use. We cannot deny that the mass, i.e., the communion of bread and wine, is a rite divinely instituted by Christ himself and that it was observed first by Christ and then by the apostles, quite simply and evangelically without any additions. But in the course of time so many human inventions were added to it that nothing except the names of the mass and communion has come down to us.

Now the additions of the early fathers who, it is reported, softly prayed one or two Psalms before blessing the bread and wine are commendable. Athanasius and Cyprian are supposed to be some of these. Those who added the *Kyrie eleison* also did well. We read that under Basil the Great, the *Kyrie eleison* was in common use by all the people. The reading of the Epistles and Gospels is necessary, too. Only it is wrong to read them in a language the common people do not understand. Later, when chanting began, the Psalms were changed into the introit; the Angelic Hymn *Gloria in Excelsis: et in terra pax*, the graduals, the alleluias, the Nicene Creed, the *Sanctus*,

the *Agnus Dei,* and the *communio* were added. All of these are unob-
jectionable, especially the ones that are sung *de tempore* [temporal
cycle] on Sundays. For these days by themselves testify to ancient
purity, the canon excepted. . . .

We will set forth the rite according to which we think that it [the
mass] should be used.

First, we approve and retain the introits for the Lord's days and
the festivals of Christ, such as Easter, Pentecost, and the Nativity,
although we prefer the Psalms from which they were taken as of
old. But for the time being we permit the accepted use. And if any
desire to approve the introits (inasmuch as they have been taken
from Psalms or other passages of Scripture) for apostles' days, for
feasts of the Virgin and of other saints, we do not condemn them. . . .

Second, we accept the *Kyrie eleison* in the form in which it has
been used until now, with the various melodies for different seasons,
together with the Angelic Hymn, *Gloria in Excelsis,* which follows it.
However the bishop [pastor] may decide to omit the latter as often
as he wishes.

Third, the prayer or collect which follows, if it is evangelical (and
those for Sunday usually are), should be retained in its accepted
form; but there should be only one. After this the Epistle is read.
Certainly the time has not yet come to attempt revision here, as
nothing unevangelical is read, except that those parts from the
Epistles of Paul in which faith is taught are read only rarely, while
the exhortations to morality are most frequently read. The Epistles
seems to have been chosen by a singularly unlearned and superstitious advocate of works. But for the service those sections in which
faith in Christ is taught should have been given preference. The latter
were certainly considered more often in the Gospels by whosoever
it was who chose these lessons. In the meantime, the sermon in the
vernacular will have to supply what is lacking. If in the future the
vernacular be used in the mass (which Christ may grant), one must
see to it that Epistles and Gospels chosen from the best and most
weighty parts of these writings be read in the mass.

Fourth, the gradual of two verses shall be sung, either together
with the Alleluia, or one of the two, as the bishop may decide. But the
Quadragesima [Lenten] graduals and others like them that exceed
two verses may be sung at home by whoever wants them. In church
we do not want to quench the spirit of the faithful with tedium. Nor
is it proper to distinguish Lent, Holy Week, or Good Friday from
other days, lest we seem to mock and ridicule Christ with half of a
mass and the one part of the sacrament. For the Alleluia is the perpetual voice of the church, just as the memorial of His passion and
victory is perpetual.

Fifth, we allow no sequences or proses [verses] unless the bishop wishes to use the short one for the Nativity of Christ: "*Grates nunc omnes.*"...

Sixth, the Gospel lesson follows, for which we neither prohibit nor prescribe candles or incense. Let these things be free.

Seventh, the custom of singing the Nicene Creed does not displease us; yet this matter should also be left in the hands of the bishop. Likewise, we do not think that it matters whether the sermon in the vernacular comes after the Creed or before the introit of the mass; although it might be argued that since the Gospel is the voice crying in the wilderness and calling unbelievers to faith, it seems particularly fitting to preach before mass. For properly speaking, the mass consists in using the Gospel and communing at the table of the Lord. Inasmuch as it belongs to believers, it should be observed apart [from unbelievers]. Yet since we are free, this argument does not bind us, especially since everything in the mass up to the Creed is ours, free and not prescribed by God; therefore it does not necessarily have anything to do with the mass.

John Calvin

John Calvin introduces sung congregational psalmody.

> John Calvin, *Articles Concerning the Organization of the Church and of Worship at Geneva Proposed by the Ministers at the Council January 16, 1537,* trans. J. K. S. Reid, in LCC 22:53–54.

There are psalms which we desire to be sung in the Church, as we have it exemplified in the ancient Church and in the evidence of Paul himself, who says it is good to sing in the congregation with mouth and heart. We are unable to compute the profit and edification which will arise from this, except after having experimented. Certainly as things are, the prayers of the faithful are so cold, that we ought to be ashamed and dismayed. The psalms can incite us to lift up our hearts to God and to move us to an ardor in invoking and exalting with praises the glory of his Name. Moreover, it will be thus appreciated of what benefit and consolation the pope and those that belong to him have deprived the Church; for he has reduced the psalms, which ought to be true spiritual songs, to a murmuring among themselves without any understanding.

This manner of proceeding seemed specially good to us, that children, who before hand have practiced some modest church song, sing in a loud distinct voice, the people listening with all attention and following heartily what is sung with the mouth, till all become accustomed to sing communally. But in order to avoid all confusion, you must not allow that anyone by his insolence, and to put the congregation to derision, should come to disturb the order you have adopted.

Church of England

In the Church of England, the Liturgy or Service of the Word becomes detached from the Eucharist when there are no communicants. Ceremonial is reduced but not eliminated.

The Booke of the Common Prayer (1549), in *First and Second Prayer Books of Edward VI* (London: J. M. Dent & Sons, 1910; spelling modernized); rubric at end of Eucharist, 229.

Upon Wednesdays and Fridays the English Litany shall be said or sung in all places, after such form as is appointed by the king's majesty's injunctions: Or as is or shall be otherwise appointed by his highness. And though there be none to communicate with the priest, yet these days (after the Litany [is] ended) the priest shall put upon him a plain alb or surplice, with a cope, and say all things at the altar (appointed to be said at the celebration of the Lord's Supper), until the offertory. And then [he] shall add one or two of the collects aforewritten, as occasion shall serve by his discretion. And then turning him to the people shall let them depart with the accustomed blessing. And the same order shall be used all other days whensoever the people be customarily assembled to pray in his church, and none [be] disposed to communicate with the priest.

The Booke of the Common Prayer (1549), in *First and Second Prayer Books of Edward VI*; "Of Ceremonies, Why Some Be Abolished and Some Retained," 287–88.

Furthermore, the most weighty cause of the abolishment of certain ceremonies was, that they were so far abused, partly by the superstitious blindness of the rude and unlearned, and partly by the insatiable avarice of such as sought more their own lucre than the glory of God; that the abuses could not well be taken away, the thing remaining still.

But now as concerning those persons, which peradventure will be offended for that some of the old ceremonies are retained still: If they consider, that without some ceremonies it is not possible to keep any order or quiet discipline in the church: they shall easily perceive just cause to reform their judgments. And if they think much that any of the old do remain, and would rather have all devised anew:

then such men (granting some ceremonies convenient to be had), surely where the old may be well used: there they cannot reasonably reprove the old (only for their age) without betraying of their own folly. For in such a case they ought rather to have reverence unto them for their antiquity, if they will declare themselves to be more studious of unity and concord, than of innovations and newfangledness, which (as much as may be with the true setting forth of Christ's religion) is always to be eschewed.

Furthermore, such shall have no just cause with the ceremonies reserved, to be offended: for as those be taken away which were most abused, and did burden men's consciences without any cause: So the other that remain are retained for a discipline and order, which (upon just causes) may be altered and changed, and therefore are not to be esteemed equal with God's law. And moreover they be neither dark nor dumb ceremonies, but are so set forth that every man may understand what they do mean, and to use what they do serve. . . . We think it convenient that every country should use such ceremonies, as they shall think best to the setting forth of God's honor, and glory.

THE PURITANS

The Puritans object to many remaining ceremonies but finally succeed in shaping the Service of the Word according to their own consensus.

The Millenary Petition (1603), in *Documents Illustrative of English Church History*, ed. Henry Gee and William John Hardy (London: Macmillan & Co., 1910), 509–10.

Our humble suit, then, unto your majesty is that these offenses following, some may be removed, some amended, some qualified:

In the Church service: that the cross in baptism, interrogatories ministered to infants, confirmation, as superfluous, may be taken away; baptism not to be ministered by women, and so explained; the cap and surplice not urged; that examination may go before the communion; that it be ministered with a sermon; that divers terms of priests, and absolution, and some other used, with the ring in marriage, and other such like in the book, may be corrected; the longsomeness of service abridged, Church songs and music moderated to better edification; that the Lord's Day be not profaned; the rest upon holy days not so strictly urged; that there may be a uniformity of doctrine prescribed; no popish opinion to be any more taught or defended; no ministers charged to teach their people to bow at the name of Jesus; that the canonical Scriptures only be read in the Church.

Concerning Church ministers: that none hereafter be admitted into the ministry but able and sufficient men, and those to preach diligently and especially upon the Lord's day; that such as be already entered and cannot preach, may either be removed, and some charitable course taken with them for their relief.

A Directory for the Publique Worship of God [Westminster Directory]
(London, 1644 [1645]); copy in University Library, Cambridge, 9–38.

Of the Assembling of the Congregation and Their Behaviour in the Publique Worship of God.

When the congregation is to meet for Publique Worship, the people (having before prepared their hearts thereunto) ought all to come, and joyne therein: not absenting themselves from the Publique Ordinances, through negligence, or upon pretence of Private meetings.

Let all enter the Assembly, not irreverently, but in a grave and seemly manner, taking their seats or places without Adoration, or Bowing themselves towards one place or other.

The Congregation being assembled: the Minister, after solemne calling on them to the worshiping of the great name of God, is to begin with prayer. . . .

Of Publique Reading of the holy Scriptures.

Reading of the Word in the Congregation being part of the Publique Worship of God, (wherein we acknowledge our dependence upon him, and subjection to him) and one means sanctified by him for the edifying of his People, is to be performed by the Pastors and Teachers. . . .

How large a portion shall be read at once, is left to the wisdome of the Minister: but it is convenient, that ordinarily one Chapter of each Testament be read at every meeting: and sometimes more, where the chapters be short, or the coherence of matter requireth it.

It is requisite that all the Canonical Books be read over in order, that the people may be better acquainted with the whole Body of the Scriptures: And ordinarily, where the Reading in either testament endeth on one Lord's Day, it is to begin the next.

Wee commend also the more frequent reading of such Scriptures, as hee that readeth shall thinke best for edification of his Hearers: as the Book of Psalmes, and such like.

When the Minister, who readeth, shall judge it necessary to expound any part of what is read, let it not bee done until the whole

Chapter, or Psalme be ended: and regard it always to be had unto the time, that neither Preaching or other Ordinance be straitned, or rendred tedious. Which Rule is to be observed in all other publique performance. . . .

Of Publike Prayer before the Sermon.
After reading of the Word (and singing of the Psalme) the Minister who is to Preach, is to endeavor to get his own, and his Hearers hearts to be rightly affected with their Sinnes, that they may all mourn in sense thereof before the Lord, and hunger and thirst after the grace of God in Jesus Christ, by proceeding to a more full Confession of sinne with shame and holy confusion of face, and to Call upon the Lord to this effect. . . .

Of the Preaching of the Word.
Preaching of the Word, being the power of God unto Salvation, and one of the greatest and most excellent Works belonging to the ministry of the Gospell, should be so performed, that the Workman need not be ashamed, but may save himself, and those that heare him. . . .

Ordinarily, the subject of his Sermon is to be some Text of Scripture, holding forth some principle of head of Religion; or suitable to some speciall occasion emergent; or he may goe on in some Chapter, Psalme, or Booke of the holy Scripture as he shall see fit. . . .

But the servant of Christ, whatever his Method be, is to perform the whole ministery: painfully, ... plainly, ... faithfully, ... wisely, ... gravely, ... with loving affection, as taught of God, and perswaded in his own heart. . . .

Of Prayer after the Sermon.
The sermon being ended, the minister is:

To give thanks . . . to pray for the continuance of the Gospell. . . . to turn the chief and most usefull heads of the Sermon into some few Petitions. . . . to pray for preparation for Death, and judgement. . . .

And because the prayer which Christ taught his Disciples is not only a Pattern of Prayer, but it selfe a most comprehensive Prayer, we recommend it also to be used in the Prayers of the Church. . . .

Every Minister is herein to apply himselfe in his Prayer before, or after his Sermon to those occasions: [of sacraments, fasts, and thanksgiving], but for the manner, he is left to his liberty, as God shall direct and inable him, in piety and wisdom to discharge his duty.

The Prayer ended, let a Psalme be sung, if with conveniency it may be done. After which (unless some other Ordinance of Christ that concerneth the congregation at that time be to follow) let the Minister dismisse the Congregation with a solemne Blessing.

Lutherans in Leipzig

The order of service in Leipzig, 1714, is noted by J. S. Bach (1685–1750).

"Order of Divine Service in Leipzig" (December 2, 1714),
trans. Arthur Mendel, in *The Bach Reader*, rev. ed., ed. Hans T. David
and Arthur Mendel (New York: W. W. Norton & Co., 1966), 70.

First Sunday in Advent: Morning
(1) Preluding
(2) *Motetta*
(3) Preluding on the Kyrie, which is performed throughout in concerted music
(4) Intoning before the altar
(5) Reading of the Epistle
(6) Singing of the Litany
(7) Preluding on [and singing of] the Chorale
(8) Reading of the Gospel
(9) Preluding on [and performance of] the principal composition [cantata]
(10) Singing of the Creed
(11) The Sermon
(12) After the Sermon, as usual, singing of several verses of a hymn
(13) Words of Institution [of the Sacrament]
(14) Preluding on [and performance of] the composition [probably the second part of the cantata]. After the same, alternate preluding and singing of chorales until the end of the Communion, *et sic porro.*

Modern Development

EVANGELISTIC CAMP MEETINGS AND WORSHIP

The frontier camp meeting reshapes Protestant worship to focus on individual religious experience.

Camp Meeting Manual

B. W. Gorham, *Camp Meeting Manual: A Practical Book for the Camp Ground* (Boston: H. V. Degen, 1854), 155–56.

As to the order of exercises and of domestic arrangements, I have generally noticed that the following worked well:

1. Rise at five, or half-past five in the morning.
2. Family prayer and breakfast from half-past six to half-past seven.
3. General prayer meeting at the altar, led by several ministers appointed by the Presiding Elder, at half-past eight, A.M.
4. Preaching at half-past ten, followed by prayer meeting to twelve, M.
5. Dine at half-past twelve, P.M.
6. Preaching at two, or half-past two, P.M., followed by prayer at the altar till five.
7. Tea at six, P.M.
8. Preaching at half-past seven, followed by prayer meeting at the altar till nine or ten.
9. All strangers to leave the ground and the people to retire at ten, or immediately thereafter.

The prayer meetings at the altar, after preaching, should be strongly manned with a good number of preachers and official members, and under the control of the Presiding Elder, who should lead the exercises from the stand, or employ some other person to do so.

Special circumstances will occasionally dictate a departure from any prescribed routine, and yet it is good to have an established order, and to adhere to it with some tenacity.

On the last night of the meeting, the services are sometimes protracted through the night. Commonly this is of doubtful utility. A very appropriate method of closing the services is, after taking the names of such as have been converted, with the view to proper future attentions to them, to administer the sacrament of the Lord's supper.

Hymn from *The Wesleyan Camp-Meeting Hymn-Book*

Hymn 94 (early nineteenth century), in *The Wesleyan Camp-Meeting Hymn-Book*, compiled by Joseph Meriam, 4th ed. (Wendell, MA: J. Metcalf, 1829), 131–32.

> What hath the world to equal this?
> The solid peace, the heavenly bliss;
> The joys immortal, love divine,
> The love of Jesus ever mine:

Greater joys I'm born to know,
From terrestrial to celestial,
When I up to Jesus go.
When I shall leave this house of clay,
Glorious angels shall convey;
Upon their golden wings shall I
Be wafted far above the sky;
There behold him free from harm,
Beauties vernal, spring eternal,
In my lovely Jesus' arms.
There in sweet silent raptures wait,
Till the saints' number is complete,
Till the last trump of God shall sound,
Break up the graves and tear the ground.
There descending with the Lamb,
Ev'ry spirit shall inherit
Bodies of eternal frame.
O tiresome world, when will it end,
When shall I see my heavenly Friend,
When will my lovely Jesus come,
And take his weary pilgrims home!
When shall I meet him in the sky,
There adore him, fall before him,
And holy, holy, holy cry.

African American Spiritual

African American Spiritual, "Steal Away" (nineteenth century).
in *Songs of Zion* (Nashville: Abingdon Press, 1981), 134.

Response:
Steal away, steal away, steal away to Jesus!
Steal away, steal away home, I ain't got long to stay here.

Leader:
1. My Lord calls me, He calls me by the thunder;
2. Green trees are bending, Poor sinner stands a-trembling;
3. Tombstones are bursting, Poor sinner stands a-trembling;
4. My Lord calls me, He calls me by the lightning, The trumpet sounds with-in-a my soul,

Response:
I ain't got long to stay here.

Charles G. Finney

The Sunday service becomes oriented to producing converts. Charles G. Finney (1792–1875) leads the way in promoting a pragmatic approach to worship and argues that, since worship forms have changed over time, nothing biblical or historical is normative except that which works at the present.

Charles G. Finney, "Measures to Promote Revivals" (1835),
in *Lectures on Revivals of Religion*, ed. William G. McLoughlin
(Cambridge, MA: Harvard University Press, 1960), 250, 256–57, 273, 276.

Our present forms of public worship, and every thing, so far as *measures* are concerned, have been arrived at *by degrees*, and *by a succession of New Measures.* . . .

Choirs. . . . O how many congregations were torn and rent in sunder, by the desire of ministers and some leading individuals to bring about an improvement in the cultivation of music, by forming choirs of singers. . . .

Instrumental Music. . . . And there are many churches now who would not tolerate an organ. They would not be half so much excited to be told that sinners are going to hell, as to be told that there is going to be an organ in the meeting house. . . .

Extemporary Prayers. How many people are there, who talk just as if the Prayer Book was of divine institution! And I suppose multitudes believe it is. And in some parts of the church a man would not be tolerated to pray without his book before him. . . .

Kneeling in Prayer. This has made a great disturbance in many parts of the country. The time has been in the Congregational churches in New England, when a man or woman would be ashamed to be seen kneeling at a prayer meeting, for fear of being taken for a Methodist. I have prayed in families where I was the only person that would kneel. The others all stood, lest they should imitate the Methodists, I suppose, and thus countenance innovations upon the established form. . . .

It is evident that we must have more exciting preaching, to meet the character and wants of the age. . . . The character of the age is changed, and these men [preachers] have not conformed to it, but retain the same stiff, dry, prosing styles of preaching that answered half a century ago.

Look at the Methodists. Many of their ministers are unlearned, in the common sense of the term, many of them taken right from the shop or farm, and yet they have gathered congregations, and pushed their way, and won souls every where. Wherever the Methodists have gone, their plain, pointed and simple but warm and animated mode of preaching has always gathered congregations. . . . We must have exciting, powerful preaching, or the devil will have the people, except what the Methodists can save. . . .

But it is just as absolutely fanatical for the Presbyterian church, or any other church, to be sticklish for her particular forms, and to act as if *they* were established by divine authority. The fact is, that God has established in no church, any particular *form*, or manner of worship, for promoting the interests of religion. The scriptures are entirely silent on these subjects, under the gospel dispensation, and the church is left to exercise her own discretion in relation to all such matters. . . .

The only thing insisted upon under the gospel dispensation, in regard to measures, is that there should be *decency and order.* . . . But I do not suppose that by "order" we are to understand any particular set mode, in which any church may have been accustomed to perform their service.

"Of Public Worship" (1844), in *The Doctrines and Discipline of the Methodist Episcopal Church*

"Of Public Worship" (1844), in *The Doctrines and Discipline of the Methodist Episcopal Church* (Cincinnati: L. Swormstedt & J. T. Mitchell, 1844), 78.

Quest. What directions shall be given for the establishment of uniformity in public worship among us, on the Lord's Day?

Answ. 1. Let the morning service consist of singing, prayer, the reading of a chapter out of the Old Testament, and another out of the New, and preaching.

2. Let the afternoon service consist of singing, prayer, the reading of one or two chapters out of the Bible, and preaching.

3. Let the evening service consist of singing, prayer, and preaching.

4. But on the days of administering the Lord's supper, the two chapters in the morning service may be omitted.

5. In administering the ordinances, and in the burial of the dead, let the form of Discipline invariably be used. Let the Lord's prayer also be used on all occasions of public worship in concluding the first prayer, and the apostolic benediction [2 Cor. 13:13] in dismissing the congregation.

6. Let the society be met, wherever it is practicable, on the sabbath day.

Fanny J. Crosby

Fanny J. Crosby becomes the most popular American hymn writer and the preeminent popular saint of her time.

Fanny J. Crosby, "Blessed Assurance" (1873), in *The Methodist Hymnal*
(Nashville: Publishing House, Methodist Episcopal Church, South, 1905), 548.

1. Blessed assurance, Jesus is mine!
   O what a foretaste of glory divine!
   Heir of salvation, purchase of God,
   Born of his Spirit, washed in his blood.
2. Perfect submission, perfect delight,
   Visions of rapture now burst on my sight,
   Angels descending, bring from above,
   Echoes of mercy, whispers of love.
3. Perfect submission, all is at rest,
   I in my Saviour am happy and best,
   Watching and waiting, looking above,
   Filled with his goodness, lost in his love.

Refrain:
This is my story, this is my song,
Praising my Saviour all the day long;
This is my story, this is my song,
Praising my Saviour all the day long.

MODERN ROMAN CATHOLICISM

Roman Catholics reform the Liturgy of the Word after Vatican II (1962–65) with greater attention to the amount of Scripture read liturgically and to the importance of preaching.

Constitution on the Sacred Liturgy

Constitution on the Sacred Liturgy, 7, 51–53
(Collegeville, MN: Liturgical Press, 1963), 31–32.

7. . . . . Christ is always present in his Church, especially in her liturgical celebrations. He is present in the Sacrifice of the Mass not only in the person of his minister . . . but especially in the eucharistic species. By his power he is present in the sacraments so that when anybody

baptizes it is really Christ himself who baptizes. He is present in his word since it is he himself who speaks when the holy scriptures are read in the Church. Lastly, he is present when the Church prays and sings, for he has promised "where two or three are gathered together in my name there am I in the midst of them" (Mt. 18:20).

51. The treasures of the Bible are to be opened up more lavishly, so that richer fare may be provided for the faithful at the table of God's word. In this way a more representative portion of the holy scriptures will be read to the people in the course of a prescribed number of years.

52. By means of the homily the mysteries of the faith and the guiding principles of the Christian life are expounded from the sacred text, during the course of the liturgical year; the homily, therefore, is to be highly esteemed as part of the liturgy itself; in fact, at those Masses which are celebrated with the assistance of the people on Sundays and feasts of obligation, it should not be omitted except for a serious reason.

53. Especially on Sundays and feasts of obligation there is to be restored, after the Gospel and the homily, "the common prayer" or "the prayer of the faithful." By this prayer, in which the people are to take part, intercession will be made for holy Church, for the civil authorities, for those oppressed by various needs, for all mankind, and for the salvation of the entire world.

Karl Rahner and Heinrich Fries

Karl Rahner and Heinrich Fries underscore the ecumenical importance of a new emphasis on the Word and its implications for Christian unity.

Karl Rahner and Heinrich Fries, *Unity of the Churches: An Actual Possibility*, trans. Ruth and Eric Gritsch (New York/Philadelphia: Paulist Press and Fortress Press, 1985), 125.

Pulpit fellowship is already being practiced in many cases; and it no longer presents a disquieting exception, even to Catholic Christians. But one really should think about this more than ever, since it is precisely a pulpit fellowship which presupposes a community of faith. Consider the reality of salvation of the Word of God; consider Christ's presence in its various forms, including the form of proclamation; finally consider the theological conformity of Word *and* Sacrament—sacrament as visible Word (*verbum visibile*), the Word as audible sacrament (*sacramentum audible*).

MODERN PROTESTANTISM

Like Roman Catholics, modern Protestants have also called for a renewed theology of the Word, the reading of Scripture, and the importance of liturgical preaching.

Evangelical Lutheran Church in America

Evangelical Lutheran Church in America, *The Use of the Means of Grace: A Statement on the Practice of Word and Sacrament* (Minneapolis: Augsburg Fortress, 1997), 6, 12–16.

1. Jesus Christ is the living and abiding Word of God. By the power of the Spirit, this very Word of God, which is Jesus Christ, is read in the Scriptures, proclaimed in preaching, announced in the forgiveness of sins, eaten and drunk in the Holy Communion, and encountered in the bodily presence of the Christian community. By the power of the Spirit active in Holy Baptism, this Word washes a people to be Christ's own Body in the world.

We have called this gift of Word and Sacrament by the name "the means of grace." The living heart of all these means is the presence of Jesus Christ through the power of the Spirit as the gift of the Father.

5. Jesus Christ is the Word of God incarnate. The proclamation of God's message to us is both Law and Gospel. The canonical Scriptures of the Old and New Testaments are the written Word of God. Through this Word in these forms, as through the sacraments, God gives faith, forgiveness of sins, and new life.

6. Sunday, the day of Christ's resurrection and of the appearances to the disciples by the crucified and risen Christ, is the primary day on which Christians gather to worship. Within this assembly, the Word is read and preached and the sacraments are celebrated.

7. The public reading of the Holy Scriptures is an indispensable part of worship, constituting the basis for the public proclamation of the Gospel.

9. The preaching of the Gospel of the crucified and risen Christ is rooted in the readings of the Scriptures in the assemblies for worship. Called and ordained ministers bear responsibility for the preached Word in the Church gathered for public worship.

10. The assembled congregation participates in proclaiming the Word of God with a common voice. It sings hymns and the texts of the liturgy. It confesses the Nicene or Apostles' Creed.

11. Music, the visual arts, and the environment of our worship spaces embody the proclamation of the Word in Lutheran churches.

CHAPTER **6**

Occasional Sacraments and Services

The occasional sacraments and services that make up this chapter are, of course, the four rites other than baptism, confirmation, and Eucharist, known as sacraments by Roman Catholic, Eastern Orthodox, and some other Christians: penance (now more frequently referred to as reconciliation and/or confession), anointing and healing of the sick, marriage, and ministry and ordination. Although funeral rites are not recognized officially as a sacrament by any Christian tradition, the chapter concludes by offering a brief overview of such rites, past and present, for the sake of completeness.

Penance, Reconciliation, Confession

CANONICAL PENANCE IN EARLY CHRISTIANITY

Scripture

Early practice is communal and only for serious offenders.

Matthew 18:15–18 (see also Luke 17:3–4;
1 Cor. 6:1–7; Gal. 6:1; Jas. 5:19–20).

If another member of the church sins against you, go and point out the fault when the two of you are alone. If the member listens to you, you have regained that one. But if you are not listened to, take one or two others along with you, so that every word may be confirmed by the evidence of two or three witnesses. If the member refuses to listen to them, tell it to the church; and if the offender refuses to listen even to the church, let such a one be to you as a Gentile and a tax collector. Truly I tell you, whatever you bind on earth will be bound in heaven, and whatever you loose on earth will be loosed in heaven.

John 20:22–23.

When he had said this, he breathed on them and said to them, "Receive the Holy Spirit. If you forgive the sins of any, they are forgiven them; if you retain the sins of any, they are retained."

1 Corinthians 5:1–5, 9–13.

It is actually reported that there is sexual immorality among you, and of a kind that is not found even among pagans; for a man is living with his father's wife. And you are arrogant! Should you not rather have mourned, so that he who has done this would have been removed from among you?

For though absent in body, I am present in spirit; and as if present I have already pronounced judgment in the name of the Lord Jesus on the man who has done such a thing. When you are assembled, and my spirit is present with the power of our Lord Jesus, you are to hand this man over to Satan for the destruction of the flesh, so that his spirit may be saved in the day of the Lord. . . .

I wrote to you in my letter not to associate with sexually immoral persons—not at all meaning the immoral of this world, or the greedy and robbers, or idolaters, since you would then need to go out of the world. But now I am writing to you not to associate with anyone who bears the name of brother or sister who is sexually immoral or greedy, or is an idolater, reviler, drunkard, or robber. Do not even eat with such a one. For what have I to do with judging those outside? Is it not those who are inside that you are to judge? God will judge those outside. "Drive out the wicked person from among you."

1 John 1:5–10

This is the message we have heard from him and proclaim to you, that God is light and in him there is no darkness at all. If we say that we have fellowship with him while we are walking in darkness, we lie and do not do what is true; but if we walk in the light as he himself is in the light, we have fellowship with one another, and the blood of Jesus his Son cleanses us from all sin.

If we say that we have no sin, we deceive ourselves, and the truth is not in us. If we confess our sins, he who is faithful and just will forgive us our sins and cleanse us from all unrighteousness. If we say that we have not sinned, we make him a liar, and his word is not in us.

Tertullian

Tertullian is our first witness to what will become known as "canonical penance," reserved for serious sins.

Tertullian, *On Penance* (203), trans. S. Thelwall, in *ANF* 3:659–65.

4. To all sins, then, committed whether by flesh or spirit, whether by deed or will, the same God who has destined penalty by means of judgment, has withal engaged to grant pardon by means of repentance, saying to the people, "Repent thee, and I will save thee;" and again, "I live, saith the Lord, and I will (have) repentance rather than death." Repentance, then, is "life," since it is preferred to "death." That repentance, O sinner, like myself (nay, rather, less than myself, for pre-eminence in sins I acknowledge to be mine), do you so hasten to, so embrace, as a shipwrecked man the protection of some plank. This will draw you forth when sunk in the waves of sins, and will bear you forward into the port of the divine clemency. . . .

6. That *baptismal* washing is a sealing of faith, which faith is begun and is commended by the faith of repentance. We are not washed *in order that* we *may* cease sinning, but *because* we *have* ceased, since in *heart* we have *been* bathed already. For the *first* baptism of a learner is *this*, a perfect fear; thenceforward, in so far as you have understanding of the Lord, faith *is* sound, the conscience having once for all embraced repentance. . . .

7. It is irksome to append mention of a *second*—nay, in that case, the *last*—hope; lest, by treating of a remedial repenting yet in reserve, we seem to be pointing to a yet further space for sinning. Far be it that any one so interpret our meaning, as if, because there is an opening for repenting, there were even now, on that account, an opening for sinning; and *as if* the redundance of celestial clemency constituted a license for human temerity. Let no one be less good because God is more so, by repeating his sin as often as he is forgiven. Otherwise be sure he will find an end of *escaping*, when he shall not find one of *sinning*. We have escaped *once*: thus far *and no farther* let us commit ourselves to perils, even if we seem likely to escape a second time. Men in general, after escaping shipwreck, thenceforward declare divorce with ship and sea; and by *cherishing* the memory of the danger, honour the benefit conferred by God, their deliverance. . . .

9. The narrower, then, the sphere of action of this second and only (remaining) repentance, the more laborious is its probation; in order that it may not be exhibited in the conscience alone, but may likewise be carried out in some (external) act. This act, which is more

usually expressed and commonly spoken of under a Greek name, is *exomologēsis* [confession] whereby we confess our sins to the Lord, not indeed as if He were ignorant of them, but inasmuch as by confession satisfaction is settled, of confession repentance is born; by repentance God is appeased. And thus *exomologēsis* is a discipline for man's prostration and humiliation, enjoining a demeanor calculated to move mercy. With regard also to the very dress and food, it commands (the penitent) to lie in sackcloth and ashes, to cover his body in mourning, to lay his spirit low in sorrows, to exchange for severe treatment the sins which he has committed; moreover, to know no food and drink but such as is plain,—not for the stomach's sake, to wit, but the soul's; for the most part, however, to feed prayers on fastings, to groan, to weep and make outcries unto the Lord your God; to bow before the feet of the presbyters, and kneel to God's dear ones; to enjoin on all the brethren to be ambassadors to bear his deprecatory supplication (before God). All this *exomologēsis* (does), that it may enhance repentance; may honour God by its fear of the (incurred) danger; may, by itself pronouncing against the sinner, stand in the stead of God's indignation, and by temporal mortification (I will not say frustrate, but) expunge eternal punishments. Therefore, while it abases the man, it raises him; while it covers him with squalor, it renders him more clean; while it accuses, it excuses; while it condemns, it absolves. The less quarter you give yourself, the more (believe me) will God give you. . . .

10. Are the judgment of men and the knowledge of God so put upon a par? Is it better to be damned in secret than absolved in public? *But you say*, "It is a miserable thing thus to come to *exomologēsis*:" Yes, for evil does bring to misery; but where repentance is to be made, the misery ceases, because it is turned into something salutary. Miserable it is to be cut, and cauterized, and racked with the pungency of some (medicinal) powder: still, the things which heal by unpleasant means do, by the benefit of the cure, excuse their own offensiveness, and make present injury bearable for the sake of the advantage to supervene.

Didascalia Apostolorum

The *Didascalia Apostolorum* provides insight into the healing and reconciling role of the bishop in the process of penance.

Didascalia Apostolorum (mid-third century), 5, ii. 11; 6, ii. 6–16; and 7, ii.18; in *The Liturgical Portions of the Didascalia*, AGLS 29, ed. Sebastian Brock and Michael Vasey (Cambridge: Grove Books, Ltd., 1982), 9–10.

For this reason then, O bishop, endeavour to be pure in your actions.

Be aware of your position, how you are placed in the likeness of God Almighty, and hold the position of God Almighty. And so sit in the church and teach as having authority to judge, on behalf of God Almighty, those who sin. For to you bishops it is said in the Gospel, "Whatever you bind on earth shall be bound in heaven."

Therefore judge as follows, O bishop; first of all, strictly, but afterwards receive a person with compassion and mercy when he promises to repent. Rebuke and chasten him, and then be entreated by him. . . . [R]eceive the person who repents and without the slightest hesitation; do not be held back from this by those who are without mercy. . . . But when you have seen someone who has sinned, be stern with him, and give orders that they take him out; and when he has gone out, let them be stern with him, and take him to task, and keep him outside the church; and then let them come in and plead for him. . . . And then, bishop, give orders for him to come in, and examine him to see whether he is repentant. And if he is worthy to be received into the church, appoint him a period of fasting according to his offence, two or three weeks—or five, or seven. And so dismiss him, so that he can depart, and say to him whatever is appropriate by way of admonition and instruction; and rebuke him, and tell him that he should pray during his fast that he may be found worthy of the forgiveness of sins. . . . So you . . . are required to act . . . in the case of those who promise to repent of their sins, excluding them from the church for a period proportionate to their offences; and afterwards receive them as merciful fathers. . . . And when the person who has sinned has repented and wept, receive him; and while the entire people are praying for him, lay hands on him and allow him henceforth to be in the church.

DEVELOPMENTS IN THE MIDDLE AGES

Finnian of Clonard

The Irish church develops a pattern of tariff penance celebrated privately and repeatedly.

Finnian of Clonard, *The Penitential of Finnian* (ca. 540),
trans. John T. McNeill and Helena M. Gamer, in *Medieval Handbooks
of Penance* (New York: Columbia University Press, 1938), 88, 91.

6. If anyone has started a quarrel and plotted in his heart to strike or kill his neighbor, if [the offender] is a cleric, he shall do penance for half a year with an allowance of bread and water and for a whole

year abstain from wine and meats, and thus he will be reconciled to the altar.

7. But if he is a layman, he shall do penance for a week, since he is a man of this world and his guilt is lighter in this world and his reward less in the world to come. . . .

23. If any cleric commits murder and kills his neighbor and he is dead, he must become an exile for ten years and do penance seven years in another region . . . and having thus completed the ten years, if he has done well and is approved by testimonial of the abbot or priest, he shall be received into his own country.

An Old Irish Table of Commutations

An Old Irish table of commutations (eighth century),
in *Medieval Handbooks of Penance*, 143.

5. Now every penance, both for severity and length of time in which one is at it, depends on the greatness of the sin and on the space of time which one perseveres in it, and on the reason for which it is done, and on the zeal with which one departs from it afterwards. For there are certain sins which do not deserve any remission of penance, however long the time that shall be asked for them, unless God Himself shortens it through death or a message of sickness; or the greatness of the work which a person lays on himself; such as are parricides and manslaughters and manstealings, and such as brigandage and druidism and satirising [defamatory verses], and such as adultery and lewdness and lying and heresy and transgression of order. For there are certain sins for which halfpenances with half-*arrea* [substitutions] atone. There are others for which an *arreum* only atones.

The Gelasian Sacramentary

Canonical penance appears still in the early medieval sacramentaries at Rome but will gradually be replaced by the more private individualized rite inherited, at least in part, from the Irish tariff system above.

The Gelasian Sacramentary (seventh century), XVI and XXXVIII,
trans. Paul F. Palmer, in *Sources of Christian Theology: Sacraments
and Forgiveness* (Westminster, MD: Newman Press, 1959), 159–62.

XVI. THE ORDER FOR THOSE DOING PUBLIC PENANCE
You receive him on the morning of Wednesday in the beginning of

Lent, and you cover him with a hair-cloth, pray for him, and enclose him from the Lord's Supper. Who on the same day is presented in the bosom of the church, and while his whole body lies prostrate on the ground, the pontiff makes prayer over him for his reconciliation on the Thursday of the Lord's Supper . . .

XXXVIII. PRAYERS ON [HOLY] THURSDAY
On this same day there is no psalmody, nor a greeting, that is, The Lord be with you *is not said: and the Reconciliation of the Penitent.*

[Three short prayers of a general character follow, after which we have the following heading.]

The Order for Those doing Public Penance
The penitent comes forth from the place where he has been doing penance, and is presented in the bosom of the church, his whole body prostrate on the ground. And a deacon makes a request in these words.

The accepted time, O venerable pontiff, is at hand, the day of divine propitiation and human salvation, in which death has received destruction and eternal life a beginning, when in the vineyard of the Lord of Hosts a planting of new shoots is to be made in such a way that the care of the old may be effected by cleansing. . . . We grow by those to be newly born, we increase by those who have returned. . . . And so there is but one opportunity of penance, which is at once of profit to individuals and of help to all in common. . . .

After this he is admonished by the bishop or by some other priest, to the effect that what he has washed away by penance he should not call back by repetition. And then the priest says these prayers over him.

Be propitious, O Lord, to our supplications, and kindly hear me who first of all have need also of Thy mercy, as one whom Thou hast set over the ministry of this office, not through choice based on merit but by the gift of Thy grace: Give me confidence in fulfilling Thy office, and Thyself be present in our ministry which is the work of Thy fatherly kindness. Through [Christ our Lord].

Bestow, we beseech Thee, O Lord, on this Thy servant, fruit worthy of penance, that by obtaining pardon for the sins he has admitted, he may be restored unharmed to Thy holy Church, from whose unity *[integritate]* he has strayed by sinning. Through the Lord.

O God who hast fashioned and most graciously refashioned the human race, who hast redeemed by the blood of Thine only Son man when cast down from eternal [blessedness] by the devil's envy, quicken now him who Thou in no way desirest to be dead to Thee, and Thou who dost not abandon what is crooked, take back what has been straightened. May the tearful sighs of this Thy servant move Thy fatherly kindness, we beseech thee, O Lord. Do Thou heal his wounds. Do Thou stretch forth Thy saving hand to him while prostrate, lest Thy Church be deprived of some portion of its body, lest Thy flock suffer loss, lest the enemy rejoice over the harm done to Thy family, lest a second death grip him who was reborn by the saving bath [of baptism]. To Thee then, O Lord, as suppliants we pour forth our prayers, to Thee our heartfelt tears. Do thou spare the one who confesses, that by Thy mercy he may not incur the punishments which now threaten him and the sentence of the judgement to come. . . .

Again for reconciling a Penitent

Almighty, everlasting God, in Thy fatherly kindness release the sins of this Thy servant who makes confession to Thee, that guilt *(reatus)* of conscience may no longer harm him unto punishment; rather may Thy indulgent love [admit him] unto pardon. Through our Lord Jesus Christ.

Almighty and merciful God, who hast placed the pardon of sins in prompt confession, succour the fallen, have mercy on those who have confessed, that those whom the chain of sins has bound, the greatness of Thy love may release *(absolvat)*. Through Christ our Lord. Amen.

O God who cleansest the hearts of those who confess to Thee, and absolvest from every bond of iniquity the consciences of those who accuse themselves, grant pardon to the guilty, and bestow a healing remedy to the wounded, that having received the remission of all their sins they may henceforth persevere in true devotion, and suffer no loss of eternal redemption. Through Christ our Lord. Amen.

Holy Lord, almighty Father, eternal God, look upon this Thy servant who has been plunged down by the hostile storms of the world, and now with tearful lamentation acknowledges his excesses, in such a way that Thou wilt lovingly accept his tears and groans, and recall him from darkness into light, and grant to the one confessing a remedy, to the penitent salvation, and to the wounded the grace of health. Nor let the enemy have power in his soul any longer, but freely accepting his confession, restore him cleansed to Thy Church, and present him again to Thy altar, so that admitted to the sacrament of reconciliation he may be worthy along with us to give thanks to Thy holy name. Through Christ our Lord. Amen.

Peter Lombard

Peter Lombard, *Four Books of Sentences*, IV (ca. 1152),
trans. Elizabeth Frances Rogers, in *Peter Lombard and the Sacramental System*
(Merrick, NY: Richwood Publishing Co., 1976), 151, 158, 171.

Distinction XIV. I. Next we must discuss penance. Penance is needful to those who are far from God, that they may come near. For it is, as Jerome says, "the second plank after shipwreck"; because if anyone by sinning sullies the robe of innocence received in baptism, he can restore it by the remedy of penance. . . . A man is allowed to do penance often, but not be baptized often. Baptism is called only a sacrament, but penance is called both a sacrament and virtue of the mind. For there is an inner penance and an outer: the outer is the sacrament, the inner is the virtue of the mind; and both are for the sake of salvation and justification. . . .

IV. From these and from many other testimonies it is clearly shown, that by penance not only once, but often, we rise from our sins, and that true penance may be done repeatedly. . . .

Distinction XVI. I. Moreover in the perfection of penance three steps are to be observed, that is compunction of the heart, confession of the mouth, satisfaction in deed. Wherefore John the goldenmouthed [Chrysostom]: "Perfect penance compels the sinner to bear all things cheerfully; in his heart contrition, in his mouth confession, in deed all humility. This is fruitful penance; that just as we offend God in three ways, that is, with the heart, the mouth, and the deed, so in three ways we make satisfaction."

Council of Florence

Council of Florence, "Decree for the Armenians" (1439), trans. from
Enchiridion Symbolorum Definitionum et Declarationum, ed. Henry Denzinger
and Adolf Schönmetzer, 33rd ed. (Freiburg: Herder, 1965), 335–36.

The fourth sacrament is penance. The matter is the acts of penitence which are distinguished in three parts. The first is contrition of the heart, to which belongs grief at sin committed with the resolution of not sinning further. The second is confession of the mouth; to which pertains that the sinner confesses all sins to his priest of which he has memory. The third is satisfaction for sins according to the guidance of a priest; which principally may be through prayers, fasting and charity. The form of this sacrament is the words of absolution which the priest pronounces when he says: "I absolve you." The minister of this sacrament is a priest having authority of absolving, either ordinarily or by commission of a superior. The effect of this sacrament is the absolution from sins.

THE PROTESTANT AND CATHOLIC REFORMATIONS

Positions both conservative and radical on penance are expressed by the various Reformers.

Martin Luther

Martin Luther, *The Babylonian Captivity of the Church* (1520), trans. A. T. W. Steinhäuser, Frederick C. Ahrens, and Abdel Ross Wentz, in LW 36:86–88.

As to the current practice of private confession, I am heartily in favor of it, even though it cannot be proved from the Scriptures. It is useful, even necessary, and I would not have it abolished. Indeed, I rejoice that it exists in the Church of Christ, for it is a cure without equal for distressed consciences. For when we have laid bare our conscience to our brother and privately made known to him the evil that lurked within, we receive from our brother's lips the word of comfort spoken by God himself. And if we accept this in faith, we find peace in the mercy of God speaking to us through our brother. There is just one thing about it that I abominate, and that is the fact that this kind of confession has been subjected to the despotism and extortion of the pontiffs. . . .

In the first place, Christ speaks in Matt. 18:[15–17] of public sins and says that if our brother hears us, when we tell him his fault, we have saved the soul of our brother, and that he is to be brought before the church only if he refuses to hear us, so that his sin can be corrected among brethren. . . .

Hence, I have no doubt but that every one is absolved from his secret sins when he has made confession, privately before any brother, either of his own accord or after being rebuked, and has sought pardon and amended his ways, no matter how much the violence of the pontiffs may rage against it. For Christ has given to every one of his believers the power to absolve even open sins. . . . Let them, moreover, permit all brothers and sisters most freely to hear the confession of secret sins, so that the sinner may make his sins known to whomever he will and seek pardon and comfort, that is, the word of Christ, by the mouth of his neighbor.

The Schleitheim Confession

The Schleitheim Confession (1527),
trans. Walter Klaassen, in *Anabaptism in Outline*
(Scottdale, PA: Herald Press, 1981), 215.

II. We have been united as follows concerning the ban. The ban shall be employed with all those who have given themselves over to the Lord, to walk after [him] in his commandments, those who have been baptized into the one body of Christ, and let themselves be called brothers or sisters, and still somehow slip and fall into error and sin, being inadvertently overtaken. The same [shall] be warned twice privately and the third time be publicly admonished before the entire congregation according to the command of Christ [Matt. 18]. But this shall be done according to the ordering of the Spirit of God before the breaking of bread, so that we may all in one spirit and in one love break and eat from one bread and drink from one cup.

Menno Simons

Menno Simons, *A Kind Admonition on Church
Discipline* (1541), trans. Leonard Verduin, in *The Complete Writings of
Menno Simons* (Scottdale, PA: Herald Press, 1974), 413.

But we do not want to expel any, but rather to receive, not to amputate, but rather to heal; not to discard, but rather to win back; not to grieve but rather to comfort; not to condemn, but rather to save.

Peter Riedeman

Peter Riedeman, *Account* (1542),
in *Anabaptism in Outline*, 221.

But as in the beginning one is received into the church by means of a sign (that is baptism), so also after he fell and was separated from the church he must likewise be received by a sign, that is through the laying on of hands, which must be done by a servant of the gospel. This indicates that he once more has part and is rooted in the grace of God. When this has taken place he is accepted again in full love.

The Council of Trent

The Council of Trent continues the Western medieval arrangements.

The Canons and Decrees of the Council of Trent (1551),
trans. Philip Schaff, in *Creeds of Christendom*, (Grand Rapids:
Baker Book House, n.d.), 2:151, 165–66.

Fourteenth Session, held November 25, 1551
Chapter VI. But, as regards the minister of this sacrament, the holy
Synod declares all those doctrines to be false, and utterly alien from
the truth of the Gospel, which perniciously extend the ministry of
the keys to any others soever besides bishops and priests. . . .

Canon VI.—If any one denieth, either that sacramental confession was instituted, or is necessary to salvation, of divine right; or
saith, that the manner of confessing to salvation, of divine right;
or saith, that the manner of confessing secretly to a priest alone,
which the Church hath ever observed from the beginning, and doth
observe, is alien from the institution and command of Christ, and is
a human invention: let him be anathema.

"The Common Form of Absolution in the Roman Ritual"

"The Common Form of Absolution in the Roman Ritual" (1614–1973),
in *Collectio Rituum pro Dioecesibus Civitatum Foederatarum Americae
Septentrionalis* (Collegeville, MN: Liturgical Press, 1964), 185.

May almighty God have mercy on you, forgive you your sins, and
bring you to life everlasting. Amen.

*Then, with his right hand elevated toward the penitent, he [the
priest] says:*

May the almighty and merciful Lord, grant you pardon, absolution, and remission of your sins. Amen

May our Lord Jesus Christ absolve you, and by his authority I
absolve you from every bond of excommunication, suspension [for
clergy only], and interdict, to the extent of my power and your need.
Finally I absolve you from your sins, in the name of the Father and
of the Son + and of the Holy Spirit. Amen.

May the Passion of our Lord Jesus Christ, the merits of the Blessed
Virgin Mary and of all the saints, and also whatever good you do and
evil you endure be cause for the remission of your sins, the increase
of grace, and the reward of everlasting life. Amen.

VATICAN II

The Second Vatican Council points to new directions, including the restoration of the corporate dimension of reconciliation.

Sacred Congregation for Divine Worship

Sacred Congregation for Divine Worship, "Decree: Rite of Penance,"
in International Commission on English in the Liturgy, *The Rites of the
Catholic Church* (Collegeville, MN: Liturgical Press, 1990), 1:523–24.

Vatican Council II decreed that "the rite and formularies for the sacrament of penance are to be revised so that they may more clearly express both the nature and effect of this sacrament" [CSL, art. 72]. In view of this the Congregation for Divine Worship has carefully prepared the new *Rite of Penance* so that the celebration of the sacrament may be more fully understood by the faithful.

In this new rite, besides the *Rite for Reconciliation of Individual Penitents,* a *Rite for Reconciliation of Several Penitents* has been drawn up to emphasize the relation of the sacrament to the community. This rite places individual confession and absolution in the context of a celebration of the word of God. Furthermore, for special occasions, a *Rite for Reconciliation of Several Penitents with General Confession and Absolution* has been composed in accordance with the Pastoral Norms on General Sacramental Absolution, issued by the Congregation for the Doctrine of the Faith, 16 June, 1972.

The Church is deeply concerned with calling the faithful to continual conversion and renewal. It desires that the baptized who have sinned should acknowledge their sins against God and their neighbor and have heartfelt repentance for them; it takes pains to prepare them to celebrate the sacrament of penance. For this reason the Church urges the faithful to attend penitential celebrations from time to time. This Congregation has therefore made regulations for such celebrations and has proposed examples or models that conferences of bishops may adapt to the needs of their own regions.

"The Formula of Absolution"

"The Formula of Absolution," in *The Rites of the Catholic Church,* 546–47.

God, the Father of mercies, through the death and resurrection of his Son has reconciled the world to himself and sent the Holy Spirit among us for the forgiveness of sins; through the ministry of the Church may God give you pardon and peace, and I absolve you from your sins in the name of the Father, and of the Son, + and of the Holy Spirit.

CONTEMPORARY PROTESTANTISM

Some Modern Protestant rites have sought to restore private confession and absolution to the place it held among the Reformers.

Evangelical Lutheran Worship

"Individual Confession and Forgiveness," in *Evangelical Lutheran Worship* (Minneapolis: Augsburg Fortress, 2006), 243–44.

Washed in water and marked with the cross, the baptized children of God are united with Christ and, through him, with other believers who together form a living community of faith. Although we are set free to live in love and faithfulness, we continue to turn away from God and from one another. Confessing our sin involves a continuing return to our baptism where our sinful self is drowned and dies; in the gift of forgiveness God raises us up again and again to new life in Jesus Christ.

Individual Confession and Forgiveness is a ministry of the church through which a person may confess sin and receive the assurance of God's forgiveness. This order may be used by itself at times when a congregation offers opportunity or people request the opportunity for confession. It may also be used in conjunction with pastoral care, such as to conclude a counseling session. There is a confidential nature to this order, in keeping with the discipline and practice of the Lutheran church.

Confession
The pastor begins:
In the name of the Father,
and of the +Son,
and of the Holy Spirit.
Response: Amen.
OR
Blessed be the holy Trinity, + one God,
who forgives all our sin,
whose mercy endures forever.
Response: Amen.
You have come to make confession before God.

You are free to confess before me, a pastor in the church of Christ,
sins of which you are aware and which trouble you.
The penitent may use the following form or pray in her/his own words.
Merciful God, I confess
that I have sinned in thought, word, and deed,
by what I have done and by what I have left undone.
*Here the penitent may confess sins that are known and that burden
her/him.*
I repent of all my sins, known and unknown.
I am truly sorry, and I pray for forgiveness.
I firmly intend to amend my life,
and to seek help in mending what is broken.
I ask for strength to turn from sin and to serve you in newness of life.
*The pastor may engage the penitent in conversation, sharing admonition, counsel, and comfort from the scriptures. Psalm 51 or Psalm 103
may be spoken together.*

Forgiveness
Addressing the penitent, the pastor may lay both hands on the penitent's head.
Cling to this promise: the word of forgiveness I speak to you comes
from God.
Name,
in obedience to the command
of our Lord Jesus Christ,
I forgive you all your sins
in the name of the Father,
and of the + Son,
and of the Holy Spirit. *Response:* Amen.
OR
Name,
by water and the Holy Spirit
God gives you a new birth,
and through the death and resurrection
of Jesus Christ,
God forgives you all your sins.
Almighty God
strengthen you in all goodness
and keep you in eternal life.
Response: Amen.
The peace of God, which passes all understanding,
keep your heart and your mind in Christ Jesus.
Response: Amen.
The pastor and the penitent may share the greeting of peace.

|

Healing and Anointing of the Sick

|

EARLY CHRISTIAN DOCUMENTS

Healing of soul and of body have a long and close affinity.

Scripture

Mark 16:18c.

"They will lay their hands on the sick, and they will recover."

James 5:14–16.

Are any among you sick? They should call for the elders of the church and have them pray over them, anointing them with oil in the name of the Lord. The prayer of faith will save the sick, and the Lord will raise them up; and anyone who has committed sins will be forgiven. Therefore confess your sins to one another, and pray for one another, so that you may be healed. The prayer of the righteous is powerful and effective.

Sarapion of Thmuis

The prayers of Sarapion provide for us what is very likely the earliest liturgical prayer for the specific blessing of oil for the sick, as well as other related elements, which may have been taken home for use by the faithful from the Sunday Eucharist.

Sarapion of Thmuis, *Prayer-Book* (ca. 350), trans. Maxwell E. Johnson,
in *The Prayers of Sarapion of Thmuis: A Liturgical, Literary, and Theological Analysis*,
OCA 249 (Rome: Pontificio Istituto Orientale, 1995), 67.

[Prayer 17] Prayer for Oil of the Sick or for Bread or for Water
Father of our Lord and Savior Jesus Christ, having all authority and power, the savior of all people, we call upon you and we implore you that healing power of your only-begotten may be sent out from heaven upon this oil. May it become to those who are anointed (or to those who receive of these your creatures) for a rejection of every

disease and every sickness, for an amulet warding off every demon, for a departing of every unclean spirit, for a taking away of every evil spirit, for a driving away of all fever and shiverings and every weakness, for good grace and forgiveness of sins, for a medicine of life and salvation, for health and wholeness of soul, body, spirit, for perfect strength.

Master, let every satanic energy, every demon, every plot of the opposing one, every blow, every lash, every pain, or every slap in the face, or shaking, or evil shadow be afraid of your holy name, which we have now called upon, and the name of the only-begotten; and let them depart from the inner and the outer parts of these your servants so that the name of Jesus Christ, the one who was crucified and risen for us, who took to himself our diseases and weaknesses, and is coming to judge the living and the dead, may be glorified. For through him (be) to you the glory and the power in holy Spirit both now and to all the ages of ages. Amen.

The Letter of Pope Innocent I to Decentius of Gubbio

This fifth-century Roman letter is as much concerned with the minister who anoints the sick as it is with the anointing itself. After Innocent, who still allowed for lay administration of anointing in emergencies, the rite will become increasingly connected to the ministry of presbyters.

The Letter of Pope Innocent I to Decentius of Gubbio, 8 (416), trans. Martin Connell, in *Church and Worship in Fifth-Century Rome: The Letter of Innocent I to Decentius of Gubbio*, AGLS 52 (Cambridge: Grove Books, Ltd., 2002), 46.

There is no doubt but that this [James 5:24] ought to be received and understood as referring to the faithful who are ailing for they are able to be anointed with the holy chrism, which has been made by the Bishop. In case of emergency, this anointing is permitted not only for priests but even for all Christians. We know that anything else that might be added would be superfluous, such as there being confusion regarding what is without a doubt able to be done by presbyters. The passage refers here to presbyters because the bishops, whose schedules are quite taken up with other things, are not able to go be with all who are sick. Still, if the Bishop is able to visit or is taken to someone who is worthy of it, let him whose very job it is to make chrism visit and bless and touch the sick with chrism without hesitation. Nonetheless, this which is a kind of sacrament cannot be poured on penitents. For how can you agree to offer this one kind of sacrament to those who are denied the rest?

MEDIEVAL DEVELOPMENT

A Carolingian Rite of Anointing the Sick

A Carolingian rite of anointing the sick (ninth century), trans. Paul F. Palmer,
in *Sources of Christian Theology: Sacraments and Forgiveness*
(Westminster, MD: Newman Press, 1959), 294–95.

Prayers for Visiting the Sick.
In the first place let the priests prepare blessed water with a sprinkling of salt, and sprinkle it over the sick person himself and over his house, with an Antiphon and Prayers.

[After six short prayers, which are taken from Alcuin's Order for Visiting the Sick, the following longer prayer, which alone has survived in the present Roman Ritual, is said.]

Then let this Prayer be said by the priests:
Lord God, who hast spoken by Thine Apostle James, saying: Is anyone sick among you? Let him call in the presbyters of the Church, and let them pray over him, anointing him with oil in the name of the Lord: and the prayer of faith shall save the sick man, and the Lord will raise him up; and if he be in sins, they shall be forgiven him: cure, we beseech Thee, our Redeemer, by the grace of the Holy Spirit, the weakness of this sick man; heal his wounds, and forgive his sins; drive out from him all pains of body and mind, and mercifully restore to him full health, both inwardly and outwardly; that recovered and healed by the help of Thy mercy, he may be strengthened to take up again his former duties of piety to Thee. Through.

And so let the ailing person bend the knee or knees, and stand at the priest's right, and let the following Antiphon be sung:
The Lord has said to his disciples: In my name cast out devils; and lay your hands on the sick, and they will be well.

[Psalm 49 is recited, the Antiphon repeated, and the following prayer is said.]

We pray our Lord Jesus Christ, and in all supplication we ask that he deign through His holy angel to visit, gladden and comfort this His servant.
The Antiphon follows: Come, O Lord, to the assistance of this sick

person, and heal him with spiritual medicine, that, restored to former health, he may return thanks to Thee in soundness of health.

[Psalm 119 is recited, followed by the Antiphon, "Heal, O Lord, this sick man, etc." Psalm 37 is introduced and concluded with a *Gloria* and repetition of the Antiphon, "Heal, O Lord."]

Peter Lombard

Further medieval development, especially in Western Christianity, makes anointing a sacrament for the dying, increasingly called "extreme unction."

Peter Lombard, *Four Books of Sentences*, IV (ca. 1152),
in *Peter Lombard and the Sacramental System*, 221–23.

Distinction XXIII. 1. Beside the preceding, there is another sacrament, that is, the unction of the sick, which is administered at the end of life, with oil consecrated by the bishop. . . .

3. The sacrament was instituted for a double purpose, namely for the remission of sins, and for the relief of bodily infirmity. Wherefore it is plain that he who receives this unction faithfully and devoutly, is relieved both in body and in soul, provided it is expedient that he be relieved in both. But if perhaps it is not expedient for him to have bodily health, he acquires in this sacrament that health which is of the soul. . . .

4. But if you apply it to the receiving of the "sacrament," it is true of some that they are not repeated or frequently received, but it is not true of others, because they are frequently received like this sacrament of unction, which is often repeated in almost every Church.

Thomas Aquinas

Thomas Aquinas reflects on the relationship between healing and forgiveness of sin in this sacrament.

Thomas Aquinas, *Summa Theologica*, Suppl. XXX (ca. 1271), trans. Fathers of the
English Dominican Province (New York: Benziger Bros., 1948), 3:2671–72.

*Article I. Whether Extreme Unction Avails for the Remission
of Sins?* . . .
I answer that, Each sacrament was instituted for the purpose of one

principal effect, though it may, in consequence, produce other effects besides. And since a sacrament causes what it signifies, the principal effect of a sacrament must be gathered from its signification. Now this sacrament is conferred by way of a kind of medicament, even just as Baptism is conferred by way of a washing, and the purpose of a medicament is to expel sickness. Hence the chief object of the institution of this sacrament is to cure the sickness of sin. . . .

Consequently we must say that the principal effect of this sacrament is the remission of sin as to its remnants, and consequently, even as to its guilt, if it find it.

THE PROTESTANT AND CATHOLIC REFORMATIONS

John Calvin

John Calvin takes vigorous exception to this shift toward extreme unction.

John Calvin, *Institutes of the Christian Religion*, IV (1559), trans. Ford Lewis Battles, in LCC 21:1467–69.

18. But that gift of healing, like the rest of the miracles, which the Lord willed to be brought forth for a time, has vanished away in order to make the new preaching of the gospel marvelous forever. Therefore, even if we grant to the full that anointing was a sacrament of those powers which were then administered by the hands of the apostles, it now has nothing to do with us, to whom the administering of such powers has not been committed. . . .

21. James wishes all sick persons to be anointed [James 5:14]; these fellows smear with their grease not the sick but half dead corpses when they are already drawing their last breath, or (as they say), *in extremis*. If in their sacrament they have a powerful medicine with which to alleviate the agony of diseases, or at least to bring some comfort to the soul, it is cruel of them never to heal in time. . . . The prayers of believers, with which the afflicted brother has been commended to God, will not be in vain. . . . Pope Innocent [I], who presided over the church at Rome in Augustine's day, established the practice that not only presbyters but also all Christians should use oil for anointing when they or their dependents should need it.

Council of Trent

The Council of Trent reaffirms the necessity of an ordained priest as minister of the sacrament.

Canons and Decrees of the Council of Trent (1551), in *The Creeds of Christendom* (Grand Rapids: Baker Book House, n.d.), 2:170,

Fourteenth Session, held November 25, 1551
Canon IV.—If any one saith, that the presbyters [*presbyteros*] of the Church, whom the blessed James exhorts to be brought to anoint the sick, are not the priests who have been ordained by a bishop, but the elders [*seniores*] in each community, and that for this cause a priest alone is not the proper minister of Extreme Unction: let him be anathema.

VATICAN II

Vatican II points to new orientations in a more broadly conceived ministry to the sick.

Constitution on the Sacred Liturgy

Constitution on the Sacred Liturgy (Collegeville, MN: Liturgical Press, 1963), 41.

73. "Extreme unction," which may also and more fittingly be called "anointing of the sick," is not a sacrament for those only who are at the point of death. Hence, as soon as any one of the faithful begins to be in danger of death from sickness or old age, the fitting time for him to receive this sacrament has certainly already arrived.

74. In addition to the separate rites for anointing of the sick and for viaticum, a continuous rite shall be prepared according to which the sick man is anointed after he has made his confession and before he receives viaticum.

75. The number of anointings is to be adapted to the occasion, and the prayers which belong to the rite of anointing are to be revised so as to correspond with the varying conditions of the sick who receive the sacrament.

Christian Marriage

MARRIAGE RITES REFLECTING LOCAL CULTURES

Scripture

Matthew 19:4–6 (see also Gen. 1:27; 2:24; Mark 10:1–12).

He answered, "Have you not read that the one who made them at the beginning 'made them male and female,' and said, 'For this reason a man shall leave his father and mother and be joined to his wife, and the two shall become one flesh'? So they are no longer two, but one flesh. Therefore what God has joined together, let no one separate."

John 2:1–2.

On the third day there was a wedding in Cana of Galilee, and the mother of Jesus was there. Jesus and his disciples had also been invited to the wedding.

Ephesians 5:31–32.

"'For this reason a man will leave his father and mother and be joined to his wife, and the two will become one flesh." This is a great mystery [*mystērion*], and I am applying it to Christ and the church.

Ignatius of Antioch

Ignatius of Antioch, "Letter to Polycarp," V, 2 (ca. 115), trans. Cyril C. Richardson, in LCC 1:119.

It is right for men and women who marry to be united with the bishop's approval. In that way their marriage will follow God's will and not the promptings of lust. Let everything be done so as to advance God's honor.

A MARRIAGE RITE FROM THE
WESTERN MIDDLE AGES

The Hadrianum

This early papal sacramentary from the eighth century at Rome, sent by
Pope Hadrian I to the emperor Charlemagne, provides texts both for the
nuptial mass and the nuptial blessing.

The Hadrianum, a Gregorian sacramentary, in Mark Searle
and Kenneth Stevenson, *Documents of the Marriage Liturgy*
(Collegeville, MN: Liturgical Press, Pueblo, 1992), 46–49.

PRAYER OVER THE GIFTS
2.
Receive, we beseech you, O Lord,
the gift we offer for the holy law of marriage;
be the guardian of the enterprise which you have given.
Through.

PREFACE
3. It is truly right and just,
fitting and for our salvation.
For you have joined people in marriage
with the sweet yoke of concord
and the unbreakable bond of peace,
so that the chaste fruitfulness of holy marriages
may serve to increase the adoptive children of God.
Your providence, O Lord, and your grace
serve to guide both things in wonderful ways:
what generation brings forth to enrich the world,
regeneration leads to the increase of the Church.
And therefore, with angels and archangels,
with thrones and dominations,
and with the whole heavenly host,
we sing the hymn of your glory,
saying without ceasing: Holy, holy, holy.

HANC IGITUR
4.
Be pleased, therefore, O Lord,
to accept the offering of your servants,
which they offer for your maidservant, N.,

whom you have deigned to bring to the age of maturity
and to the day of marriage.
On her behalf
we pour out our prayers to your majesty,
that you would mercifully grant her
to be united with her husband . . . .

BLESSING
6.
O God,
you made all things out of nothing by your power.
When you had laid the foundations of the universe,
you created man in the image of God,
and made woman as man's inseparable helper,
bringing the woman's body into being
out of the man's flesh,
teaching us thereby
that what it had pleased to create
out of an original unity
must never be put asunder.
O God,
you have consecrated the bond of marriage
with such an excellent mystery
as to prefigure in the covenant of marriage
the sacrament of Christ and his Church.

7.
O God,
through you a woman is joined to her husband
and society is chiefly ordered by that blessing
which was neither lost by original sin
nor washed away in the flood.

8a
Look with kindness upon your maidservant,
who is to be joined in marriage,
and who now seeks the help of your protection.

8b
May her yoke be one of love and peace.

8c
May she marry in Christ,
faithful and chaste.

8d
May she remain an imitator of holy women:

8e
amiable to her husband, like Rachel;
wise, like Rebecca;
long-lived and faithful, like Sarah.

9a
May the author of lies never subvert her behavior;
may she remain steadfast in fidelity
and in keeping the commandments.

9b
Loyal to one marriage bed,
may she flee all unlawful relations.

9c
Let her shore up her weakness
with the strength of discipline.

9d
May she be sober and modest,
her honor above reproach,
learned in heavenly wisdom.

10a
May she be fruitful with children,
a person of integrity
and beyond suspicion.

10b
And may she come at last
to enjoy the repose of the blessed
and to the heavenly kingdom.

10c
May she see her children's children
to the third and fourth generation,
and come to a desired old age.
Through.

10d
The peace of the Lord be with you always.

TO CONCLUDE
11. We beseech you, almighty God,
to accompany with your love
what your providence has established,
so that those who are joined in lawful wedlock
may be preserved by you in lasting peace.
Through.

MARRIAGE AS ONE OF SEVEN SACRAMENTS

Marriage makes it onto the list of seven sacraments.

Peter Lombard

Peter Lombard, *Four Books of Sentences*, IV (ca. 1152),
in *Peter Lombard and the Sacramental System*, 243.

Distinction XXVI. 1. "Although the other sacraments took their rise after sin and on account of sin, we read that the sacrament of marriage was instituted by the Lord before sin, yet not as a remedy, but as a duty." . . .

2. Now the institution of marriage is twofold: one was instituted before sin in paradise as a duty, that there might be a blameless couch and honorable nuptials; as a result of which they might conceive without passion and bring forth without pain; the other was instituted after sin outside paradise for a remedy, to prevent unlawful desires; the first that nature might be multiplied; the second, that nature might be protected, and sin repressed. For even before sin God said: "Increase and multiply" and again after sin, when most men had been destroyed by the deluge. But Augustine testified that before sin marriage was instituted for a duty, and after sin allowed for a remedy, when he says: "What is a duty for the sound is a remedy for the sick." For the infirmity of incontinence which exists in the flesh that is dead through sin, is protected by honorable marriage lest it fall into the ruin of vice. If the first men had not sinned, they and their descendants would have united without the incentive of the flesh and the heat of passion; and as any good deed deserves reward, so their union would have been good and worthy of reward. But because on account of sin the law of deadly concupiscence has beset our members, without which there is no carnal union, an evil union is reprehensible unless it be excused by the blessings of marriage. . . .

6. Since therefore marriage is a sacrament, it is also a sacred sign and of a sacred thing, namely, of the union of Christ and the Church, as the Apostle says: It is written, he says: "A man shall leave father and mother and shall cling to his wife, and they shall be two in one flesh. This is a great sacrament, but I speak of Christ and of the Church" [Eph. 5:31–32].

Marriage Vows in the Vernacular

Marriage vows in the vernacular, in *Manual of York Use* (fourteenth century), University Library, Cambridge, England (MS Ee.iv.19), pp. 23, 23B, 24 (spelling and punctuation modernized).

[Name] will you have this woman to your wife, and love her, and worship her and keep her in health and in sickness, and in all other degrees, be to her as a husband should be to his wife, and all other forsake, and hold you only to her to your life's end? . . . I will. . . .

[Name] will you have this man to your husband, and to be buxom to him, love him, obey to him, and worship him, serve him, and keep him in health and in sickness, and in all other degrees, be to him as a wife should be to her husband, and all other to forsake for him, and hold you only to him till your life's end? . . . I will. . . .

Here I take you [name] to my wedded wife, to hold and to have at bed and at board, for fairer for [fouler], for better for worse, in sickness and in health, till death us do part, if holy Church it will ordain, and thereto I plight you my troth....

Here I take you [name] to my wedded husband, to hold and to have at bed and at board, for fairer for [fouler], for better for worse, in sickness and in health, till death us do part, if holy Church it will ordain, and thereto I plight you my troth....

With this ring I wed you, and with this gold and silver I honor you, and with this gift I endow you.

John Calvin

John Calvin, *Institutes of the Christian Religion*, IV (1559), trans. Ford Lewis Battles, in LCC 21:1480–83.

34. The last one is marriage. All men admit that it was instituted by God [Gen. 2:21–24; Matt. 19:4ff.]; but no man ever saw it administered as a sacrament until the time of Gregory [VII]. And what sober man would ever have thought it such? Marriage is a good and holy ordinance of God; and farming, building, cobbling, and barbering are lawful ordinances of God, and yet are not sacraments. For it is

required that a sacrament be not only a work of God but an outward ceremony appointed by God to confirm a promise. Even children can discern that there is no such thing in matrimony.

36. The term "sacrament" deceived them. But was it right that the whole church should suffer the punishment of their ignorance? Paul had said "mystery." The translator [of the Latin version] could have left this word, as one not unfamiliar to Latin ears, or rendered it as "secret." He preferred to use the word "sacrament" [Eph. 5:32, Vulgate], but in the same sense that the word "mystery" had been used by Paul.

Council of Trent

Canons and Decrees of the Council of Trent (1563), in *The Creeds of Christendom* (Grand Rapids: Baker Book House, n.d.), 2:197.

Twenty-Fourth Session, held November 11, 1563.
Canon X.—If any one saith, that the marriage state is to be placed above the state of virginity, or of celibacy, and that it is not better and more blessed to remain in virginity, or in celibacy, than to be united in matrimony: let him be anathema.

Rituale Romanum

This rite for the celebration of the sacrament of matrimony was the official Roman Catholic marriage rite until after the reforms of the Second Vatican Council.

Rituale Romanum (1614), *The Roman Ritual* (1614), in *Documents of the Marriage Liturgy*, 184–88.

1.
After publishing the banns on three feast days, as aforesaid, and if no lawful impediment stands in the way, the parish priest who is to celebrate the marriage, being vested in surplice and white stole and attended by at least one cleric likewise vested in a surplice and carrying the book and the vessel of holy water with its sprinkler, shall, in the presence of two or three witnesses, in the church, ask the man and the woman separately, preferably in the presence of their parents or relatives, the question about their consent to the marriage, using the vernacular tongue and the following form:
N., will you take N.,
here present,

to be your lawful wife,
according to the rite of holy mother Church?
The bridegroom answers:
I will.
Then the priest asks the bride:
N., will you take N.,
here present,
to be your lawful husband,
according to the rite of holy mother Church?
The bride answers:
I will.
The consent of one does not suffice; it must be of both. And it must be expressed in some sensible sign, either by the parties themselves or through an intermediary.

2.
Having understood the mutual consent of the parties, the priest orders them to join their right hands, saying:
I join you in matrimony,
in the name of the Father +
and of the Son
and of the Holy Spirit.
Or other words may be used according to the received rite of each province. Afterwards, he sprinkles them with holy water.

3.
Then he blesses the ring.
BLESSING OF THE RING
V. Our help is in the name of the Lord.
R. Who made heaven and earth.
V. Lord, hear my prayer.
R. And let my cry come to you.
V. The Lord be with you.
R. And also with you.
Let us pray:
Bless +, O Lord,
this ring which we bless + in your name,
so that she who shall wear it,
remaining totally faithful to her husband,
may remain in peace and in your will,
and live always in mutual charity.
Through Christ, etc.
Then the priest sprinkles the ring with holy water in the form of a cross.

4.

Receiving the ring from the priest's hand, the bridegroom places it on the ring finger of his bride's left hand, while the priest says:
In the name of the Father +,
and of the Son, and of the Holy Spirit.
Amen.

5.

Then he adds:
V. Confirm, O God, what you have wrought among us.
R. From your holy temple, which is in Jerusalem.
Kyrie eleison.
Christe eleison.
Kyrie eleison.
Our Father. *silently*
V. And lead us not into temptation.
R. But deliver us from evil.
V. Save your servants.
R. Who put their trust in you, my God.
V. Lord, send them help from your holy place.
R. And defend them out of Sion.
V. Be a tower of strength to them, O Lord.
R. In the face of the enemy.
V. Lord, hear my prayer.
R. And let my cry come to you.
V. The Lord be with you.
R. And also with you.
Let us pray:
Look down, we beseech you, O Lord,
upon these your servants,
and graciously assist this ordinance of yours,
which you have provided
for the propagation of the human race;
that those who are joined together
by your authority
may be preserved by your help.
Through Christ our Lord.
Amen.

6.

When all this is done, and if the marriage is to be blessed, the parish priest celebrates the Mass for Bride and Groom, as found in the Roman Missal, observing everything prescribed there.

7.

Moreover, if, besides the above, some provinces are accustomed to using other laudable customs and ceremonies in the celebration of the sacrament of matrimony, the holy Council of Trent desires that they should be retained.

8.

When everything has been completed, the parish priest enters in the register of marriages, in his own hand, the names of the couple, of the witnesses and the other things required; and that he, or some other priest delegated either by him or by the ordinary, has celebrated the marriage.

MARRIAGE AFTER THE REFORMATION

The purposes of marriage enunciated in medieval documents survive the Reformation.

The Book of Common Prayer

The Book of Common Prayer (1559), in *Documents of the Marriage Liturgy*, 216–26.

THE FOURME OF SOLEMPNIZACION OF MATRIMONYE
First, the banes must be asked thre seuerall Sondaies or holy daies, in the tyme of seruice, the people beyng present, after the accustomed maner.

And yf the persons that would be maryed dwell in diuerse Paryshes, the banes must be asked in both Parishes and the Curate of the one Paryshe shall not solempnize matrimonye betwyxt them, wythout a certifycate of the banes beyng thryse asked, from the Curate of the other Parysh.

I
At the daie appoincted for solempnizacyon of Matrimonye, the persones to be maryed shal come into the body of the Churche, wyth theyr frendes and neighbours. And there the Pryest shall thus saye.

1.

Dearely beloued frendes,
we are gathered together here in the sight of God,
and in the face of his congregacion,

to ioyne together this man and this woman
in holy matrimony,
which is an honorable state,
instytuted of God in Paradise,
in the time of manes innocencie,
signifiyng vnto vs the mistical vnion
that is betwixt Christ and his Churche:
which holy state Christe adourned and beautified
with his presence and firste miracle
that he wrought in Cana of Galile,
and is commended of sainct Paul
to be honourable emong all men,
and therfore is not to be enterprised,
nor taken in hande
vnaduisedly, lightly or wantonly,
to satisfye mennes carnall lustes and appetytes,
lyke brute beastes that haue no vnderstandyng;
but reuerently, discretely, aduisedly,
soberly, and in the feare of God,
duely consideryng the causes
for the which matrimony was ordeined.
One was the procreation of children,
to be brought vp in the feare
and nurtoure of the Lorde,
and praise of God.
Secondly,
it was ordeined for a remedy agaynste sinne
and to auoide fornication,
that suche persones
as haue not the gifte of continencie might mary,
and kepe themselues vndefiled membres of Christes body.
Thirdly,
for the mutual societie, helpe, and comfort,
that the one ought to haue of the other,
bothe in prosperity and aduersitye,
into the whiche holy state
these two persones present,
come nowe to be ioyned.
Therefore
if any man can shewe any iust cause,
why thei may not lawfully be iouned together
let hym now speake,
or els hereafter for euer holde his peace.

2.
And also speakynge to the persons that shalbe maryed, he shall saie.
I require and charge you
(as you wil aunswere at the dreadful day of iudgement,
when the secretes of all hartes shalbe disclosed)
that if either of you doe knowe any impedyment,
why ye may not be lawfully ioyned together
in Matrimony,
that ye confesse it.
For be ye well assured,
that so many as be coupled together,
otherwyse than Goddes worde doeth allowe,
are not ioyned together by God,
neither is their Matrimonye lawfull.
At whyche day of Maryage, if any man do allege and declare any
impediment, why they may not be coupled together in matrymony by
Gods law, or the lawes of thys realme, and wyll be bound, and suf-
ficient sureties with him, to the parties, or els put in a cautyon to the
ful value of suche charges, as the persons to be maryed do susteine, to
proue hys allegation: then the solempnization must be deferred vnto
suche tyme as the truthe be tried. If no impediment be alledged, then
shall the curate saye vnto the man,

3.
N., wilt thou haue thys woman to thy wedded wyfe,[1]
to lyue together after Goddes ordynaunce
in the holye estate of Matrimony?
Wylt thou loue her, comforte her,
honour, and kepe her,
in sickenes, and in healthe?
And forsakyng al other,
kepe the onely to her,
so long as you both shall liue?
The man shall aunswere,
I will.
Then shall the Priest saye to the woman,
N., wilt thou haue this man to thy wedded housband,
to lyue together after Goddes ordynaunce
in the holy estate of matrimony?
Wilt thou obey hym and serue him,
loue, honour, and kepe him,
in sycknes, and in health?

1. Sarum, I.3.

And forsakynge al other,
kepe the onely to him
so long as ye bothe shal liue?
The woman shall aunswere,
I will.
Then shall the Minister saie,

4.
Who geueth this woman to be maried vnto this man?[2]
And the Minister, receiuyng the woman at her father or frendes handes,
shall cause the man to take the woman by the right hand, and so either
to geue their trouth to other, the man first saying.

5.
I, N., take the, N.,[3]
to my wedded wyfe,
to haue and to hold from thys day forward,
for better, for worse,
for richer, for porer,
in sickenes, and in healthe,
to loue and to cheryshe,
tyll death vs departe;
according to Gods holy ordinaunce,
and therto I plight the my trouth.
Then shall they louse their handes, and the woman takyng againe the
man by the right hande, shall saie.
I, N., take the, N.,
to my wedded husbande,
to haue and to holde,
from this day forward,
for better, for worse,
for richer, for porer,
in sickenes, and in health,
to loue, cherish, and to obey,
till death vs departe;
accordynge to Godes holy ordinaunce,
and therto I geue the my trouth.

6.
Then shall they again louse theyr handes, and the man shal geue vnto
the woman a ring, laying the same vpon the booke, with the accus-
tomed dutie to the Priest and Clerke. And the Priest taking the ryng,

2. Sarum, I.4 (York).
3. Sarum, I.4.

shal delyuer it vnto the man, to put it vpon the fourth finger of the
womans left hand. And the man taught by the Priest, shal say.
With this ring I the wed:
with my body I the worship:
and with all my worldly goodes, I the endow.
In the name of the Father,
and of the Sonne,
and of the holy Ghost.
Amen.
Then the man leauyng the ryng vpon the fourth finger of the womans
left hande, the Minister shall saye.
O eternall God,
creatoure and preseruer of all mankynd,
giuer of all spirytuall grace,
the aucthour of euerlastyng life:
send thy blessyng vpon these thy seruauntes,
thys man and this woman,
whom we blesse in thy name,
that as Isaac and Rebecca
lyued faithfully together:
So these persons may surely performe
and kepe the vow and couenaunt betwixte them made,
whereof this ring geuen, and receiued,
is a token and pledge,
and may euer remain
in perfect loue and peace together,
and liue according vnto thy lawes,
through Jesus Christ our Lorde.
Amen.

7.
Then shal the Priest ioyne their right handes together and say.
Those whome God hath ioyned together,
let no man put a sonder.

8.
Then shall the Minister speak unto the people.
For asmuche as N. and N.
haue consented together in holy wedlocke,
and haue witnessed the same before God,
and thys company,
and therto haue giuen and pledged,
their trouth eyther to other,
and haue declared the same

by geuyyng and receiuyng of a ryng,
and by ioynyng of hands
I pronounce that thei be man and wife together.
In the name of the father,
of the sonne
and of the holy Ghost.
Amen.

MODERN RITES AND THEOLOGY

Roman Catholic

"Rite of Marriage," in *The Rites of the Catholic Church*, 1:726–31.

INTRODUCTION
23. All stand, including the bride and bridegroom, and the priest
addresses them in these or similar words:
My dear friends,* you have come together in this church so that
the Lord may seal and strengthen your love in the presence of the
Church's minister and this community. Christ abundantly blesses
this love. He has already consecrated you in baptism and now he
enriches and strengthens you by a special sacrament so that you
may assume the duties of marriage in mutual and lasting fidelity. And so, in the presence of the Church, I ask you to state your
intentions.

*At the discretion of the priest, other words which seem more
suitable under the circumstances, such as **friends** or **dearly beloved**
or **brethren** may be used. This also applies to parallel instances in
the liturgy.

QUESTIONS
24. The priest then questions them about their freedom of choice,
faithfulness to each other, and the acceptance and upbringing of
children:

N. and N., have you come here freely and without reservation to
give yourselves to each other in marriage?

Will you love and honor each other as man and wife for the rest
of your lives?

The following question may be omitted if, for example, the couple
is advanced in years.

Will you accept children lovingly from God, and bring them up
according to the law of Christ and his Church?

Each answers the questions separately.

CONSENT

25. The priest invites the couple to declare their consent:

Since it is your intention to enter into marriage, join your right hands, and declare your consent before God and his Church.

They join hands.

The bridegroom says:

I, N., take you, N., to be my wife. I promise to be true to you in good times and in bad, in sickness and in health. I will love you and honor you all the days of my life.

The bride says:

I, N., take you, N., to be my husband. I promise to be true to you in good times and in bad, in sickness and in health. I will love you and honor you all the days of my life.

If, however, it seems preferable for pastoral reasons, the priest may obtain consent from the couple through questions.

First he asks the bridegroom:

N., do you take N. to be your wife? Do you promise to be true to her in good times and in bad, in sickness and in health, to love her and honor her all the days of your life?

The bridegroom: **I do.**

Then he asks the bride:

N., do you take N. to be your husband? Do you promise to be true to him in good times and in bad, in sickness and in health, to love him and honor him all the days of your life?

The bride: **I do.**

If pastoral necessity demands it, the conference of bishops may decree, in virtue of the faculty in no. 17, that the priest should always obtain the consent of the couple through questions.

In the dioceses of the United States, the following form may also be used:

I, N., take you, N., for my lawful wife, to have and to hold, from this day forward, for better, for worse, for richer, for poorer, in sickness and in health, until death do us part.

I, N., take you, N., for my lawful husband, to have and to hold, from this day forward, for better, for worse, for richer, for poorer, in sickness and in health, until death do us part.

If it seems preferable for pastoral reasons for the priest to obtain consent from the couple through questions, in the dioceses of the United States the following alternative form may be used:

N., do you take N. for your lawful wife (husband), to have and to hold, from this day forward, for better, for worse, for richer, for poorer, in sickness and in health, until death do you part?

The bride (bridegroom): **I do.**

26. Receiving their consent, the priest says:

You have declared your consent before the Church. May the Lord in his goodness strengthen your consent and fill you both with his blessings. What God has joined, men must not divide.

R: Amen.

BLESSING OF RINGS

27. Priest:

May the Lord bless + these rings which you give to each other as the sign of your love and fidelity.

R: Amen.

Other forms of the blessing of the rings, nos. 110 or 111, may be chosen.

EXCHANGE OF RINGS

28. The bridegroom places his wife's ring on her ring finger. He may say:

N., take this ring as a sign of my love and fidelity. In the name of the Father, and of the Son, and of the Holy Spirit.

The bride places her husband's ring on his ring finger. She may say:

N., take this ring as a sign of my love and fidelity. In the name of the Father, and of the Son, and of the Holy Spirit.

GENERAL INTERCESSIONS

29. The general intercessions (prayer of the faithful) follow, using formulas approved by the conference of bishops. If the rubrics call for it, the profession of faith is said after the general intercessions.

LITURGY OF THE EUCHARIST

30. The Order of Mass is followed, with the following changes. During the offertory, the bride and bridegroom may bring the bread and wine to the altar.

31. Proper preface (see nos. 115–117).

32. When the Roman canon is used, the special **Hanc igitur** is said (no. 118).

NUPTIAL BLESSING

33. After the Lord's Prayer, the prayer **Deliver us** is omitted. The priest faces the bride and bridegroom and, with hands joined, says:

My dear friends, let us turn to the Lord and pray that he will bless with his grace this woman (or N.) now married in Christ to this man (or N.) and that (through the sacrament of the body and blood of Christ,) he will unite in love the couple he has joined in this holy bond.

extends his

Father, by your power you have made everything out of nothing. In the beginning you created the universe and made mankind in your own likeness. You gave man the constant help of woman so that man and woman should no longer be two, but one flesh, and you teach us that what you have united may never be divided.

Or:

Father, you have made the union of man and wife so holy a mystery that it symbolizes the marriage of Christ and his Church.

Or:

Father, by your plan man and woman are united, and married life has been established as the one blessing that was not forfeited by original sin or washed away in the flood.

Look with love upon this woman, your daughter, now joined to her husband in marriage. She asks your blessing. Give her the grace of love and peace. May she always follow the example of the holy women whose praises are sung in the scriptures.

May her husband put his trust in her and recognize that she is his equal and the heir with him to the life of grace. May he always honor her and love her as Christ loves his bride, the Church.

Father, keep them always true to your commandments. Keep them faithful in marriage and let them be living examples of Christian life.

Give them the strength which comes from the gospel so that they may be witnesses of Christ to others. (Bless them with children and help them to be good parents. May they live to see their children's children.) And, after a happy old age, grant them fullness of life with the saints in the kingdom of heaven.

We ask this through Christ our Lord.

R: Amen.

A Contemporary Protestant Rite

Rite of Marriage, in *Evangelical Lutheran Worship*, 286–91.

Marriage
Marriage is a gift of God, intended for the joy and mutual strength of those who enter it and for the well-being of the whole human family. God created us male and female and blessed humankind with the gifts of companionship, the capacity to love, and the care and nurture of children. Jesus affirmed the covenant of marriage and revealed God's own self-giving love on the cross. The Holy Spirit helps those

who are united in marriage to be living signs of God's grace, love, and faithfulness.

Marriage is also a human estate, with vows publicly witnessed. The church in worship surrounds these promises with the gathering of God's people, the witness of the word of God, and prayers of blessing and intercession.

GATHERING

Entrance
The assembly stands as the ministers and the wedding group enter. Music—hymn, song, psalm, instrumental music—may accompany the entrance.

Greeting
The presiding minister and the assembly greet each other.
The grace of our Lord Jesus Christ, the love of God,
and the communion of the Holy Spirit be with you all.
And also with you.

Declaration of Intention
The minister addresses the couple in these or similar words, asking each person in turn:
Name , will you have *name* to be your *wife/husband,* to live together in the covenant of marriage? Will you love *her/him,* comfort *her/him,* honor and keep *her/him,* in sickness and in health, and, forsaking all others, be faithful to *her/him* as long as you both shall live?
Response: I will.
The minister may address the assembly in these or similar words.
Will all of you, by God's grace, uphold and care for *name* and *name* in their life together?
We will.

Prayer of the Day
The presiding minister leads the following or another prayer of the day.
Let us pray.
Gracious God, you sent your Son Jesus Christ into the world to reveal your love to all people. Enrich *name* and *name* with every good gift, that their life together may show forth your love; and grant that at the last we may all celebrate with Christ the marriage feast that has no end; in the name of Jesus Christ our Lord. **Amen.**

WORD

Readings
The assembly is seated. Two or three scripture readings are proclaimed. When the service includes communion, the last is a reading from the gospels. Responses may include a psalm in response to a reading from the Old Testament, a sung acclamation preceding the reading of the gospel, or other appropriate hymns, songs, and psalms.

Sermon
Silence for reflection follows.

Hymn of the Day
A hymn of the day may be sung.

MARRIAGE

Vows
The couple may join hands. Each promises faithfulness to the other in these or similar words.

I take you, *name* , to be my *wife/husband* from this day forward,
to join with you and share all that is to come,
and I promise to be faithful to you until death parts us.
OR
In the presence of God and this community,
I, *name* , take you, *name* , to be my wife/husband;
to have and to hold from this day forward,
in joy and in sorrow, in plenty and in want,
in sickness and in health,
to love and to cherish, as long as we both shall live.
This is my solemn vow.

Giving of Rings
The couple may exchange rings with these or similar words.
Name , I give you this ring as a sign of my love and faithfulness.
OR
Name , I give you this ring as a symbol of my vow.
With all that I am, and all that I have, I honor you,
in the name of the Father, and of the Son, and of the Holy Spirit.

Acclamation
The presiding minister addresses the assembly.

Name and *name* , by their promises before God and in the presence of this assembly, have joined themselves to one another as husband and wife. Those whom God has joined together let no one separate.

Amen. Thanks be to God.

The assembly may offer acclamation with applause. A sung acclamation, hymn, or other music may follow.

Other symbols of marriage may be given or used at this time.

Marriage Blessing

The couple may kneel. The presiding minister may extend a hand over the couple while praying for God's blessing in the following or similar words.

Most gracious God, we give you thanks for your tender love in sending Jesus Christ to come among us, to be born of a human mother, and to endure the cross for our sake, that we may have abundance of life.

By the power of your Holy Spirit pour out the abundance of your blessing on *name* and *name* . Defend them from every enemy. Lead them into all peace. Let your love be a seal upon their hearts, a mantle about their shoulders, and a crown upon their foreheads.

Bless them so that their lives together may bear witness to your love. Bless them in their work and in their companionship; in their sleeping and in their waking; in their joys and in their sorrows; in their life and in their death.

Finally, in your mercy, bring them to that table where your saints feast forever in your heavenly home, through Jesus Christ our Lord, who lives and reigns with you and the Holy Spirit, one God, now and forever.

Amen.

Parents or others may speak additional words of blessing and encouragement at this time.

Prayers of Intercession

The assembly stands. Prayers of intercession for the world and its needs may be prayed.

Each petition may end:

Gracious and faithful God,

hear our prayer.

The presiding minister concludes the prayers, and the assembly responds **Amen.**

A service with communion continues with the peace. After the presiding minister greets the assembly, the couple may greet each other with the kiss of peace, and the assembly may greet one another in peace.

Ministry and Ordination

EARLY PATTERNS

Biblical texts provide a variety of ministries.

Scripture

Acts 6:2b–6.

"It is not right that we should neglect the word of God in order to wait on tables. Therefore, friends, select from among yourselves seven men of good standing, full of the Spirit and of wisdom, whom we may appoint to this task, while we, for our part, will devote ourselves to prayer and to serving the word." . . . They had these men stand before the apostles, who prayed and laid their hands on them.

Acts 20:17, 28.

From Miletus he [Paul] sent a message to Ephesus, asking the elders [*presbyterous*] of the church to meet him. . . .
    "Keep watch over yourselves and over all the flock, of which the Holy Spirit has made you overseers [*episkopous*], to shepherd the church of God that he obtained with the blood of his own Son."

Romans 16:1–7.

I commend to you our sister Phoebe, a deacon of the church at Cenchreae, so that you may welcome her in the Lord as is fitting for the saints, and help her in whatever she may require from you, for she has been a benefactor of many and of myself as well. Greet Prisca and Aquila, who work with me in Christ Jesus, and who risked their necks for my life, to whom not only I give thanks, but also all the churches of the Gentiles. Greet also the church in their house. Greet my beloved Epaenetus, who was the first convert in Asia for Christ. Greet Mary, who has worked very hard among you. Greet Andronicus and Junia, my relatives who were in prison with me; they are prominent among the apostles, and they were in Christ before I was.

1 Corinthians 12: 4–11, 27–31a.

Now there are varieties of gifts, but the same Spirit; and there are varieties of services, but the same Lord; and there are varieties of activities, but it is the same God who activates all of them in everyone. To each is given the manifestation of the Spirit for the common good. To one is given through the Spirit the utterance of wisdom, and to another the utterance of knowledge according to the same Spirit, to another faith by the same Spirit, to another gifts of healing by the one Spirit, to another the working of miracles, to another prophecy, to another the discernment of spirits, to another various kinds of tongues, to another the interpretation of tongues. All these are activated by one and the same Spirit, who allots to each one individually just as the Spirit chooses. . . .

Now you are the body of Christ and individually members of it. And God has appointed in the church first apostles, second prophets, third teachers; then deeds of power, then gifts of healing, forms of assistance, forms of leadership, various kinds of tongues. Are all apostles? Are all prophets? Are all teachers? Do all work miracles? Do all possess gifts of healing? Do all speak in tongues? Do all interpret? But strive for the greater gifts.

Ephesians 4:11–13.

The gifts he gave were that some would be apostles, some prophets, some evangelists, some pastors and teachers, to equip the saints for the work of ministry, for building up the body of Christ, until all of us come to the unity of the faith and of the knowledge of the Son of God, to maturity, to the measure of the full stature of Christ.

1 Timothy 3:1–13.

The saying is sure: whoever aspires to the office of bishop desires a noble task. Now a bishop must be above reproach, married only once, temperate, sensible, respectable, hospitable, an apt teacher, not a drunkard, not violent but gentle, not quarrelsome, and not a lover of money. He must manage his own household well, keeping his children submissive and respectful in every way— for if someone does not know how to manage his own household, how can he take care of God's church? He must not be a recent convert, or he may be puffed up with conceit and fall into the condemnation of the devil. Moreover, he must be well thought of by outsiders, so that he may not fall into disgrace and the snare of the devil.

Deacons likewise must be serious, not double-tongued, not

indulging in much wine, not greedy for money; they must hold fast to the mystery of the faith with a clear conscience. And let them first be tested; then, if they prove themselves blameless, let them serve as deacons. Women likewise must be serious, not slanderers, but temperate, faithful in all things. Let deacons be married only once, and let them manage their children and their households well; for those who serve well as deacons gain a good standing for themselves and great boldness in the faith that is in Christ Jesus.

1 Timothy 4:12–16.

Let no one despise your youth, but set the believers an example in speech and conduct, in love, in faith, in purity. Until I arrive, give attention to the public reading of scripture, to exhorting, to teaching. Do not neglect the gift that is in you, which was given to you through prophecy with the laying on of hands by the council of elders. Put these things into practice, devote yourself to them, so that all may see your progress. Pay close attention to yourself and to your teaching; continue in these things, for in doing this you will save both yourself and your hearers.

THE PRE-NICENE AND POST-NICENE PERIOD

In the first four centuries of the Common Era, the threefold pattern of bishop, presbyter, and deacon, together with other ministries, becomes gradually standardized.

Clement's First Letter

The Letter of the Church at Rome to the Church of Corinth, Commonly Called Clement's First Letter, 40–43 (ca. 96), trans. Cyril C. Richardson, in LCC 1:62–63.

40. Now that this is clear to us and we have peered into the depths of the divine knowledge, we are bound to do in an orderly fashion all that the Master has bidden us to do at the proper times he set. He ordered sacrifices and services to be performed; and required this to be done, not in a careless and disorderly way, but at the times and seasons he fixed. Where he wants them performed, and by whom, he himself fixed by his supreme will, so that everything should be done in a holy way and with his approval, and should be acceptable to his will. Those, therefore, who make their offerings at the time set, win his approval and blessing. For they follow the Master's orders and do no wrong. The high priest is given his particular duties: the priests

are assigned their special place, while on the Levites particular tasks are imposed. The layman is bound by the layman's code.

41. "Each of us," brothers, "in his own rank"[4] must win God's approval and have a clear conscience. We must not transgress the rules laid down for our ministry, but must perform it reverently. Not everywhere, brothers, are the different sacrifices—the daily ones, the freewill offerings, and those for sins and trespasses—offered, but only in Jerusalem. And even there sacrifices are not made at any point, but only in front of the sanctuary, at the altar, after the high priest and the ministers mentioned have inspected the offering for blemishes. Those, therefore, who act in any way at variance with his will, suffer the penalty of death. You see, brothers, the more knowledge we are given, the greater risks we run.

42. The apostles received the gospel for us from the Lord Jesus Christ; Jesus, the Christ, was sent from God. Thus Christ is from God and the apostles from Christ. In both instances the orderly procedure depends on God's will. And so the apostles, after receiving their orders and being fully convinced by the resurrection of our Lord Jesus Christ and assured by God's word, went out in the confidence of the Holy Spirit to preach the good news that God's Kingdom was about to come. They preached in country and city, and appointed their first converts, after testing them by the Spirit, to be the bishops and deacons of future believers. Nor was this any novelty, for Scripture had mentioned bishops and deacons long before. For this is what Scripture says somewhere: "I will appoint their bishops in righteousness and their deacons in faith."[5]

43. And is it any wonder that those Christians whom God had entrusted with such a duty should have appointed the officers mentioned? For the blessed Moses too, "who was a faithful servant in all God's house,"[6] recorded in the sacred books all the orders given to him, and the rest of the prophets followed in his train by testifying with him to his legislation. Now, when rivalry for the priesthood arose and the tribes started quarreling as to which of them should be honored with this glorious privilege, Moses bid the twelve tribal chiefs bring him rods, on each of which was written the name of one of the tribes. These he took and bound, sealing them with the rings of the tribal leaders; and he put them in the tent of testimony on God's table. Then he shut the tent and put seals on the keys just as he had on the rods. And he told them: "Brothers, the tribe whose rod puts forth buds is the one God has chosen for the priesthood and for his ministry." Early the next morning he called all Israel together, six

4. 1 Cor. 15:23.
5. Isa. 60:17.
6. Num. 12:7; Heb. 3:5.

hundred thousand strong, and showed the seals to the tribal chiefs and opened the tent of testimony and brought out the rods. And it was discovered that Aaron's rod had not only budded, but was actually bearing fruit. What do you think, dear friends? Did not Moses know in advance that this was going to happen? Why certainly. But he acted the way he did in order to forestall anarchy in Israel, and so that the name of the true and only God might be glorified. To Him be the glory forever and ever. Amen.

The Didache

The Didache, X, XI, and XV (late first or early second century), trans. Cyril C. Richardson, in LCC 1:176, 178.

X. In the case of prophets, however, you should let them give thanks in their own way.

XI. Now, about the apostles and prophets: Act in line with the gospel precept. Welcome every apostle on arriving, as if he were the Lord. But he must stay not beyond one day. In case of necessity, however, the next day too. If he stays three days, he is a false prophet. On departing, an apostle must not accept anything save sufficient food to carry him till his next lodging. If he asks for money he is a false prophet.

XV. You must, then, elect for yourselves bishops and deacons who are a credit to the Lord, men who are gentle, generous, faithful, and well tried. For their ministry to you is identical with that of the prophets and teachers. You must not, therefore, despise them, for along with the prophets and teachers they enjoy a place of honor among you.

Ignatius of Antioch

Ignatius of Antioch is the first to articulate what comes to be recognized universally as the "mon" or "monarchical episcopacy," that is, the rule of one bishop.

Ignatius of Antioch, *Letter to the Magnesians*, 6 (ca. 115), trans. Cyril C. Richardson, in LCC 1:95.

Let the bishop preside in God's place, and the presbyters take the place of the apostolic council, and let the deacons (my special favorites) be entrusted with the ministry of Jesus Christ who was with the Father from eternity and appeared at the end [of the world].

Ignatius of Antioch, *Letter to the Trallians*, 2–3 (ca. 115),
trans. Cyril C. Richardson, in LCC 1:99.

It is essential, therefore, to act in no way without the bishop, just as
you are doing. Rather submit even to the presbytery as to the apostles
of Jesus Christ. He is our Hope, and if we live in union with him now,
we shall gain eternal life. Those too who are deacons of Jesus Christ's
"mysteries" must give complete satisfaction to everyone. For they do
not serve mere food and drink, but minister to God's Church. They
must therefore avoid leaving themselves open to criticism, as they
would shun fire.

Correspondingly, everyone must show the deacons respect. They
represent Jesus Christ, just as the bishop has the role of the Father,
and the presbyters are like God's council and an apostolic band. You
cannot have a church without these.

Ignatius of Antioch, *Letter to the Smyrnaeans* 8 (ca. 115),
trans. Cyril C. Richardson, in LCC 1:115.

Flee from schism as the source of mischief. You should all follow
the bishop as Jesus Christ did the Father. Follow, too, the presbytery
as you would the apostles; and respect the deacons as you would
God's law. Nobody must do anything that has to do with the Church
without the bishop's approval. You should regard that Eucharist
as valid [authentic] which is celebrated either by the bishop or by
someone he authorizes. Where the bishop is present, there let the
congregation gather, just as where Jesus Christ is, there is the Catholic Church. Without the bishop's supervision, no baptisms or love
feasts are permitted.

Didascalia Apostolorum

This mid-third-century Syrian source includes women among those
ordained as deacons (or deaconesses), underscores their ministries, and
gives them a place of honor as representing the Holy Spirit in the life of the
church, just as the male deacon represents Christ.

Didascalia Apostolorum (mid-third century), 9 and 16,
in *The Liturgical Portions of the Didascalia*, 11 and 22–23.

9. [L]et him be honoured by you as God, for the bishop sits for you
in the position of God Almighty. Now the deacon stands in the position of Christ, and you should love him. And the deaconess, in the

position of the Holy Spirit, shall be honored by you. The presbyters shall be to you in the likeness of the apostles; and the orphans and widows shall be considered by you in the likeness of the altar.

16. For this reason, O bishop, appoint for yourself workers of righteousness as helpers who can co-operate with you, for salvation. Of those who are pleasing to you out of all the people, you should choose and appoint as deacons: a man for the performance of most things that are necessary, but a woman for the ministry of women. For there are houses where you cannot send a deacon to the women, on account of the heathen; but you can send a deaconess. Also, because in many other matters too the office of a woman, a deaconess, is required. In the first place, when women go down into the baptismal water: those who go down into the water ought to be anointed by a deaconess with the oil of anointing; and where there is no woman at hand, and especially no deaconess, he who baptizes must of necessity anoint the woman who is being baptized. But where there is a woman, and especially a deaconess, present, it is not fitting that women should be seen by men, but with the imposition of hand you should anoint the head only. As of old priests and kings were anointed in Israel, so do you likewise, with the imposition of hand, anoint the head of those who receive baptism, whether it be of men or of women; and afterwards, whether you yourself baptize, or you tell the deacons or presbyters to baptize, let a woman, a deaconess, anoint the women, as we have already said. But let a man pronounce over them the invocation of the divine names in the water. And when the woman who is being baptized has come up from the water, let the deaconess receive her and teach and instruct her how the seal of baptism ought to be kept unbroken in purity and holiness. For this reason we say that the ministry of a woman, a deaconess, is particularly needed and important. For our Lord and Saviour was also ministered to by women ministers, "Mary Magdalene, and Mary the daughter of James and mother of Jose, and the mother of the sons of Zebedee," with other women as well. And you too need the ministry of the deaconess for many things; for a deaconess is needed to go into the houses of the heathen where there are believing women, and to visit those who are sick, ministering to them in whatever way they require, and to bathe those who have begun to recover from sickness.

Apostolic Tradition

The so-called *Apostolic Tradition* probably did not assume its final form until sometime in the mid to late fourth century, with the earliest version, the Verona Latin manuscript, dated to ca. 500. Further, with the exception of the prayer for the ordination of the bishop and presbyter, most of the following is supplied only by later manuscripts in Sahidic Coptic (ca. 700) and/or Ethiopic (ca. 1295). The prayer for the ordination of the bishop in the modern Roman Rite has been adapted from the prayer for the bishop here.

Apostolic Tradition, 2–3, 7–13, trans. Geoffrey J. Cuming, in *Hippolytus: A Text for Students* (Bramcote, Notts.: Grove Books, 1976), 8–15.

Of Bishops

2. Let him be ordained bishop who has been chosen by all the people; and when he has been named and accepted by all, let the people assemble, together with the presbytery and those bishops who are present, on the Lord's day. When all give consent, they shall lay hands on him, and the presbytery shall stand by and be still. And all shall keep silence, praying in their hearts for the descent of the Spirit; after which one of the bishops present, being asked by all, shall lay his hand on him who is being ordained bishop, and pray, saying thus:

3. God and Father of our Lord Jesus Christ, Father of mercies and God of all comfort, you dwell on high and look on that which is lowly; you know all things before they come to pass; you gave ordinances in the Church through the word of your grace; you foreordained from the beginning of a race of righteous men from Abraham; you appointed princes and priests, and did not leave your sanctuary without a ministry. From the beginning of the age it was your good pleasure to be glorified in those whom you have chosen: now pour forth that power which is from you, of the princely Spirit which you granted through your beloved Son Jesus Christ to your holy apostles who established the Church in every place as your sanctuary, to the unceasing glory and praise of your name.

You who know the hearts of all, bestow upon this your servant, whom you have chosen for the episcopate, to feed your holy flock and to exercise the high-priesthood before you blamelessly, serving night and day; to propitiate your countenance unceasingly, and to offer to you the gifts of your holy Church; and by the spirit of high-priesthood to have the power to forgive sins according to your command, to confer orders according to your bidding, to loose every bond according to the power which you gave to the apostles, to please you in gentleness and a pure heart, offering to you a sweet-smelling savour; through your child Jesus Christ our Lord, with whom be glory and power and honour to you, with the holy Spirit, both now and to the ages of ages. Amen.

Of Presbyters

7. And when a presbyter is ordained, the bishop shall lay his hand on his head, the presbyters also touching him; and he shall say according to what was said above, as we said before about the bishop, praying and saying:

God and Father of our Lord Jesus Christ, look upon this your servant, and impart the Spirit of grace and counsel of the presbyterate, that he may help and govern your people with a pure heart; just as you looked upon your chosen people, and commanded Moses to choose presbyters whom you filled with your Spirit which you granted to your servant. And now, Lord, grant the Spirit of your grace to be preserved unfailingly in us, and make us worthy to minister to you in faith and in simplicity of heart, praising you through your child Christ Jesus; through whom be glory and power to you with the holy Spirit, in the holy Church, both now and to the ages of ages. Amen.

Of Deacons

8. And when a deacon is ordained, let him be chosen according to what was said above, the bishop alone laying on hands, in the same way as we also directed above. In the ordination of a deacon, the bishop alone shall lay on hands, because he is not being ordained to the priesthood, but to the service of the bishop, to do what is ordered by him. For he does not share in the counsel of the presbyterate, but administers and informs the bishop of what is fitting; he does not receive the common spirit of seniority in which the presbyters share, but that which is entrusted to him under the bishop's authority. For this reason the bishop alone shall ordain a deacon; but on a presbyter the presbyters alone shall lay hands, because of the common and like spirit of their order. For a presbyter has authority only to receive; he has not authority to give. For this reason he does not ordain the clergy, but at the ordination of a presbyter he seals, while the bishop ordains.

Over a deacon, then, (the bishop) shall say thus:

God, who created all things and ordered them by your Word, Father of our Lord Jesus Christ, whom you sent to serve your will and make known to us your desire, give the holy Spirit of grace and caring and diligence to this your servant whom you have chosen to serve your Church and to present in your holy of holies that which is offered to you by your appointed high-priest to the glory of your name; that serving blamelessly and purely, he may attain to the rank of a higher order, and praise and glorify you through your Son Jesus Christ our Lord; through whom be glory and power and praise to you, with the holy Spirit, now and always and to the ages of ages. Amen.

Of Confessors

9. But a confessor, if he was in chains for the name of the Lord shall not have hands laid on him for the diaconate or the presbyterate, for he has the honour of the presbyterate by his confession. But if he is appointed bishop, hands shall be laid on him.

But if there is a confessor who was not brought before the authorities, nor punished with chains, nor shut up in prison, nor condemned to any other penalty, but has only been derided on occasion for the name of our Lord and punished with a domestic punishment: if he confessed, let hands be laid on him for any order of which he is worthy.

And the bishop shall give thanks according to what we said above. It is not at all necessary for him to utter the same words as we said above, as though reciting them from memory, when giving thanks to God; but let each pray according to his ability. If indeed anyone has the ability to pray at length and with a solemn prayer, it is good. But if anyone, when he prays, utters a brief prayer, do not prevent him. Only, he must pray what is sound and orthodox.

Of Widows

10. When a widow is appointed, she is not ordained, but is chosen by name. If her husband has been dead a long time, let her not be taken on trust; even if she is old, let her be tested for a time, for often the passions grow old with him who makes a place for them in himself. A widow shall not be appointed by word only, and shall join the rest. But hands shall not be laid on her, because she does not offer the offering, nor has she a liturgical duty. Ordination is for the clergy, on account of their liturgical duties; but a widow is appointed for prayer, which belongs to all.

Of A Reader

11. A reader is appointed by the bishop giving him the book, for he does not have hands laid on him.

Of A Virgin

12. Hands shall not be laid on a virgin: her choice alone makes her a virgin.

Of A Subdeacon

13. Hands shall not be laid on a subdeacon, but he shall be named in order that he may follow the deacons.

Of Gifts Of Healing

14. If anyone says, "I have received a gift of healing by a revelation,"

hands shall not be laid on him, for the facts themselves will show whether he has spoken the truth.

The Prayers of Sarapion of Thmuis

The ordination prayers in this Egyptian liturgical document, especially for deacons and bishops, show considerable theological development, with the ordination of deacons related explicitly to the appointment of the seven in Acts 6, and the association of apostolic succession with the bishop. Further, rather than election, laying on of hands, and prayer for the necessary gifts of the Spirit constituting ordination proper, the prayer for the bishop asks explicitly that he be "made" a bishop.

The Prayers of Sarapion of Thmuis, 12–14 (ca. 350),
in *The Prayers of Sarapion of Thmuis*, 59–61.

[12]Laying on of Hands for the Appointment of Deacons
Father of the only-begotten, you sent your Son and ordered the events upon earth. You gave canons and orders to the church for the advantage and salvation of the flocks. You elected bishops and presbyters and deacons for the service of your catholic church. Through your only-begotten you elected the seven deacons and graciously gave holy Spirit to them. Appoint also this one a deacon of your catholic church. Graciously give him a spirit of knowledge and discernment that he may be able to minister purely and blamelessly in this service in the middle of your holy people. Through your only-begotten Jesus Christ, through whom (be) to you the glory and the power in holy Spirit both now and to all the ages of ages. Amen.

[13]Laying on of Hands for the Appointment of Presbyters
Master, God of the heavens, Father of your only-begotten, we extend (our) hand(s) upon this man and we pray that the Spirit of truth may come to him. Graciously give him insight and knowledge and a good heart. Let divine Spirit come to be in him that he might be able to govern your people, to act as an ambassador of your divine words, and to reconcile your people to you, the uncreated God. From the spirit of Moses you graciously gave holy Spirit to the elect ones. Distribute holy Spirit also to this one from the Spirit of the only-begotten for the gift of wisdom and knowledge and right faith, that he may be able to serve you with a pure conscience. Through your only-begotten Jesus Christ, through whom (be) to you the glory and the power in holy Spirit both now and to all the ages of ages. Amen.

[14]Laying on of Hands for the Appointment of the Bishop
God of truth, you sent the Lord Jesus for the benefit of the whole

world. Through him you elected the apostles, appointing holy bishops from generation to generation. Make this one also a living bishop, a holy bishop of the succession of the apostles, and give to him grace and divine Spirit, which you graciously gave to all of your genuine servants and prophets and patriarchs. Make him worthy to shepherd your flock and let him continue both blamelessly and without stumbling in the episcopate. Through your only-begotten Jesus Christ, through whom (be) to you the glory and the power in holy Spirit both now and to all the ages of ages. Amen.

THE MEDIEVAL PERIOD IN EAST AND WEST

The Ordination of a Bishop in the Roman Rite

Since the fullness of orders was believed to belong to the episcopate, the "high priesthood," this prayer from the Roman Rite, and the following from the Byzantine Rite, for the ordination of a bishop provide concrete examples of this theological understanding.

> *The Verona [or Leonine] Sacramentary*, trans. Paul Bradshaw,
> in *Ordination Rites of the Ancient Churches of East and West*
> (Collegeville, MN: Liturgical Press, Pueblo, 1990), 215–16.

CONSECRATION OF BISHOPS

Hear, Lord, the prayers of your humble people, that what is to be carried out by our ministry may be established further by your power; through. . . .

[Then follow texts for the Secret and the Hanc Igitur of the ordination mass.]

Assist [us], merciful God, so that what is done by our obedient office may be established by your blessing; through. . . .

Be gracious, Lord, to our supplications, and with the horn of priestly grace inclined over these your servants pour out upon them the power of your benediction; through. . . .

God of all the honors, God of all the worthy ranks, which serve to your glory in hallowed orders; God who in private familiar converse with Moses your servant also made a decree, among the other patterns of heavenly worship, concerning the disposition of priestly vesture; and commanded that Aaron your chosen one should wear a mystical robe during the sacred rites, so that the posterity to come might have an understanding of the meaning of the patterns of the former things, lest the knowledge of your teaching be lost in any age; and as among the ancients the very outward sign of these symbols obtained reverence, also among us there might be a knowledge of them more certain than types and shadows. For the adornment of our mind is as the vesture of that earlier priesthood; and the dignity of robes no longer commends to us the pontifical glory, but the splendor of spirits, since even those very things, which then pleased fleshly vision, depended rather on these truths which in them were to be understood.

And, therefore, to these your servants, whom you have chosen for the ministry of the high-priesthood, we beseech you, O Lord, that you would bestow this grace; that whatsoever it was that those veils signified in radiance of gold, in sparkling of jewels, in variety of diverse workmanship, this may show forth in the conduct and deeds of these men. Complete the fullness of your mystery in your priests, and equipped with all the adornments of glory, hallow them with the dew of heavenly unction. May it flow down, O Lord, richly upon their head; may it run down below the mouth; may it go down to the uttermost parts of the whole body, so that the power of your Spirit may both fill them within and surround them without. May there abound in them constancy of faith, purity of love, sincerity of peace. Grant to them an episcopal throne to rule your Church and entire people. Be their strength; be their might; be their stay. Multiply upon them your blessing and grace, so that fitted by your aid always to obtain your mercy, they may by your grace be devoted to you; through. . . .

The Ordination of a Bishop in the Byzantine Rite

The ordination of a bishop in the Byzantine Rite, in *Ordination Rites of the Ancient Churches of East and West*, 133-34.

After the Trisagion, when the cantors have come down from the ambo, the archbishop stands on the step before the holy table, and there is given to him the scroll on which is written: The divine grace, which always heals that which is infirm and supplies what is lacking, appoints the presbyter N., beloved by God, as bishop. Let us pray therefore that the grace of the Holy Spirit may come upon him.

And he reads it in the hearing of all, having his hand on the head of the ordinand. And after the reading of "The divine grace," the people say, Lord have mercy, *three times.*

And the archbishop, opening the Gospel, lays it on his head and neck, the other bishops standing around and touching the holy Gospel, and making three crosses on his head and laying his hand on him, he prays thus: Sovereign Lord, our God, who have established by your illustrious apostle Paul the hierarchy of ranks and orders for the service of your venerable and pure mysteries at your holy altar—first apostles, second prophets, third teachers—O Lord of all, strengthen by the advent, power, and grace of your Holy Spirit him who has been elected to undertake the gospel and the high-priestly dignity, by the hand of me, a sinner, and by that of the bishops who minister with me, as you strengthened your holy prophets, as you anointed kings, as you sanctified high priests. And give him an irreproachable high-priesthood, and adorning him with all sanctity, make him holy so that he may be worthy to pray for the salvation of the people and to be heard by you. For your name is hallowed and your kingdom glorified. . . .

And after the "Amen," one of the bishops present performs the diaconal prayer, thus: In peace let us pray to the Lord.

For peace from above and the salvation of our souls, let us pray to the Lord.

For the peace of the whole world, the welfare of the holy churches, and the unity of all, let us pray to the Lord.

For our archbishop N., his priesthood, succor, perseverance, peace, and his salvation, and the works of his hands, let us pray to the Lord.

For N., now appointed bishop, and his salvation, let us pray to the Lord.

That our loving God will bestow on him a spotless and irreproachable high-priesthood, let us pray.

For our most pious and divinely-protected emperor, for this city, for our delivery, help, save, and have mercy, at the intercession of our all-holy, immaculate Lady, the mother of God.

And while this prayer is being said by the bishop, the archbishop, holding his hand in the same way on the head of the ordinand, prays thus: Lord our God, who, because human nature cannot sustain the essence of your divinity, by your dispensation have established teachers subject to the same passions as ourselves who approach your throne to offer you sacrifice and oblation for all your people; Lord, make him who has been made dispenser of the high-priestly grace to be an imitator of you, the true shepherd, giving his life for your sheep, guide of the blind, light of those in darkness, corrector of the ignorant, lamp in the world, so that, after having formed in this present life the souls who have been entrusted to him, he may stand before your judgment-seat without shame and receive the great reward which you have prepared for those who have striven for the preaching of your gospel. (*Aloud:*) For yours are mercy and salvation. . . .

And after the "Amen," the patriarch takes the Gospel and sets it down on the holy table, and then, having put the omophorion on the

newly ordained, he kisses him, as do all the bishops, and the archbishop
ascends with him to the throne, and the rest of the liturgy is completed.

Peter Lombard

This text and the following one are concerned with establishing the sacramentality of ordination.

Peter Lombard, *Four Books of Sentences*, IV (ca. 1152),
in *Peter Lombard and the Sacramental System*, 224.

Distinction XXIV. 1. Now we come to the consideration of holy ordination. There are seven grades or orders of spiritual office, as is clearly taught us in the words of the holy Fathers, and as is shown by the example of our head, that is Jesus Christ, who performed in his own person the duties of them all, and left the same orders to be observed in his body which is the Church.

2. And there are seven on account of the sevenfold grace of the holy Spirit, and those who do not participate in this grace, enter the ecclesiastical grades unworthily. But when men in whose minds the sevenfold grace of the holy Spirit is diffused, enter the ecclesiastical orders, they are believed to receive a fuller grace ill the very promotion to the spiritual rank.

3. (See Chapter 1, p. 8.)

Council of Florence

Council of Florence, "Decree for the Armenians" (1439), trans. from
Enchiridion Symbolorum Definitionum et Declarationum, 336.

The sixth sacrament is ordination. The matter is according to the order which is conferred: for a presbyter it is passed on through a chalice with wine and a paten with bread; for a deacon through the giving of books of the Gospels; for a subdeacon through an empty chalice placed on an empty paten; and likewise for the others the things pertaining to the assignments of their ministries. The form for a priest is: "Receive the power for the offering of sacrifice in the Church for the living and the dead, in the name of the Father and of the Son and of the Holy Spirit." And thus for the other forms of order, according as they are contained in the Roman Pontifical. The ordinary minister of this sacrament is a bishop. The effect is the increase of grace, that whoever is ordained may be a fit minister.

THE PROTESTANT AND CATHOLIC REFORMATIONS

The Protestant Reformation challenges ministry as power and calls for equality on the basis of baptism.

Martin Luther

Martin Luther, *To the Christian Nobility of the German Nation concerning the Reform of the Christian Estate* (1520), trans. Charles M. Jacobs and James Atkinson, in LW 44:128, 129.

Suppose a group of earnest Christian laymen were taken prisoner and set down in a desert without an episcopally ordained priest among them. And suppose they were to come to a common mind there and then in the desert and elect one of their number, whether he were married or not, and charge him to baptize, say mass, pronounce absolution, and preach the gospel. Such a man would be as truly a priest as though he had been ordained by all the bishops and popes in the world. . . .

For whoever comes out of the water of baptism can boast that he is already a consecrated priest, bishop and pope, although of course it is not seemly that just anybody should exercise such office. Because we are priests of equal standing, no one must push himself forward and take it upon himself, without our consent and election, to do that for which we all have equal authority. For no one dare take upon himself what is common to all without the authority and consent of the community. And should it happen that a person chosen for such office were deposed for abuse of trust, he would then be exactly what he was before. Therefore a priest in Christendom is nothing else but an office-holder. . . .

There is no true, basic difference between laymen and priests, princes and bishops, between religious and secular, except for the sake of office and work, but not for the sake of status. They are all of the spiritual estate, all are truly priests, bishops, and popes. But they do not all have the same work to do.

Martin Bucer

Martin Bucer, "Sermon on the Good Shepherd" (ca. 1550), trans. E. C. Whitaker, in *Martin Bucer and the Book of Common Prayer* (Great Wakering: Mayhew-McCrimmon, 1974), in ACC 55:178–80.

Brethren, you have heard both in your canonical examination and now in the sermon and in the sacred lessons which have been read from the Apostles and the gospels, how great is the dignity and the responsibility of this office to which you have been called and are now in the name of our Lord Jesus Christ to be solemnly instituted. . . . Consider now how great is the treasure which is committed to you: for the sheep are Christ's, and he has bought them for himself at the price of his own life: the church to which you are to administer even to eternal life is his bride, his body.

The Council of Trent

The Catholic Reformation at Trent reaffirms the traditional Western approach to the various orders of ordained ministry leading to priesthood in service to the celebration of the Eucharist.

The Council of Trent, Session 23 (July 1563), I, II, and III,
trans. H. Schroeder, in *The Canons and Decrees of the Council
of Trent* (St. Louis: B. Herder Book Co., 1941), 160–61.

Chapter I: The Institution of the Priesthood of the New Law
Sacrifice and priesthood are by the ordinance of God so united that both have existed in every law. Since therefore in the New Testament the Catholic Church has received from the institution of Christ the holy, visible sacrifice of the Eucharist, it must also be confessed that there in that Church a new, visible and eternal priesthood, into which the old has been translated. That this was instituted by the same Lord our Savior, and that to the Apostles and their successors in the priesthood was given the power to consecrating, offering and administering His body and blood, as also of forgiving and retaining sins, is shown by the Sacred Scriptures and has always been taught by the tradition of the Catholic Church.

Chapter II: The Seven Orders
But since the ministry of so a priesthood is something divine, that it might be exercised in a more worthy manner and with greater veneration, it was consistent that in the most well-ordered arrangement of the Church there should be several distinct orders of ministers, who by virtue of their office should minister to the priesthood, so distributed that those already having the clerical tonsure should ascend through the minor to the major orders. For the Sacred Scriptures mention unmistakably not only the priests but also the deacons, and teach in the most definite words what is especially to be observed in their ordination; and from the very beginning of the Church the names of the following orders and the duties proper to each one are known to have been in use, namely, those of the subdeacon, acolyte,

exorcist, lector and porter, though these were not of equal rank; for the subdeacon is classed among the major orders by the Fathers and holy councils, in which we also read very often or other inferior orders.

Chapter III: The Order of the Priesthood Is Truly a Sacrament
Since from the testimony of Scripture, Apostolic tradition and the unanimous agreement of the Fathers it is clear that grace is conferred by sacred ordination, which is performed by words and outward signs, no one ought to doubt that order is truly and properly one of the seven sacraments of holy Church. . . .

MODERN APPROACHES

Roman Catholic Rite for the Ordination of a Bishop

Revised by decree of the Second Vatican Council, modern Roman Catholic ordination rites focus both on the restoration of the office of bishop as an "order" in the church as well as on the traditional threefold office of bishop, presbyter, and deacon. The following current prayer for the ordination of a bishop is taken directly from the so-called *Apostolic Tradition* (see page 320). Hence, a more deliberate patristic model for holy orders was employed.

Roman Catholic rite for the ordination of a bishop,
trans. International Committee on English in the Liturgy,
in *The Rites of the Catholic Church*, 2:3–92.

Laying on of Hands
The principal consecrator lays his hands upon the head of the bishop-elect, in silence. After him, all other bishops present do the same.

Book of the Gospels
Candidate kneels before the bishop.
Then the principal consecrator places the open Book of the Gospels upon the head of the bishop-elect; two deacons, standing at either side of the bishop-elect, hold the Book of the Gospels above his head until the prayer of consecration is completed.

Prayers of Consecration
Principal Consecrator:
God the Father of our Lord Jesus Christ,
Father of mercies and God of all consolation,
you dwell in heaven,
yet look with compassion on all that is humble.

You know all things before they come to be;
by your gracious word
you have established the plan of your Church.
From the beginning
you chose the descendants of Abraham
    to be your holy nation.
You established rulers and priests,
and did not leave your sanctuary
    without ministers to serve you.
From the creation of the world
you have been pleased to be glorified
by those whom you have chosen.

The following part of the prayers is recited by all the consecrating bishops, with hands joined.

So now pour out upon this chosen one
that power which is from you,
the governing Spirit
whom you gave to your beloved Son, Jesus Christ,
the Spirit given by him to the holy apostles,
who founded the Church in every place
    to be your temple for the
unceasing glory and praise of your name.

Then the principal consecrator continues alone:

Father, you know all hearts.
You have chosen your servant for the office of bishop.
May he be a shepherd to your holy flock,
and a high priest blameless in your sight,
ministering to you night and day;
may he always gain the blessing of your favor
and offer the gifts of your holy Church.
Through the Spirit who gives the grace of high priesthood
grant him the power
to forgive sins as you have commanded,
to assign ministries as you have decreed,
and to loose every bond by the authority which you
gave to your apostles.
May he be pleasing to you by his gentleness
    and purity of heart,
presenting a fragrant offering to you,
through Jesus Christ your Son,
through whom glory and power and honor are yours
with the Holy Spirit
in your holy Church,
now and forever.
Amen.

Anointing of the Bishop's Head
Principal Consecrator: God has brought you to share the high priesthood of Christ. May he pour out on you the oil of mystical anointing and enrich you with spiritual blessing.

Presentation of the Book of the Gospels
Principal Consecrator: Receive the Gospel and preach the word of God with unfailing patience and sound teaching.

Investiture with Ring, Miter, and Pastoral Staff
Principal Consecrator: Take this ring, the seal of your fidelity. With faith and love protect the bride of God, his holy Church.
Place the miter on the new bishop's head in silence.
Principal Consecrator: Take this staff as a sign of your pastoral office: keep watch over the whole flock in which the Holy Spirit has appointed you to shepherd the Church of God.

Seating of the Bishop
If the new bishop is in his own church, the principal consecrator invites him to occupy the chair. If the new bishop is not in his own church, his is invited by the principal consecrator to take the first place among the concelebrating bishops.

Baptism, Eucharist, and Ministry

As with baptism (see pp. 175–76) and Eucharist (see pp. 249–51), so the section on ministry in this ecumenical document shows a remarkable degree of convergence, both on the traditional threefold office of bishop, presbyter, and deacon and on the meaning of ordination itself.

World Council of Churches, *Baptism, Eucharist, and Ministry*,
Faith and Order Paper 111 (Geneva: World Council of Churches, 1982),
paragraphs III.A.22–25; IV.A.34; B.46; V.A.39; B.41; VI.51–55.

22. Although there is no single New Testament pattern, although the Spirit has many times led the Church to adapt its ministries to contextual needs, and although other forms of the ordained ministry have been blessed with the gifts of the Holy Spirit, nevertheless the threefold ministry of bishop, presbyter and deacon may serve today as an expression of the unity we seek and also as a means for achieving it. Historically, it is true to say, the threefold ministry became the generally accepted pattern in the Church of the early centuries and is still retained today by many churches . . .

23. The Church as the body of Christ and the eschatological people of God is constituted by the Holy Spirit through a diversity of gifts or ministries. Among these gifts a ministry of *episkopé* is necessary to express and safeguard the unity of the body. Every church needs this ministry of unity in some form in order to be the Church of God, the one body of Christ, a sign of the unity of all in the Kingdom.

24. The threefold pattern stands evidently in need of reform. In some churches the collegial dimension of leadership in the eucharistic community has suffered diminution. In others, the function of deacons has been reduced to an assistant role in the celebration of the liturgy: they have ceased to fulfill any function with regard to the diaconal witness of the Church. In general, the relation of the presbyterate to the episcopal ministry has been discussed throughout the centuries, and the degree of the presbyter's participation in the episcopal ministry is still for many an unresolved question of far-reaching ecumenical importance. In some cases, churches which have not formally kept the threefold form have, in fact, maintained certain of its original patterns.

25. The traditional threefold pattern thus raises questions for all the churches. Churches maintaining the threefold pattern will need to ask how its potential can be fully developed for the most effective witness of the Church in this world. In this task churches not having the threefold pattern should also participate. They will further need to ask themselves whether the threefold pattern as developed does not have a powerful claim to be accepted by them.

IV. SUCCESSION IN THE APOSTOLIC TRADITION
A. Apostolic Tradition in the Church

34. . . . Apostolic tradition in the Church means continuity in the permanent characteristics of the Church of the apostles: witness to the apostolic faith, proclamation and fresh interpretation of the Gospel, celebration of baptism and the eucharist, the transmission of ministerial responsibilities, communion in prayer, love, joy and suffering, service to the sick and the needy, unity among the local churches and sharing the gifts which the Lord has given to each.

B. Succession of the Apostolic Ministry

35. The primary manifestation of apostolic succession is to be found in the apostolic tradition of the Church as a whole. The succession is an expression of the permanence and, therefore, of the continuity of Christ's own mission in which the Church participates. Within the Church the ordained ministry has a particular task of preserving and actualizing the apostolic faith. The orderly transmission of the

ordained ministry is therefore a powerful expression of the continuity of the Church throughout history; it also underlines the calling of the ordained minister as guardian of the faith. . . .

36. Under the particular historical circumstances of the growing Church in the early centuries, the succession of bishops became one of the ways, together with the transmission of the Gospel and the life of the community, in which the apostolic tradition of the Church was expressed. This succession was understood as serving, symbolizing and guarding the continuity of the apostolic faith and communion.

V. ORDINATION
A. The Meaning of Ordination
39. The Church ordains certain of its members for the ministry in the name of Christ by the invocation of the Spirit and the laying on of hands (I Tim. 4:14; II Tim. 1:6); in so doing it seeks to continue the mission of the apostles and to remain faithful to their teaching. The act of ordination by those who are appointed for this ministry attests the bond of the Church with Jesus Christ and the apostolic witness, recalling that it is the risen Lord who is the true ordainer and bestows the gift. In ordaining, the Church, under the inspiration of the Holy Spirit, provides for the faithful proclamation of the Gospel and humble service in the name of Christ. The laying on of hands is the sign of the gift of the Spirit, rendering visible the fact that the ministry was instituted in the revelation accomplished in Christ, and reminding the Church to look to him as the source of its commission. This ordination, however, can have different intentions according to the specific tasks of bishops, presbyters and deacons as indicated in the liturgies of ordination.

B. The Act of Ordination
41. A long and early Christian tradition places ordination in the context of worship and especially of the eucharist. Such a place for the service of ordination preserves the understanding of ordination as an act of the whole community, and not of a certain order within it or of the individual ordained. The act of ordination by the laying on of hands of those appointed to do so is at one and the same time invocation of the Holy Spirit (epiklesis); sacramental sign; acknowledgment of gifts and commitment.

VI. TOWARDS THE MUTUAL RECOGNITION OF THE ORDAINED MINISTRIES
51. In order to advance towards the mutual recognition of ministries, deliberate efforts are required. All churches need to examine

the forms of ordained ministry and the degree to which the churches are faithful to its original intentions. Churches must be prepared to renew their understanding and their practice of the ordained ministry.

52. Among the issues that need to be worked on as churches move towards mutual recognition of ministries, that of apostolic succession is of particular importance. Churches in ecumenical conversations can recognize their respective ordained ministries if they are mutually assured of their intention to transmit the ministry of Word and sacrament in continuity with apostolic times. The act of transmission should be performed in accordance with the apostolic tradition, which includes the invocation of the Spirit and the laying on of hands.

53. In order to achieve mutual recognition, different steps are required of different churches. For example:

a) Churches which have preserved the episcopal succession are asked to recognize both the apostolic content of the ordained ministry which exists in churches which have not maintained such succession and also the existence in these churches of a ministry of episkopé in various forms.

b) Churches without the episcopal succession, and living in faithful continuity with the apostolic faith and mission, have a ministry of Word and sacrament, as is evident from the belief, practice, and life of those churches. These churches are asked to realize that the continuity with the Church of the apostles finds profound expression in the successive laying on of hands by bishops and that, though they may not lack the continuity of the apostolic tradition, this sign will strengthen and deepen that continuity. They may need to recover the sign of the episcopal succession.

54. Some churches ordain both men and women, others ordain only men. Differences on this issue raise obstacles to the mutual recognition of ministries. But those obstacles must not be regarded as substantive hindrance for further efforts towards mutual recognition. Openness to each other holds the possibility that the Spirit may well speak to one church through the insights of another. Ecumenical consideration, therefore, should encourage, not restrain, the facing of this question.

55. The mutual recognition of churches and their ministries implies decision by the appropriate authorities and a liturgical act from which point unity would be publicly manifest. Several forms of such public act have been proposed: mutual laying on of hands, eucharistic concelebration, solemn worship without a particular rite of recognition, the reading of a text of union during the course of a celebration. No one liturgical form would be absolutely required, but

in any case it would be necessary to proclaim the accomplishment of mutual recognition publicly. The common celebration of the eucharist would certainly be the place for such an act.

Christian Burial

EARLY TEXTS

The Prayers of Sarapion of Thmuis

The Prayers of Sarapion of Thmuis offers us the first written text for a Christian funeral, specifically here for the burial procession.

The Prayers of Sarapion of Thmuis 18 (ca. 350),
in *The Prayers of Sarapion of Thmuis*, 65.

[18] Prayer for One Who Has Died and Is Being Carried Out
God, you have the power of life and death, God of the spirits and Master of all flesh, God of the dead and of the living. You lead down to the doors of Hades and you lead up. You create the human spirit in a person and take the souls of the saints and give them rest. You, who alone are incorruptible and unchangeable and eternal, are the one who changes and turns and transforms your creatures as it is right and beneficial. We pray to you for the sleep and rest of this your (male or female) servant. Give rest to his soul, his spirit, in green pastures, in the inner rooms of rest with Abraham, Isaac, and Jacob and all your saints. And raise (his) body on the appointed day according to your truthful promises so that you may give to him according to the worthy inheritance(s) in your holy pastures. Do not remember his transgressions and his sins, but make his departure to be peaceful and blessed. Heal the griefs of those who carry (him) with a spirit of consolation and give us all a good end. Through your only-begotten Jesus Christ, through whom (be) to you the glory and the power in holy Spirit to the ages of ages. Amen.

Augustine of Hippo

Augustine of Hippo, *Confessions*, IX (ca. 400), trans. Albert C. Outler, in LCC 7:197.

32. So, when the body [of Monica, his mother] was carried forth, we both went and returned without tears. For neither in those prayers which we poured forth to thee, when the sacrifice of our redemption was offered up to thee for her—with the body placed by the side of the grave as the custom is there, before it is lowered down into it—neither in those prayers did I weep. But I was most grievously sad in secret all the day, and with a troubled mind entreated thee, as I could, to heal my sorrow; but thou didst not.

The Anaphora of St. John Chrysostom

Commemoration of and intercession for the departed in eucharistic prayers, in *The Anaphora of St. John Chrysostom*, in *PEER*, 134.

We offer you this reasonable service also for those who rest in faith, <forefathers,> Fathers, patriarchs, prophets, apostles, preachers, evangelists, martyrs, confessors, ascetics, and all the righteous <spirits> perfected in faith; *(aloud)* especially our all-holy, immaculate, highly glorious, Blessed Lady, Mother of God and ever-Virgin Mary; <*diptychs of the dead;*> Saint John the <prophet,> forerunner, and Baptist, and the holy, <glorious,> and honored Apostles; and this saint whose memorial we are keeping; and all your saints: at their entreaties, look on us, O God.

And remember all those who have fallen asleep in hope of resurrection to eternal life, <*he remembers them by name*> and grant them rest where the light of your own countenance looks upon them.

The Roman *Canon Missae*

Commemoration of and intercession for the departed in eucharistic prayers, in the Roman *Canon Missae*, in *PEER*, 165.

Memento etiam—Remember also, Lord, the names of those who have gone before us with the sign of faith, and sleep in the sleep of peace. We beseech you to grant to them and to all who rest in Christ a place of restoration, light, and peace; through Christ our Lord.

MEDIEVAL AND REFORMATION-ERA TEXTS

The Requiem Mass according to the Roman Rite

Selections from the propers for the requiem Mass according to the Roman Rite, trans. Gaspar Lefebvre, in *Saint Andrew Daily Missal with Vespers for Sundays and Feasts* (Bruges, Belgium: Biblica, 1962), 1585–91.

Introit
Eternal rest give unto them, O Lord: and let perpetual light shine upon them. *Ps.* A hymn, O God, becometh Thee in Sion; and a vow shall be paid to Thee in Jerusalem: hear my prayer: all flesh shall come to Thee. – Eternal rest.

Gradual
Eternal rest give unto them, O Lord: and let perpetual light shine upon them. *V.* The just shall be in everlasting remembrance: he shall not fear the evil hearing.

Tract
Absolve, O Lord, the souls of all the faithful departed from every bond of sin. *V.* And by the help of your grace may they be enabled to escape the avenging judgment. *V.* And enjoy the happiness of ever-lasting life.

Sequence: Dies Irae (See the next document.)

Offertory
O Lord Jesus Christ, King of glory, deliver the souls of all the faith-ful departed from the pains of hell and from the deep pit: deliver them from the lion's mouth, that hell may not swallow them up, and may they not fall into darkness; but may the holy standard-bearer, Michael, lead them into the holy Light; Which You promised to Abraham and to his seed of old. *V.* We offer to You, Lord, sacrifices and prayers: do You receive them in behalf of those souls whom we commemorate this day. Grant them, O Lord, to pass from death to that life; Which You promised to Abraham and to his seed of old.

Communion
May light eternal shine upon them, O Lord. With Thy saints for ever, for Thou art merciful. *V.* Eternal rest grant them, O Lord; and let perpetual light shine upon them. With Thy saints for ever, for Thou art merciful.

Responsory: Libera Me

Deliver me, Lord, from ever-lasting death in that awful day: * When the heavens and the earth shall be moved: When You will come to judge the world by fire. V. Dread and trembling have laid hold upon me, and I fear exceedingly because of the judgment and the wrath to come. * When the heavens and the earth shall be moved. V. O that day, that day of wrath, of sore distress and of all wretchedness, that great and exceeding bitter day. When you will come to judge the world with fire. V. Eternal rest grant to them, O Lord; and let perpetual light shine upon them.

Thomas of Celano (possibly)

Thomas of Celano (possibly), *Dies Irae* (thirteenth century), trans. William J. Irons and Isaac Williams, in *The Hymnal 1940* (New York: Church Pension Fund, 1940), 468.

Day of wrath! O day of mourning!
See fulfilled the prophets' warning,
Heav'n and earth in ashes burning!
O what fear man's bosom rendeth,
When from heav'n the Judge descendeth,
On whose sentence all dependeth!
Wondrous sound the trumpet flingeth,
Through earth's sepulchres it ringeth,
All before the throne it bringeth!
. . . .
Worthless are my prayers and sighing,
Yet, good Lord, in grace complying,
Rescue me from fires undying!
With thy favored sheep, O place me!
Nor among the goats abase me;
But to thy right hand upraise me.
While the wicked are confounded,
Doomed to flames of woe unbounded,
Call me with thy saints surrounded.
Low I kneel, with heart submission;
See, like ashes, my contrition;
Help me, in my last condition.
Ah that day of tears and mourning!
From the dust of earth returning,
Man for judgment must prepare him;
Spare, O God, in mercy spare him!
Lord, all pitying, Jesus blest,
Grant them thine eternal rest!

Martin Luther

Martin Luther, "Preface to the Burial Hymns" (1542), trans. Paul Zeller Strodach and Ulrich S. Leupold, in LW 53:326–27.

Nor do we sing any dirges or doleful songs over our dead and at the grave, but comforting hymns of the forgiveness of sins, of rest, sleep, life, and of the resurrection of departed Christians so that our faith may be strengthened and the people be moved to true devotion.

For it is meet and right that we should conduct these funerals with proper decorum in order to honor and praise that joyous article of our faith, namely, the resurrection of the dead, and in order to defy Death, that terrible foe who so shamefully and in so many horrible ways goes on to devour us. . . .

All this is done so that the article of the resurrection may be firmly implanted in us. For it is our lasting, blessed, and eternal comfort and joy against death, hell, devil, and every woe.

John Knox

John Knox, *The Forme of Prayers* (1556), ed. William D. Maxwell, in *The Liturgical Portions of the Genevan Service Book* (London: Faith Press, 1965), 161 (spelling modernized).

Of Burial

The corpse is reverently brought to the grave, accompanied with the congregation, without any further ceremonies, which being buried, the minister goes to the church, if it be not far off, and makes some comfortable exhortation to the people, touching death, and resurrection.

EIGHTEENTH CENTURY

John Wesley

John Wesley describes here a Moravian burial in Germany, which would be influential in Methodist rites.

John Wesley, *Journal* (1738), in *The Works of John Wesley*, vol. 18: *Journal and Diaries*, ed. W. Reginald Ward and Richard P. Heitzenrater (Nashville: Abingdon Press, 1988), 269.

[Herrnhut] Tue. 8. [August 1738] A child was buried. The burying ground (called by them *Gottes Acker*, i.e. God's ground) lies a few hundred yards out of the town, under the side of a little wood. There are distinct squares in it for married men and unmarried; for married and unmarried women; for male and female children, and for widows. The corpse was carried from the chapel, the children walking first; next the "orphan-father" (so they call him who has the chief care of the orphan-house) with the minister of Berthelsdorf; then four children bearing the corpse, and after them, Martin Dober and the father of the child. Then followed the men, and last the women and girls. They all sung as they went. Being come into the square where the male children are buried, the men stood on two sides of it, the boys on the third, and the women and girls on the fourth. There they sung again; after which the minister used (I think, read) a short prayer, and concluded with that blessing, "Unto God's gracious mercy and protection I commit you."

Seeing the father (a plain man, a tailor by trade) looking at the grave, I asked, "How do you find yourself?" He said, "Praised be the Lord, never better. He has taken the soul of my child to himself. I have seen, according to my desire, his body committed to holy ground. And I know that when it is raised again, both he and I shall be ever with the Lord."

THE MODERN PERIOD

Constitution on the Sacred Liturgy

Constitution on the Sacred Liturgy (Collegeville, MN: Liturgical Press, 1963), 43.

81. The rite for the burial of the dead should express more clearly the paschal character of Christian death, and should correspond more closely to the circumstances and traditions found in various regions. This holds good also for the liturgical color to be used.

CHAPTER 7

Liturgy and Time

Often described by anthropologists and ritual-studies practitioners as reflecting the sanctification of time, both daily prayer (often referred to as the liturgy of the hours and/or the divine office) and the liturgical year are concerned, indeed, about the use of time in the ongoing sanctification of life in Christ. The first part of this chapter traces the origins and development of daily prayer, related to the Pauline command that Christians are to "pray without ceasing" (1 Thess. 5:7) as that prayer becomes attached to fixed hours of the day: morning, noon, and evening and/or the third, sixth, and ninth hours, with prayer during the night as well.

Originally the prayer of the whole church in East and West—especially as it comes to be celebrated morning and evening in the great "cathedral offices" of the fourth century—in the medieval period, praying the canonical hours, as they are called (vigils, lauds, prime, terce, sext, none, vespers, and compline), becomes largely a monastic observance, inspired by the cathedral and monastic synthesis of the Roman Divine Office by Benedict of Nursia in his famous Rule. Together with various Reformation attempts to restore the office to the life of the church in general (especially the work of Thomas Cranmer), this part of the chapter concludes with examples of family prayer, mostly among Reformed Christians, and the reform of the liturgy of the hours at the Second Vatican Council.

The second part of the chapter provides an overview of the origins and evolution of the liturgical year, with particular attention given to the original Christian feast of Sunday, the development of Pascha (Easter), and the paschal cycle concluding fifty days later with the solemn feast of Pentecost. The origins and theology of Epiphany, Christmas, and Advent (the order of their appearance historically) appears next. This is followed by texts showing the development of the sanctoral cycle (the cycle of saints' feasts) from the early cult of the martyrs to medieval overgrowth and Reformation-era pruning, to contemporary reform and the ecumenical recovery of the place of various "saints" in the calendar, although subordinated clearly to the priority of the temporal cycle (Advent, Christmas, Lent, and Easter seasons).

| DAILY PRAYER |

|

The First Three Centuries

|

SCRIPTURE

Biblical texts suggest patterns of daily prayer to early Christians.

Select Texts

Exodus 29:38–39.

Now this is what you shall offer on the altar: two lambs a year old regularly each day. One lamb you shall offer in the morning, and the other lamb you shall offer in the evening.

Psalm 55:17.

Evening and morning and at noon
I utter my complaint and moan,
and he will hear my voice.

Psalm 119:62, 164.

At midnight I rise to praise you,
because of your righteous ordinances.
. . . .
Seven times a day I praise you
for your righteous ordinances.

Psalm 141:2.

Let my prayer be counted as
incense before you,
and the lifting up of my hands
as an evening sacrifice.

Daniel 6:10.

Daniel . . . continued to go to his house, which had windows in its upper room open toward Jerusalem, and to get down on his knees three times a day to pray to his God and praise him, just as he had done previously.

Acts 2:15; 10:9; 3:1; 16:25.

[Pentecost] Indeed, these are not drunk, as you suppose, for it is only nine o'clock in the morning. . . .

About noon the next day, as they were on their journey and approaching the city [Caesarea], Peter went up on the roof to pray. . . .

One day Peter and John were going up to the temple at the hour of prayer, at three o'clock in the afternoon. . . .

About midnight Paul and Silas were praying and singing hymns to God, and the prisoners were listening to them [at Philippi].

1 Thessalonians 5:17.

Pray without ceasing.

SYRIA

The Didache

The Didache, VIII (late first or early second century), trans. Cyril C. Richardson, in LCC 1:174.

You must not pray like the hypocrites, but "pray as follows" as the Lord bids us in his gospel:

"Our Father in heaven, hallowed be your name; your Kingdom come; your will be done on earth as it is in heaven; give us today our bread for the morrow; and forgive us our debts as we forgive our debtors. And do not lead us into temptation, but save us from the evil one, for yours is the power and the glory forever."

You should pray in this way three times a day.

EGYPT

Clement of Alexandria

Clement of Alexandria, *Stromata or Miscellanies*, VII, 7 (ca. 200),
trans. William Wilson, in *ANF* 11:534.

Prayer is, then, to speak more boldly, converse with God. Though whispering, consequently, and not opening the lips, we speak in silence, yet we cry inwardly. For God hears continually all the inward converse. So also we raise the head and lift the hands to heaven, and set the feet in motion at the closing utterance of the prayer, following the eagerness of the spirit directed towards the intellectual essence; and endeavouring to abstract the body from the earth, along with the discourse, raising the soul aloft, winged with longing for better things, we compel it to advance to the region of holiness, magnanimously despising the chain of the flesh. . . .

Now, if some assign definite hours for our prayer—as, for or example, the third, and sixth, and ninth—yet the Gnostic [here, true Christian] prays throughout his whole life, endeavouring by prayer to have fellowship with God. And, briefly, having reached to this, he leaves behind him all that is of no service, as having now received the perfection of the man that acts by love.

Origen

Origen, *On Prayer*, XII, 2 (ca. 233), trans. John Ernest Leonard Oulton, in LCC 2:261–62.

That man "prays without ceasing" (virtuous deeds or commandments fulfilled being included as part of prayer) who combines with the prayer the needful deeds and the prayer with the fitting actions. For thus alone can we accept "pray without ceasing" as a practicable saying, if we speak of the whole life of the saint as one great unbroken prayer: of which prayer that which is commonly called prayer is a part. This ought to be engaged in not less than three times every day, as is clear from the case of Daniel, who when great danger hung over him "prayed three times a day." . . . The final one is indicated in the words "the lifting up of my hands as the evening sacrifice" (Ps. 141:2). Indeed we shall not fittingly pass even the night time without this prayer: for David says, "At midnight did I rise to give thanks unto thee for the judgments of thy righteousness" (Ps. 119:62); and "Paul," as is stated in the Acts of the Apostles, "about midnight" in company with "Silas," at Philippi, "was praying and singing hymns unto God," so that even the "prisoners listened to them."

NORTH AFRICA

By the third century, five daily hours for prayer are commended to devout Christians in North Africa.

Tertullian

Tertullian. *On Prayer*, XXV–XXVI (ca. 200), trans. S. Thelwall, in *ANF* 3:689–90.

Touching the time, however, the extrinsic observance of certain hours will not be unprofitable—those common hours, I mean, which mark the intervals of the day—the third, the sixth, the ninth—which we may find in the Scriptures to have been more solemn than the rest. The first infusion of the Holy Spirit into the congregated disciples took place at "the third hour." Peter, on the day on which he experienced the vision of Universal Community, (exhibited) in that small vessel, had ascended into the more lofty parts of the house, for prayer's sake "at the sixth hour." The same (apostle) was going into the temple, with John, "at the ninth hour," when he restored the paralytic to his health. Albeit these practices stand simply without any precept for their observance, still it may be granted a good thing to establish some definite presumption, which may both add stringency to the admonition to pray, and may, as it were by a law, tear us out from our businesses unto such a duty; so that—what we read to have been observed by Daniel also, in accordance (of course) with Israel's discipline—we pray at least not less than thrice in the day, debtors as we are to Three—Father, Son, and Holy Spirit: of course, in addition to our regular prayers which are due, without any admonition, on the entrance of light and of night. But, withal, it becomes believers not to take food, and not to go to the bath, before interposing a prayer; for the refreshments and nourishments of the spirit are to be held prior to those of the flesh, and things heavenly prior to things earthly.

You will not dismiss a brother who has entered your house without prayer.—"Have you seen," says *Scripture*, "a brother? You have seen your Lord"; —especially "a stranger," lest perhaps he be "an angel." But again, when received yourself by brethren, you will not make earthly refreshments prior to heavenly, for your faith will forthwith be judged. Or else how will you—according to the precept—say, "Peace to this *house*," unless you exchange mutual peace with them who are *in* the house?

Cyprian of Carthage

Cyprian of Carthage, *On the Lord's Prayer*, XXXIV–XXXVI
(ca. 251), in *ANF* 5:456–57.

And in discharging the duties of prayer, we find that the three children with Daniel, being strong in faith and victorious in captivity, observed the third, sixth, and ninth hour, as it were, for a sacrament of the Trinity, which in the last times had to be manifested. For both the first hour in its progress to the third shows forth the consummated number of the Trinity, and also the fourth proceeding to the sixth declares another Trinity; and when from the seventh the ninth is completed, the perfect Trinity is numbered every three hours, which spaces of hours the worshippers of God in time past having spiritually decided on, made use of for determined and lawful times for prayer. And subsequently the thing was manifested, that these things were of old Sacraments, in that anciently righteous men prayed in this manner. For upon the disciples at the third hour the Holy Spirit descended, who fulfilled the grace of the Lord's promise. Moreover, at the sixth hour, Peter, going up unto the house-top, was instructed as well by the sign as by the word of God admonishing him to receive all to the grace of salvation, whereas he was previously doubtful of the receiving of the Gentiles to baptism. And from the sixth hour to the ninth, the Lord, being crucified, washed away our sins by His blood; and that He might redeem and quicken us, He then accomplished His victory by His passion.

But for us, beloved brethren, besides the hours of prayer observed of old, both the times and the sacraments have now increased in number. For we must also pray in the morning, that the Lord's resurrection may be celebrated by morning prayer. And this formerly the Holy Spirit pointed out in the Psalms, saying, "My King, and my God, because unto Thee will I cry; O Lord, in the morning shalt Thou hear my voice; in the morning will I stand before Thee, and will look up to Thee." And again, the Lord speaks by the mouth of the prophet: "Early in the morning shall they watch for me, saying, Let us go, and return unto the Lord our God." Also at the sunsetting and at the decline of day, of necessity we must pray again. For since Christ is the true sun and the true day, as the worldly sun and worldly day depart, when we pray and ask that light may return to us again, we pray for the advent of Christ, which shall give us the grace of everlasting light. Moreover, the Holy Spirit in the Psalms manifests that Christ is called the day. "The stone," says He, "which the builders rejected, is become the head of the corner. This is the Lord's doing; and it is marvellous in our eyes. This is the day which the Lord hath made; let us walk and rejoice in it." Also the prophet Malachi testifies that He is called the Sun, when he says, "But to you that fear the name of the Lord shall the Sun of righteousness arise, and there is healing in His wings." But if in the Holy Scriptures the true sun and the true day is Christ, there is no hour excepted for Christians wherein God ought not frequently and always to be worshipped; so that we who are in Christ—that is, in the true Sun and the true Day—should be instant throughout the entire day in petitions, and should pray; and when, by the law of the world, the revolving night, recurring in its alternate changes, succeeds, there can be no harm arising from the darkness of night to those who pray, because the children of light have the day even in the night. For when is he without light who has light in his heart? or when has not he the sun and the day, whose Sun and Day is Christ?

Let not us, then, who are in Christ—that is, always in the lights cease from praying even during night. Thus the widow Anna, without intermission praying and watching, persevered in deserving well of God, as it is written in the Gospel: "She departed not," it says, "from the temple, serving with fastings and prayers night and day." . . . Let there be no failure of prayers in the hours of night—no idle and reckless waste of the occasions of prayer. New-created and new-born of the Spirit by the mercy of God, let us imitate what we shall one day be. Since in the kingdom we shall possess day alone, without intervention of night, let us so watch in the night as if in the daylight. Since we are to pray and give thanks to God for ever, let us not cease in this life also to pray and give thanks.

ROME

Apostolic Tradition

As we have seen repeatedly, great caution must be taken with regard to the date, provenance, and authorship of this particular document. Again, it is included at this place simply because of the traditional, though no longer universally accepted, view that it reflects early third-century Roman practice.

Apostolic Tradition, XLI (ca. 217), trans. Geoffrey J. Cuming,
in *Hippolytus: A Text for Students* (Bramcote, Notts.: Grove Books, 1976), 28–31.

The deacons and priests shall assemble daily at the place which the bishop appoints for them. Let the deacons not fail to assemble at all times, unless illness hinders them. When all have assembled, let them teach those who are in the church, and in this way, when they have prayed, let each one go to the work which falls to him. . . .

But if instruction in the word of God is given, each one should choose to go to that place, reckoning in his heart that it is God whom he hears in the instructor.

For he who prays in the church will be able to pass by the wickedness of the day. . . . Therefore let each one be diligent in coming to the church, the place where the holy Spirit flourishes. If there is a day when there is no instruction, let each one, when he is at home, take up a holy book and read in it sufficiently what seems to him to bring profit.

Let every faithful man and woman, when they have risen from sleep *in the morning*, before they touch any work at all, wash their hands and pray to God, and so go to their work. . . .

And if you are at home, pray at the *third hour* and bless God. But if you are somewhere else at that moment, pray to God in your heart. For at that hour Christ was nailed to the tree. For this reason also in the Old (Testament) the Law prescribed that the shewbread should be offered continually as a type of the body and blood of Christ; and the slaughter of the lamb without reason is this type of the perfect lamb. For Christ is the shepherd, and also the bread which came down from heaven.

Pray likewise at the time of the *sixth hour*. For when Christ was nailed to the wood of the cross, the day was divided, and darkness fell. And so at that hour let them pray a powerful prayer, imitating the voice of him who prayed and made all creation dark for the unbelieving Jews.

And at the *ninth hour* let them pray also a great prayer and a great blessing, to know the way in which the soul of the righteous blesses God who does not lie, who remembered his saints and sent his word to give them light. For at that hour Christ was pierced in his side and poured out water and blood; giving light to the rest of time of the day, he brought it to evening. Then, in beginning to sleep and making the beginning of another day, he fulfilled the type of the resurrection.

Pray before your body rests on the bed. Rise about *midnight*, wash your hands with water, and pray. If your wife is present also, pray both together; if she is not yet among the faithful, go apart into another room and pray, and go back to bed again. Do not be lazy about praying. He who is bound in the marriage-bond is not defiled. . . .

For the elders who gave us the tradition taught us that at that hour all creation is still for a moment, to praise the Lord; stars, trees, waters stop for an instant, and all the host of angels (which) ministers to him praises God with the souls of the righteous in this hour. That is why believers should take good care to pray at this hour.

Bearing witness to this, the Lord says thus, "Lo, about midnight a shout was made of men saying, Lo, the bridegroom comes; rise to meet him." And he goes on, saying "Watch therefore, for you know not at what hour he comes."

And likewise rise about *cockcrow*, and pray. For at that hour, as the cock crew, the children of Israel denied Christ, whom we know by faith, our eyes looking towards that day in the hope of eternal light at the resurrection of the dead.

And if you act so, all you faithful, and remember these things, and teach them in your turn, and encourage the catechumens, you will not be able to be tempted or to perish, since you have Christ always in memory.

|
The Fourth, Fifth, and Sixth Centuries
|

The parochial (parish) office or cathedral office involving a variety of ministries becomes an important daily form of public worship after persecution ends. Morning and evening public prayer, plus a vigil Saturday night, become common.

ANTIOCHIA

Eusebius of Caesarea

Eusebius of Caesarea, "Commentary on Psalm 64:10" (ca. 337), in PG 23:640, in Robert Taft, *The Liturgy of the Hours in East and West: The Origins of the Divine Office and Its Meaning for Today* (Collegeville, MN: Liturgical Press, 1986), 33.

Rightly, it is no ordinary sign of the power of God, that throughout the whole world, in the churches of God, hymns, praises, and truly divine delights are offered to God at the morning going forth of the sun and at evening time. For indeed the delights of God are the hymns poured forth everywhere on earth in his Church, both morning and evening. On account of which it is said somewhere: "May my praise be pleasing to him"; again, "the lifting of my hands as an evening sacrifice," and "may my prayer be as incense in your sight." And so these delights turn out to be a sign of the Savior.

Apostolic Constitutions

Apostolic Constitutions, 2, 59; 8, 34, 35 (ca. 375),
trans. James Donaldson, in *ANF* 7:422–23, 496.

When thou instructest the people, O bishop, command and exhort them to come constantly to church morning and evening every day, and by no means to forsake it on any account, but to assemble together continually; neither to diminish the Church by withdrawing themselves, and causing the body of Christ to be without its member. For it is not only spoken concerning the priests, but let every one of the laity hearken to it as concerning himself, considering that it is said by the Lord: "He that is not with me is against me, and he that gathereth not with me scattereth abroad" [Matt. 12:30]. Do not you therefore scatter yourselves abroad, who are the members of Christ, by not assembling together, since you have Christ your head, according to His promise, present, and communicating to you. Be not careless of yourselves, neither deprive your Saviour of His own members, neither divide His body nor disperse His members, neither prefer the occasions of this life to the word of God; but assemble yourselves together every day, morning and evening, singing psalms and praying in the Lord's house: in the morning saying the sixty-[third] Psalm, and in the evening the hundred and forty-[first], but principally on the Sabbath-day. And on the day of our Lord's resurrection, which is the Lord's day, meet more diligently, sending praise to God that made the universe by Jesus, and sent Him to us, and condescended to let Him suffer, and raised Him from the dead. Otherwise what apology will he make to God who does not assemble on that day to hear the saving word concerning the resurrection, on which we pray thrice standing in memory of Him who arose in three days, in which is performed the reading of the prophets, the preaching of the Gospel, the oblation of the sacrifice, the gift of the holy food? . . .

If it be not possible to assemble either in the church or in a house, let every one by himself sing, and read, and pray, or two or three together. For "where two or three are gathered together in my name, there am I in the midst of them" [Matt. 18:20]. Let not one of the faithful pray with a catechumen, no, not in the house: for it is not reasonable that he who is admitted should be polluted with one not admitted. Let not one of the godly pray with an heretic, no, not in the house. For "what fellowship hath light with darkness?" . . .

I James, the brother of Christ according to the flesh, but His servant as the only begotten God, and one appointed bishop of Jerusalem by the Lord Himself, and the Apostles, do ordain thus: When it is evening, thou, O bishop, shalt assemble the church; and after the repetition of the psalm at the lighting up the lights, the deacon shall bid prayers for the catechumens, the energumens, the illuminated, and the penitents, as we have formerly said. But after the dismission of these, the deacon shall say: So many as are of the faithful, let us pray to the Lord.

John Chrysostom

John Chrysostom, *Baptismal Instructions*, XVII–XVIII (388), trans. Paul W. Harkins, in *St. John Chrysostom: Baptismal Instructions*, in ACW 31:126–27.

And I urge you to show great zeal by gathering here in the church at dawn to make your prayers and confessions to the God of all things, and to thank Him for the gifts He has already given. Beseech Him to deign to lend you from now on His powerful aid in guarding this treasure; strengthened with this aid, let each one leave the church to take up his daily tasks, one hastening to work with his hands, another hurrying to his military post, and still another to his post in the government. However, let each one approach his daily task with fear and anguish, and spend his working hours in the knowledge that at evening he should return here to the church, render an account to the Master of his whole day, and beg forgiveness for his falls. . . .

This is the reason why each evening we must beg pardon from the Master for all these faults. This is why we must flee to the loving-kindness of God and make our appeal to Him. Then we must spend the hours of the night soberly, and in this way meet the confessions of the dawn. If each of us manages his own life in this way, he will be able to cross the sea of this life without danger and to deserve the loving-kindness of the Master. And when the hour for gathering in church summons him, let him hold this gathering and all spiritual things in higher regard than anything else. In this way we shall manage the goods we have in our hands and keep them secure.

John Chrysostom, "Homily 26 on the Acts of the Apostles" (ca. 400), trans. J. Walker, J. Sheppard, and H. Browne, in *NPNF¹* 11:172–73.

Not for this was the night made, that we should sleep all through it and be idle. . . . [At night] Sleep hath invaded and defeated nature: it is the image of death, the image of the end of all things. . . . All this is enough to arouse the soul, and lead it to reflect on the end of all things.

Here indeed my discourse is for both men and women. Bend

thy knees, send forth groans, beseech thy Master to be merciful: He is more moved by prayers in the night, when thou makest the time for rest a time for mourning. . . . After such vigils come sweet slumbers and wondrous revelations. Do this, thou also the man, not the woman only. Let thy house be a Church, consisting of men and women. . . . If thou hast children wake up them also, and let thy house altogether become a Church through the night: but if they be tender, and cannot endure the watching, let them stay for the first or second prayer, and then send them to rest: only stir up thyself, establish thyself in the habit.

JERUSALEM

The holy places in Jerusalem provide locations for daily worship of monks and virgins, lay people, and clergy, each with different roles.

Egeria

Egeria, *Pilgrimage of Egeria*, XXIV–XXV (ca. 384), trans. John Wilkinson, in *Egeria's Travels* (London: SPCK, 1971), 123–26.

Loving sisters, I am sure it will interest you to know about the daily services they have in the holy places, and I must tell you about them. All the doors of the Anastasis [place of the resurrection] are opened before cock-crow each day, and the "*monazontes* and *parthenae*" [monks and virgins], as they call them here, come in, and also some lay men and women, at least those who are willing to wake at such an early hour. From then until daybreak they join in singing the refrains to the hymns, psalms, and antiphons. There is a prayer between each of the hymns, since there are two or three presbyters and deacons each day by rota, who are there with the monazontes and say the prayers between all the hymns and antiphons.

As soon as *dawn* comes, they start the Morning Hymns, and the bishop with his clergy comes and joins them. He goes straight into the cave [the tomb], and inside the screen he first says the Prayer for All (mentioning any names he wishes) and blesses the catechumens, and then another prayer and blesses the faithful. Then he comes outside the screen, and everyone comes up to kiss his hand. He blesses them one by one, and goes out, and by the time the dismissal takes place it is already day.

Again *at midday* everyone comes into the Anastasis and says psalms and antiphons until a message is sent to the bishop. Again he enters, and, without taking his seat, goes straight inside the screen in the Anastasis (which is to say into the cave where he went in the early morning), and again, after a prayer, he blesses the faithful and comes outside the screen, and again they come to kiss his hand.

At *three o'clock* they do once more what they did at midday, but at *four o'clock* they have *Lychnicon*, as they call it, or in our language, Lucernare. All the people congregate once more in the Anastasis, and the lamps and candles are all lit, which makes it very bright. The fire is brought not from outside, but from the cave—inside the screen—where a lamp is always burning night and day. For some time they have the Lucernare psalms and antiphons; then they send for the bishop, who enters and sits in the chief seat. The presbyters also come and sit in their places, and the hymns and antiphons go on. Then, when they have finished singing everything which is appointed, the bishop rises and goes in front of the screen (i.e., the cave). One of the deacons makes the normal commemoration of individuals, and each time he mentions a name a large group of boys responds, *Kyrie eleison* (in our language, "Lord, have mercy"). Their voices are very loud. As soon as the deacon has done his part, the bishop says a prayer and prays the Prayer for All. Up to this point the faithful and the catechumens are praying together, but now the deacon calls every catechumen to stand where he is and bow his head, and the bishop says the blessing over the catechumens from his place. There is another prayer, after which the deacon calls for all the faithful to bow their head, and the bishop says the blessing over the faithful from his place. Thus the dismissal takes place at the Anastasis, and they all come up one by one to kiss the bishop's hand.

Then, singing hymns, they take the bishop from the Anastasis to the Cross, and everyone goes with him. On arrival he says one prayer and blesses the catechumens, then another and blesses the faithful. Then again the bishop and all the people go Behind the Cross, and do there what they did Before the Cross; and in both places they come to kiss the bishop's hand, as they did in the Anastasis. Great glass lanterns are burning everywhere, and there are many candles in front of the Anastasis, and also Before and Behind the Cross. By the end of all this it is dusk. So these are the services held every weekday at the Cross and at the Anastasis.

But on the seventh day, *the Lord's Day*, there gather in the court-yard *before cock-crow* all the people, as many as can get in, as if it was Easter. The courtyard is the "basilica" beside the Anastasis, that is to say, out of doors, and lamps have been hung there for them. Those who are afraid they may not arrive in time for cockcrow come early, and sit waiting there singing hymns and antiphons, and they have prayers between, since there are always presbyters and deacons there ready for the vigil, because so many people collect there, and it is not usual to open the holy places before cock-crow.

Soon the first cock crows, and at that the bishop enters, and goes into the cave in the Anastasis. The doors are all opened, and all the people come into the Anastasis, which is already ablaze with lamps. When they are inside, a psalm is said by one of the presbyters, with everyone responding, and it is followed by a prayer; then a psalm is said by one of the deacons, and other prayer; then a third psalm is said by one of the clergy, a third prayer, and the Commemoration of All. After these three psalms and prayers they take censers into the cave of the Anastasis, so that the whole Anastasis basilica is filled with the smell. Then the bishop, standing inside the screen, takes the Gospel book and goes to the door, where he himself reads the account of the Lord's resurrection. At the beginning of the reading the whole assembly groans and laments at all that the Lord underwent for us, and the way they weep would move even the hardest heart to tears. When the Gospel is finished, the bishop comes out, and is taken with singing to the Cross, and they all go with him. They have one psalm there and a prayer, then he blesses the people, and that is the dismissal. As the bishop goes out, everyone comes to kiss his hand.

Then straight away the bishop retires to his house, and all the monazontes go back into the Anastasis to sing psalms and antiphons until daybreak. There are prayers between all these psalms and antiphons, and presbyters and deacons take their turn every day at the Anastasis to keep vigil with the people. Some lay men and women like to stay on there till daybreak, but others prefer to go home again to bed for some sleep. . . .

Except on the special days, which we shall be describing below, this order is observed on every day of the year. What I found most impressive about all this was that the psalms and antiphons they use are always appropriate, whether at night, in the early morning, at the day prayers at midday or three o'clock, or at Lucernare. Everything is suitable, appropriate, and relevant to what is being done.

EGYPT

Although the Egyptian tradition knew the pattern of the cathedral or parochial office, it is the monastic office as it developed in Egypt that exerted a great amount of influence on the development of similar forms of prayer elsewhere.

Cassian

Egyptian monastics set a pattern of an evening and early morning office with twelve psalms at each as established by high authority.

John Cassian, *Institutes*, II, 3–6 (ca. 420), trans. Edgar C. S. Gibson, in *NPNF²* 11:205, 207.

And so throughout the whole of Egypt and the Thebaid, where monasteries are not founded at the fancy of every man who renounces the world, but through a succession of fathers and their traditions last even to the present day, or are founded so to last, in these we have noticed that a prescribed system of prayers is observed in their evening assemblies and nocturnal vigils. . . .

So, as we said, throughout the whole of Egypt and the Thebaid the number of Psalms is fixed at twelve both at Vespers and in the office of Nocturns, in such a way that at the close two lessons follow, one from the Old and the other from the New Testament. And this arrangement, fixed ever so long ago, has continued unbroken to the present day throughout so many ages, in all the monasteries of those districts, because it is said that it was no appointment of man's invention, but was brought down from heaven to the fathers by the ministry of an angel.

As they were going to celebrate their daily rites and prayers, one rose up in the midst to chant the Psalms to the Lord. And while they were all sitting (as is still the custom in Egypt), with their minds intently fixed on the words of the chanter, when he had sung eleven Psalms, separated by prayers introduced between them, verse after verse being evenly enunciated, he finished the twelfth with a response of Alleluia, and then, by his sudden disappearance from the eyes of all, put an end at once to their discussion and their service.

Whereupon the venerable assembly of the Fathers understood that by Divine Providence a general rule had been fixed for the congregations of the brethren through the angel's direction, and so decreed that this number should be preserved both in their evening and in their nocturnal services; and when they added to these two lessons, one from the Old and one from the New Testament, they added them simply as extras and of their own appointment, only for those who liked, and who were eager to gain by constant study a mind well stored with Holy Scripture. But on Saturday and Sunday they read them both from the New Testament; viz., one from the Epistles or the Acts of the Apostles, and one from the Gospel. And this also those do whose concern is the reading and the recollection of the Scriptures, from Easter to Whitsuntide.

CAPPADOCIA

Basil of Caesarea

Basil of Caesarea witnesses to the fact that within the East a cycle of eight daily offices has developed in the fourth century.

Basil of Caesarea, *The Long Rules*, XXXVII (358–64),
trans. M. Monica Wagner, in *Saint Basil: Ascetical Works*, in FC 9:309–10.

Prayers are recited *early in the morning* so that the first movements of the soul and the mind may be consecrated to God and that we may take up no other consideration before we have been cheered and heartened by the thought of God, as it is written: "I remembered God and was delighted" and that the body may not busy itself with tasks before we have fulfilled the words: "To thee will I pray, O Lord; in the morning thou shalt hear my voice. In the morning I will stand before thee and will see" [Ps. 5:3]. Again *at the third hour* the brethren must assemble and betake themselves to prayer, even if they may have dispersed to their various employments. Recalling to mind the gift of the Spirit bestowed upon the Apostles at this third hour, all should worship together, so that they also may become worthy to receive the gift of sanctity, and they should implore the guidance of the Holy Spirit and His instruction in what is good and useful. . . .

But, if some, perhaps, are not in attendance because the nature or place of their work keeps them at too great a distance, they are strictly obliged to carry out wherever they are, with promptitude, all that is prescribed for common observance, for "where there are two or three gathered together in my name," says the Lord, "there am I in the midst of them" [Matt. 18:20]. It is also our judgment that prayer is necessary *at the sixth hour*, in imitation of the saints who say: "Evening and morning and at noon I will speak and declare; and he shall hear my voice" [Ps. 55:17]. And so that we may be saved from invasion and the noonday Devil, at this time, also, the [ninety-first] Psalm will be recited. *The ninth hour*, however, was appointed as a compulsory time for prayer by the Apostles themselves in the Acts where it is related that "Peter and John went up to the temple at the ninth hour of prayer." *When the day's work is ended*, thanksgiving should be offered for what has been granted us or for what we have done rightly therein and confession made of our omissions whether voluntary or involuntary, or of a secret fault, if we chance to have committed any in words or deeds, or in the heart itself; for by prayer we propitiate God for all our misdemeanors. The examination of our past actions is a great help toward not falling into like faults again; wherefore the Psalmist says: "the things you say in your hearts, be sorry for them upon your beds" [4:4].

Again, *at nightfall,* we must ask that our rest be sinless and untroubled by dreams. At this hour, also, the ninetieth Psalm should be recited. Paul and Silas, furthermore, have handed down to us the practice of compulsory prayer at *midnight,* as the history of the Acts declares: "And at midnight Paul and Silas praised God." The Psalmist also says: "I rose at midnight to give praise to thee for the judgments of thy justifications" [119:62]. Then, too, we *must anticipate the dawn* by prayer, so that the day may not find us in slumber and in bed.

ROME

Benedict of Nursia

The Western pattern of eight daily offices is fixed by Benedict in the sixth century.

Benedict of Nursia, *The Rule,* VIII, XVI, XVIII (ca. 530), trans. Owen Chadwick, in LCC 12:304–5, 307, 309.

In the winter time, that is from the first of November until Easter, having regard to different circumstances, they shall rise at 2 o'clock in the morning, that they may have time to rest till after midnight, and the time of digestion is past. What time remains after the office is done, they may use in studying the psalms and lessons if they do not yet know them thoroughly.

From Easter to the first of November, they shall so arrange the night office as to leave a very short interval after it (so that the brothers may go out for the needs of nature) and then begin Lauds at break of day. . . .

"Seven times a day have I praised thee," said the prophet [Ps. 119:164]. We shall perform this consecrated number of seven if we offer prayer (the duty of our profession) at the hours of Lauds, Prime, Terce, Sext, None, Vespers, and Compline. It was of these day hours that he said: "Seven times a day have I praised thee." Elsewhere the same prophet makes mention of the night office, "at midnight I rose to confess to thee." At these times, therefore, let us render praise to our creator "for the judgments of his justice"—that is, Lauds, Prime, Terce, Sext, None, Vespers, Compline: and let us rise at night to confess to him. . . .

These are the arrangements for the psalmody at the day offices.

The remaining psalms are to be distributed equally among the seven night offices, dividing the longer psalms and always assigning twelve for each night.

Notwithstanding, we hereby declare that if anyone does not approve of the present distribution of psalms, he may appoint otherwise, if he thinks better: provided he takes care that the whole psalter, of a hundred and fifty psalms, be sung every week, and that they begin it again at the night office each Sunday. It is a mean devotion if monks should in a week sing less than the whole Psalter with the usual canticles. We read that our holy fathers bravely recited the Psalter in a single day; God grant that we, their degenerate sons, may do the like in seven.

The Western Middle Ages

The office in the West becomes both increasingly privatized and obligatory for monks and diocesan clergy alike.

The Rule of St. Chrodegang of Metz

The Rule of St. Chrodegang of Metz (d. 766), chapter 4; trans. Pierre Salmon, in *The Breviary through the Centuries* (Collegeville, MN: Liturgical Press, 1962), 9.

That all should come to the divine office at all the canonical hours.
At the hour for the divine office, as soon as the signal is heard, those who are close enough to the building to be able to get there for the office must drop whatever they have in hand and hurry there with all possible speed. And, if anyone is from the church, so that he cannot get there for the canonical hours, and the bishop or the archdeacon agrees that such is the situation, he shall perform the work of God right where he is at the time, with reverent fear. And the archdeacon or the head guardian of the church shall see to it that the signals are sounded at the proper time.

Thomas Aquinas

In those twice-a-year "Quodlibetal Disputations," in which a teacher would be asked to respond to any topic of interest, Thomas Aquinas responds to various questions regarding the obligations surrounding the praying of the divine office.

Thomas Aquinas, *Quaestiones quodlibetales* III, q. 13, a. 2; *Quaestiones quodlibetales* VI, q. 5, a. 2; and *Quaestiones quodlibetales* V, q. 14, a. 1; in *Quaestiones de Quolibet*, in vol. 2, *Sancti Thomae Opera Omnia Iussu Leonis XIII P. M. Edita* 25 (Rome: Commissio Leonina, 1996), 286–88, 302–3, and 394–95, trans. Nathaniel Marx for this volume.

Quaestiones quodlibetales III, q. 13, a. 2: **Question:** Whether one who omits to say the divine office quietly to himself can be assigned some other penance for such an omission, or whether he must be required to repeat what he omitted.

Objection: It seems that one who omits to say the divine office must be charged with saying it again. For whoever is bound to satisfy a specific debt cannot be freed unless the same debt is paid back. If, therefore, anyone has this duty of saying the divine office, it seems that he cannot be released unless this debt has been paid.

On the contrary: Opposed to this is that *penances are arbitrary;* therefore for the sin of such an omission, any penalty at all can be imposed at the discretion of the priest.

Response: In every divine office there is this common feature: that it pertains to the praise of God and to the petitions of the faithful; but one office is distinguished from another by a difference of time and place. For it has been reasonably established that God is praised in various ways suitable to times and places. And therefore, just as suitability to place must be observed in the performance of the divine office, so also must suitability to time; and this would be impossible to observe if it were necessary to impose upon the offender that he say the hours which he omitted. For then he might say at Compline: *Star of light now having risen,*[1] and during Eastertide say the office of the Lord's Passion, which would be absurd. Thus, it does not seem to be the case that one who omits the divine office should be charged with repeating those same hours, but with something else pertaining to divine praise, such as saying the seven penitential psalms, or an entire Psalter, or something larger according to the magnitude of the offense.

Reply to the objection: Since the duty of the office has been neglected with respect to time, it is now impossible to pay back this debt with respect to time, and therefore, since it is impossible to do this, he must be enjoined to some other penance.

Quaestiones quodlibetales VI, q. 5, a. 2: **Question:** Regarding the fulfillment of the office, whether a cleric holding a benefice, with or

---

1. Hymn at the office of prime.

without a post, may be required to say the office of the dead while appearing in choir.

Objection: It seems that a cleric with benefice may be required to say the office of the dead while appearing in choir. For one who receives someone else's temporal goods is required to repay him in spiritual goods; but such a cleric accepts the goods of those who have died; therefore he is required to say the office of the dead for them.

On the contrary: Opposed to this is that one who receives less is held to less; and the cleric who remains in choir receives less than those who take up residence in a church and receive daily distributions; therefore he is not required to say the office of the dead in the same way as they.

Response: A cleric, inasmuch as he is a cleric and especially as he has been established in sacred orders, is required to say the canonical hours. Indeed, it seems that such persons have been claimed for divine praise, as it says in Isaiah 43: *Everyone who is called by my name, for my praise I created them;*[2] and inasmuch as the cleric is a beneficiary in this church, he is required to say the office according to the way of this church. It should be considered, therefore, that the office of the dead is said in a church whenever it ordinarily pertains to the church's office, just as in the whole church the office for the dead is said on All Souls Day while in some particular church there may be in addition to this a special custom, perhaps that the office of the dead is ordinarily said once a week or in some other way according to a fixed time. In this way, a cleric with benefice, including one appearing in choir, is bound in any church at all to say the office of the dead, and by this he makes satisfaction to the dead from whom he has received goods. Truly, at times the office of the dead is said extraordinarily in a church, on account of some specially emerging cause, say at the request of some person or something of the like; and a cleric appearing in choir is not bound to the office of the dead for such a reason.

Reply to the objection: Through this the response to the objection is clear.

Quaestiones quodlibetales V, q. 14, a. 1: **Question:** Whether it is lawful for a cleric bound to the canonical hours to say the following day's matins at night.

Objection: It seems that it is not. For as it says in Ecclesiasticus 21: *a babbler and a fool will regard no time;*[3] and such a cleric does not heed the time in saying matins. Indeed, since the day begins at

---

2. Isa. 43:7.
3. Sirach 20:7.

midnight, it appears that he is saying the following day's matins on the preceding day. Therefore it seems that this pertains to wantonness and foolishness and thus appears to be a sin.

On the contrary: Opposed to this is that God is more merciful than any human being whatsoever; yet no human being charges a debtor with a crime if the debtor pays back the debt ahead of time; therefore much less would God do so.

Response: The intention of the one who anticipates the time in the saying of matins or any of the canonical hours must be considered here. For if he does this on account of wantonness, namely in order to sleep more peacefully and to be free for pleasure, he is not without sin. However, if he does this because of the necessity of licit and honorable business—such as when a cleric or a teacher is obliged to view his readings at night, or on account of something else of this sort—he can lawfully say matins in the evening and anticipate the time in the saying of the other canonical hours. Indeed, this very thing happens in the church on solemnities, for it is better to render unto to God from both sides—that is, both due praise and other honorable offices—than that one of these be hindered by the other.

Reply to the objection: As far as contracts and other things of that sort go, the day begins at midnight; but as far as the ecclesiastical office and the most solemn celebrations go, the day begins at vespers; hence if anyone says matins after having said vespers and compline, this now pertains to the following day.

|

Reformation and Later Developments

|

The most familiar pattern for daily prayer by this time in the West is the monastic office, which several Reformers adapt.

THE REFORMATION

Martin Luther

Martin Luther, *Formula Missae* (1523), trans. Paul Zeller Strodach
and Ulrich S. Leupold, in LW 53:37–39.

As for the other days which are called weekdays, I see nothing that we cannot put up with, provided the [weekday] masses be discontinued.

For Matins with its three lessons, the [minor] hours, Vespers, and Compline *de tempore* consist—with the exception of the propers for the Saints' days—of nothing but divine words of Scripture. And it is seemly, nay necessary, that the boys should get accustomed to reading and hearing the Psalms and lessons from the Holy Scripture. If anything should be changed, the bishop may reduce the great length [of the services] according to his own judgment so that three Psalms may be sung for Matins and three for Vespers with one or two responsories. These matters are best left to the discretion of the bishop. He should choose the best of the responsories and antiphons and appoint them from Sunday to Sunday throughout the week, taking care lest the people should either be bored by too much repetition of the same or confused by too many changes in the chants and lessons. The whole Psalter, Psalm by Psalm, should remain in use, and the entire Scripture, lesson by lesson, should continue to be read to the people. But we must take care—as I have elsewhere explained—lest the people sing only with their lips, like sounding pipes or harps [1 Cor. 14:7], and without understanding. Daily lessons must therefore be appointed, one in the morning from the New or Old Testament, another for Vespers from the other Testament with an exposition in the vernacular. That this rite is an ancient one is proven by both the custom itself and by the words *homilia* in Matins and *capitulum* in Vespers and in the other [canonical] hours, namely, that the Christians as often as they gathered together read something and then had it interpreted in the vernacular in the manner Paul describes in I Corinthians 14 [:26–27]. But when evil times came and there was a lack of prophets and interpreters, all that was left after the lessons and *capitula* was the response, "Thanks be to God." And then, in place of the interpretation, lessons, Psalms, hymns, and other things were added in boring repetition. Although the hymns and the *Te Deum laudamus* at least confirm the same thing as the *Deo gratias*, namely, that after the exposition and homilies they used to praise God and give thanks for the revealed truth of his words. That is the kind of vernacular songs I should like us to have.

Martin Luther, *The German Mass* (1526), trans. Augustus Steimle
and Ulrich S. Leupold, in LW 53:89–90.

This is what I have to say concerning the daily service and instruction in the Word of God, which serves primarily to train the young and challenge the unlearned. For those who itch for new things will soon be sated and tired with it all, as they were heretofore in the Latin service. There was singing and reading in the churches every day, and yet the churches remained deserted and empty. Already they do the same in the German service. Therefore, it is best to plan the services in the interest of the young and such of the unlearned as may happen to come. With the others neither law nor order, neither scolding nor coaxing, will help. Allow them to leave those things in the service alone which they refuse to do willingly and gladly. God is not pleased with unwilling services; they are futile and vain.

Christian Gerber

Christian Gerber, *Historie der Kirchen Ceremonien in Sachsen* (1732), quoted in Günther Stiller, *Johann Sebastian Bach and Liturgical Life in Leipzig*, trans. Herbert J. A. Bouman, Daniel F. Poellot, and Hilton C. Oswald (St. Louis: Concordia Press, 1984), 55.

Happy is he who can live in a city where worship is conducted publicly every day. In this respect, the inhabitants of Dresden and Leipzig are fortunate, because in these two cities preaching and prayer services are held every day, so that they are enriched with all speech and knowledge and are not lacking in any spiritual gift.

Francisco de Quiñones

Francisco de Quiñones, Preface, *Breviarium Romanae Curiae* (1535 and 1536), trans. from both 1535 and 1536 editions in the sequence used by Thomas Cranmer; texts in *Cranmer's Liturgical Projects*, ed. J. Wickham Legg (London: Henry Bradshaw Society, 1915), 50:168–82.

[1536] Nothing was ever worked out by human cleverness so completely from the beginning but that it was possible to be restored more perfectly after the judgments of many; this we have seen to have happened especially in the restoration of the church according to the primitive church. . . .

[1535] And truly if one may consider carefully what manner of praying was passed down formerly from most people, he discovers the reasonable character of all the hours to be clear.

[1536] But the fact is that I do not know how through what neglect of the stipulated practice of praying that little by little it departed from that most sacred practice put in place by the ancient fathers.

[1535] Now at first the books of holy scripture, which were appointed for reading through in the times of the year, scarcely began but they were passed over for prayers.

For example could be the book of Genesis, which is begun in Septuagesima, and the book of Isaiah, which in Advent, of which scarcely a single chapter is read through, and in the same means others of the Old Testament books we taste rather than we read.

[1535, 1536] The order became so complex, the calculation of the prayers so difficult, that sometimes it was little less work in finding what was laid down than after finding it, in reading it.

[1535, 1536] Which perception of things, happily having pondered, Pope Clement VII, when he considered it to be his duty . . . has encouraged me, and given authority, that with as much care and diligence as is possible, to distribute the prayers of the hours rationally, and to take away, as I have said, the difficulties and so dispose, that clergy in major orders may be more conveniently attracted to praying.

[1535] Antiphons, chapters, responses, and many hymns and other things of that sort which are a hindrance to the reading of sacred scripture are omitted; the breviary consists of psalms and sacred scripture of the Old and New Testaments, and histories of the saints which we have gathered from approved and serious greek and latin authors.

The First and Second Prayer Books of Edward VI

"The Preface," *The Booke of the Common Prayer* (1549), in *The First and Second Prayer Books of Edward VI* (London: J. M. Dent & Sons, 1910; spelling, capitalization, and punctuation modernized), 3–5.

There was never any thing by the wit of man so well devised, or so surely established, which (in continuance of time) hath not been corrupted: as (among other things) it may plainly appear by the common prayers in the Church, commonly called divine service: the first original and ground whereof . . . was . . . that all the whole Bible (or the greatest part thereof) should be read over once in the year. . . . And further, that the people (by daily hearing of holy scripture read in the Church) should continually profit more and more in the knowledge of God, and be the more inflamed with the love of his true religion. But these many years passed this Godly and decent order of the ancient fathers, hath been so altered, broken, and neglected . . . that commonly when any book of the Bible was begun: before three or four chapters were read out, all the rest were unread. And in this sort the book of Isaiah was begun in Advent, and the book of Genesis in Septuagesima; but they were only begun, and never read through. . . . Many times, there was more business to find out what should be read, then to read it when it was found out.

These inconveniences therefore considered: here is set forth such an order, whereby the same shall be redressed. And for a readiness in this matter, here is drawn out a Calendar for that purpose, which is plain and easy to be understood, wherein (so much as may be) the reading of holy scripture is so set forth, that all things shall be in order, without breaking one piece thereof from another. For this cause be cut off anthems, responds, invitatories, and such like things, as did break the continual course of the reading of the scripture. . . .

Yet it is not meant, but when men say matins and evensong privately, they may say the same in any language that they themselves do understand.

"The Table and Kalender," *The Booke of the Common Prayer* (1549),
in *The First and Second Prayer Books of Edward VI*, 6.

The Psalter shall be read through once every month, and because that some months, be longer than some other be; it is thought good, to make them even by this means.

"The Preface," *The Booke of Common Prayer* (1552), in
The First and Second Prayer Books of Edward VI, 323.

And all priests and deacons shall be bound to say daily the morning and evening prayer, either privately or openly, except they be letted [prevented] by preaching, studying of divinity, or by some other urgent cause.

And the curate that ministers in every parish church or chapel, being at home, and not being otherwise reasonably letted, shall say the same in the parish church or chapel where he ministers, and shall toll a bell thereto, a convenient time before he begin, that such as be disposed may come to hear God's word, and to pray with him.

"The Order How the Rest of Holy Scripture
(Beside the Psalter) Is Appointed to Be Read," in *The First
and Second Prayer Books of Edward VI*, 329.

The Old Testament is appointed for the first lessons, at morning and evening prayer, and shall be read through every year once, except certain books and chapters, which be least edifying, and might best be spared, and therefore be left unread.

The New Testament is appointed for the second lessons, at morning and evening prayer, and shall be read over orderly every year thrice, beside the epistles and gospels: except the Apocalypse, out of the which there be only certain lessons appointed, upon divers proper feasts.

Church of Scotland

Family worship on a daily basis becomes an important part of Christian devotion.

Church of Scotland, *The Directory for Family-Worship*, I, II, IV (1647),
in *The Confession of Faith; . . . Directories for Public and Family Worship*
(Philadelphia: Towar and Hogan, 1829), 595–96.

Besides the publick worship in congregations, mercifully established in this land in great purity, it is expedient and necessary that secret worship of each person alone, and private worship of families, be pressed and set up; that with national reformation, the profession and power of godliness, both personal and domestick, be advanced.

I. And first, for secret worship, it is most necessary . . . to perform this duty morning and evening, and at other occasions. . . .

II. The ordinary duties comprehended under the exercise of piety, which should be in families, when they are convened to this effect, are these: First, Prayer and praises performed with a special reference as well to the publick condition of the kirk of God in this kingdom, as to the present case of the family, and every member thereof. Next, Reading of the scriptures, with catechising in a plain way, that the understandings of the simpler may be the better enabled to profit under the publick ordinances, and they made more capable to understand the scriptures when they are read; together with godly conferences tending to the edification of all members in the most holy faith: as also, admonition and rebuke, upon just reasons, from those who have authority in the family. . . .

IV. The head of the family is to take care that none of the family withdraw himself from any part of family-worship.

LATER DEVELOPMENTS

John Wesley

John Wesley combines set forms and extempore daily prayer.

John Wesley, letter of September 10, 1784, bound with *Sunday Service* (1784), in
John Wesley's Sunday Service (Nashville: United Methodist Publishing House, 1984), n.p.

And I have prepared a liturgy little differing from that of the church of England (I think, the best constituted national church in the world) which I advise all the travelling-preachers to use, on the Lord's day, in all their congregations, reading the litany only on Wednesdays and Fridays, and praying extempore on all other days. I also advise the elders to administer the supper of the Lord on every Lord's day.

John Wesley, Letter of September 9, 1784, bound with
Sunday Service (1784), in *John Wesley's Sunday Service.*

Many Psalms left out, and many parts of the others, as being highly improper for the mouths of a Christian Congregation.

Charles G. Finney

The midweek prayer meeting recovers some of the characteristics of the early people's office (frequent use of familiar hymns and prayers) and leads to transformation of society (abolition of slavery, temperance movements, etc.).

Charles G. Finney, *Lectures on Revivals of Religion* (1835), ed. William G. McLoughlin
(Cambridge, MA: Harvard University Press, 1960), 259.

Female Prayer Meetings. Within the last few years [1830s], female prayer meetings have been extensively opposed in this state [New York]. What dreadful things! A minister, now dead, said that when he first attempted to establish these meetings, he had all the clergy around opposed to him. "Set women to praying? Why, the next thing, I suppose, will be to set them preaching." And serious apprehensions were entertained for the safety of Zion, if women should be allowed to get together to pray. And even now, they are not tolerated in some churches.

General Instruction on the Liturgy of the Hours

The liturgy of the hours is reformed by Roman Catholics in the 1970s.

General Instruction on the Liturgy of the Hours, with Commentary
by A. M. Roguet, XXIX, CXXVI, CXLIII, trans. Peter Coughlan
and Peter Purdue (London: Geoffrey Chapman, 1971), 27, 45, 48.

They are to give due importance to the Hours which are the two hinges on which this Liturgy turns, that is, Lauds as morning prayer and Vespers; let them take care not to omit these hours, unless for a serious reason.

They are also to carry out faithfully the Office of Readings, which is above all the liturgical celebration of the word of God. . . .

That the day may be completely sanctified, they will desire to recite the middle Hour and Compline, thus commending themselves to God and completing the entire "Opus Dei" before going to bed. . . .

The psalms are distributed over a four-week cycle. In this cycle, a very small number of psalms are omitted, while the traditionally more important ones are repeated more frequently. Lauds, Vespers and Compline have psalms corresponding with their respective Hour. . . .

The reading of scripture in the Liturgy of the Hours is linked with and completes the reading at Mass; in this way the history of salvation is viewed as a whole.

| THE LITURGICAL YEAR |

| The Christian Week |

THE BEGINNING OF SUNDAY OBSERVANCE

Hints of the observance of Sunday as the occasion for Christian worship appear in the New Testament.

Scripture

1 Corinthians 16:2.

On the first day of every week, each of you is to put aside and save whatever extra you earn, so that collections need not be taken when I come.

Acts 20:7, 11.

On the first day of the week, when we met to break bread, Paul . . . continued speaking until midnight. . . . Then Paul went upstairs, and after he had broken bread and eaten, he continued to converse with them until dawn; then he left [Troas].

Revelation 1:10.

I was in the spirit on the Lord's day [*kyriakē hēmera*], and I heard behind me a loud voice like a trumpet.

EARLY DEVELOPMENT OF SUNDAY

References to Sunday become more common in the second century.

Pliny the Younger

The term *stato die* in the following might not be Sunday but could be a reference to the Sabbath instead.

> Pliny the Younger, "Letter 10" (ca. 112), trans. Henry Bettenson, in *Documents of the Christian Church* (New York: Oxford University Press, 1947), 6.

On an appointed day, they had been accustomed to meet before daybreak [*stato die ante lucem*], and to recite a hymn antiphonally to Christ, as to a god, and to bind themselves by an oath [*sacramentum*], not for the commission of any crime but to abstain from theft, robbery, adultery, and breach of faith, and not to deny a deposit when it was claimed. After the conclusion of this ceremony it was their custom to depart and meet again to take food; but it was ordinary and harmless food.

The Didache

> *The Didache*, XIV (late first or early second century), trans. Cyril C. Richardson, in LCC 1:178.

On every Lord's Day—his special day [*kyriakên de kyriou*, literally "Lord's Day of the Lord"]—come together and break bread and give thanks, first confessing your sins so that your sacrifice may be pure.

The Epistle of Barnabas

> *The Epistle of Barnabas*, XV, 8–9 (late first or early second century), trans. Krisopp Lake, in *Apostolic Fathers* (Cambridge: Harvard University Press, 1965), 1:395–96.

The present sabbaths are not acceptable to me, but that which I have made, in which I will give rest to all things and make the beginning of an eighth day, that is the beginning of another world. Wherefore we also celebrate with gladness the eighth day in which Jesus also rose from the dead, and was made manifest, and ascended into Heaven.

Ignatius of Antioch

> Ignatius of Antioch, *To the Magnesians*, IX (ca. 115), trans. Cyril C. Richardson, in LCC 1:96.

Those, then, who lived by ancient practices arrived at a new hope. They ceased to keep the Sabbath and lived by the Lord's Day [*kyriakēn*] on which our life as well as theirs shone forth, thanks to Him and his death, though some deny this.

Justin Martyr

Justin Martyr, *First Apology,* LXVII (ca. 155), trans.
Edward Rochie Hardy, in LCC 1:287–88.

We all hold this common gathering on Sunday [*hēliou hēmeran*], since it is the first day, on which God transforming darkness and matter made the universe, and Jesus Christ our Saviour rose from the dead on the same day. For they crucified him on the day before Saturday, and on the day after Saturday, he appeared to his apostles and disciples and taught them these things which I have passed on to you also for your serious consideration.

Codex Justinianus

In 321 Sunday is recognized as the day of rest by imperial decree.

Codex Justinianus, III, xii, 3 (321), trans. Henry Bettenson, in *Documents of the Christian Church* (New York: Oxford University Press, 1947), 27.

Constantine to Elpidius. All judges, city-people and craftsmen shall rest on the venerable day of the Sun. But countrymen may without hindrance attend to agriculture, since it often happens that this is the most suitable day for sowing grain or planting vines, so that the opportunity afforded by divine providence may not be lost, for the right season is of short duration. 7 March 321.

Development of Other Days of the Week

Wednesdays and Fridays become fast days.

Scripture

The following text refers to the Jewish custom of fasting on Mondays and Thursdays.

Luke 18:11–12.

The Pharisee, standing by himself, was praying thus, "God, I thank you that I am not like other people: thieves, rogues, adulterers, or even like this tax collector. I fast twice a week; I give a tenth of all my income."

The Didache

This selection and the next note that Wednesdays and Fridays become fast days.

The Didache, VIII (late first or early second century), trans. Cyril C. Richardson, in LCC 1:174.

Your fasts must not be identical with those of the hypocrites. They fast on Mondays and Thursdays; but you should fast on Wednesdays and Fridays.

Apostolic Constitutions

Apostolic Constitutions, VII, 23 (ca. 375), trans. James Donaldson, in *ANF* 7:469.

But do you . . . fast . . . on the fourth day of the week, and on the day of Preparation, because on the fourth day the condemnation went out against the Lord, Judas then promising to betray him for money; and you must fast on the day of Preparation, because on that day the Lord suffered the death of the cross under Pontius Pilate.

Tertullian

Saturday retains a quasi-liturgical significance.

Tertullian, *On Prayer*, XXIII (ca. 205), trans. S. Thelwall, in *ANF* 3:689.

In the mater of *kneeling* also prayer is subject to diversity of observance, through the fact of some few who abstain from kneeling on the Sabbath. . . . We, however (just as we have received), only on the day of the Lord's Resurrection ought to not only guard against kneeling, but [also against] every posture and office of solicitude.

Apostolic Constitutions

Apostolic Constitutions, VII, 23 (ca. 375), trans. James Donaldson, in *ANF* 7:469.

But keep the Sabbath and the Lord's day festival; because the former is the memorial of the creation, the latter of the resurrection. But there is one only Sabbath to be observed by you in the whole year, which is that of our Lord's burial, on which men ought to keep a fast, but not a festival. For inasmuch as the Creator was then under the earth, the sorrow for Him is more forcible than the joy of the creation; for the Creator is more honorable by nature and dignity than His own creatures.

Feasts and Seasons

JEWISH ROOTS

Scripture

The Pascha is central for Judaism and Christianity.

Exodus 12:6–8.

You shall keep it [the lamb] until the fourteenth day of this month; then the whole assembled congregation of Israel shall slaughter it at twilight. They shall take some of the blood and put it on the two doorposts and the lintel of the houses in which they eat it. They shall eat the lamb that same night; they shall eat it roasted over the fire with unleavened bread and bitter herbs.

1 Corinthians 5:7–8.

Clean out the old yeast so that you may be a new batch, as you really are unleavened. For our paschal lamb, Christ, has been sacrificed. Therefore, let us celebrate the festival, not with the old yeast, the yeast of malice and evil, but with the unleavened bread of sincerity and truth.

EASTER AND PASSOVER

The Quartodeciman controversy rages over whether Easter should be observed always on Sunday or on the same day of the week as the Jewish Passover.

Eusebius

Eusebius, *The History of the Church*, V, 23–24 (323), trans. G. A. Williamson, in *The History of the Church: From Christ to Constantine* (Baltimore: Penguin Classics, 1965), 229–30.

It was at that stage [late second century] that a controversy of great significance took place, because all the Asian dioceses thought that in accordance with ancient tradition they ought to observe the fourteenth day of the lunar month [Nisan] as the beginning of the Paschal festival—the day on which the Jews had been commanded to sacrifice the lamb: on that day, no matter which day of the week it might be, they must without fail bring the fast to an end. But nowhere else in the world was it customary to arrange their celebrations in that way: in accordance with apostolic tradition, they preserved the view which still prevails, that it was improper to end the fast on any day other than that of our Saviour's resurrection. So synods and conferences of bishops were convened, and without a dissentient voice, drew up a decree of the Church, in the form of letters addressed to Christians everywhere, that never on any day other than the Lord's Day should the mystery of the Lord's resurrection from the dead be celebrated, and that on that day alone we should observe the end of the Paschal fast.

Melito of Sardis

Melito of Sardis, *On the Pascha*, 46, 67–69, 71, selected, annotated, and introduced by Raniero Cantalamessa, in *Easter in the Early Church: An Anthology of Jewish and Christian Texts*, trans. and ed. James M. Quigley and Joseph T. Lienhard (Collegeville, MN: Liturgical Press, 1993), 43–45.

46. Now that you have heard the explanation of the type and of its corresponding reality, listen also to what went into making up the mystery. What is the Pascha? Its name is taken from an accompanying circumstance: *paschein* (to keep Pascha) comes from *pathein* (to suffer). Therefore learn who the sufferer is and who he is who suffers along with the sufferer, and why the Lord is present on the earth in order to clothe himself with the sufferer and carry him off to the heights of heaven.

67. For, having been himself led as a lamb and slain as a sheep, he ransomed us from the world's service as from the land of Egypt and freed us from the devil's slavery as from the hand of Pharoah; and he marked our souls with his own Spirit and the members of our body with his own blood.

68. It is he that clothed death with shame and put the devil into mourning as Moses did Pharoah. It is he that struck down crime and made injustice childless as Moses did Egypt. It is he that delivered us from slavery to liberty, from darkness to light, from death to life, from tyranny to eternal royalty, and made us a new *priesthood* and an eternal *people personal* (to him).

69. He is the Pascha of our salvation.

71. He is the lamb being slain; he is the lamb that is speechless, he is the one born from Mary the lovely ewe-lamb, he is the one taken from the flock and dragged to slaughter and sacrificed at evening and buried in the night; who on the tree was not broken, in the earth was not dissolved, arose from the dead, and raised up mortals from the grave below.

ELABORATION OF THE PASCHA

Third-century documents show elaboration of the Christian Pascha.

Tertullian

Tertullian, *On Baptism*, XIX (ca. 205), trans. S. Thelwall, in *ANF* 3:678.

The Passover [Pascha] affords a more than usually solemn day for baptism; when, withal, the Lord's passion in which we are baptized, was completed. Nor will it be incongruous to interpret figuratively the fact that, when the Lord was about to celebrate the last Passover, He said to the disciples who were sent to make preparation, "Ye will meet a man bearing water." He points out the place for celebrating the Passover by the sign of water.

Didascalia Apostolorum

Didascalia Apostolorum, XXI (mid-third century), trans. R. Hugh Connolly, in *Didascalia Apostolorum* (Oxford: Clarendon Press, 1969), 190.

Especially incumbent on you therefore is the fast of the Friday and of the Sabbath; and likewise the vigil and watching of the Sabbath, and the reading of the Scriptures, and psalms, and prayer and intercession for them that have sinned, and the expectation and hope of the resurrection of our Lord Jesus, until the third hour in the night after the Sabbath. And then offer your oblations; and thereafter eat and make good cheer, and rejoice and be glad, because that the earnest of our resurrection, Christ, is risen.

Origen of Alexandria

Pascha as "passage" is added to the growing interpretation of the feast.

Origen of Alexandria, *On the Pascha*, 1, trans. Raniero Cantalamessa, in *Easter in the Early Church* (Collegeville, MN: The Liturgical Press, 1993), 53.

Most, if not all, of the brethren, think that Pascha is named Pascha from the passion of the Savior. However, the feast in question is not called precisely Pascha by the Hebrews, but *phas[h]*. The name of this feast is constituted by the three letters phi, alpha, and sigma, plus the rougher Hebrew aspirate. Translated it means "passage." Since it is on this feast that the people goes forth from Egypt, it is logical to call it *phas[h]*. . . . And so, if any of our people in the company of the Hebrews makes the rash statement that the Pascha is so named beause of the passion of the Savior, they will ridicule him for being completely ignorant of the meaning of the appellation.

Dionysius of Alexandria

Dionysius describes the various prepaschal fasting practices known to him and provides the first witness to a one-week preparatory fast.

Dionysius of Alexandria, *Letter to Basilides*, 1, trans. Raniero Cantalamessa, in *Easter in the Early Church*, 60–61.

You sent to me, my most faithful and learned son, to inquire at what hour one ought to end the fast before Easter. For you say that some of the brethren maintain one should do so at cockcrow: and some at evening. For the brethren in Rome, so they say, await cockcrow: but concerning those in the Pentapolis you said (they broke the fast) sooner. And you ask me to set an exact limit and definite hour, which is both difficult and risky. For it will be acknowledged by all alike that one ought to start the feast and the gladness after the time of our Lord's resurrection, up till then humbling our souls with fastings. . . .

As things stand thus, we pronounce this decision for those who inquire to a nicety at what hour or what half-hour, or quarter of an hour, they should begin their rejoicing at the resurrection of our Lord from the dead: those who are premature and relax before midnight, though near it, we censure as remiss and wanting in self-restraint; for they drop out of the race just before the end as the wise man says: "that which is within a little in life is not little." And those who put off and endure to the furthest and persevere till the fourth watch, when our Saviour appeared to those who were sailing, "walking on the sea," . . . we shall approve as generous and painstaking. And those midway who stop as they were moved or as they were able, let us not treat altogether severely. For not all continue during the six days of the fast either equally or similarly: but some remain without food till cockcrow on all the days, and some on two, or three, or four, and some on none of them. And for those who strictly persist in these prolonged fasts and then are distressed and almost faint, there is some pardon if they take something sooner. But if some, so far from prolonging their fast do not fast at all, but feed luxuriously during the earlier days of the week, and then, when they come to the last two and prolong their fast on them alone, viz. on Friday and Saturday, think they are performing some great feat by continuing till dawn, I do not hold they have exercised an equal discipline with those who have practiced it for longer periods.

FOURTH-CENTURY DEVELOPMENTS ON PASCHA

The Council of Nicaea

The date of Easter is determined for all churches by the Council of Nicaea.

The Council of Nicaea, *Decree on Easter*,
trans. Raniero Cantalamessa, in *Easter in the Early Church*, 63–64.

When . . . in the course of examining the matter of the need for the whole (Church) under heaven to keep the Pascha harmoniously, the three parts of the empire were found acting in harmony with the Romans and Alexandrians, and only one region, that of the Orient, disagreed, it was decided that, putting aside all contention and contradiction, the brethren in the Orient too should do as the Romans and Alexandrians and all the rest do, so that all in harmony on the same day may send up their prayers on the holy day of the Pascha. And, while disagreeing with the others, those of the Orient subscribed.

Egeria

Pascha (like Epiphany and Pentecost) splits into a series of separate commemorations during the fourth century.

Egeria, *Travels*, XXX–XXXVIII (ca. 384), trans. John Wilkinson,
in *Egeria's Travels* (London: SPCK, 1971), 132–38.

Sunday is the beginning of the Easter week or, as they call it here [Jerusalem], "The Great Week." . . . [Sunday] the bishop and all the people rise from their places, and start off on foot down from the summit of the Mount of Olives. All the people go before him with psalms and antiphons, all the time repeating, "Blessed is he that cometh in the name of the Lord." . . .

Wednesday is exactly like Monday and Tuesday . . . but at night . . . a presbyter . . . reads the passage about Judas Iscariot going to the Jews and fixing what they must pay him to betray the Lord. The people groan and lament at this reading in a way that would make you weep to hear them. . . .

Thursday . . . everyone receives Communion. . . . When the cocks begin to crow, everyone leaves the Imbomon [place of the Ascension], and comes down with singing to the place where the Lord prayed. . . . From there all of them, including the smallest children, now go down with singing and conduct the bishop to Gethsemane. . . .

[Friday] The Bishop's chair is placed on Golgotha Behind the Cross (the cross there now), and he takes his seat. A table is placed before him with a cloth on it, and the deacons stand round, and there is brought to him a gold and silver box containing the holy Wood of the Cross. It is opened, and the Wood of the Cross and the Title [inscription] are taken out and placed on the table. . . . [A]ll the people, catechumens as well as faithful, come up one by one to the table. They stoop down over it, kiss the Wood, and move on.

Saturday . . . they keep their paschal vigil like us.

Augustine

Augustine, *Letter 55: To Januarius* (ca. 400), trans. Wilfrid Parsons,
in *Augustine: Letters*, vol. 1 (1–182); in FC 12:279, 283.

Note, therefore, the three sacred days of His Crucifixion, Burial and Resurrection. . . .

Since it is clear from the Gospel on what days the Lord was

crucified and rested in the tomb and rose again, there is added, through the councils of the fathers, the requirement of retaining those same days, and the whole Christian world is convinced that the pasch should be celebrated in that way.

THE SEASON OF LENT

Following the Council of Nicaea and the adoption of Easter baptism, the season of Lent becomes the time for the final preparation of candidates for baptism (the elect, *competentes*, or *phōtizomenoi*), the reconciliation of penitents, and the preparation of all the faithful. For examples of prebaptismal catechesis during Lent, as well as descriptions of the rites of Christian initiation at Easter, see chapter 3, pages 121–23.

Cyril of Jerusalem

Cyril of Jerusalem, *Procatechesis*, IV (ca. 350), trans. William Telfer, in LCC 4:68.

You have a long period of grace, forty days for repentance. You have plenty of time to discard and wash thoroughly your soul's apparel, and so to clothe yourself and come back. . . . For though the water will receive you, the Holy Spirit will not.

Augustine

Augustine, *Letter 55: To Januarius* (ca. 400), in *Augustine: Letters*; in FC 12:283–84.

The forty-day fast of Lent draws its authority from the Old Testament, from the fasts of Moses and Elias, and from the Gospel, because the Lord fasted that many days, showing that the Gospel is not at variance with the Law and the Prophets. . . . In what part of the year, then, could the observance of Lent be more appropriately instituted than that adjoining, so to speak, and touching on the Lord's Passion?

Leo the Great

The sermons of Pope Leo I, in the mid-fifth century, clearly demonstrate the threefold orientation of Lent: the preparation of the faithful, the penitents, and those elected to baptism.

Leo the Great, *Sermons* 39.2–3 and 49.3, in *NPNF²* 12:152–53 and 161.

39.2. Accordingly, dearly-beloved, that we may be able to overcome all our enemies, let us seek Divine aid by the observance of the heavenly bidding, knowing that we cannot otherwise prevail against our adversaries, unless we prevail against our own selves. For we have many encounters with our own selves: the flesh desires one thing against the spirit, and the spirit another thing against the flesh. . . . For knowing that the most hollowed days of Lent are now at hand, in the keeping of which all past slothfulnesses are chastised, all negligences alerted for, they direct all the force of their spite on this one thing, that they who intend to celebrate the Lord's holy Passover may be found unclean in some matter, and that cause of offence may arise where propitiation ought to have been obtained.

39.3. As we approach then, dearly-beloved, the beginning of Lent, which is a time for the more careful serving of the Lord, because we are, as it were, entering on a kind of contest in good works, let us prepare our souls for fighting with temptations, and understand that the more zealous we are for our salvation, the more determined must be the assaults of our opponents. But "stronger is He that is in us than He that is against us," and through Him are we powerful in whose strength we rely: because it was for this that the Lord allowed Himself to be tempted by the tempter, that we might be taught by His example as well as fortified by His aid. For He conquered the adversary, as ye have heard, by quotations from the law, not by actual strength, that by this very thing He might do greater honour to man, and inflict a greater punishment on the adversary by conquering the enemy of the human race not now as God but as Man. He fought then, therefore, that we too might fight thereafter: He conquered that we too might likewise conquer. For there are no works of power, dearly-beloved, without the trials of temptations, there is no faith without proof, no contest without a foe, no victory without conflict. This life of ours is in the midst of snares, in the midst of battles; if we do not wish to be deceived, we must watch: if we want to overcome, we must fight.

49. 3. And, dearly-beloved, no season requires and bestows this fortitude more than the present, when by the observance of a special strictness a habit is acquired which must be persevered in. For it is well known to you that this is the time when throughout the world the devil waxes furious, and the Christian army has to combat him, and any that have grown lukewarm and slothful, or that are absorbed in worldly cares, must now be furnished with spiritual armour and their ardour kindled for the fray by the heavenly trumpet, inasmuch as he, through whose envy death came into the world,

is now consumed with the strongest jealousy and now tortured with the greatest vexation. For he sees whole tribes of the human race brought in afresh to the adoption of God's sons and the offspring of the New Birth multiplied through the virgin fertility of the Church. He sees himself robbed of all his tyrannic power, and driven from the hearts of those he once possessed, while from either sex thousands of the old, the young, the middle-aged are snatched away from him, and no one is debarred by sin either of his own or original, where justification is not paid for deserts, but simply given as a free gift. He sees, too, those that have lapsed, and have been deceived by his treacherous snares, washed in the tears of penitence and, by the Apostle's key unlocking the gates of mercy, admitted to the benefit of reconciliation. He feels, moreover, that the day of the Lord's Passion is at hand, and that he is crushed by the power of that cross which in Christ, Who was free from all debt of sin, was the world's ransom and not the penalty of sin.

PENTECOST

Pentecost, the great fifty days following Easter, culminates in the Day of Pentecost.

Scripture

Leviticus 23:15–16.

And from the day after the sabbath, from the day on which you bring the sheaf of the elevation offering, you shall count off seven weeks; they shall be complete. You shall count until the day after the seventh sabbath, fifty days; then you shall present an offering of new grain to the LORD.

Acts 1:8–9.

"But you will receive power when the Holy Spirit has come upon you; and you will be my witnesses in Jerusalem, in all Judea and Samaria, and to the ends of the earth." When he had said this, as they were watching, he was lifted up, and a cloud took him out of their sight.

Acts 2:1–4.

When the day of Pentecost had come, they were all together in one place. And suddenly from heaven there came a sound like the rush of a violent wind, and it filled the entire house where they were sitting. Divided tongues, as of fire, appeared among them, and a tongue rested on each of them. All of them were filled with the Holy Spirit and began to speak in other languages, as the Spirit gave them ability.

Tertullian

Tertullian, *On Baptism*, XIX (ca. 205), trans. S. Thelwall, in *ANF* 3:678.

After that [the Pascha], Pentecost is a most joyous space for conferring baptisms; wherein, too, the resurrection of the Lord was repeatedly proved among the disciples, and the hope of the advent of the Lord indirectly pointed to, in that, at that time, when he had been received back into the heavens, the angels told the apostles that "He would so come, as He had withal ascended into the heavens"; at Pentecost, of course. But, moreover, when Jeremiah says, "And I will gather them together from the extremities of the land in the feast-day," he signifies the day of the Passover and of the Pentecost which is properly a "feast-day."

Tertullian, *De Corona*, III (ca. 211), trans. S. Thelwall, in *ANF* 3:94.

As often as the anniversary [of a death] comes round, we make offerings for the dead as birthday honours. We count fasting or kneeling in worship on the Lord's day to be unlawful. We rejoice in the same privilege also from Easter to Pentecost.

Augustine of Hippo

Augustine of Hippo, *Letter 55: To Januarius* (ca. 400),
in *Augustine: Letters*; in FC 12:284–85.

These days after the Lord's Resurrection form a period, not of labor, but of peace and joy. That is why there is no fasting and we pray standing, which is a sign of resurrection. This practice is observed at the altar on all Sundays, and the Alleluia is sung, to indicate that our future occupation is to be no other than the praise of God. . . .

Easter and Pentecost are feasts with the strongest Scriptural authority. The observance of forty days before Easter rests on the decree of the Church, and by the same authority the eight days of the neophytes [newly baptized who underwent eight days of instruction after Easter] are distinguished from other days, so that the eighth harmonizes with the first.

Eusebius

Eusebius, *Life of Constantine*, IV, 64 (ca. 338), trans. E. C. Richardson, in *NPNF²* 1:557.

All these events occurred during a most important festival, I mean the august and holy solemnity of Pentecost, which is distinguished by a period of seven weeks, and sealed with that one day on which the holy Scriptures attest the ascension of our common Saviour into heaven, and the descent of the Holy Spirit among men.

Apostolic Constitutions

By the end of the fourth century, Ascension is distinct from the Day of Pentecost.

Apostolic Constitutions, V, 19 (ca. 375), trans. James Donaldson, in *ANF* 7:447–48.

And again, from the first Lord's day count forty days, from the Lord's day till the fifth day of the week, and celebrate the feast of the ascension of the Lord, whereon He finished all His dispensation and constitution, and returned to that God and Father that sent Him, and sat down at the right hand of power, and remains there until His enemies are put under His feet; who also will come at the consummation of the world with power and great glory, to judge the quick and the dead, and to recompense to every one according to his works.

EPIPHANY

The manifestation of God in Jesus Christ, or Epiphany, commemorates Jesus' baptism and first sign.

Scripture

John 1:5.

The light shines [*phainei*] in the darkness, and the darkness did not overcome it.

John 1:9.

The true light, which enlightens everyone, was coming into the world.

John 1:32–34 (see also Matt. 3:1–17; Mark 1:4–11; Luke 3:21–22).

And John testified, "I saw the Spirit descending from heaven like a dove, and it remained on him. I myself did not know him, but the one who sent me to baptize with water said to me, 'He on whom you see the Spirit descend and remain is the one who baptizes with the Holy Spirit.' And I myself have seen and have testified that this is the Son of God."

John 2:11.

Jesus did this, the first of his signs, in Cana of Galilee, and revealed [*ephanerōsen*] his glory and his disciples believed in him.

1 Timothy 3:16.

He was revealed [*ephanerōthē*] in flesh,
vindicated in spirit,
seen by angels,
proclaimed among Gentiles,
believed in throughout the world,
taken up in glory.

Clement of Alexandria

Clement of Alexandria, *Miscellanies*, 1, 21 (ca. 200),
trans. William Wilson, in *ANF* 2:333.

And the followers of Basilides [a Gnostic] hold the day of his [Jesus'] baptism as a festival, spending the night before in readings.

And they say it was the fifteenth year of Tiberius Caesar, the fifteenth day of the month Tubi; and some that it was the eleventh [January 6] of the same month.

John Chrysostom

John Chrysostom, *Sermon Preached at Antioch, January 6, 387*,
trans. from *Sancti Patris Nostri Joannis Chrysostomi, opera o
mnia quae exstant* (Paris: Gaume Fratres, 1834), 2:436.

But why is it not the day on which he was born, but the day on which he was baptized, that is called Epiphany? For this is the day on which he was baptized, and made holy the nature of the waters. . . . Why then is this day called Epiphany? Because it was not when he was born that he became manifest to all, but when he was baptized; for up to this day he was unknown to the multitudes.

John Chrysostom, *Sermon Preached on December 20, 386*, trans. from *Sancti Patris Nostri Joannis Chrysostomi, opera omnia quae exstant*, 1:608.

For if Christ had not been born into flesh, He would not have been baptized, which is the Theophany [Orthodox term for Epiphany], He would not have been crucified [some texts add: and would not have risen] which is the Pascha, He would not have sent down the Spirit, which is the Pentecost.

John Cassian

John Cassian, *Conferences*, X, 2 (ca. 428), trans. E. C. S. Gibson, in *NPNF²* 11:401.

In the country of Egypt this custom is by ancient tradition observed that—when Epiphany is past, which the priests of that province regard as the time, both for our Lord's baptism and also of His birth in the flesh, and so celebrate the commemoration of either mystery not separately as in the Western provinces but on the single festival of this day—letters are sent from the Bishop of Alexandria through all the Churches of Egypt, by which the beginnning of Lent and the day of Easter are pointed out not only in all the cities but also in the monasteries.

CHRISTMAS

Although its documentary evidence suggests that Christmas appears originally in Rome about 330 CE, recent scholarship has suggested its origins may be earlier and in North Africa.

Philocalian Martyrology

Philocalian Martyrology (ca. 354); line included in a list of commemorations, trans. from A. Allan McArthur, *The Evolution of the Christian Year* (London: SCM Press, 1953), 42.

[December 25] The birth of Christ in Bethlehem of Judea.

John Chrysostom

John Chrysostom, *Sermon Preached at Antioch, December 25, 386*,
trans. Albert D. Alexander, cited by McArthur,
in *The Evolution of the Christian Year*, 49–50.

And moreover it is not yet the tenth year since this day has become clearly known to us. . . . And so this day too, which has been known from of old to the inhabitants of the West and has now been brought to us, not many years ago, has developed so quickly and has manifestly proved so fruitful. . . . And the star brought the Magi from the East.

Apostolic Constitutions

Apostolic Constitutions, VIII, 33 (ca. 375), in *ANF* 7:495.

Let them [slaves] rest on the festival of His birth, because on it the unexpected favour was granted to men, that Jesus Christ, the Logos of God, should be born of the Virgin Mary, for the salvation of the world. Let them rest on the feast of the Epiphany, because on it a manifestation took place of the divinity of Christ, for the Father bore testimony to him at the baptism; and the Paraclete, in the form of a dove, pointed out to the bystanders Him to whom testimony was borne.

ADVENT

Council of Saragossa

It is possible that the Advent season of preparation for Christmas in the West was originally a time of preparation for Epiphany, and, perhaps, even as preparation of candidates for the celebration of baptisms on Epiphany.

Council of Saragossa (380), trans. from McArthur,
in *The Evolution of the Christian Year*, 56.

From December 17 until the day of Epiphany, which is January 6, it is not permitted to be absent from church.

Maximus of Turin

As shown by Maximus of Turin, in North Italy, as elsewhere in both East and West, Advent was understood as a season of preparation for celebrating the nativity on December 25. At Rome, on the other hand, from the time of Gregory the Great on (590–604), Advent was eschatological in focus.

Maximus of Turin, *Sermo* LX.3, trans. Boniface Ramsey, in ACW 50 (New York: Newman Press, 1989), 145.

Before many days, then, let us make our hearts pure, let us cleanse our consciences and purify our spirit, and, shining and without stain, let us celebrate the coming of the spotless Lord, so that the birthday of Him whose birth was known to be from a spotless virgin may be observed by spotless servants. For whoever is dirty or polluted on that day will not observe the birthday of Christ and fulfill his obligation. Although he is bodily present at the Lord's festivity, yet in mind he is separated by a great distance from the Savior. The impure cannot keep company with the holy, nor the avaricious with the merciful, nor the corrupt with the virgin.

Bernard of Clairvaux

Bernard summarizes the theology of the final form of a Roman four-week Advent before Christmas in the West as oriented to three comings of Christ: past, present, and future.

Bernard of Clairvaux, *Sermo* 5, in *Adventu Domini*, 1–3: Opera Omnia, Edit. Cisterc. 4 (1966), 188–90; in *The Liturgy of the Hours* (New York: Catholic Book Publishing Company, 1975), 1:169

We know that there are three comings of the Lord. The third lies between the other two. It is invisible, while the other two are visible. In the first coming he was seen on earth, dwelling among men; he himself testifies that they saw him and hated him. In the final coming all flesh will see the salvation of our God, and they will look on him whom they pierced. The intermediate coming is a hidden one; in it only the elect see the Lord within their own selves, and they are saved. In his first coming our Lord came in our flesh and in our weakness; in this middle coming he comes in spirit and in power; in the final coming he will be seen in glory and majesty.

In case someone should think that what we say about this middle coming is sheer invention, listen to what our Lord himself says: If anyone loves me, he will keep my word, and my Father will love him, and we will come to him. There is another passage of Scripture which reads: He who fears God will do good, but something further has been said about the one who loves, that is, that he will keep God's word. Where is God's word to be kept? Obviously in the heart, as the prophet says: I have hidden your words in my heart, so that I may not sin against you.

Keep God's word in this way. Let it enter into your very being, let it take possession of your desires and your whole way of life. Feed on goodness, and your soul will delight in its richness. Remember to eat your bread, or your heart will wither away. Fill your soul with richness and strength.

Because this coming lies between the other two, it is like a road on which we travel from the first coming to the last. In the first, Christ was our redemption; in the last, he will appear as our life; in this middle coming, he is our rest and consolation.

FEASTS OF THE SAINTS

Martyrs, as those who most perfectly imitated Christ in his passion, were the first to be included on the liturgical calendars of local churches.

The Martyrdom of Polycarp

The Martyrdom of Polycarp, XVIII (ca. 156), trans. Massey H. Shepherd Jr., in LCC 1:156.

So we later took up his bones, more precious than costly stones and more valuable than gold, and laid them away in a suitable place. There the Lord will permit us, so far as possible, to gather together in joy and gladness to celebrate the day of his martyrdom as a birthday, in memory of those athletes who have gone before, and to train and make ready those who are to come hereafter.

Ambrose of Milan

Writing to his sister, Ambrose describes the discovery of the intact bodies of the martyrs Protasius and Gervasius, their translation to his basilica, and what he said to the church at Milan on this occasion.

Ambrose of Milan, Letter 22, in *NPNF²* 10:437–38.

2. Why should I use many words? God favoured us, for even the clergy were afraid who were bidden to clear away the earth from the spot before the chancel screen of SS. Felix and Nabor. I found the fitting signs, and on bringing in some on whom hands were to be laid, the power of the holy martyrs became so manifest, that even

whilst I was still silent, one was seized and thrown prostrate at the holy burial-place. We found two men of marvellous stature, such as those of ancient days. All the bones were perfect, and there was much blood. During the whole of those two days there was an enormous concourse of people. Briefly we arranged the whole in order, and as evening was now coming on transferred them to the basilica of Fausta, where watch was kept during the night, and some received the laying on of hands. On the following day we translated the relics to the basilica called Ambrosian. During the translation a blind man was healed. I addressed the people then as follows:

3. When I considered the immense and unprecedented numbers of you who are here gathered together, and the gifts of divine grace which have shone forth in the holy martyrs, I must confess that I felt myself unequal to this task, and that I could not express in words what we can scarcely conceive in our minds or take in with our eyes. But when the course of holy Scripture began to be read, the Holy Spirit Who spake in the prophets granted me to utter something worthy of so great a gathering, of your expectations, and of the merits of the holy martyrs.

9. . . . Not without reason do many call this the resurrection of the martyrs. I do not say whether they have risen for themselves, for us certainly the martyrs have risen. You know—nay, you have yourselves seen—that many are cleansed from evil spirits, that very many also, having touched with their hands the robe of the saints, are freed from those ailments which oppressed them; you see that the miracles of old time are renewed, when through the coming of the Lord Jesus grace was more largely shed forth upon the earth, and that many bodies are healed as it were by the shadow of the holy bodies. How many napkins are passed about! how many garments, laid upon the holy relics and endowed with healing power, are claimed! All are glad to touch even the outside thread, and whosoever touches will be made whole.

12. The glorious relics are taken out of an ignoble burying-place, the trophies are displayed under heaven. The tomb is wet with blood. The marks of the bloody triumph are present, the relics are found undisturbed in their order, the head separated from the body. Old men now repeat that they once heard the names of these martyrs and read their titles. The city which had carried off the martyrs of other places had lost her own. Though this be the gift of God, yet I cannot deny the favour which the Lord Jesus has granted to the time of my priesthood, and since I myself am not worthy to be a martyr, I have obtained these matryrs for you.

13. Let these triumphant victims be brought to the place where Christ is the victim. But He upon the altar, Who suffered for all; they

beneath the altar, who were redeemed by His Passion. I had destined this place for myself, for it is fitting that the priest should rest there where he has been wont to offer, but I yield the right hand portion to the sacred victims; that place was due to the martyrs. Let us, then, deposit the sacred relics, and lay them up in a worthy resting-place, and let us celebrate the whole day with faithful devotion.

|

Medieval Elaboration of the Sanctoral and Temporal Cycles

|

Innocent III

Innocent gives the first full rationale for the use of liturgical colors followed at Rome.

> Innocent III (pope 1198–1216), *Concerning the Holy Mystery of the Altar*, LXV (ca. 1195), trans. from PL 217:799-802.

There are four principal colors by which the Roman Church distinguishes vestments according to the proper sacred days: white, red, black, and green. In the laws of garments, four colors had been appointed (Ex. 28): gold and violet, purple and scarlet. White is worn in vestments for feasts of confessors and virgins, red in solemnities of apostles and martyrs. Hence the bride says in the Song of Songs: "My beloved is fair and ruddy, chosen from thousands" (Song of Solomon 5). White is used for confessors and virgins, red for martyrs and apostles. Such are the flowers, roses and lilies of the valley.

White garb is used in festivals of confessors and virgins because of completeness and innocence. For those belonging to him of Nazareth are made white and they walk always in white with him: "They are virgins and follow wherever the Lamb goes" (Rev. 14). On account of this, white is used in the solemnities following [births of Christ and John the Baptist, Epiphany, Presentation, Maundy Thursday, Easter, Ascension, and at the consecration of a bishop or a church], certainly in the solemnities of the angels, of whose brightness God asked Lucifer: "Where were you when the morning stars praised me?" (Job 38). . . .

Red, on the other hand, is used in vestments for the feasts of the apostles and martyrs, on account of the blood of their suffering which they shed for Christ. For "they are those who have come through great tribulation, and have washed their garments in the blood of the Lamb" (Rev. 7). It is used in the feast of the cross, through which Christ poured out his blood for us, hence the Prophet: "Why is your clothing red, as one who treads grapes in a winepress?" (Isa. 63). Or in the feast of the cross it is better to use white when it is not the feast of the passion but of the discovery or the exaltation.

In Pentecost the fervor of the Holy Spirit appeared over the apostles in tongues of fire. "There appeared to them scattered tongues as of fire seated on each of them" (Acts 2). The prophet says: "He sent fire from heaven into my bones" (Lam. 1). For the martyrdoms of the apostles Peter and Paul, red may be used; however, for the conversion (of Paul) and the chair (of Peter) white is used. Likewise for the birth of St. John (the Baptist), white may be used; for his beheading, however, red is used. When the feast is celebrated of someone who was both martyr and virgin, martyrdom takes preference over virginity, since it is the most perfect sign of love, wherefore Truth says: "Greater love no one can have, than that he should lay down his life for his friends" (John 15). On account of which in the commemoration of All Saints at certain times red garments are used; others, indeed, such as the Roman curia, use white, not so much of themselves but because the Church says of this feast, that the saints, according to the Apocalypse of John (ch. 7), stand "before the Lamb, clothed in white robes with palms in their hands."

Black vestments are used in days of affliction and abstinence, for sins and for the dead. Black is used during Advent until the vigil of the Nativity and from Septuagesima to Easter eve. The bride ironically says in the Song of Songs: "I am black, but beautiful, daughters of Jerusalem, like the tents of Kedar, as the tent-curtains of Shalmah. Do not despise me, who may be dark, because the sun has discolored me" (Song of Solomon 1).

For Holy Innocents some use black; others contend red garments ought to be used. This is on account of sorrow, because "a voice is heard in Ramah with much lamenting and wailing, Rachel weeping for her children and not wishing to be consoled, because they no longer are" (Jer. 31). Because of this, songs of joy are not sung and a golden miter is not worn. This is on account of martyrdom, commemorating which the Church says: "Under the throne of God the saints cry out: Vindicate our blood which is shed, our God" (Luke 18; Rev. 6). Because of this sorrow, silent is the joy of songs, the miter which is worn is not decorated with gold, but on account of the martyrs red vestments are used. Today we use violet on the Fourth Sunday of Lent because of joy which the gold rose signifies. The Roman pontifex carries a miter decorated with gold cloth, but on account of the abstinence of black, at the same time violet vestments are used.

It remains that in weekdays and common days *green* vestments may be used, since green is the color intermediate between white, black, and red. This color is expressed when it is said: "Henna with nard, nard and saffron" (Song of Solomon 4).

To these four, others are related: to red the color of scarlet, to black violet, to green saffron. A few use rose for martyrs, scarlet for confessors, and white for virgins.

Erasmus of Rotterdam

The Renaissance humanist Disederius Erasmus strongly critiques the overgrowth in and the use of the cult of the saints in the late Middle Ages.

Erasmus of Rotterdam (ca. 1466–1536), *The Praise of Folly* (1511), trans. Clarence H. Miller (New Haven and London: Yale University Press, 1979), 62–63, 65–67.

But there can be no question at all that another group is entirely enlisted "under my banner": those who delight in hearing or telling miracles and monstrous lies. They can never get enough of such tales whenever strange horrors are told about apparitions, ghosts, specters, dead souls, and thousands of such marvels as these. And the further such tall tales are from the truth, the more easily they gain credence and the more delicately they tickle the ears of the listeners.

Besides, they are not only wonderfully useful in relieving the boredom of the passing hours, but they also produce a fine profit, especially for priests and preachers.

Closely related to such men are those who have adopted the very foolish (but nevertheless quite agreeable) belief that if they look at a painting or statue of that huge Polyphemus Christopher, they will not die on that day; or, if they address a statue of Barbara with the prescribed words, they will return from battle unharmed; or, if they accost Erasmus on certain days, with certain wax tapers, and in certain little formulas of prayer, they will soon become rich. Moreover, in George they have discovered a new Hercules. . . .

But what do men end up asking from these saints except things that pertain to folly? Just think, among all the votive tablets that you see covering the walls and even the ceilings of some churches, have you ever seen anyone who escaped from folly or who became the least bit wiser? One saved his life by swimming. Another was stabbed by an enemy but recovered. Another, with no less luck than bravery, fled from the battle while the rest were fighting. Another who had been hung on the gallows fell down by the favor of some saint friendly to thieves, so that he could proceed in his career of disburdening those who are sadly overburdened by their riches. Another escaped by breaking out of jail. Another, much to the chagrin of his physician, recovered from a fever. For another, a poisonous potion, because it worked as a purge, was curative rather than fatal, though his wife (who lost her effort and expense) was not exactly overjoyed at the result. Another, whose wagon had overturned, drove his horses home uninjured. Another, buried by the collapse of a building, was not killed. Another, caught by a husband, managed to get away. No one gives thanks for escaping from folly. To lack all wisdom is so very agreeable that mortals will pray to be delivered from anything rather than from folly.

But why have I embarked on this vast sea of superstitions?

> Not if I had a hundred tongues, a hundred mouths,
>   A voice of iron, could I survey all kinds
> Of fools, or run through all the forms of folly.

So rife, so teeming with such delusions is the entire life of all Christians everywhere. And yet priests are not unwilling to allow and even foster such delusions because they are not unaware of how many emoluments accumulate from this source. In the midst of all this, if some odious wiseman should stand up and sing out the true state of affairs: "You will not die badly if you live well. You redeem your sins if to the coin you add a hatred of evil deeds, then tears, vigils, prayers, fasts, and if you change your whole way of life. This saint will help you if you imitate his life"—if that wiseman were to growl out such assertions and more like them, look how much happiness he would immediately take away from the minds of mortals, look at the confusion he would throw them into!

|

Reformation Pruning of the Calendar

|

THE LUTHERAN REFORMATION

Martin Luther

The liturgical year is retained but simplified.

Martin Luther, *Formula Missae* (1523), trans. Paul Zeller Strodach, in LW 53:23.

But we at Wittenberg intend to observe only the Lord's days and the festivals of the Lord. We think that all the feasts of the saints should be abrogated, or if anything in them deserves it, it should be brought into the Sunday sermon. We regard the feasts of Purification and Annunciation as feasts of Christ, even as Epiphany and Circumcision. Instead of the feasts of St. Stephen and of St. John the Evangelist, we are pleased to use the office of the Nativity. The feasts of the Holy Cross shall be anathema. Let others act according to their own conscience or in consideration of the weakness of some—whatever the Spirit may suggest.

Martin Luther, *German Mass* (1526), trans. Augustus Steimle, in LW 53:68, 90.

For the Epistles and Gospels we have retained the customary division according to the church year, because we do not find anything especially reprehensible in this use. . . . We . . . have no objection to others who take up the complete books of the evangelists [continuous reading]. . . .

But on the festivals, such as Christmas, Easter, Pentecost, St. Michael's, Purification, and the like, we must continue to use Latin until we have enough German songs. This work is just beginning. . . .

Lent, Palm Sunday, and Holy Week shall be retained, not to force anyone to fast, but to preserve the Passion history and the Gospels appointed for that season. This, however, does not include the Lenten veil, throwing of palms, veiling of pictures, and whatever else there is of such tomfoolery. . . . Holy Week shall be like any other week save that the Passion history [shall] be explained every day for an hour . . . and that the sacrament [shall] be given to everyone who desires it.

THE CHURCH OF ENGLAND

The Booke of the Common Prayer

The Book of Common Prayer provides propers for the temporal cycle and only for New Testament saints.

The Booke of the Common Prayer (1549); bracketed items disappear in 1552 title; in *The First and Second Prayer Books of Edward VI* (London: J. M. Dent & Sons, 1910), 32–211 (spelling modernized).

The [introits,] collects, epistles, and gospels, to be used at the celebration of the Lord's Supper and Holy Communion through the Year: [with Proper Psalms and Lessons for Divers Feasts and Days.]

The first Sunday in Advent . . . [second, third, fourth]

Christmas Day; At Matins; At the First Communion; At the Second Communion

St. Stephen's Day

St. John Evangelist's Day

The Innocents' Day

The Sunday after Christmas Day

The Circumcision of Christ

The Epiphany

The first Sunday after the Epiphany . . . [second, third, fourth, fifth]

The Sunday called Septuagesima

The Sunday called Sexagesima

The Sunday called Quinquagesima

The First day of Lent, commonly called Ash-Wednesday

The first Sunday in Lent . . . [second, third, fourth, fifth]

The Sunday next before Easter

Monday before Easter . . . [Tuesday, Wednesday, Thursday]

On Good Friday

Easter Eve

Easter Day

Monday in Easter Week . . . [Tuesday]

The first Sunday after Easter . . . [second, third, fourth, fifth]

The Ascension Day

The Sunday after the Ascension

Whitsunday

Monday in Whitsun week . . . [Tuesday]

Trinity Sunday

First Sunday after Trinity Sunday [. . . Twenty-fifth]

St. Andrew's Day

St. Thomas the Apostle

The Conversion of Saint Paul

The Purification of Saint Mary the Virgin

Saint Mathias' Day

The Annunciation of the Virgin Mary

Saint Mark's Day

Saint Philip and James

Saint Barnabas, Apostle

Saint John Baptist

Saint Peter's Day

Saint Mary Magdalene

Saint James the Apostle

Saint Bartholomew

Saint Matthew

Saint Michael and All Angels

Saint Luke Evangelist
Simon and Jude, Apostles
All Saints

THE CHURCH OF SCOTLAND

"The Book of Discipline"

The Church of Scotland not only prunes the calendar of saints but deletes even Christmas and Epiphany.

The Church of Scotland, "The Book of Discipline" (1560), in *John Knox's History of the Reformation in Scotland* (London: Thomas Nelson & Sons, 1949), 2:281.

We understand whatsoever men, by laws, councils, or constitutions have imposed upon the conscience of men, without the expressed commandment of God's Word; such as vows of chastity, forswearing of marriage, binding of men and women to several and disguised apparels, to the superstitious observation of fasting days, difference of meat for conscience sake, prayer for the dead, and keeping of holy days of certain saints commanded by man, such as be all those that the Papists have invented, as the feasts, as they term them, of apostles, martyrs, virgins, of Christmas, circumcision, epiphany, purification, and other fond feasts of our Lady. Which things, because in God's Scriptures they neither have commandment nor assurance, we judge utterly to be abolished from this realm; affirming farther, that the obstinate maintainers and teachers of such abominations ought not to escape the punishment of the civil magistrate.

THE PURITANS

A Directory for the Publique Worship of God

The Puritans focus on the Lord's Day and on responding to God's present actions to the exclusion of other feasts altogether.

A Directory for the Publique Worship of God, Throughout the Three Kingdoms of England, Scotland, and Ireland . . . [Westminster Directory] (London: 1644 [1645]). Copy in University Library, Cambridge, 56, 85.

The Lord's day ought to be so remembered beforehand, as that all worldly businesse of our ordinary Callings may be so ordered, and so timely and seasonably laid aside, as they may not be impediments to the due sanctifying of the Day when it comes.

The whole Day is to be celebrated as holy to the Lord, both in publique and private, as being the Christian Sabbath. To which end, it is requisite, that there be a holy cessation, or resting all the day, from all unnecessary labours; and an abstaining, not onely from all sports and pastimes, but also from all worldly words and thoughts. . . .

There is no Day commanded in Scripture to be kept holy under the Gospell, but the Lord's Day, which is the Christian Sabbath.

Festivall days, vulgarly called Holy daies, having no warrant in the Word of God, are not to be continued.

Neverthelesse, it is lawfull and necessary upon speciall emergent occasions, to separate a day or daies for Publique Fasting or Thanksgiving, as the severall eminent and extraordinary dispensations of Gods providence shall administer cause and opportunity to his people.

THE CATHOLIC CHURCH

The Council of Trent

The Council of Trent, Session XXII.III (1562), trans. H. J. Schroeder, in *The Canons and Decrees of the Council of Trent* (St. Louis: Herder, 1941), 146.

Masses in Honor of the Saints: And though the Church has been accustomed to celebrate at times certain masses in honor and memory of the saints, she does not teach that sacrifice is offered to them but to God alone who crowned them; whence, the priest does not say: "To thee, Peter or Paul, I offer sacrifice," but giving thanks to God for their victories, he implores their favor that they may vouchsafe to intercede for us in heaven whose memory we celebrate on earth.

The Council of Trent, Session XXV (1563), in *The Canons and Decrees of the Council of Trent*, 215–17.

On the Invocation, Veneration, and Relics of Saints, and on Sacred Images: The holy council commands all bishops and others who hold the office of teaching. . . they above all instruct the faithful diligently in matters relating to intercession and invocation of the saints, the veneration of relics, and the legitimate use of images, teaching them that the saints who reign together with Christ offer up their prayers to God for men, that it is good and beneficial suppliantly to invoke them and to have recourse to their prayers, assistance and support in order to obtain favors from God through His Son, Jesus Christ our Lord, who alone is our redeemer and savior. . . .

Also that the holy bodies of the holy martyrs and of others living with Christ . . . are to be venerated by the faithful, through which many benefits are bestowed by God on men. . . .

Moreover, that the images of Christ, of the Virgin Mother of God, and of the other saints are to be placed and retained especially in the churches and that due honor and veneration is to be given them; not, however, that any divinity or virtue is believed to be in them . . . but because the honor which is shown them is referred to the prototypes which they represent, so that by means of the images which we kiss and before which we uncover the head and prostrate ourselves, we adore Christ and venerate the saints whose likeness they bear. . . .

. . . Furthermore, in the invocation of the saints, the veneration of relics, and the sacred use of images, all superstition shall be removed, all filthy quest for gain eliminated, and all lasciviousness avoided, so that images shall not be painted and adorned with a seductive charm, or the celebration of saints and the visitation of relics be perverted by the people into boisterous festivities and drunkenness, as if the festivals in honor of the saints are to be celebrated with revelry and with no sense of decency.

METHODISM

John Wesley

John Wesley's calendar takes a pragmatic approach.

John Wesley, letter bound with *The Sunday Service*, dated September 9, 1784, in *John Wesley's Sunday Service* (Nashville: United Methodist Publishing House, 1984), n.p.

Most of the holy-days (so called) are omitted, as at present answering no valuable end.

John Wesley, "The Collects, Epistles, and Gospels to be used throughout the Year," from *The Sunday Service of the Methodists in North America* (London, 1784), 27–124.

The First Sunday in Advent . . . [Second, Third, Fourth]
The Nativity of our Lord, or the Birth-day Of CHRIST, commonly called Christmas-day
The First Sunday after Christmas . . . [Second to Fifteenth]
The Sunday next before Easter
GOOD-FRIDAY
EASTER-DAY

The First Sunday after Easter . . . [Second to Fifth]
The Ascension-day
Sunday after Ascension-day
Whit-Sunday
Trinity-Sunday
First Sunday after Trinity . . . [Second to Twenty-fifth Sunday after Trinity]

Modern Developments

ROMAN CATHOLIC

The Roman Calendar

The norms and principles in the current Roman Catholic liturgical calendar restore the priority of the temporal cycle over the sanctoral cycle.

The Roman Calendar: Text and Commentary (Washington, DC:
United States Catholic Conference, 1976), 5, 28.

The Church celebrates the paschal mystery on the first day of the week, known as the Lord's Day or Sunday. This follows a tradition handed down from the Apostles, which took its origin from the day of Christ's resurrection. This Sunday should be considered the original feast day.

Because of its special importance, the celebration of Sunday is replaced only by solemnities or feasts of the Lord. The Sundays of Advent, Lent, and the Easter season, however, take precedence over all solemnities and feasts of the Lord. Solemnities that occur on these Sundays are observed on the preceding Saturday.

Based on the Constitution on the Liturgy, the principles for revising the sanctoral cycle are:

1. The number of devotional feasts was lessened.
2. The history of the lives of those saints found in the 1960 calendar was subjected to critical study.
3. Only saints of important significance were chosen.
4. The days for the observance of the feasts were examined.
5. The calendar was made universal in order to contain, as far as possible, saints from every race and period of time.

PROTESTANTISM

The Book of Common Prayer

The rediscovery of a richer and ecumenically based sanctoral cycle of feasts and commemorations has been a characteristic of contemporary liturgical renewal among Anglicans, Lutherans, and others. The following list for the month of August in *The Book of Common Prayer* provides an example of this rediscovery from within the Anglican tradition.

The Book of Common Prayer (New York: Church Hymnal Corp., 1979), 26.

August
1
2
3
4
5
6 **The Transfiguration of Our Lord Jesus Christ**
7 John Mason Neale, Priest, 1866
8 Dominic, Priest and Friar, 1221
9
10 Lawrence, Deacon, and Martyr at Rome, 258
11 Clare, Abbess at Assisi, 1253
12
13 Jeremy Taylor, Bishop of Down, Connor, and Dromore, 1667
14
15 **Saint Mary the Virgin, Mother of Our Lord Jesus Christ**
16
17
18 William Porcher DuBose, Priest, 1918
19
20 Bernard, Abbot of Clairvaux, 1153
21
22
23
24 **Saint Bartholomew the Apostle**
25 Louis, King of France, 1270
26
27
28 Augustine, Bishop of Hippo, 430
29
30
31 Aidan, Bishop of Lindisfarne, 651

Permissions

Ambrose of Milan, *On the Sacraments,* trans. T. Thompson, *St. Ambrose "On the Mysteries" and the Treatise "On the Sacraments"* (London: SPCK, 1919), used by permission of SPCK.

Thomas Aquinas, *Summa Theologiae,* from *St. Thomas Aquinas: Summa Theologiae,* vol. 57: *Baptism and Confirmation (3a. 33–72),* ed. J. J. Cunningham (New York: McGraw Hill, 1975). Reprinted with the permission of Cambridge University Press.

Augustine, *Letter 55: To Januarius* (ca. 400), trans. Wilfrid Parsons, in *Augustine: Letters,* vol. 1 (1–182); in *Fathers of the Church: A New Translation.* Washington, DC: Catholic University of America, vol. 12. Used with permission of the Catholic University of America Press, Washington, DC.

Michael B. Aune, "Liturgy and Theology: Rethinking the Relationship: Part 2" *Worship* 81, no. 2 (2007), used by permission of Liturgical Press.

John Baillie, John T. McNeill, and Henry P. Van Dusen, ed. *Library of Christian Classics* (Philadelphia: Westminster Press; London: SCM Press). Extracts from *Library of Christian Classics* are copyright © SCM Press and are reproduced by permission of Westminster John Knox Press and SCM Press.

Karl Barth, *The Teaching of the Church regarding Baptism,* trans. Ernest A. Payne (London: SCM Press, 1948; repr. Eugene, OR: Wipf and Stock Publishers, 2006), used by permission of Wipf and Stock Publishers. www.wipfandstock.com.

Basil of Caesarea, *The Long Rules,* XXXVII (358–64), trans. M. Monica Wagner, in *Saint Basil: Ascetical Works,* in *Fathers of the Church: A New Translation.* Washington, DC: Catholic University of America, vol. 9. Used with permission of the Catholic University of America Press, Washington, DC.

Teresa Berger, *Fragments of Real Presence: Liturgical Traditions in the Hands of Women* (New York: Herder & Herder, 2005), used by permission.

Bernard of Clairvaux, *Sermo 5,* in *Adventu Domini,* 1–3: Opera Omnia, Edit. Cisterc. 4 (1966), excerpt from the English translation of the sermon by Bernard of Clairvaux from *The Liturgy of the Hours* © 1974, ICEL. Used by permission of ICEL. All rights reserved.

Henry Bettenson, trans., *Documents of the Christian Church* (New York: Oxford University Press, 1947), used by permission of Oxford University Press.

Paul Bradshaw, sources trans., *Ordination Rites of the Ancient Churches of East and West* (Collegeville, MN: Liturgical Press, Pueblo, 1990), used by permission.

Sebastian Brock and Michael Vasey, trans., *Didascalia Apostolorum, The Liturgical Portions of the Didascalia,* AGLS 29 (Cambridge: Grove Books, Ltd., 1982), used by permission of Grove Books (www.grovebooks.co.uk).

permission of Open Court Publishing Company, a division of Carus Publishing Company, Chicago, IL, from *Religion within the Limits* by Immanuel Kant, copyright © 1934 Open Court Publishing Company and © 1960 Harper & Brothers.

Aidan Kavanagh, "Christian Initiation in Post-Conciliar Catholicism: A Brief Report," in *Living Water, Sealing Spirit: Readings on Christian Initiation,* ed. Maxwell E. Johnson (Collegeville, MN: Liturgical Press, Pueblo, 1995), used by permission of Liturgical Press.

Aidan Kavanagh, *On Liturgical Theology* (New York: Pueblo, 1984), used by permission of Liturgical Press.

Edward Kilmartin, *Christian Liturgy I. Theology* (Kansas City, MO: Sheed & Ward, 1988), used by permission of Sheed & Ward, an imprint of Rowman & Littlefield Publishers, Inc.

Walter Klaassen, trans., *Anabaptism in Outline* (Scottdale, PA: Herald Press, 1981), used by permission of Herald Press.

Kirsopp Lake, trans., *The Epistle of Barnabas*, in *Apostolic Fathers*, vol. 1. Reprinted by permission of the publisher and the Trustees of the Loeb Classical Library from *Apostolic Fatthers: Volume 1*, Loeb Classical Library˙ Volume 24, translated by Kirsopp Lake, pp. 395-396, Cambridge, Mass.: Harvard University Press, copyright © by the President and Fellows of Harvard College. The Loeb Classical Library˙ is a registered trademark of the Presidents and Fellows of Harvard College.

Gordon Lathrop, *What Are the Essentials of Christian Worship? Open Questions in Worship*, vol. 1. Copyright © 1994 Augsburg Fortress Publishers. Reproduced by permission.

Leo I, *De Ascensione Domini* II, in *Benedictine Daily Prayer: A Short Breviary,* ed. Maxwell E. Johnson (Collegeville, MN: Liturgical Press, 2006), used by permission of Liturgical Press.

Lutheran World Federation, *Nairobi Statement on Worship and Culture* (Geneva: Lutheran World Federation, 1996), used by permission of Lutheran World Federation.

Luther's Works, vols. 36 and 53 (Philadelphia/St. Louis: Concordia Publishing House), volume 36 copyright © 1959 and volume 53 copyright © 1965 Fortress Press, 2011 Evangelical Lutheran Church in America, admin. Augsburg Fortress. Reproduced by permission.

Manual of York Use (fourteenth century), University Library, Cambridge, England (MS Ee.iv.19), reproduced by kind permission of the Syndics of Cambridge University Library.

Maximus of Turin, *Sermo LX*, in *The Sermons of St. Maximus of Turin,* translated and annotated by Boniface Ramsey, O.P. Copyright © 1989 by Boniface Ramsey, O.P. Paulist Press, Inc., Mahwah, NJ. Reprinted by permission of Paulist Press, Inc. www.paulistpress.com.

A. Allan McArthur, primary sources trans., in *The Evolution of the Christian Year* (London: SCM Press, 1953), used by permission of Hymns Ancient & Modern Ltd.

Killian McDonnell, trans., *Sub Tuum Praesidium*, in "The Marian Liturgical Tradition," in *Between Memory and Hope: Readings on the Liturgical Year,* ed.

Maxwell E. Johnson (Collegeville, MN: Liturgical Press, Pueblo, 2000), used by permission of Liturgical Press.

John T. McNeill and Helena M. Gamer, trans., *Medieval Handbooks of Penance* (New York: Columbia University Press, 1938), reprinted with the permission of Columbia University Press.

Arthur Mende, trans., "Order of Divine Service in Leipzig," in *The Bach Reader*, revised edition, edited by Hans T. David and Arthur Mendel. Copyright © 1966, 1945 by W. W. Norton & Company, Inc. Used by permission of W. W. Norton & Company, Inc.

Nathan D. Mitchell, "The Amen Corner: Being Good and Being Beautiful" *Worship* 74, no. 6 (Nov. 2000), used by permission.

Nathan D. Mitchell, *Meeting Mystery: Liturgy, Worship, and Sacraments* (Maryknoll, NY: Orbis Books, 2006), used with permission.

David N. Power, *Unsearchable Riches: The Symbolic Nature of Liturgy* (New York: Pueblo, 1984; repr. Eugene, OR: Wipf and Stock Publishers, 2008), used by permission of Wipf and Stock Publishers. www.wipfandstock.com.

Francisco de Quiñones, Preface, *Breviarium Romanae Curiae* (1535 and 1536), trans. from both 1535 and 1536 editions in the sequence used by Thomas Cranmer; texts in *Cranmer's Liturgical Projects*, ed. J. Wickham Legg (London: Henry Bradshaw Society, 1915), used with permission of Boydell and Brewer Ltd.

Karl Rahner, *The Church and the Sacraments*, Quaestiones Disputatae 9 (London: Burnes and Oates, Ltd., 1986), reproduced by kind permission of Continuum International Publishing Group.

Roman Catholic Church, *General Instruction on the Liturgy of the Hours,* trans. Peter Coughlan and Peter Purdue, in *Liturgy of the Hours: The General Instruction,* with commentary by A. M. Roguet (London: Geoffrey Chapman, 1971). Reprinted with the permission of the Continuum International Publishing Group.

Roman Catholic Church, excerpts from the English translation of *Rite of Marriage* © *1969, International Committee on English in the Liturgy, Inc. (ICEL),* excerpts from the English translation of *Rite of Penance* © *1974,* ICEL; excerpts from the English translation of *The Ordination of Deacons, Priests, and Bishops* © *1975,* ICEL; excerpts from the English translation of *The Roman Calendar* © *1975,* ICEL; excerpts from the English translation of *Rite of Christian Initiation of Adults* © *1985* ICEL; used by permission of ICEL. All rights reserved.

Melanie Ross, "Joseph's Britches Revisited: Reflections on Method in Liturgical Theology," *Worship* 80, no. 6 (2006), used by permission.

Susan A. Ross, "God's Embodiment and Women," in *Freeing Theology: The Essentials of Theology in Feminist Perspective,* ed. Catherine Mowry LaCugna. Copyright © 1993 by HarperCollins Publishers, Inc. Reprinted by permission of HarperCollins Publishers.

Don E. Saliers, *Worship as Theology: Foretaste of Glory Divine* (Nashville: Abingdon Press, 1994), used with permission of Abingdon Press.

Edward Schillebeeckx, *Christ the Sacrament of the Encounter with God,* trans. Paul Barrett, et al. (New York: Sheed & Ward, 1963), reprinted by kind permission of Sheed & Ward, an imprint of Rowman & Littlefield Publishers, Inc., and Continuum International Publishing Group.

Suggestions for Further Reading

Liturgical History and Methodology

Adam, Adolf. *Foundations of Liturgy: An Introduction to Its History and Practice.* Collegeville, MN: Liturgical Press, Pueblo 1992.

Baldovin, John. *Reforming the Liturgy: A Response to Critics.* Collegeville, MN: Liturgical Press, Pueblo, 2008.

Bradshaw, Paul F. *The Search for the Origins of Christian Worship: Sources and Methods for the Study of Early Liturgy.* Second Revised and Enlarged Edition. London: SPCK, 2002.

———. *Early Christian Worship: A Basic Introduction to Ideas and Practice.* London: SPCK, 1996.

———, ed. *The New Westminster Dictionary of Liturgy and Worship.* Louisville and London: Westminster John Knox Press, 2002.

Bugnini, Annibale. *The Reform of the Liturgy 1948–1975.* Collegeville, MN: Liturgical Press, 1990.

Chupungco, Anscar J., ed. *Handbook for Liturgical Studies.* 5 vols. Collegeville, MN: Liturgical Press, Pueblo, 1997–2000.

Harper, John. *The Forms and Orders of Western Liturgy: From the Tenth to the Eighteenth Century.* New York: Oxford University Press, 1991.

Klauser, Theodore. *A Short History of the Western Liturgy: An Account and Some Reflections.* London/New York: Oxford University Press, 1969.

Martimort, A. G., et al., eds. *The Church at Prayer.* 4 vols. Collegeville, MN: Liturgical Press, 1986.

Palazzo, Eric. *A History of Liturgical Books from the Beginning to the Thirteenth Century.* Collegeville, MN: Liturgical Press, Pueblo, 1998.

Senn, Frank C. *Christian Liturgy: Catholic and Evangelical.* Minneapolis: Augsburg Fortress, 1997.

Taft, Robert F. *Beyond East and West: Problems in Liturgical Understanding.* 2nd revised and enlarged edition. Rome: Edizioni Christiana Analecta, 1997.

———. *The Byzantine Rite: A Short History.* Collegeville, MN: Liturgical Press, 1992.

Vogel, Cyrille. *Medieval Liturgy: An Introduction to the Sources,* ed. William G. Storey and Niels K. Rasmussen. Washington, DC: Pastoral Press, 1986.

Wainwright, Geoffrey, and Karen Westerfield-Tucker, eds. *The Oxford History of Christian Worship.* New York: Oxford University Press, 2006.

Wegman, Hermann. *Christian Worship in East and West: A Study Guide to Liturgical History.* Collegeville, MN: Liturgical Press, Pueblo, 1985.

White, James F. *A Brief History of Christian Worship.* Nashville: Abingdon Press, 1993.

———. *Protestant Worship: Traditions in Transition.* Louisville, KY: Westminster/ John Knox Press, 1989.

Sacraments in General

Chauvet, Louis-Marie. *The Sacraments: The Word of God at the Mercy of the Body.* Collegeville, MN: Liturgical Press, Pueblo, 2001.

——. *Symbol and Sacrament: A Sacramental Reintepretation of Christian Existence.* Collegeville, MN: Liturgical Press, Pueblo, 1995.

Empereur, James, and Eduardo Fernández, eds. *La Vida Sacra: Contemporary Hispanic Sacramental Theology.* Lanham, MD: Rowman & Littlefield, 2006.

Jenson, Robert. *Visible Words.* Philadelphia: Fortress Press, 1978.

Mitchell, Nathan. *Meeting Mystery: Liturgy, Worship, Sacraments.* Maryknoll, NY: Orbis, 2007.

Osborne, Kenan B. *Sacramental Theology: A General Introduction.* Mahwah, NJ: Paulist Press, 1988.

Rahner, Karl. *The Church and the Sacraments.* London: Burns & Oates, 1963.

Schillebeeckx, Edward. *Christ the Sacrament of the Encounter with God.* New York: Sheed & Ward, 1963.

Schmemann, Alexander. *For the Life of the World.* Crestwood, NY: St. Vladimir's Seminary Press, 1973.

Smolarski, Dennis C. *Sacred Mysteries: Sacramental Principles and Liturgical Practice.* New York: Paulist Press, 1995.

Vorgrimler, Herbert. *Sacramental Theology.* Collegeville, MN: Liturgical Press, Pueblo, 1992.

White, James F. *Sacraments as God's Self Giving.* Nashville: Abingdon Press, 1983.

——. *The Sacraments in Protestant Practice and Faith.* Nashville: Abingdon Press, 1999.

Liturgical Theology

Aune, Michael B. "Liturgy and Theology: Rethinking the Relationship." Part 1: *Worship* 81, no. 1 (2007): 46–68; Part 2: *Worship* 81, no. 2 (2007): 141–69.

Fagerberg, David W. *Theologia Prima: What Is Liturgical Theology?* 2nd ed. Hillenbrand Books. Chicago: Liturgy Training Publications, 2004.

Kavanagh, Aidan. *On Liturgical Theology.* Collegeville, MN: Liturgical Press, Pueblo, 1984.

Kilmartin, Edward. *Christian Liturgy: Theology and Practice.* Kansas City, MO: Sheed & Ward, 1988.

Lathrop, Gordon. *Holy Things: A Liturgical Theology.* Minneapolis: Fortress Press, 1993.

Mazza, Enrico. *Mystagogy: A Theology of Liturgy in the Patristic Age.* New York: Pueblo, 1989.

Mitchell, Nathan D. *Meeting Mystery: Liturgy, Worship, Sacraments.* Maryknoll, NY: Orbis, 2007.

Schmemann, Alexander. *Introduction to Liturgical Theology.* London: Faith Press, 1966.

Spinks, Bryan D., ed. *The Place of Christ in Liturgical Prayer: Trinity, Christology, and Liturgical Theology.* Collegeville, MN: Liturgical Press, Pueblo, 2008.

Vogel, Dwight W., ed. *Primary Sources of Liturgical Theology: A Reader.* Collegeville, MN: Liturgical Press, Pueblo, 2000.

Wainwright, Geoffrey. *Doxology: The Praise of God in Worship, Doctrine and Life.* New York: Oxford, 1980.

Christian Initiation

Austin, Gerard. *The Rite of Confirmation: Anointing with the Spirit.* New York: Pueblo Publishing Co., 1985.

Best, Thomas F., ed. *Baptism Today: Understanding, Practice, Ecumenical Reflections.* World Council of Churches, Faith and Order Paper 207. Collegeville, MN: Pueblo, 2008.

Ferguson, Everett. *Baptism in the Early Church: History, Theology, and Liturgy in the First Five Centuries.* Grand Rapids: Eerdmans, 2009.

Fisher, J. D. C. *Christian Initiation: The Reformation Period.* London: Alcuin Club, 1970. Repr., Chicago: Liturgy Training Publications, Hillenbrand Books, 2007.

———. *Christian Initiation: Baptism in the Medieval West.* London: SPCK, 1963. Repr. Chicago: Liturgy Training Publications, Hillenbrand Books, 2004.

Johnson, Maxwell E. *Images of Baptism.* Forum Essays 6. Chicago: Liturgy Training Publications, 2001.

———, ed. *Living Water, Sealing Spirit: Readings on Christian Initiation.* Collegeville, MN: Liturgical Press, Pueblo, 1995.

———. *The Rites of Christian Initiation: Their Evolution and Interpretation.* Rev. and expanded ed. Collegeville, MN: Liturgical Press, Pueblo, 2007.

Kavanagh, Aidan. *Confirmation: Origins and Reform.* New York: Pueblo Publishing Co., 1988.

———. *The Shape of Baptism.* New York: Pueblo Publishing Co., 1978.

Kreider, Alan. *The Change of Conversion and the Origin of Christendom.* Harrisburg, PA: Trinity Press Int., 1999.

Turner, Paul. *When Other Christians Become Catholic.* Collegeville, MN: Liturgical Press, Pueblo, 2007.

Wood, Susan K. *One Baptism: Ecumenical Dimensions of the Doctrine of Baptism.* Collegeville, MN: Liturgical Press, Michael Glazier, 2009.

Yamane, David, and Sarah MacMillan, *Real Stories of Christian Initiation.* Collegeville, MN: Liturgical Press, 2006.

Yarnold, Edward J. *The Awe-Inspiring Rites of Initiation: The Origins of the R.C.I.A.* 2nd ed. Collegeville, MN: Liturgical Press, 1994.

The Eucharist

See also works listed in the first three sections of these "Suggestions for Further Reading."

Bradshaw, Paul F., ed. *Essays on Early Eastern Eucharistic Prayers.* Collegeville, MN: Liturgical Press, Pueblo, 1997.

———. *Eucharistic Origins.* Oxford/New York: Oxford Publishing House, 2004.

Brillioth, Yngve. *Eucharistic Faith and Practice: Evangelical and Catholic.* London: SPCK, 1930.

Jasper, R. C. D., and Geoffrey Cuming. *Prayers of the Eucharist: Early and Reformed.* 3rd ed. New York: Pueblo Publishing Co., 1987.

Johnson, Maxwell E., ed. *Issues in Eucharistic Praying in East and West: Essays in Liturgical and Theological Analysis*. Collegeville, MN: Liturgical Press, Pueblo, 2011.

Jungmann, Joseph. *The Mass of the Roman Rite*. 2 vols. New York: Benziger Bros., 1951–1955.

Kilmartin, Edward J. *The Eucharist in the West: History and Theology*. Collegeville, MN: Liturgical Press, Pueblo, 1998.

Macy, Gary. *The Banquet's Wisdom: A Short History of the Theologies of the Lord's Supper*. Mahwah, NJ: Paulist Press, 1992.

Mazza, Enrico. *The Celebration of the Eucharist: The Origin of the Rite and the Development of Its Interpretation*. Collegeville, MN: Liturgical Press, Pueblo, 1999.

——. *The Eucharistic Prayers of the Roman Rite*. New York; Pueblo, 1986.

McKenna, John H. *The Eucharistic Epiclesis: A Detailed History from the Patristic to the Modern Era*. Chicago: Liturgy Training Publications; Mundelein, IL: Hillenbrand Books, 2009.

Mitchell, Nathan D. *Cult and Controversy: The Worship of the Eucharist Outside of Mass*. New York: Pueblo, 1982.

——. *Eucharist as Sacrament of Initiation*. Forum Essays. Chicago: Liturgy Training Publications, 1994.

——. *Real Presence: The Work of Eucharist*. Expanded ed. Chicago: Liturgy Training Publications, 2001.

Schmemann, Alexander. *The Eucharist: Sacrament of the Kingdom*. Crestwood, NY: St. Vladimir's Seminary Press, 1988.

Seasoltz, R. Kevin, ed. *Living Bread, Saving Cup: Readings on the Eucharist*. Collegeville, MN: Liturgical Press, 1987.

Stevenson, Kenneth. *Eucharist and Offering*. New York: Pueblo, 1986.

The Liturgy of the Word

Brightman, F. E. *The English Rite*. 2 vols. London: Rivingtons, 1921.

Cabié, Robert. *The Church at Prayer*, vol. 2: *The Eucharist*. Collegeville, MN: Liturgical Press, 1986.

Cuming, G. J. *A History of Anglican Liturgy*. 2nd ed. London: Macmillan & Co., 1982.

——. *The Godly Order*. London: Alcuin Club/SPCK, 1983.

Davies, Horton. *The Worship of the English Puritans*. London: Dacre Press, 1948.

Jungmann, Joseph A. *The Mass of the Roman Rite*. 2 vols. New York: Benziger Bros., 1951–1955.

——. *The Liturgy of the Word*. Collegeville, MN: Liturgical Press, 1966.

Old, Hughes Oliphant. *Worship That Is Reformed according to Scripture*. Atlanta: John Knox Press, 1984.

——. *The Patristic Roots of Reformed Worship*. Zurich: Theologischer Verlag, 1975.

Reed, Luther D. *The Lutheran Liturgy*. Philadelphia: Fortess Press, 1960.

Van Dijk, S. J. P., and J. H. Walker. *The Origins of the Modern Roman Liturgy*. London: Darton, Longman & Todd, 1960.

White, James F. *Protestant Worship: Traditions in Transition*. Louisville, KY: Westminster/John Knox Press, 1989.

Occasional Services

Bradshaw, Paul F. *Ordination Rites of the Ancient Churches: East and West*. New York: Pueblo Publishing Co., 1990.

Cooke, Bernard J. *Ministry to Word and Sacraments: History and Theology*. Philadelphia: Fortress Press, 1980.

Dallen, James. *The Reconciling Community: The Rite of Penance*. New York: Pueblo Publishing Co., 1986.

Favazza, Joseph A. *The Order of Penitents: Historical Roots and Pastoral Future*. Collegeville, MN: Liturgical Press, 1988.

Gusmer, Charles W. *And You Visited Me: Sacramental Ministry to the Sick and Dying*. New York: Pueblo Publishing Co., 1984.

Larson-Miller, Lizette. *The Sacrament of the Anointing of the Sick*. Lex Orandi Series. Collegeville, MN: Liturgical Press, 2005.

Rowell, Geoffrey. *The Liturgy of Christian Burial*. London: Alcuin/SPCK, 1982.

Rutherford, Richard, and Tony Barr. *The Death of a Christian: The Order of Christian Funerals*. Collegeville, MN: Liturgical Press, Pueblo, 1990.

Searle, Mark, and Kenneth Stevenson, eds. *Documents of the Marriage Liturgy*. Collegeville, MN: Liturgical Press, Pueblo, 1992.

Stevenson, Kenneth. *Nuptial Blessing*. London: Alcuin/SPCK, 1982.

Vos, Wiebe, and Geoffrey Wainwright, eds. *Ordination Rites*. Rotterdam: Liturgical Ecumenical Trust, 1980.

Wood, Susan. *Sacramental Orders*. Lex Orandi Series. Collegeville, MN: Liturgical Press, 2000.

Daily Prayer

Bradshaw, Paul F. *Daily Prayer in the Early Church*. London: Alcuin Club/SPCK, 1981.

———. *Two Ways of Praying*. Maryville, TN: Order of Saint Luke Publications, 2008.

Guiver, George. *Company of Voices*. New York: Pueblo Publishing Co., 1988.

Liturgy of the Hours: The General Instruction, with commentary by A. M. Roguet, OP. Trans. Peter Coughlan and Peter Purdue. London: Geoffrey Chapman, 1971.

Salmon, Pierre. *The Breviary through the Centuries*. Collegeville, MN: Liturgical Press, 1962.

Taft, Robert. *The Liturgy of the Hours in East and West*. Collegeville, MN: Liturgical Press, 1986.

The Liturgical Year

Adam, Adolf. *The Liturgical Year*. New York: Pueblo Publishing Co., 1981.

Alexander, J. Neil. *Waiting for the Coming: The Liturgical Meaning of Advent, Christmas, Epiphany*. Washington, DC: Pastoral Press, 1993.

Bradshaw, Paul F., and Maxwell E. Johnson. *The Origins of Feasts, Fasts, and Seasons in the Early Church*. London: SPCK, 2011.

Brown, Peter. *The Cult of the Saints: Its Rise and Function in Latin Christianity*. Chicago: University of Chicago Press, 1981.

Connell, Martin. *Eternity Today: On the Liturgical Year*. 2 vols. New York and London: Continuum, 2006.

Johnson, Maxwell E., ed. *Between Memory and Hope: Readings on the Liturgical Year*. Collegeville, MN: Liturgical Press, Pueblo, 2000.

McArthur, A. Allan. *The Evolution of the Christian Year*. London: SCM Press, 1953.

Nocent, Adrian. *The Liturgical Year*. 4 vols. Collegeville, MN: Liturgical Press, 1977.

Pfatteicher, Philip E. *New Book of Festivals and Commemorations: A Proposed Common Calendar of Saints*. Minneapolis: Fortress Press, 2008.

Rordorf, Willy. *Sunday*. Philadelphia: Westminster Press, 1968.

Stevenson, Kenneth. *Jerusalem Revisited: The Liturgical Meaning of Holy Week*. Portland: Pastoral Press, 1988.

Talley, Thomas J. *The Origins of the Liturgical Year*. New York: Pueblo Publishing Co., 1986.

Index

CPSIA information can be obtained at www.ICGtesting.com
Printed in the USA
BVOW061918060312

284584BV00002B/52/P